Built as a City

Built as a City

God and the Urban World Today

by

David Sheppard

HODDER AND STOUGHTON
LONDON SYDNEY AUCKLAND TORONTO

Jerusalem, built as a city which is bound firmly together,
to which the tribes go up, the tribes of the Lord,
as was decreed for Israel, to give thanks to the name of
    the Lord.

There thrones for judgment were set,
the thrones of the house of David.
Pray for the peace of Jerusalem!
'May they prosper who love you!
Peace be within your walls, and security within your
    towers!'
For my brethren and companions' sake I will say,
'Peace be within you!'
For the sake of the house of the Lord our God,
I will seek your good.

PSALM 122. *Revised Standard Version*

British Library C.I.P.

Sheppard, David
  Built as a city : God and the urban world today.
  ——(Hodder Christian paperbacks)
  1. City churches——Great Britain
  I. Title
  274.1   BV637

Hodder and Stoughton Editorial Office: 47 Bedford Square, London WC1B 3DP

CONTENTS

3. OUR INHERITANCE: URBANISATION

4. LEVELS, LANGUAGE AND LEARNING: THE AIMS OF EDUCATION

5. PRIORITY AREAS

6. POWER AND POWERLESSNESS

7. RESPONSES TO INDUSTRIAL LIFE

8. THE CHURCH'S TASK

9. THE GOSPEL FOR THE CITY

PROLOGUE

TEN years on the divided city of which I wrote in *Built as a City* is yet more deeply divided.

It is still substantially true that the Church has been unable to establish a strong, locally rooted Christian presence among the groups that society leaves without voice or power. The poor often feel that the Christ the Churches preach is not for them. They do not see us standing for justice in a way which may lead to our own disadvantage.

The inner city has become a regular topic, sometimes an irritant, in the consciousness of comfortable Britain. That consciousness makes many people long to help, yet feel helpless about how to go about it. We need to understand better, to stop blaming the poor and to commit ourselves to bringing about the changes that are within our power. When we do, we learn fresh truths from Christ, who is in special ways to be found close to the poor.

Understanding how a great city has been built up is hard work. A city is not built by magic. Nor will it be mended by magic. The story is a complex one; urban disadvantage is not caused simply by bad housing, or lack of jobs, or low pay, or poor schooling, or lack of good health care or inefficient transport, or sparse and ill-placed facilities, but by a confusing interlocking of all these. We are tempted to give up when a subject becomes complex and confusing. Love of our neighbour calls us to 'hang in there' until we begin to understand.

Built as a City relates some history and some experience drawn from twenty years living and working in London's inner city. It attempts to look at the interlocking causes of deprivation.

For the last nine years I have served in Liverpool. From the North-West of England we are inclined to look at London and the South-East as the affluent part of Britain. But there is a very large part of London, especially in the inner city, where both black and white people do not share that undoubted affluence and opportunity which the South-East enjoys. In 1981 the Brixton and Toxteth riots shocked comfortable Britain. They sprang out of a deep sense of alienation: people felt themselves deserted, unvalued; 'No one hears us.'

Deprivation and the division of our nation have accelerated sharply during these last ten years. In *this* book unemployment appears as a serious threat. By the time I wrote *Bias to the Poor* out of my Liverpool experience, unemployment was filling the horizon of every urban working-class community. At the heart of the problem lies the decline of manual work. By 1981 there were almost 2.5 million fewer manual jobs in Britain than in 1970. Employment in manufacturing industry has collapsed in the old cities. In London it dropped by 40% between 1961 and 1975. The pressure for wealth creation as a nation and for higher productivity has led to the displacement of labour by capital invested in new technology. It needs to be said that unless we invested in at least some new technology we should be unable to compete at all with other countries. But the effect of these changes on the weakest groups in the labour market has not been faced.

A dual labour market has come into being: one, highly trained and highly paid, is ready to move, perhaps to the 'Sun Belt' of the M4 corridor, employers preferring new machines on new sites to reinvesting and redirecting workforces in the old cities.

The other part of the labour market is found in what I describe as 'the community of the left behind'. Age or lack of skills makes job-seekers vulnerable; they cannot compete with skilled workers. They do not see the value of moving house away from family and community when mass unemployment is nationwide. Government ministers and employers repeatedly talk of the need for young people to 'get mobile'. They seem blind to the damage which such mobility does to inner city communities. Such mobility is highly selective; it is the self-confident who will move.

The jobs which continue to exist in London and the other old cities increasingly go to commuters rather than inner city people. It is quite often said that more people are in work, and that therefore new jobs have been created. The majority of these will often be part-time jobs for women. The proper call for small businesses to develop will need a massive response to catch up with the relentless tide of closures which the old industrial and commercial cities have witnessed.

For school-leavers, going to work has traditionally been their introduction to the adult world. For the vast majority in inner city areas that introduction does not now exist. Urban areas with 95% youth unemployment are breeding alienation, with a destructive influence flowing back into schools where even eleven-year-olds ask what is the point of working. It would be one matter for all parts of the nation to be facing austerity in a time of economic recession. It is an altogether sharper challenge to the Christian to recognise that the burden falls on entirely predictable groups – those who are most powerless.

The Archbishop of Canterbury has appointed a two-year Commission on Urban Priority Areas. Our task is to listen to those who live and work in inner city areas and corporation housing estates round the edge of the cities; it is to look again at the task of the Church, to make recommendations for fresh action and to raise public policy questions.

We shall help no one if we are not realistic. The human picture of inner city life is increasingly gloomy; yet there are persistent and strong flickers of hope to be seen. For years there have been prophecies of the total extinction of the Church in inner city areas. Against all the odds little centres of resistance to apathy and materialism have survived. The danger of thinking in terms of survival is that a backs-to-the-wall mentality develops, concerned only with inward-looking Church life. My impression is that a growing number of churches in Urban Priority Areas give a much higher priority than before to looking outside church buildings and activities; they involve themselves in the life, needs and joys of the community in which God has placed them. For example, Church people in one corporation housing estate on the edge of Liverpool have re-ordered the church building so that it can be a drop-in centre for anyone, open every day of the week. And they have been among the prime movers in getting the whole community involved in a festival day each summer.

One of the two day visits of the Archbishop's Commission to inner city areas was paid to the Bishop of Stepney's area. We saw large and unsuitable church buildings, small congregations, massive human needs: one member of the Commission, often critical of the Church's performance, said to me, 'What other body could bring together such a variety of marvellous people?'

Again my impression is that more people in comfortable Britain are seeing the point that they have more power than they supposed to help disadvantaged people by the policies they follow in their working life. I think of a manager who insists on the figures being brought to him each month of how many black people have applied for posts, at what levels they have applied and what has happened to their applications.

A growing number, too, of Christians in other parts of the Church have shown themselves willing to release clergy and lay workers to go where the needs are greater.

If the Church wants to call the nation to new priorities, we must reflect those priorities in Church manpower and money. If a much greater commitment is made to Urban Priority Areas, it will be costly to the Church in other areas; at the same time it will help the Church to question its assumptions and its priorities.

One of the assumptions has often been that the Christian gospel is first and foremost a personal matter. It is indeed personal; equally it is corporate. It is about changing both human hearts and social structures. God sets us in families and communities. It is part of the lesson the big city has to teach us that being 'members one of another' will always involve others, and not simply those of like mind and similar background.

The Church is both a spiritual community and a springboard for social action. A belief that Jesus's teaching about the Kingdom of God relates to this world as well as to the next will lead Christians to involvement in community and into politics. In a meeting of Latin American Bishops an attack was made on Christian leaders espousing left-wing ideologies. Bishop Schmitz of Peru replied, 'Let him who is without an ideology cast the first stone.' Those who avoid all political involvement tacitly agree to the status quo or to the policies of the government of the day. Like it or not, all of us take up a political stance.

The present government's policies since 1979 have hit those with least power and least voice very hard. Public spending cuts have reduced the Rate Support Grant massively; even when the Urban Programme is taken into account, this has weakened the capacity of local government to act and often pushes those who are hurt into the arms of those who offer more extreme answers. At the same time heavy tax relief is granted to those buying their own home on mortgages. They receive more public money than council tenants. It is fashionable to say that urban problems are not solved by throwing money at them. A major initiative was taken by the Conservative Secretary of State for the Environment, Peter Walker, in the 1970s in setting up the Inner Areas Study. Following on from this the Labour Secretary of State, Peter Shore, in 1977 started a multi-pronged attack on the inner city problem with the hope of diverting major resources this way. It cannot be claimed that the plan failed, because it was never tried. What happened was that the problem grew worse and the resources were reduced.

Most of all the conscious abandonment of a full employment policy has sharpened the patterns of powerlessness and dependence which afflict so many who live in Urban Priority Areas.

The repeated emphasis is that we have to increase the size of the national cake before the poor can receive a better slice of it. To use another metaphor this policy relies on what in World Development terms has been called 'trickle down'. There is no evidence that in the United States, which has the largest 'cake' in the world, or in Britain in years when this country was the wealthiest, the poor received a proper share. That would require a new political will.

Those who are deprived don't expect Christians to be able to have a magic wand to remove their disadvantages. If we claim to come in the name of Jesus, they do expect us to lose our innocence, and to involve ourselves deeply in community life and public debate. If we fail, they may still come to see us as true allies. What they and we will know to be sin is indifference or withdrawal.

We know that evil will continue to be present in the world. That does not mean that we must put up with it. All of us are called to change the course of events. All of us have some influence over the events which offer great opportunities to some and great disadvantages to others. We are 'members one of another'. We need a new vision, if our nation is to be united – a vision of whole-hearted service, which never ignores the disadvantaged.

This book is not simply about what the Church should do in the inner city. It is about the attitudes, beliefs and priorities of the whole Church.

David Sheppard
Liverpool 1984

One

THE PRESSURES OF THE CITY

CITY FACTS AND FACTORS

THE city stands for choice. This is its attraction, its dilemma, and its contradiction. Many city-dwellers find they have no power to choose. They are sucked into big cities by forces with which it seems impossible to argue. They arrive in their millions.

So in London seventy persons per acre is the rule for housing density on most large new estates, compared with 10 per acre in some privately-owned housing in the suburbs. In Singapore they are building for 1,800 persons per acre and in Hong Kong for 2,000.

Such is the pressure of life in the city today.

My focus in this book will be on the big city and especially on those groups of city dwellers who feel themselves most hemmed in and powerless. The issues I shall raise will be somewhat different from those in smaller industrial towns and cities. They have what is socially a more mixed community, and more people are likely to belong to formal leisure-time associations such as evening classes, cricket clubs or churches. 'Smaller' in modern urban terms probably means any city of less than 500,000. Beyond a certain size, a whole further range of problems appears to develop in a city.

I hope this does not mean that what I write will be irrelevant to smaller industrial towns and cities. But, because my own experience is of London and Liverpool, and because there are issues which are different in kind as well as in scale, I shall concentrate on the big city.

Nine months spent in Australia after I had worked for seven years in London gave me a strong sense that cities like Brisbane, Adelaide and Perth, whose populations numbered 500,000 to 800,000, did not seem to face the same kind of problems that London did. On the other hand, both Sydney and Melbourne, with two millions each, did have the pressures of a big city. Why not restrict all cities to a million or less, I have wondered. If only we could!

Many city dwellers *chose* to migrate to the city. But there are great compulsive forces that seem to suck other men into cities in their millions. In most migrations there is a powerful persuader that encourages people to leave home. Sometimes it is persecution; for example the Asians expelled from Uganda in 1972/3. The Jews of Anatevka in the play *Fiddler on the Roof* did not choose to go and settle in New York, Warsaw or Jerusalem. They were pushed.

Rural Poverty

Rural poverty is the main cause of movement to the city. In 1950, one million people left their homes in eastern Brazil. They did not choose to go to Rio de Janeiro or Sao Paulo any more than the millions who flock into Calcutta or those who seek work in Johannesburg choose those cities. Rural poverty drives them just as it drove the Irish to London, Liverpool, Glasgow or New York, and just as it has driven Pakistanis, Indians or West Indians to Britain. There will soon be twenty Calcuttas in the developing world. There are serious issues here that must be tackled. In Calcutta a million people live in bustees with one tap for each fifty families. In Sao Paulo, where 250,000 new city dwellers may arrive every year, public services have broken down to such an extent that poor people take three hours to get to work and three hours to get home from work.

The United States and Russia would acknowledge similar

stresses in their cities. Communism and capitalism both offer material plenty, but neither has any adequate message about quality of living. Neither has solved the problem that big cities segregate society deeply and allow whole 'communities of the left behind' to develop even in the most affluent states. The black ghettos of North American cities have grown up in the wealthiest society in the world. As I have listened to descriptions of the barriers which prevent people developing their potential in these ghettos, I have had a strong feeling that it was areas of London which were being portrayed — and I do not mean in a racial sense.

Society today is expressed in urban living, so trying to understand what the big city does to people and what Christ's mission within it is is not a marginal subject for Christians. Urban mission is one of the priorities today in God's work. If we fail here, if we ignore the city and its pressures, there is no gospel which we can preach anywhere else with integrity. 'In Europe at the time of the industrial revolution the Church failed to meet the challenge. It must not fail again.'[1] But has it the ability and insight to cope with the facts of the city and the pressures those facts create?

GOD'S PURPOSE FOR THE CITY

IN the Old Testament dream, every man should sit under his vine and his fig tree.[2] But the Bible's teaching about creation does not encourage us to withdraw from the attempt to make the city a good place. God the Creator has a purpose for the city. Romantic thought about creation takes our imaginations to oceans, sunsets and mountain ranges.

But the great chapters about creation in the Bible, generally reach their climax when they speak of the inhabited world of men. For example, Wisdom speaks as a person in Proverbs, chapter 8. Wisdom was beside God at the creation like a master workman. 'I was daily His delight, rejoicing before Him always, rejoicing in His inhabited world, and delighting in the sons of men.' Man is given dominion over all things in this universe and is told from the very beginning to subdue the earth.[3] He is called to be God's partner in making the world what He wants it to be.

Creation

There are two accounts of the creation in the first two chapters of Genesis, taking up the story from different points of view. In chapter 1, God's own creative activity includes forming and naming. In chapter 2, man is enlisted to help. He does the naming. In that way he takes a full share in the continuing creation of the world. Naming for the Hebrew did not mean simply attaching an arbitrary label. It meant conferring on something its essential meaning and significance.[4] From the beginning man was to be a responsible partner. When we act responsibly and plan and build cities where community and human warmth develop, we are sharing with God in His work of creation.

Belief in God is difficult for many because of earthquakes, wars and other destructive events. But they are more likely to believe if, along with an acknowledgment of evil, they have some experience of goodness and purpose in the world around them. They can understand something of what Christians mean, when we say that they are made 'in the image of God', if they have some experience of putting their own stamp on their environment. Often city dwellers find it more difficult to believe in a God who is good and purposeful than people from town and country.

There are certainly parts of cities which are the product of good planning. Wise government has made the effort to enable people to know that they have a part in maintaining the life of the community. Other parts of cities are the product of indifference and calculated greed in those who wield power. They are also the product of a fatalism, almost unconscious, on the part of good men who have given up the effort to make the city warm and human. The city traps people. Millions all over the world feel this. They then begin to feel that nothing they think or say will ever change anything. Christians who hope that people will make conscious, responsible choices to serve the living God must not withdraw from the complex issues of the city. They must commit themselves to help make it the liberating organism a city can be. A book about urban mission cannot therefore be only about the life of the Church. It must look too at the sociology of that which is 'built as a city'.

The big city is like a machine in which several cog wheels have different functions. If the machine is to work properly each of the cog wheels must engage with the next. If we look at housing or education or industry in totally separate compartments, we shall end up with half truths. The same is true of the Gospel. It must not only contain 'Church Truth' about spiritual or religious matters. Unless that cog wheel engages with 'World Truth' or 'Urban Truth', it will not have any effect on the machine which is the big city. The powerless and the voiceless in the big city will not take our gospel seriously unless it grapples with the issues within community life and with justice.

Good and Evil

The big city throws into relief significant developments both of good and evil. This is true not only of economic life but also of the intellectual and the artistic areas. Constant contact with other men frees the human mind and makes easy the exchange of ideas. It 'permits the accumulation of enormous quantities of human raw material whose synthesis is to the glory of human intelligence'.[5] To use such a phrase is not to contradict a desire to give glory to God. The same Psalm, which speaks of man as little less than a god and as master over all the creatures, begins and ends with the same phrase, 'O Lord our sovereign, how glorious is Thy name in all the earth.'[6]

Harvey Cox wrote a more optimistic book about *The Secular City* in 1965 than he might write now. Its optimism should be taken critically but seriously. It celebrated the modern city as 'Technopolis'. This has a culture quite distinct from what 'tribal' man and 'town' man knew. As an illustration he pictured 'technopolitan man' sitting at a giant switchboard of relationships. Through relationships made at work, in the community and through a thousand interest groups, technopolitan man can communicate with all kinds of people. Immense variety of culture, entertainment, education and opportunity is at his finger tips. This means that he has to learn to choose, not only from among fifty films, plays or concerts, but from among many more people than 'town' man ever knew. If some personal relationships are to have real depth and meaning, many others must be kept 'functional'. He should not feel guilty that he only knows the supermarket cashier or the man who reads the gas meter in a 'functional' way.

Harvey Cox rejected the dismay which a group of ministers expressed after a survey on new 'high rise' dwellings. They found that few people wanted to meet their neighbours and that they had no interest in community groups. He claimed that for them to be anonymous is good and necessary, that they must resist efforts to produce a kind of 'village togetherness', if they are to maintain any human relationships at all. Anonymity, he said, rescues a man from the life of a village where everyone will always know that he is John Smith's son. It sets him free to be himself and choose what relationships he will, rather than have them forced on him by the chance of who his next door neighbour is.

Liberating

If you know how to 'work the switchboard', how to make varied relationships, living in the city is a liberating experience. When we lived in London, we could choose a circle of friends who gave us insight across class and race barriers. The world was marvellously open to us, and all within a radius of ten miles! That was all very well for us. My wife and I have lived in Islington, Canning Town, Peckham and now Liverpool since we were married. Each time we moved, we were free to choose where to live. Most of our neighbours in these inner city areas were not able to make choices about where to live. Harvey Cox's rejection of the value of neighbourhood life stems from the experience of more sophisticated people, who consciously determine their needs and aims. For many others, particularly the elderly and those who have achieved less educationally, the city becomes a terrifyingly lonely place. If there is not the warmth of a human community in the neighbourhood, there is a feeling of 'lostness' that can be overwhelming.

A WORD ON THE MASS MEDIA

MY experience in London suggests that there is a link between greater affluence and a loss of community strength. Those who knew a strong sense of belonging in terraced streets have been encouraged by advertisers to see progress in terms of commodities for the home. More domestic appliances, colour television, a new or second car, all tend to make someone more of an individual who becomes less conscious of being an active member of a community. Hire purchase payments make more and more overtime necessary and there is less and less time for participation in community life. 'Nothing makes markets like a family' say the advertisers. That sounds as though they will be an influence for good. But a family loses something if it has lost the sense of community.

Television brings the issues of the whole global village into our living-rooms. We are emotionally, yet despairingly, involved.[7] We acknowledge that these great issues need to be tackled. But they overwhelm us. We don't see what we can possibly do to help, and feel ourselves to be helpless bystanders. In *The Uses of Literacy* Richard Hoggart wrote in 1957[8] of the effect of the mass media, particularly on people for whom it was a new experience to have the money and the leisure time to do what they wanted. He believed the greatest damage is done by the trivialising of everything. 'Good' values like freedom, equality and progress are never questioned. They are turned into so much candyfloss. Freedom is always 'freedom from', never 'freedom for'.

'Everyone's entitled to his own opinion.'

'Wouldn't you do the same in his place?'

'Well it brings in the money, doesn't it?'

'It doesn't matter what you believe so long as your heart's in the right place.'

These attitudes may spell tolerance, but it is the sort of tolerance that leads to a refusal to be committed beyond the limited familiar areas of life. There is no real risk involved. Equality as it is presented in the mass media, encourages people to believe that success in life is all a matter of luck. It tends to undervalue the need for sheer effort in the use of our minds and to minimise the need to take unpopular decisions and to show self-discipline. Progress is often presented in terms of growth rates, which in turn are interpreted in terms of consumer goods. The popular media over-simplify issues. Their rules are to present 'short, unconnected and pepped-up items'.

When serious debate on television intrudes into an evening's entertainment, the politician or the commentator — or those who take part in religious programmes — are in a major dilemma. To tackle great matters in a four-minute comment usually produces answers which are four minutes deep. The viewer becomes no more than a voyeur, as Hoggart wrote more recently. 'Tragedy and comedy become aesthetic objects mediated through technology and of roughly the same weight or weightlessness, since they are not connected to any decision by us.'[9] The sense of unreality extends to the needs of the city in which we live. We see bad housing, we know that children are given inadequate opportunity, but we feel powerless to do anything about it.

There is much more that should be said about the mass media, but this is not the book in which to do it. What is relevant here is the contribution to the sense of powerlessness made by the mass media, especially in life in the city.

WITHDRAWAL

WITHDRAWAL is perhaps the most damaging attitude of our times. People who have access to power, who 'know how to work the switchboard', and who have great abilities, could offer them to the community, but avoid the issues by withdrawing from them. Specialism in profession and jobs is one of the causes of this. The need for a very high degree of skill in his own field often stretches a professional man to his limits. This increases the tendency to keep life in carefully separated compartments. He defers to other specialists in their field. He doesn't have any view about public values, because that's not his subject. The managing director, or the leader of the council, ought to be, above anything else, the guardian of the overall vision, but the need to stay in business or in office dominates his time, so he just isn't available. It is perhaps this that provides the justification of a Christian minister's offering of his insight in matters whch are not his expertise. The city desperately needs a 'generalist' view, an overall vision.

The sense of powerlessness is perhaps greatest for the wives of professional men. They are usually well educated and intelligent. They often live in commuter zones where life is self-contained and where issues are difficult to identify and don't relate to life as they experience it. Economically they know they take most out of the city. At the same time, they feel more powerless than most to contribute personally to its well being. Keeping life in separate compartments, holding increasingly private values, and living in segregated zones of a city, together make withdrawal seem the only possible response to their situation.

This inevitability about urban life is just what needs to be challenged most. Bigness, or 'the system', is blamed, though very quickly the failures of other systems are declared. We assert that as a country we are doing all we can. Class barriers are lessening, we say. Everyone has the same opportunity to get on, if he has the ability and works hard, we say. I don't believe this is true. Nor do I believe that the dehumanising effects of the big city are inevitable. I believe we can identify and appreciate some of the major causes of the dehumanisation process, and that we can fight back.

When I arrived in Islington in 1955 as a green young curate, I said to a friend, 'I don't believe the leader type live round here.' I have long been ashamed of that remark. In the first place I have no doubt at all that there is ample intelligence and ability in working class areas if it is given the opportunity to develop. Secondly I realise that what I meant was, 'People like me don't live round here.' I made the assumption that my public school and university background had given me, that within the community there were whole sections which could be thought of as 'leaders' and 'led'. Thirdly, I realised that such assumptions encouraged dependence in those who were influenced by such leaders, while discouraging the more independent minded from real involvement.

Different Cultures

What helped me as much as anything to change this assumption was to see the parallel with Europeans from one culture serving in another, for example in India or Indonesia or Uganda. To go to such an area from Europe, imagining that you know everything and that they can't help themselves, would destroy the value of going. Of a variety of Americans going to a mythical country in South-East Asia in *The Ugly American,* the majority spend their time among 'influential people'. Then follow those who are anxious that the nationals should understand just how much Uncle Sam is doing for them. Only a retired engineer, and one or two others like a Middle-West chicken farmer try to understand the people of the country, offer the skills they have to help, but wait for the people of the country to take a lead in developing their own country in their own way.[10]

If I were called to serve in developing countries, I hope I would know that I was going from a different culture and background to a different culture and background. I would expect to learn quite as much from going as I would be able to give. The same is true for someone coming as I was from a professional family's culture to a working class culture. I realised that I came not from a superior to an inferior, but from a different to a different way of life. In speaking of valuing working class culture, I am not denigrating the culture of other social groups. There are great virtues among the values which we describe as 'middle class'. Some values are quite neutral, and may or may not be appropriate in other social groupings, others need to be challenged. The point is the *difference* rather than assuming that one culture is superior.

The experience of being immersed in a different culture and learning to respect its values caused me to question a great many assumptions. Parents who stay close to their children when they come back from university with the new culture of another generation often have a similar enlarging experience of being faced with a 'counter culture'. This experience can stimulate new awareness of the world around you, new significance in your job, a new sense of the variety in people, new wonder in marriage, new consciousness of yourself. This, at least, was my experience. It helped me to realise that the world is a bigger place than it seems if I stay hemmed in by a circle of people who all have the same sort of experience and background. The clash of cultures can be marvellously creative. In the city we need the insights of everyone who can add to our vision.

Unequal Opportunities

Young people who rebel against the system claim that only when they stand outside it do they see with clarity what it is doing to people. Then the unequal opportunities it offers to different sections in the country seem crystal clear. They feel that their parents cannot afford to face the implications, because they believe that their advantages in life rest on the disadvantages of others. They determine to stay true to their ideals in a way which they feel that their parents and the institutional Church have failed to do. The vision is both true *and* over simple. The attack is often made on all institutions. It is true that many organisations set out to serve people, but become institutionalised in such a way that they insist that those who want their benefits must first fit in with their system. Many young people bring a spontaneity which demands that we discover real needs, and break through an institution's rules in order to meet those needs. But it is a mistake to believe that all institutions as such would be better swept away.

A person with this 'new consciousness' of society has three commandments: Do no violence to yourself; No one judges anyone else; Take full personal responsibility. If he wants to take on some issue, his whole life style must fit. He takes full personal responsibility for getting things changed. But there is one important proviso. His actions must not include doing violence to himself.[11]

I understand that determination to keep personal ideals uncompromised. That can be done without rejecting all institutions and all allies. There can be honourable alliances to achieve short or medium term goals between those who do not agree about every issue in life. Getting barriers moved in the big city needs all the allies we can get, and a lot of time. Institutions are needed to maintain continuity and trust, not only from authorities who offer public money, but from those who wonder who they can trust. The city is littered with broken promises made, for example, to young people by those who responded spontaneously to the needs they saw. A year or two later they have gone. Often sadly it would have been better if they had not raised hopes at all, if they were not going to sustain their work.

Social work bodies, voluntary agencies, settlements and the institutional Church need constantly to be reformed so that they actually serve people, rather than simply maintain their life. Such reform needs the vision of those who have perhaps seen the system's failures most clearly because they have stepped outside it. Some will find they can serve within such institutions; others can bring pressure to bear on them. What they cannot afford to do, if they really want the well-being of the big city, is to write off the institutions, or to believe that a revolution which destroys the whole system will by magic produce a better life. Revolution is only another sort of withdrawal because it refuses to attempt the hard grind of working out, persuading and sustaining that real policies which help real people demand.

Disillusionment

Middle-aged caution can crush ideals. But the ideals will only lead to greater disillusionment if the reality of the big city is not faced. Must we then accept that man is only the victim of the forces which psychology and sociology describe? Is he a prisoner of the past? The Resurrection of Christ is God's great event which comes 'out of the future'. It could not have been predicted from any of the events

which went before. It claims that in partnership with the
living Christ, man can take his values from the future and
expect to see the present changed by them. The Resurrection
is 'a history making event in the light of which all other
history is illumined, called in question and transformed'.[12]
The Biblical view of the city is both to acknowledge the evil
which is in it, and to catch and strengthen the vision of the
City of God. Like all visions, it will be rejected by practical
men, unless we are prepared to do the hard work of translat-
ing vision into limited objectives which can actually be
reached now.

The New Jerusalem comes finally not by man's effort's
but by God's. That is an assertion that God is not a prisoner
of the forces He has created. To worship such a transcendent God should bring a sense of proportion and of
humour to our life in the very imperfect city we live in.[13] It
rescues us from the sense of powerlessness and helps us to
face our calling. We are made in the image of God. We too
are to transcend the forces which dehumanise. We can make
choices which effect our destiny and that of others. We are
not to withdraw.

SEGREGATED CITIES

THE sharp divisions of large cities into single class communities means that each social group is the loser. The
group forgets its responsibilities to the others and each is
ignorant of what can be learned from another. A Christian
group in commuter belt Surrey studied 'What we are contributing to the death of inner London'. It was right to speak
in those terms. Acceptance of segregation means that we

understand each other less and less. The city which should be the place which enables us to communicate widely across the social barriers becomes more and more sharply a place of 'them' and 'us'.

A zone for professional people, a zone for the middle classes, a zone for the working classes and a zone for the poor means that each group can communicate with members of their own class more conveniently. But they will become increasingly ignorant of what other groups are saying. The dream of a city, 'An organism for communication, *our* city which we all have in common'[14] is lost. We live so near to each other, but we don't know each other.

The tragedy of every very large city is that communications between social groups have broken down. When we speak simply of 'them' from whichever side of the barrier we speak, we have little understanding and, very often, little respect for 'them'. If 'charity' has become a dirty word in the English language, it is because we have lost the capacity to have respect for people. Churches, missions, settlements, teachers and social workers, indeed a great army of 'educators', has descended on working class London in the last hundred years. A huge amount of 'caring' has been offered and given. That is beyond dispute. But few believed that working class people could take responsibility for developing their own community, or expected that local leaders could emerge from within church and society without their first being 'elevated' out of their own culture into middle class culture. My experience in inner London and Liverpool makes me reject this assumption, for ability and intelligence are present in every part of the community.

There is something about life in large working class communities, let alone in stress areas of real poverty, which blocks the development of intelligence and reduces people's ability. Those young people who do achieve well in school or at work usually want to buy their own home. The housing stock we have allowed to develop, whole zones of council estates here, expensive districts there, modest priced houses out there, forces them out of their own district to which they could give so much. This increases the segregation of the city, and the sense of powerlessness in the community they have left behind.

Everyone has a certain feeling of powerlessness about life in the big city. That should not blind us to the fact that some groups are, in real terms of being able to make choices, faced with powerlessness of a quite different order, and to a much greater degree. That 'special' powerlessness relates to lack of access to real wealth. The debate is frequently conducted about what wages men earn. It is assumed that opportunity for a full share in our common life is open to working class people now, because most receive good earnings. Later in the book I shall attempt to shift the ground to a discussion of what real wealth is. But at the heart of the debate is the question of power and powerlessness. There are scarce resources in the big city (for example, land, good jobs, good teachers). The most powerful have the greatest access to these scarce resources. But what of the powerlessness of the 'have-nots'?

Powerlessness Corrupts

Power corrupts, but powerlessness corrupts also. The big city has its most disastrous effects when particular groups within the community feel impotent and unable to change anything or even to have access to the processes of making decisions which affect their lives.

An extreme example of this impotence is to be seen in some groups of the black community in London. One evening in 1970 I visited an all black youth club. I was met with hostility, repeatedly asked, 'Would you like to tell us why you have come here'? There were long descriptions of how in housing, in jobs, in schools, black people did not receive a fair deal. (I have heard word for word the same complaints from white people who have the same sense that they are at the bottom of society's layers: 'If you go for a job and tell them your address is E.16, they just don't want to know.') In the youth club there was much talk of overthrowing this corrupt society, but there was no suggestion as to how any progress could be made, or what to put in place of society as we know it.

A few weeks later I spent an evening with a dozen responsible leaders in the black community from different parts of London. Again, the most lasting impression I took away was of a sense of impotence. It took over an hour to get past the subject of the police and the way they were said to push black people around. There was one other white man present. He said that it was as though people wanted to go to see a man who lived in a big house. When they knocked at the door, the man sent the butler to get rid of them. They focused the frustration and anger which they really felt against the owner on the butler because he was the only person they could reach. The police are in the butler's place. Black or white people, who feel shut out from the places where the decisions are taken and where power is wielded, must press to see the owner of the house, the group with power, and to take an increasing share in making decisions which affect their destiny.

Industry is the most obvious place where one group has made decisions and possessed power while others have felt unable to share in that power. The influence of the roles people play in industry reaches very widely into the rest of their lives. 'The capitalist will give you sport, welfare and charity and everything but one thing, and that is power,' said Ernest Bevin in 1934.[15] 'He will hold on to that, the power to give you the sack, to impose his will and withold from you the means of sustenance. Such power is unwarrantable.' Working class people feel that they don't ask you to share in the decision making — unless you are a 'promising' lad. Then you are invited to cross the floor to the management side and leave your 'mates'.

THE WORKING CLASSES

I MUST set out to define what I mean by the 'working class'. Many object to the phrase. Class is a sore spot in British life. Many do not want to see it faced and discussed. There are further difficulties. It is regarded as fair to say, '*I'm* working class'. For someone else to say of that person, '*He's* working class' is thought to be patronising. Nevertheless, class divisions will not run away because we affect to ignore them. A very large number of people think of themselves as 'working class'. It is for them a description to be proud of. They would use no other phrase. I therefore use the description that a very large number of my friends who live in urban and industrial areas would use of themselves. It would, however, be more accurate to speak of the working classes.

No one definition about relation to the means of production, or about which jobs people do will be adequate. How people feel about their position in society has to do with 'status' as well as 'class'. To understand the differences which are still felt means attempting to enter the world of attitudes to education, to industry, to the decision making processes in society.

On the one hand 'working class' is not another name for

'the poor'. My focus will not be primarily on the 'problem families' with whom social workers spend most of their time. They will come into the picture, because they live within the same districts. But nothing has been more misleading than the identification of the mission of the Church and of other 'educators' in working class London with the idea of a mission to the poor. Thank God, people are called to serve prostitutes, drug addicts, meths drinkers and homeless families. But these particular needs are not the majority needs in working class areas and never have been. One of the factors which has masked the failures of the Church was that, in days of real poverty, the poorest people came to the activities the Church promoted just because there was nowhere else to go. 'My dad was out of work for fifteen years before the war', a member of the Mayflower Family Centre told me. 'It was luxury to come round here and have a chair to sit on.'

A Step Up

On the other hand, some manual workers try to draw away from any sense of belonging to the working classes. Mr. Lloyd moved to Woodford, a largely middle class suburb.[16] He said that he had come quite a long way from being a Shadwell boy earning five shillings a week to having his own house out in Woodford. 'Coming a long way' wasn't referring to miles (it is only nine stations on the London Underground). He saw Woodford as a step up the ladder. He and his wife started their married life in two rooms in Bow. The house came up for sale, but he could not afford to buy it. After that he said to his wife, 'I'm going to work hellish hard for the next five years. You help me, and I promise you, you'll have your own house.' Six years later he paid the deposit on a small house in Leytonstone and, to start with, let off half of it. Later he could afford the deposit for their present house. 'It's a good feeling that you've achieved something. Something you've done, something you're proud of. I could have stayed in the East End, but it didn't appeal to me. I wanted something better for my family. There's always something better than what you've got if only you're prepared to work for it.'

We have to look a little closer at working class attitudes if we are going to understand what belonging to the working classes means. A useful way of seeing the different attitudes of the manual workers who make up more than half the population of Britain, is by three different reactions to powerlessness. The 'traditional' working classes usually took up one of two attitudes. The first was 'deferential'. The deferential accepts that others are the leaders in society. He, or very likely she, recognises authentic leadership in those who claim to pursue the interest of the whole firm or of the whole nation, as opposed to 'sectional' or 'class' interests. The second attitude was 'proletarian'. Historically its most highly developed forms seem to be associated with industries like mining, docking and shipbuilding. There is pride in doing 'men's work'. of being the people on whom the whole nation's structure is built. With this goes a sense of shared experience and a belief that powerlessness can only be removed by standing together, the 'solidarity' of the workers. A third attitude has been described as 'privatised'. A privatised worker has a very loose sense of attachment to his job or his fellow workers. Work is seen as a means to an end, and the end is the development of his private life and that of his family.[17]

Out of Date?

There are those who suggest that the whole idea of class divisions is rapidly becoming out of date. They point out that Marx was mistaken in his distinctive theory of the evolution of the working class as the decisive revolutionary force. Instead of making class divisions sharper, the evolution has blurred the lines. Economic growth has brought higher living standards all round. In the best firms the division between 'staff' and 'workers' is much less. New suburbs and new towns produce communities which are made up of 'new middle class' and 'new working class'. The theory is that increasingly, the working class instead of seeing the middle classes as their enemies in the class war are themselves adopting bourgeois ways.

Embourgeoisement has been studied a great deal. One of the reasons is the politicians' concentration on marginal seats in elections. Both Conservative and Labour leaders believe that they must capture the 'middle ground' in the electorate that hovers between 'right' and 'left'. In other words, this is where a vital source of power is seen to lie. It is also studied because there is a deep need for reassurance that our society is moving in a 'just' direction, and that there may be hopes for an end of class conflict. The middle ground is therefore bound to be given great attention at election times. But it would be dangerous to forget areas like Inner London and housing estates like Dagenham, on the east border of London, where working class solidarity is still a very real concept among large numbers of people. Here the majority are used to thinking within a framework of receiving weekly money, of having little choice over housing, the kind of job they do, or schooling for their children. They generally see authority and those with access to power as set over and against them.

The typical view of a working class district for a hundred years was one of endless roofs and chimneys. The terraced street is ideal for the spur of the moment, casual conversation. It makes for friendship, even if it is only doorstep friendship. People have not usually asked neighbours in, perhaps because of the overcrowding (the sitting room being also the kitchen, wash room and drying room, plus the probability of another family living upstairs), perhaps because of the need to establish some privacy. A friend of mine lived in half a terraced house in the streets around the Mayflower Family Centre where we lived and worked in Canning Town in east London. 'My brother lives in the next street', he told me. 'He's lived there twenty years. He's never been inside my house and I've never been inside his. We're good friends, mind. We meet every Saturday in the pub.' Now they live on the fifth floor of a tall block of flats, only a stone's throw from where the terraced street stood. His wife said to me. 'There's no one to talk to up here. Only the birds.' They have more space than they used to have, and a very pleasant living room. They could entertain in it, but that would need planning, and would be something quite new to them. Neighbourliness doesn't happen automatically as it did in the terraced street. They only pass one other door on the way to the lift and there are separate lifts for odd and even floors. So they never see the neighbours who are above them or below them.

High Density Living

Tall blocks of flats highlight many of the problems of high density living, and add some problems of their own. They have been built under the pressure that we must at all cost clear up our slums and urgently build the largest possible number of dwellings. The Housing Minister who achieves 400,000 new houses a year is thought of as a success. The result is that we have built afresh huge, one class quarters, and have created living conditions which may well cause people to feel as hemmed in as in the old tenements. 'Those blocks are like filing cabinets where some council official has decided the working class should be stacked away', said a man in one of these areas.

A shorter working week would mean a man having much unused energy, but a high rise flat provides no garden and no shed. Children and young people want room to live and of course will increasingly expect more from life. Frustration when reasonable hopes are raised is the soil in which violence is often bred.[18] There seems a strong possibility that social mobility, such as Woodford-bound Mr. Lloyd could experience by working hard, is become less possible in Inner London. This is because of the exodus of so many skilled manual jobs, and by the price of private housing. Social mobility has been assumed to be one of the crucial elements in a stable industrial society.[19] It is true that the coherence of class groups has diminished. Some manual workers have moved towards middle class attitudes. Some white collar workers, according to their status, have moved towards working class attitudes to their job.[20] But the diminishing of clear cut lines of classes does not eliminate either the reality of class consciousness or the fact that there is a conflict of interests.[21]

It is not clear just what is being claimed by those who see distinctive working class consciousness lessening. Is it a good thing or a bad thing? Are 'middle class' values what we hope everyone will have? If the process accelerates, what is urban life going to be like in ten years' time? Increasing cash would offer more consumer goods. These are seen by some not as a be-all and end-all of life, but as a way of release from the grind which prevented them from sharing in the richer experiences of life. Together with the increasing affluence, if growth continues, the sense of being hemmed in is likely to increase. Education offers the promise of a full life, which for many people remains unfulfilled. Engels observed one important factor in the 1870s and 1880s when he tried to explain why the British working class were not more militant.[22] It was that Britain was the leading industrial nation of the world. Emigration to the colonies and the

growing economy were major safety valves against the sense
of being hemmed in. Such safety valves are no longer available. We have to work for a fuller life which all can share
within our cities.

Christian Values

Christian values are bound to criticise any objectives which
measure progress simply by access to more consumer goods.
They criticise also a way of life which assumes as inevitable
that people should see work only as a boring means to an
end. They challenge an assumption that it is part of
modern life to be less involved with corporate life both at
work and in the community. Christian values must balance
talk about working class solidarity by reminding people of
human solidarity. But there often needs to be a step along
the way. Because some groups have felt relatively powerless,
they have to discover strength first through an assertion of
their own solidarity. Then they are often heard to be making
two conflicting demands; one is, 'Leave us alone. Our life
and culture is as good as yours. We're happy to develop on
our own.' The other is. 'We want a share in the common
future. Give us the opportunity to develop.' At different
stages both demands must be heard. The enemies which
cause both are inequality of opportunity and segregation.

Integration is not brought about by one dominant group
'bringing them up to our standards'. True integration asserts
that there is solidarity in one human race in our common
humanity. We are all poorer if we do not enable other
groups to be strong, and if we do not build bridges in order
to concern ourselves with them and their interests. This will
mean stimulating the life of a great variety of community
groups among those who feel powerless. We must watch for
and encourage flickers of fire which look as though they may
burn up into a strong fire of human and community warmth.

We must strengthen them and give them the resources they need. Community-life may often express itself in ways we find different, assertive and disturbing. But a boiling, vital, pluralist city is alive. It will throw up new groupings, new expressions of democracy, demanding new responses from state and Church. We must encourage such groups to be strong and then to see that they can have a stake in a common future. To strengthen the sense of belonging to a distinctive group can give a sense of real security. And it is when a man has some security, in this sense, that he more readily asks fundamental questions about life:

Who am I?
What's really going on around me?
What is my heritage?
What sort of culture do I really believe in?
What other cultures can I learn from?
What do I value most?

When we ask, 'Is God in the big city?' the doubter asks in return, 'What kind of God is He?' Belief or unbelief in a God who can change things is bound up with that which the doubters have seen in the lives of believers. Sometimes most Church members in working class areas seem to come from among those whose attitude to life is what has been called either privatised or deferential. They seem to be more among those who have withdrawn than among those who are ready to fight back.

People who live in the working class areas I have described experience the weight of great impersonal pressures upon them. These can stop a man from making the choices he wants to, and can eventually rob him of the confidence that he can make decisions at all. It is a testimony to the toughness and adaptability of the human spirit that we can list as working class characteristics, endurance, expressiveness, humour, openness, solidarity, compassion, as well as the bad things which confront us in working class life in the big city. But a man made in the image of God is not meant just to adapt to his environment. The God I believe in denies that heredity plus environment equals you. He transcends the pressures of environment and wants to set men free to do so too. He is often indignant about the framework in which we cause one another to live. Christians should often be indignant too, not with the indignation which means that you 'blow your top' and storm out of the room feeling better that you've got it off your chest, but the burning indignation which steadily works at changing things that are wrong.

But has the Church been able to make its presence felt in the past in this way? Has it changed the things that are wrong? Can it do so now? These are fundamental questions when we are dealing with life in areas 'built as a city', so we must now turn to an analysis of the strength and characteristics of church life.

Two

CHURCH LIFE IN THE CITY

CHURCH-GOING TODAY

GREAT efforts have been made over the years, by many churches in urban and industrial areas. Manpower, church buildings, mission halls, settlements and community centres have been brought in on a large scale. But in spite of it all locally rooted churches with strong local leadership are rarely to be seen.

If it can be shown that visible response to the Church is on a totally different scale in working class areas from middle class areas, who can we blame? There are four possibilities:

Working class people —presumably for being harder hearted than others.

God — for not sending revival to these areas of society.

The Church — for not learning how to be an effective vehicle of the Gospel.

Society — for what it has done to those who are trapped by the forces of the big city.

When people say in this context, 'The Gospel is the same and people are the same the world over', logic is going to lead them to choose one of the first two possibilities. Yet both answers would be a contradiction of Christ's attitude to people who worked with their hands in the days of the Gospels.

The third possibility — that is the suggestion that the Church has not learnt to be an effective vehicle for the gospel — must be taken seriously. Instead of learning from St. Paul who said he became like a Jew to win Jews and like a Gentile to win Gentiles,[1] we have tried to have a blueprint of church life, and then expected every social group to fit in with our ways. There *is* one Gospel, but both its presentation and its outworkings should have a different flavour in different cultures and social groupings within a nation no less than in, for example, Asia and Europe.

The fourth possibility of blame — society's allowing people to be trapped by the forces of the city — is not one which the Church can lightly shrug off. It has reflected within itself the sense of fatalism and withdrawal felt by so many. The cutting edge of the Gospel challenges the values and priorities of society, and the Church has too often withdrawn to a wholly 'spiritual' Gospel.

When I came to Inner London as a new curate in 1955, I believed that if only the Gospel was truly preached, it would produce the same results whatever the area. All my ministry since then has been in the inner city — in Islington, then in Canning Town and now based on Peckham. This experience has made me, as I have already hinted, question much more deeply what the Gospel is and what its implications are. And it has made me expect different kinds of results in different areas.

Local Membership

Whatever yardstick is used, the evidence is massive that indigenous church life based on local adult membership and leadership is very weak in working class areas of big cities. This assertion is often questioned by those who live in what I call by comparison the church-going belt. They often retort, 'But *we* don't have strong membership. Unbelief is not just there. It is everywhere.' I must therefore try to justify the assertion I make both from my own experience and from wider evidence. If what I say is true, the Church in all areas may have important lessons to learn from our experience in the working class areas. I say 'important', because there are many other groups in all areas which stand outside the reach of the Church's influence. The attempts of the churches of all denominations to grapple with an almost wholly unchurched situation may be more relevant to those elsewhere than at first appears likely.

To think simply in terms of church attendance statistics is generally unhelpful. It is one thing to call a man to become a responsible partner in a movement to change the world, beginning with himself. It may be a very different matter to ask him to become a member of a twentieth-century church congregation. Nevertheless numbers in church present measureable evidence, and at least show *something* of what impact the Church may be having in a neighbourhood.

The chapel was crowded for my licensing as Warden of the Mayflower Family Centre in Canning Town. Two hundred and fifty or more people were there — bishop, local clergy and people from neighbouring churches, a strong party from Islington, where I had been a curate. As the crowd drifted away after the cup of tea which followed the service, I turned my mind to the local reality hidden by that crowd in the chapel. There were six regular communicants, and perhaps twenty might come to our best attended evening service.

At the Mayflower Family Centre we were given far larger resources than most parishes can possibly provide — some ten full-time staff (of whom two were clergy), a nursery school, open youth clubs, organisations for the elderly, groups emerging in various local homes. Twelve years later the electoral roll of adults who had come to church once a month or more frequently during the last six months numbered 110. This included twenty-seven married couples who lived within a mile of the Centre. Seven were over sixty years of age. We had a promising, but young church.

Great Occasions

I list the church-going numbers lest it is supposed that the strong staff and many activities of a centre like the Mayflower lead to massive church-going. Large numbers at occasional 'great-occasions' can mask the fact that the great majority in these areas have no serious adult commitment to the Church at all.

It is not, I think, an exaggeration to suggest that, on average, half the congregation in a working class parish either would not think of themselves as belonging to the main stream of working class life, or travel to church from the suburbs. If that is right the figure for reasonably occasional adult church-going in Inner London and the large council estates is not more than 0·5%

When it first dawned on me that few working class people came to the Church of England, my hopes were that the Salvation Army or the Baptists or the Mission halls would succeed where we failed. This hope didn't survive long. My first visits to Salvation Army halls in East London discovered that one had twelve adult members, of whom only one was a man; the next had eight, of whom one was a man. As with other denominations, strong congregations are not generally to be found until you reach the more middle class districts. In Canning Town there was a well-organised Free Evangelical Church with a membership of some thirty adults, all of whom had once come from the neighbourhood, but all now lived at least two miles away and travelled back for their church life. Taking five Missions or Mission halls I know in East London, the number of church-going couples under sixty-five who live within a mile or so of all five could be counted on the fingers of one hand. The Free Churches in Inner London do rather less well in terms of members than the Church of England.

Free Churches

The churches which are organised on a more congregational
basis have to find most of the money for maintenance and
for paying their ministers and other staff. This has meant
that many Free Churches have moved out to the suburbs
when the members of their congregations have moved out.
It also means that those which remain are struggling constantly to raise enough money to keep going. For example, a
young man told me that he had completed his training for
the Baptist ministry. He believed himself called to serve in
working class Inner London. But there was no Baptist
church in such a district which could afford an assistant minister. The local church had to be able to raise £600 a year
before the London Baptist Association would help with the
rest of his salary. No church was in a position to do that at
that moment in time. So he was forced either to go and serve
in a flourishing church in the church-going belt, or to delay
his ordination, which in fact he chose to do.

It is part of its parochial dream that the Church of England commits itself to serve neighbourhoods whether there
is church-going response or not. Members of strong congregations would resent paying their diocesan 'quota' (and
their secular taxes) much less if they realised that it is an
expression of the Christian truth that we are 'members one
of another'.[2] It is no accident that it is the Church of England and the Roman Catholics who have the greatest opportunities today to serve urban and industrial districts. The
Roman Catholic situation and history must be considered
later. The Church of England is 'in business' in working
class areas for three reasons. First we maintain the parochial
dream. Secondly we believe, sometimes reluctantly and
sometimes only in theory, in the truth that we are 'members
one of another'[3] and should help one another with man-

power and money. Thirdly, which is no merit of ours, we have very large resources handled by the Church Commissioners.

Church-going numbers do not tell the whole story. But it is hard to escape the conclusion that the Church is more at ease with some social groupings than others. Many Christians like to say, 'We get a good cross section in our church.' It is a painful exercise to ask with some care what a good cross section of a neighbourhood should be. We do not like to acknowledge that such a factor as social class could affect whether people will join the Church or not. We like to assert that differences of social class are becoming less and less in the country as a whole. But consider a survey of four areas in Liverpool made in 1966.[4] Areas A and B are working class inner city areas. Area C is middle class and further out from the centre. Area D is middle-upper class on the outskirts of the city. The age at which those interviewed had left school shows dramatically the educational differences between them. How many were still at school on their sixteenth birthday?

Area A	Area B	Area C	Area D
0%	12%	28%	77%

This does not show that no one in Area A ever stayed at school till they were sixteen. It does suggest that all those who stayed at school till they were sixteen were likely to have moved out of the district by the time they were adult. Church membership in the four areas shows the same sort of pattern as has been shown in south east London. What is perhaps significant also in the Liverpool survey is that basic questions about belief in God and life after death produced the same sort of answers, whatever the area. In other words, they had the same religious awareness, but widely different response to the Church as an institution.

Manual Workers

In Area A only one out of thirty-four interviewed could be said not to come within a broad definition of manual workers. He was a foreman. In Area D no heads of household were manual workers. The difference between the two working class areas should also be noted. It would be possible for quite lively church work to be going on among the minority who had stayed at school after the age of sixteen in Area B and to be totally missing out on the main population group. The kind of programme a church's youth work offers will often show which section of the community it is going to draw from. If, for example, it runs highly programmed and obviously educational evenings of study and discussion, it is likely to attract those who do well at school, and who have perhaps already decided to move out of the area.

The distinctions between different groups in working class communities are subtle and difficult to define. In part one the descriptions privatised, deferential and proletarian were used. I set myself the uncomfortable task of putting the 109 adults in the Mayflower's 1967 voting list as honestly as I could under these headings. Staff and residents in the settlement were not on the voting list. All but two lived in the borough of Newham.

Middle class	22
Privatised	22
Deferential	7
Proletarian	58

This was in an area where there was scarcely any owner-occupied property. We had deliberately tried to build up a common life which was in tune with the neighbourhood. In many districts the Church has developed a character which appeals to those who dissent from the life of the neighbour-

hood. The vicar of one parish, which has kept the flag flying
more bravely than most, said that probably over 80% of the
congregation were not representative of the neighbourhood.
In one breath they would firmly claim that they were working class people from the district. In the next, they would
show that they strongly dissented from the style of life of
most people in the neighbourhood. They were individuals
who had the strength of character and conviction (and lack
of group sense) to break away from the group, or did so for
some other reason (perhaps because they were lonely or unhappy). Obviously the Church ought to minister to the 'aspiring' minority in working class areas and certainly to the
lonely and unhappy. The point which needs to be made is
that often a church may be developing its life without
having any points of contact with the majority of its parishioners. It is at that point that serious questions have to be
asked about whether the gospel we proclaim by our presence,
our activities, our words and worship is Christ's gospel, or
whether it has been so overlaid by our cultural inheritance
that we hide Him or misrepresent Him.

The emphasis has been on areas which are mainly or
wholly working class. In some areas, where working class
people are in the minority, the Church's life also passes
them by. A curate in a seaside Lancashire town told me that
no one had ever come to the church from Victory Avenue.
A curate in south London asked what could possibly be
done in his parish about this problem. A strong church life
was maintained, drawing members from the middle class
sections of the parish. But he didn't feel he could possibly
bring people from the working class estate to the church.
They would not feel at home.

In many mixed parishes there is an estate or a Victory
Avenue, from which few find their way to the church. No
congregation true to the oneness of the Christian Gospel can
rest easily in the face of such a situation.

THE ROMAN CATHOLICS

'THE Roman Catholics hold on to their people better than we do.' That is true enough. Before we ask why, it is interesting to note the phrase we use. Apparently the best we hope for is that we shall 'hold on to our people'. When I first came to London as a curate, a vicar said to me, 'The strategy of the parish has to be like a pyramid. There must be a very broad base of children's work ...' He never finished the sentence. It would have been difficult to do so out loud, because the way it ends is '... so that if we're lucky, some may still come to us when they're adults.' Jesus began by calling adults to be His followers. We can scarcely claim that we are engaged in evangelism unless adults are becoming new disciples.

No one suggests that on any scale the Roman Catholic Church is winning adults who are not already members of other denominations or are Catholics who have lapsed recently. But it is true that they hold on to working class people better than any other Christian group does. The Roman Catholic Church in this country has a history which is not just different from the history of the Church of England, or of the English Free Churches. It is also quite different from that of the Roman Catholic Church in other countries. Pope Pius XI said that the scandal of the nineteenth century was the gulf between the Church and the working classes. In Italy the Church was bound up in men's minds with the temporal rule of the Papacy. Italian aspirations towards nationalism meant for many the rejection of the Church. The powerful Italian Communist party gives evidence of where a huge number of working class people's allegiance lies. Surveys of French church-going led F. Boulard to say that large towns everywhere present a great problem to Christianity. A considerable proportion is always made up of non-practising Catholics; 'among certain social classes abstention [from worship] is almost unanimous.'

Some figures quoted of church-going practice of factory workers in European cities include:

| Marseilles (1953) | 3·3% |
| Paris (St. Hippolyte district 1951) | 2·5% |

Figures of adults of all social groupings attending Mass include:

Marseilles (1953)	9·8% (21 and over)
Toulouse (1953)	10·8% (23 and over)
Madrid and suburbs (1942)	17·5% (18 and over)[5]

In March 1965 the Vatican's weekly *Osservatore della Domenica* estimated that the church-going figures among the working classes in cities in Catholic countries rarely rose to 10% and were usually far below that. Figures of 3% or 5% were very normal.

The 'Irish Poor'

The history of the Roman Catholic Church in English and Scottish working class areas is bound up with that of the 'Irish poor'. The Irish flooded into Liverpool, Manchester, Glasgow, Birmingham and London to provide cheap labour. In the 1840s alone no fewer than 400,000 came. At first the English Roman Catholic Church didn't know what

to do. Catholic emancipation had only just been achieved.
English priests were likely to be 'chaplains to noblemen, by
instinct men of the private chapel and the library'.[6] They
knew they would be out of their depth in serving Irish
labourers trying to survive the worst jobs and housing in
Britain. They brought priests from Ireland to serve their own
people. In Ireland there was, and is, no big city in which the
urban poor would have become estranged as in Marseilles or
Paris. Furthermore, the Roman Catholic Church in Ireland
had never been identified with the ruling class. Rather it
had been seen to stand with Irishmen in their perennial
campaign to get rid of English rule. When the Irish poor
came to England it was inconceivable for a long time that
their boss at work would be a Roman Catholic. The old
aristocratic families would not have become dock owners
or mill owners. The Church and its priests were not in
any sense identified (as the Church of England and the
Free Churches were) with the middle classes who held the
whip-hand in industry.

The Irish lived in the very worst quarters of the big cities.
They were in a comparable position with West Indian labourers when they came to British cities in the 1950s and 1960s.
They met considerable hostility from the English poor and
working classes. When jobs were short or when owners were
trying to break a strike, the 'cheap labour' which was
brought in was not likely to be popular. The threat of
'Popery' could easily raise English hostility. There were
'race riots' in Peckham as recently as 1930 — meaning English v. Irish. The Irish suffered all the culture shock of a
move from slow-moving country life to the bewildering
mass of humanity of the cities. Their only strength was in
their own community, and they retreated into it. Within that
community, they found the strength of their Church. It
became a rallying point for people cut off from their roots.
The arrival in their midst — or coming over with them — of

an Irish priest meant that there was a man who had 'had an education', and was the focus of their hopes in the middle of their miseries and struggles. God, the Church and the priest were clearly on their side. Sometimes this led to the Irish priest becoming something of a dictator. He was tempted to build his empires, and keeping people's faith simple and dependent seemed likely to hold them loyal to the church.

Shortage of Money

The leading English Catholics, many from the old aristocratic families who had held to their faith since the Reformation, were keen to consolidate the position of the Roman Catholic Church in English society. They were not at all sure how they regarded this influx of uncouth Irishmen. It was not likely to attract the respect of educated Englishmen of their Church. The great ecclesiastical architect Pugin kept designing ornate Catholic chapels, only to find that his plans were set aside or drastically cut back for shortage of money. To his disgust cheaper materials were chosen: 'They actually propose deal and plaster,' he wrote, '. . . ere long they will advocate a *new service* suited to these conventicles — a sort of *Catholicised Methodism*.' He was appalled at the Irish priests; 'Why, Sir, when they wear my chasubles, they don't look like priests, and what's worst, the chasubles don't look like chasubles.'[7]

Cardinal Manning who was Archbishop of Westminster from 1865–92 believed that his true duty lay with the working man. Roman Catholic history has given him a poor name beside John Henry Newman, but from the standpoint of the history of the Church and the working classes, Manning's leadership was very important. Newman said that the Church regarded this world and all that is in it as dust and ashes compared with the value of a single soul. Unless she

could do good to souls, it was no use her doing anything. [8]
Manning, however, cared deeply about the position of the
labouring man in this world. He was the only bishop to
appear on the Exeter Hall platform at a meeting supporting
the agricultural labouring man, whose life he had come to
know when he was a Church of England vicar in Sussex. He
was able to intervene with some effect in the 1889 Dock
Strike. Manning wanted to keep religion simple. He did not
believe that the role of Christianity was to stretch the cap-
acities of all men. He did not want to damage the simple
faith of the poor. For example, he was opposed to mixed
marriages on any terms, because he felt that making unions
with those brought up outside the Roman Catholic fold
would weaken the simplicity of their inherited faith.

The emphasis of the Roman Catholic Church in working
class areas is to take the community, the family and the
children very seriously, and then, it might be said, to 'free
wheel' gently along. Church schools have been their first
priority. The approach to a new estate or new town includes building a Church school. For example the comparatively new parish which covers Abbey Wood. Old
Belvedere and Thamesmead had a church school from the
beginning. The parish has over 30,000 people in it but is
referred to as a parish with 3,500 Catholics, 850 of them
are practising (about 2·5% of the whole population) and 700
to 750 come to three places within the parish where Mass
is said every Sunday. In the beginning in the new town of
Thamesmead there were lots of house meetings. The parish
priest said that people found it very difficult to articulate
their thoughts. 'Now I tend more to catechise. People ask
for that.' At the same time he was convinced that many
members of the Church wanted to be involved in Church,
social or community life, and over two hundred adults were
engaged on a regular basis in such a way. There were
three local social committees which ran cheap dances on a

non-profit basis, and three social welfare committees.
They sent £400 to a parish in Peru during 1972. The
biggest social club in the district was run by the Roman
Catholic Church. On a Saturday night 500 or 600 members
would come. Nearly four fifths of these were non-
Catholics.

Social Cohesion

Such a parish nurtures the strong social cohesion which
originally came from being an immigrant group who rallied
to the Church as their point of reference and strength. Some
members of the Young Christian Workers would feel that
the efforts which go into the social club, for example, are not
sufficiently 'apostolic'. Here is posed a central question
which every church in urban and industrial areas has to
face; how can the Church present the challenge of Christ,
and the need to grow as a thinking Christian and still
be — and remain — a Church of and for the district?

Visiting a Young Christian Workers' leaders' meeting in a
Roman Catholic parish in Rotherhithe, I saw a determined
attempt to hold those two aims together. Ten young people
around twenty years of age were present (five men and five
women). The curate was there, but said nothing unless they
referred to him (which they did in discussing a Youth Mass
for which they had been responsible). I said nothing until I
was asked to comment on the meeting at the end of the
evening. The pattern was the regular Y.C.W. programme.
First there was a Gospel Enquiry. Most members contributed devotional thoughts about Christ and what He
wanted them to be. They stuck closely to the verses from St.
John which they had read. Next came Facts of the Week
when members spoke about issues at work. In each case they
were to do with personal relationships. Then they discussed
the youth service and went on to review a dance run par-

ticularly for school leavers. They spoke freely of what had gone wrong, of their own responsibility and of the need to encourage the members of the Junior Y.C.W. to take more of a lead.

The group was very relaxed. Several were extremely articulate. I felt that most were either already doing non-manual jobs or would be likely to gain promotion and that they would probably want to buy a house of their own. This is very relevant to the future of that Church in Rotherhithe, as there is no moderate-priced private property for sale anywhere in the district.

FIVE FACETS OF MOVEMENT

ANGLICANS and Free Churchmen have often endorsed the Jesuit dictum: 'Give us a child until he's five (or eleven), and we'll hold him', when appealing for massive programmes for Church schools and for children's activities at church. What they ignore is that the Roman Catholic policy is set within an Irish community which in a broad way feels that it belongs with the Roman Catholic Church and supports its children's allegiance to it. They are wise enough to take concern for the interests of that community. The Church of England and the Free Churches have no such relationship to the working class community. If anything, it is rather the opposite. English working class people largely regard the churches as belonging to another social grouping. They regard the Roman Catholic Church as a sectarian (I do not use the world in any unpleasant sense) body which ministers to the Catholic population. The English working class community has long been estranged from the churches. The Roman Catholic Church does not make adult converts from that community at a higher level than any other church.

This is not to say that all the efforts we put into Church schools and Sunday School and Bible Class work are misplaced. They root a church's work in the neighbourhood, and are frequently the only points of contact with the majority social group in the area. But we should not expect massive children's work to be any more effective than it has been down the years in establishing self-rooting adult churches, unless we effectively bring the gospel to adults at the same time. It is of the nature of most church life that it tends to make people more 'respectable'. It therefore also attracts to itself those who are the more 'respectable' members of the community. This is something the Church must face and examine. In urban and industrial areas it is particularly susceptible to the loss of members through moving out of the district. Churches in every area suffer through movement from the district. The difference is that in suburbs, towns and the country, church members move in as well as move out. In urban and industrial areas there is no 'inward' movement.

The fact that, after all the effort that has been made with children and young people, they move out of the area, is the main complaint of urban and industrial area churches. A mission on a large housing estate claimed that they would have a congregation of 300 if their young people could have found housing in the area. Twenty members from one moderate sized congregation in Peckham moved out of the district in 1971. Young married couples are often forced to move out of the area because there is nowhere to live. Often such mobility is accepted as an unquestionable fact of life. There is however cause and effect, and five factors emerge:

Mobility.

Churches often appeal only to a minority social grouping.

Christian behaviour is confused with middle class behaviour.

Christian morality is often limited to personal behaviour.

Withdrawal from 'the world' often cuts Christians off from their community.

Mobility

There is much vague talk about 'high mobility' as though it may be assumed that every Englishman moves out of his present district every five years or so. Two forms of mobility need to be carefully distinguished. There is a mobility which arises because someone can't get on the housing list or because his job demands that he moves or because his street is demolished. Some workers are more willing than others to move because their work situation changes. When workers were made redundant in south east London areas many white collar workers and managerial workers were willing to consider moving house in order to find a new job. Manual workers were much less likely to want to move. No unskilled worker would consider moving.[9] Many parishes in inner city areas and, for example, in a housing estate like Dagenham have found that the great majority of young couples have been forced to move when they are married. This is because they have no chance of getting on their lengthy borough housing list, because there simply isn't room or because the planners made no allowance for natural growth in a community.

'Social mobility' describes a quite different process. People move out to a 'nicer' district, or perhaps stay, and change the way they furnish their house and their whole style of life. This is because they want to 'better themselves', or to provide 'something better for their children'. One can well understand the profound human desire to 'go up in the world' this represents.

Minority Appeal

Churches often appeal only to a minority social grouping. A church which appeals to the young people who are better behaved, do well with books, like a highly organised programme, is almost certainly appealing to those who are going to move out of the district anyway. A survey in Pittsburgh in 1948 set out to discover how new members had been brought into the churches: $1 \cdot 1\%$ of initial contacts was provided by advertising; 11% began with contacts with an organisation of the church; 17% resulted from pastoral contacts by the clergy; 60% were recruited through 'contacts with friendly members'. This is just how we would hope churches would grow. But Gibson Winter's comment on the figures is penetrating and right.[10] Like attracts like. A congregation which, for instance, likes purposeful study and classical and church music will be unlikely to attract adults or young people who are in sympathy with the spontaneous, unbookish, non-institutional life of working class districts. Often the church acts as a reference group for those who are socially mobile, who don't feel at ease in their own district.

Middle Class Behaviour

Christian behaviour is confused with middle class behaviour. It is very natural for a new Christian to assume that the behaviour of the church people he meets is the way a Christian should behave in every situation. If he is a working class man, cut off from the majority of his fellows in this Christian adventure, he is often hopelessly outnumbered by the middle class members of the church. Few are able to be as objective as the shop steward who said that churches require you to do a crash course in middle class behaviour, rather than to learn Christian maturity. Once a working class man takes up middle class behaviour patterns, he is a major step nearer emigrating either mentally or physically from the social grouping in which he has grown up and the district in which he lives.

Christianity is a real education. Saving up, hard work, planning for the future are solid virtues if not necessarily Christian ones only. But education needs to acknowledge that there are other values. Openness, community sense and spontaneity are equally important — and perhaps rather more in step with the Sermon on the Mount. Christians should look critically both at working class values and at middle class values in the light of our best understanding of the Gospel and the teaching of the Bible.

Christian Morality

Christian morality is often limited to personal behaviour. A look at surface evils may mean that a man sees hooliganism, dishonesty at work, crude swearing, open sexual immorality and drunkenness. He may feel that he can shield his children from these by moving to a 'better' district. (He doesn't always notice that the evils there are as powerful, if more subtle and discreet.) Sometimes it may be necessary to remove a boy or girl, or a family, from their environment in order to give them a chance to build a new life. Two things need to be said about this; first, a sharp distinction should be made between mainstream working class life in what may often be termed a 'rough district' and those pockets within it where crime, non-payment of rent and work-shy attitudes are accepted as normal. These attitudes are not normal among the majority of families in urban and industrial areas. Secondly, even in the case of a difficult family we should ask much more searching questions before removing someone from his environment. George Burton, the Senior Youth Leader at the Mayflower, who had grown up in Townhead in Glasgow in the years of the Depression, was frequently asked by teenagers if he would help make arrangements for them to leave an impossible situation at home. Almost invariably he refused to do so, as he believed that the problems needed to be worked out in the situation. His own experience of running away from home at fifteen had proved to him that he hadn't escaped from his own problems by removing himself from the environment.[11]

Some Christian teaching has mentioned only personal sins, whereas the Bible includes social sins in its categories of evil for which we are responsible. For example, many Gospel sermons have been preached on the text. 'Come now let us reason together,' says the Lord. 'Though your sins are as scarlet, they shall be white as snow.'[12] The sins listed in those sermons are generally personal sins. In Isaiah's sermon on that occasion not one 'personal' sin was mentioned; he talked about pursuing justice; championing the oppressed; giving the orphan his rights; pleading the widow's cause. Christian morality includes all these. To practise it brings a strong sense of responsibility to those in a man's own neighbourhood. It often means that he senses a call to stay in the district to make whatever contribution he can to the root causes which lie beneath symptoms like hooliganism, even if this means very difficult questions for his wife and family.

Cut-off Christians

Withdrawal from 'the world' often cuts Christians off from their community. The worldly 'spirit of the age' can choke the influence of Christ in a man. Some Christians have presumed that they can escape from it by making their social contacts more and more exclusively with other Christians in leisure time and on holiday. But worldliness is an attitude of mind. Indeed, one of its most insidious forms is when the atmosphere in a group is of contempt for, or condescension to another group of neighbours. To be deeply involved in joining hands with other men of goodwill in trying to serve one's own community is much more likely to guard against the spirit of the age than does withdrawal from that community. Withdrawal from social contact with neighbours from the concerns of the district means that the natural forces which so often move a family out of an area are much less likely to be questioned.

When members move out and the numbers left behind are comparatively small, there is a strong motive for those who have moved to promise to travel back to help with the problems of leadership. This continuing process has meant first that they don't get properly involved in their new community; that they are most unlikely to lead any of their new neighbours into the life of the local church in their new district; that their church life becomes divorced from their home life; that the church to which they travel begins to lean on outside leadership.

A number of churches find that the majority of their Church Council, Deacons, Trustees or Club leaders live outside the district. It is very doubtful if a middle class church council can plan the right sort of programme for a working class district. Even if it could, its understandable determination to keep things going is likely to prevent local leadership from emerging. The alternative calls for a brave act of faith. It depends on some Christians choosing not to move out of the area. Others will rightly move away, and throw themselves into the life of the new neighbourhood. If they cut their links with their former church, the number of members may be smaller, but the challenge to local people to take responsibility is firmly put, and the church is more likely to be a church of the district.

The dependence on those who have to travel means that a spontaneous common life has to give way to meetings which happen at fixed points in the diary. In Canning Town we had to learn not to be bound by 'that ... diary', and to be available for spontaneous moments when a group might want to go out together, or to sit down to talk seriously. Even if leading members still live in the district, there is the temptation to put on the kind of programme which they want, rather than what will help the church to be the church of and for the district.

Running Out of Steam

The first time I went to a famous Baptist church in a working class district, I was delighted to hear a superb performance of Mozart's Exultate Jubilate. It was performed by a robed choir in a vast church building in the middle of a most dignified church service. Yet I was bound to ask if that service was helping them to be the Church in that district — or that district to believe that the Church could be for them.

Many Baptist, Primitive Methodist, Church of England and Pentecostal churches got away to a flying start at some point in their history. For ten or twenty years they were in a marvellous sense the Church of the neighbourhood. Then they gradually ran out of steam; members moved out of the district; others became absorbed in church life; they pressed that their church should have standards of buildings and worship like other churches; they insisted that the young people should be a credit to the Church. There is nothing wrong with any one of these processes in the lives of individuals. Nevertheless, between them they have destroyed the

effectiveness of many churches for the majority grouping
in the area. Respectable routine took over.

It is a process which happens in secular groups too. An
outstanding leader initiates a new movement. All is excitement and growth. The leader dies or moves, and routine
takes over, together with a wistful longing that the new
leader could be the same as the former one. Routine can also
remove the vitality from a new idea which sparks off a
movement. We find it difficult to produce an organisation
which expects to go on bearing new ideas and plans for
change.

The desire to have a church of and for the neighbourhood
is not an argument for the third rate in church buildings or
in worship or in content. It does not argue against having
standards. It argues for the excellence which is appropriate
to the community that *that* church is called to serve.

Standards

'Standards' is a key word in this debate. Appropriate
standards in church life and in Christian behaviour in a working class area like Canning Town cannot be measured
against those which are appropriate for the church in residential Woodford. In each case Christians have to ask what
they and the Church are meant to be for their neighbours'
sake, before they can talk about what standards are right. It
is extremely difficult to judge right standards for a church or
a school or a club unless you live in its area — and are involved in its character of life. The way of the New Testament Church was that people shared in a common life
which was open to others to join if they would. The question
thus becomes crucial, 'On whose terms do they join?' Some
churches say in effect, 'Anyone is welcome here, provided he
fits in with our standards.' The New Testament Christian
wrestled with the difficult question of how you took into

account what 'weaker brothers' wanted, what Jews wanted and what Greeks wanted. 'Whatever you are doing, do all for the honour of God; give no offence to Jews or Greeks or to the church of God. For my part I always try to meet everyone halfway, regarding not my own good, but the good of the many that they may be saved.'[13]

YOUTH WORK

THE standards we hold in front of ourselves dictate the whole programme of a church. This is most plainly seen in Youth Work. A Parochial Church Council refused the offer of a 100% grant for a qualified youth leader after some years of anxious debate. One member told me that the feelings which decided it were never really brought out into the open. He was sure that they were 'We don't want kids like that on our church premises'. They believed that they were defending standards. Were these the right standards if they influenced church people to keep the teenagers of their immediate area out of church premises? To that, we must say No.

Youth club policy often reveals our fears about ourselves as well as about young people. The ethos of the Temperance Movement which has been so influential is that it takes a hard struggle to keep yourself from being pulled down to *their* standards. So when young people come to youth organisations, we must insist on standards. The only alternative that can be contemplated is of chaos with no discipline at all.

Our fears make us pose opposites; *either* you have discipline and insist that they behave as decent youngsters behave *or* you allow chaos and have no standards at all. We must ask the same questions again: What standards are appropriate to the young people we set out to serve? On whose terms do they join? What kind of discipline does this particular leader need to hold with these particular youngsters?

Discipline

Discipline may be described as holding the reins. That involves knowing how to use the reins, and this includes both tightening and loosening. A Boys' Brigade officer said, 'I couldn't cope with the problems of control of an open youth club. The discipline of the Boys' Brigade gives me just the leg up I need. Then I can cope.' It was a humble and sensible remark. Other leaders are able to hold the reins much more loosely with groups of youngsters who would never join a uniformed organisation. In the youth club situation any leader who can't crack the whip when he needs to had better give up. But he can work for standards by different means. One leader may say to would-be members at the entrance door, 'If you join this club you will be expected to behave like . . .' Another may meet them more on their terms. He believes that they will gradually feel new values as they associate with those who have standards which they can see tested in a common life which they share.

The Albemarle Report on the Youth Service in 1958 said that the first reason for running a youth club was 'association'. The majority of youth leaders prior to that Report had agreed over the years that the first reason was challenge, or activity. Albemarle was right in its major change of direction. 'Association in itself may be useless for young people, or it may be immensely educational, according to the

imagination of the leadership.'[14] The style of life of a youth
club ought not to depend on the wish of the Church Council
or the Management Committee that its members should be a
credit to the club. This is a natural wish. Neighbours and
other members of the church (who subscribed to provide the
hall) are very likely to complain that the church has no
standards, if the rougher youngsters of a neighbourhood
come to the club. They don't behave very well when they
leave the club late at night or on outings or when they go
away for weekends.

George Burton wrote me a note in 1961. He had taken a
crowd of teenagers camping, and had fallen foul of other
groups of Christians; 'I find that I am up against the code of
behaviour that is expected of the grammar school and above
type. If I spent my time watching that the tent pegs didn't get
broken ... that they cleaned behind the ears ... and teaching them to respect other people's property ... and to say
thank you and very sorry ... I would not be doing the job
God has called me to.' To some eyes it might have been
hooliganism; to his it was being boisterous. They stayed up
till the early hours of the morning, not disturbing other
people, but making a noise. There were strong criticisms by
standards of other camping parties. George Burton asserted
that by his standards their behaviour was exemplary. The
weekend had been full of good conversations. Four young
people had run the catering themselves. One young man he
hoped would be a youth leader had started in a bad mood,
but had organised the complete taking down and packing up
of everything. Groups of young people like these present
great problems to those who have the job of managing conference centres or church halls. To their credit those of
whom George complained made a determined attempt to
welcome such groups, without being foolishly soft with
them. They agreed with George that people matter more
than things. Other centres for young people insist on such

standards of behaviour that many groups of urban youngsters would never want to go again.

Same Atmosphere

At All Saints, Poplar the youth club was run with much the
same atmosphere as in that at the Mayflower. On a busy
night they would hope to have twelve to twenty helpers in the
club. A number would be local adults; rather more might be
the staff of the parish and perhaps some nurses from Poplar
Hospital. In the shared experiences of the common life,
there would be natural moments when discussions about life
and about God would happen. A bad accident on East India
Dock Road when one member was killed and another badly
hurt led to a series of discussions. They included one in the
ward when twenty club members insisted on visiting the
patient.

On a smaller scale there are the same possibilities and the
same issues are at stake. A curate was greatly encouraged
when a group of teenagers he spent time with began decorating the church hall. As they worked, they talked un-
selfconsciously about Christian faith. But the vicar's wife
was upset when they made tea in the kitchen of the hall. It
wasn't a club night. The hall belonged to a women's working
party that night.

Often it has been the fear of giving offence to church
members and neighbours which has dictated policy. It is
true that in reaction against a church-for-its-own-sake attitude some clergy go to the other extreme. The congregation
then feel they are simply to be told off for being middle class
and respectable. Visiting a Borstal boy may seem much
more exciting than caring for an elderly church member who
can't get out and about. There is a tension to be held here.
On the one hand there should be proper care and respect for
church members and their opinions. But on the other, the

whole congregation must take seriously its call to be a church of and for the district. The life of the church should be shaped to hold that tension.

If a church's youth work is run primarily for the young people who grow up through Sunday School, choir, Bible class or uniformed organisations, a social pattern will generally have appeared by the age of fourteen. The great majority is likely to be of those who achieve well in school. Those who haven't done well in school can too often feel that to join a Christian group means abandoning their mates and their culture. Ken and Charlie had, as sincerely as they knew how, committed themselves to Christ. For them it included coming into the company of people whose social background, style of life and values were utterly foreign. The group of Christian young people seemed to them to be anti-life. Ken and Charlie had been dislocated from the ties where they had felt able to develop as people. 'As a Christian you lose your identity', they said. They felt left in a kind of no-man's-land. [15]

THE GOSPEL IN WORDS

CHRISTIANS can fall into two opposite traps. The one is to emphasise so strongly that we come to a district to learn, that we end up believing we have nothing distinctively Christian to give. The other is to be so confident that we know what the standards are and what the Gospel says for every situation that we believe we can preach the Gospel by words only, without involving ourselves in the life and struggles of a neighbourhood.

The Sydney City Mission, opening a fine new set of buildings on a new housing estate, declared that all the work was to be directly evangelistic. They would not be caught up in pastoral work. This is in step with what has always been the official policy of the London City Mission. This was brought about no doubt partly for tactful reasons in response to edgy vicars, who complained that they were trespassing in their parish. The theory was that when people had been converted to Christ through the London City Mission they would be passed on to churches. It may have been tactful, but it led to a serious untruth. The preaching of the gospel in an area cannot be separated from the building up of a responsible Christian fellowship in that area. For that fellowship will be the Church in that area, and therefore the main agent of future evangelising. God's concern for the good of the whole neighbourhood combines both the preaching and the creation of the fellowship.

But the idea persists in many strands of Christian effort that the gospel can be presented by words alone. So London City Missionaries, clergy, ministers and church workers faithfully knock on doors. I wonder if they know any more than I did when I was a curate how to follow up a good visit to someone who is not ready to come to church yet. Evangelism through leaflets, newspapers, television, radio, invitations to strangers in the street to come to a service or a meeting — all these by-pass the time-consuming, costly involvement of establishing continuing relationships with people. The proclamation of the gospel in spoken word or in the liturgy or in drama or in print, all have a vital part in the communication of the gospel. But that communication will only make sense to people who have grown up outside the Church if they have felt something of what Christian living and loving mean through personal relationships, and if they have had more than a passing contact with an active Christian community.

Some churches see the special evangelistic service — or the Parish Communion or the Family Service — as the one moment when neighbours can be invited to hear the gospel. Fierce loyalty to preaching alone as being God's way of winning men to Christ has persisted. A minister quoted to me the Authorised Version of 1 Corinthians 1:21, 'It pleased God by the foolishness of preaching to save them that believe.' The sense in which he interpreted it was that, in the eyes of men, preaching is a very foolish way to convey the gospel, but God honours and blesses those who loyally stick to it. More modern translations would not have allowed this text to be pressed into service in this way. The Revised Version says, 'It was God's good pleasure through the foolishness of *the* preaching.' The Revised Standard Version says, 'The folly of what we preach' — not 'how we preach'; and the New English Bible, 'The folly of the Gospel.' What men stumble over is not the method of preaching, but the content of what is preached.

The Pattern Crusade

Many evangelical Christians hope that a preacher like Billy Graham can reach those who are right outside the life of the Church. John Pollock describes the 1959 Crusade in Sydney as 'The pattern crusade'. He claims that 'Billy Graham reached the working man too, but only where the local clergy were prepared to work on the assumption that he would'.[16] I spent some weeks working in Sydney in 1963. Several of those weeks were spent working in the parish which John Pollock quotes as his evidence for this claim. My impression was that church life was weaker in the inner city in Sydney than in any other area I knew. A senior Sydney clergyman, himself fully committed to supporting Billy Graham, said of the 1959 Crusade, 'Very few working class people came.' When Billy Graham was in London in

1966 we worked very hard to run coach parties from Canning Town to hear him. For a number of people he brought just the right challenge to prod them into getting off the fence and committing themselves to Jesus Christ. In every case they were those who had strong links with Christians at the Mayflower.

The answers to a questionnaire after the Billy Graham Crusade for five weeks at Earl's Court in 1966 showed that a very limited number of east Londoners were prepared to go to such meetings. I wrote to the Church of England parishes in east London which I knew were enthusiastic about supporting the Crusade and to the Free Churches and Mission Halls who were likewise enthusiastic supporters. I had replies from nine Church of England parishes and twenty-seven Free Churches. Non-church-goers over the age of twenty-one who attended totalled 694 (526 Church of England, 168 Free Churches). Of adult enquirers fifty-nine made a profession of acceptance of Christ and thirty-six of re-dedication.[17] The impact was marginal. This is not a criticism of Billy Graham. The same might be said of most Christian efforts in these areas. As I understand it, a preacher like that is called to be a reaper. It is no judgment on him if he fails to reap where others have failed to sow. It is high time we acknowledged that all the services and meetings in the world will not win a hearing from those right outside the Church. They will want to know about Christianity only when they meet Christians who care about them and about the issues in life which matter to them, and who are prepared at the right moment to answer up about their faith.

Fair Model

The parish of St. Mary's, Islington, where I was a curate is a fair model of much orthodox church life in urban and industrial areas. Its strengths included: a strong belief in the power of Christ today; loyalty to the Bible; a warm welcome to the fellowship for those who came to us; a determined fight for standards of behaviour; courageous personal discipleship; great care with baptisms, weddings and funerals; faithful visiting of homes by staff and by some of the congregation; compassion for individuals; individual care for immigrants who were newly arriving; concern for children and for the elderly.

St. Mary's Church had been bombed during the 1939–45 war and was rebuilt on the same grand scale while I was working there. A loyal group, perhaps thirty to forty in number, had bravely kept the flag flying during those difficult years. Some of these had moved away to the suburbs but continued to come back to support the church where they had grown up. An able and vigorous vicar, together with a paid staff of two curates and a woman worker, had encouraged students and nurses to come, partly so that they could help establish the youth and children's organisations and the visiting programme which the life of a busy parish seemed to demand. The students and nurses also played an influential part in determining the character of the Young People's Fellowship to which they belonged.

Leadership in the parish was largely either in the hands of the paid staff or of those who were imported into the neighbourhood. As young people grew up within the church organisations, the patterns of leadership to which they looked were patterns which would have been suitable in a middle class town parish. In the years since I was there, there has been an open youth club which has drawn many more youngsters from the majority group in the district. The 'tidy' programme for Sunday School, Bible Class and Youth Fellowship which I knew attracted a majority of those who are at home with books, who were getting on better at school, and who liked routine to their programme. The youngsters who represented the majority in the area either never came, or drifted away because they didn't like the type of programme. We all like to be noticed, and if in a Bible Class, for example, only those who are good at reading are noticed, it is not surprising if the others behave badly to attract attention, or just leave. The few who do stay fit more and more into the patterns imposed by those who are overwhelmingly the majority in the church group, even though they are a tiny minority in the area where the church building stands.

No Common Life

The result of this pattern of youth work was an adult congregation who would largely have found it unnatural to be relaxed at, say, an Islington wedding party, or involved in secular groups who wanted to ask questions about the neighbourhood, like housing, or education, or play facilities. The congregation prayed for their neighbours; some of them would go visiting. But nowhere did they share in common life with them. When I made friends and talked seriously about Christ with a man who lived in my street, there was no next meeting point where he could meet Christians from within his own milieu. The staff had endless slight contacts with neighbours in visiting and through baptisms, weddings and funerals. But we didn't know what to do next unless someone was willing to come straight into the circle of fully committed Christians and their activities.

CLERGY TEAMS

IT was and is the belief of many Anglo-Catholics that colour, beauty, music and nothing but the best of it, would lift men's hearts to God when their horizons were bounded by a drab world. It would be as misleading to suggest that the Liturgy of the Holy Communion by itself wins men for Christ, as to claim this for preaching by itself (though there are exceptions which prove both rules). When the excitement of participation in the Liturgy is part of the whole ministry of the Church and it is one which takes the common life of the faithful and the life of the whole community seriously, the experience is a dramatic one. People are learning because they feel that God is great and true. Participating as servers and choir members and in processions and ceremonial acts means that they are learning from shared experience.

Many of the strong clergy teams which have worked in east and south London lived in clergy houses. The rules of life which have been greatly relaxed in more recent years derived something from the Officers' Mess after both World Wars. There was disciplined prayer, clockwork organisation, faithful visiting and service to the poor. A staff meeting was a military planning exercise where often the idea was out of place that clergy might think as colleagues through their assumptions, their mistakes and the lessons they ought to be learning from the district. Perhaps experience in the army or the navy strengthened the idea that the clergy were the officers and local people were 'other ranks',

dependent upon them for ideas and instructions. When there
were very large staffs, local Christians must have assumed
that they weren't expected to take responsibility unless the
staff was unusually determined to prod them into doing
so.

Perhaps the best example of the survival of the large staffs
which several working class parishes once had was All
Saints, Poplar. Its post-war 'heyday' was in the early 1950s.
There was then a paid staff of fourteen. Numbers are
perhaps. worth mentioning because memories of packed
churches are so often recalled. Mark Hodson kept a note-
book when he was rector. It included numbers at the Parish
Communion on a number of Sundays, and the time during
the service at which they arrived. On November 25th, 1951,
73 were present at the beginning, 104 at the Gospel, 142 at
the sermon, 163 after the sermon![18] This is the largest
number quoted for an ordinary Sunday. Much was made of
great events during the year. The Passion play (which expected to sell 1,600 tickets five times over to fill Poplar
Town Hall) and the pantomime had parts for as many local
people as possible. Establishing a centre of strength made
wide contacts and major events possible. Four times a year
the whole communicant list was visited immediately before
great Church festivals. At its best this Church life produced
a relaxed atmosphere in which Poplar people felt involved
in the life of the Church. Cell groups flourished at times, and
their members knew their faith well.

Some members of the staff tried hard to enable local
people to take a lead. Yet with hindsight it seems that
largely it was a case of the staff deciding and the people
following. Wholesale redevelopment of Poplar meant that
many moved away. There was no longer a staff on such a
scale. Some members felt resentful that there was no longer
a staff member to turn to at every moment. But gradually a
smaller body of local Christians have learned that they are

involved in a partnership with the full-time workers and that they have to accept responsibility together for decisions, and for working them out.

More Vulnerable

A common life in tune with the district can develop in a very small church set-up too. Sometimes a youth group meets in a vicarage cellar, or wherever a Dormobile takes them. Or an adult group develops as they go round different homes. The small church set-up is much more vulnerable to change of purpose when a new vicar or minister comes, or to the year when a dozen adults move out of the district. It is more dependent too on having reliable members; a large set-up is able to carry the many members who at regular intervals take six months off from contact with the Church. There are many who will only find their way into the worshipping life of a church if they can take their own time (however erratic that may happen to be) in learning to share a common life with Christians. That time may be three, four, five or six years.

If large-scale church life is developed a strong staff needs to be maintained over a good period of years. The team at St. Mary's, Woolwich, in the 1960s was strong enough. A great variety of imaginative contacts with the district was established; but too many changes happened too rapidly. If the goal is to break fresh ground, seeing adults become decisive Christians and then begin to flex their muscles in taking the lead, seven or eight years is a very short time.[19]

One clergyman looked back on his time as a curate in a traditional and hard working staff in the 1950s, and recalled that the staff's attitude was that if you wanted a job done properly, you must do it yourself. When we discussed whether groups which local people would lead were encouraged, he said they were not. 'You had to keep control.

You were frightened that things would get out of hand.'
Repeatedly clergy respond to suggestions that local people
should take responsibility with, 'Don't you find that they
prefer you to do it?' or 'I find people won't take a lead
round here.'

Wesley's Risk

Two hundred years ago John Wesley took the risk and persuaded working class men and women to run class meetings.
The history of the Labour movement and experience of
Community Development today shows that where working
people are trusted and stretched, with the right sort of enabling support, they have great abilities as leaders in their
communities. The unwillingness of local people to take responsibility is due to the fact that, for so long, education has
made them feel failures, rather than having given them the
confidence that is needed to exercise responsibility. And for
those same long years clergy have believed, sometimes
wanted to believe, that they must hold the strings in their
own hand. Churches which are run like that are very likely
not to meet working class people other than the more deferential who doff their cap to the vicar.

The attitude has often sprung from failing to distinguish
between the independent-minded working classes and the
dependent poor. We have not quite rid ourselves of the emphasis on poverty of some of our own appeal literature; it
has led us to think of districts where the majority are well
able to take responsibility in their own community as wholly
poverty-stricken and delinquent. It is a proper part of the
proclaiming of the Kingdom of God to challenge local
people who are happy enough in their own lives to join
hands in serving those whom their neighbours often write
off as problem families.

In urban areas there are many who are properly described

as the dependent poor. Christ has commanded His Church to care especially for them. Clergy and ministers do not help by trying to be amateur social workers. Part of their calling is to discover, in consultation with professional social workers, what the Church can do in partnership with statutory and other voluntary bodies. Their job is then to keep the needs of the poor in the minds of their congregations. This needs to be done in a way which doesn't simply make church members anxious, but helps them to know what they can do. The Church can often be a connecting bridge between professional social workers and willing good neighbours.

For Support

There will still be individuals who come to a parish staff for counselling and support. One of the advantages of working as a team is that colleagues can tell someone when he is becoming over-involved, and help him out. I am grateful to my vicar who asked me as a curate when I was trying to be a daily amateur psychiatrist to one man, 'How many like him do you think you can carry?' The art of counselling includes referring people on to someone more qualified, when you are out of your depth. There will be some who are dependent already. A woman with two children who had been deserted came to a church worker. For a time she came to every church event. When there were staff changes, she would disappear for perhaps six months, until she was confident in another staff member to whom she could relate. If the local church really is an expression of the body of Christ, the job of clergy and other staff is as far as possible not to let people become dependent on them alone. Rather it is to encourage mutual responsibility and independence. But some like that young mother will find they cannot make relationships except with those they recognise as professionals.

Many people need a great deal of support. That doesn't contradict one of the themes of this book, that God's purpose is that all should be treated as valuable and responsible people. In Canning Town we ran a meeting for the Mums, about thirty-five of them. This was a euphemism for the Grans, for almost all were over sixty. At first I thought of it as a group who were the responsibility of a member of staff who should visit and cheer them up. We hoped that their Wednesday meeting was a happy time when they would take away some fresh grasp of what God's love meant from a brief service. A new staff member came, Coral Dunn. We discussed her work regularly. After two or three months, talking about the Mums, she said, 'I can see twenty-two leaders in that group.' She saw her job as enabling each of them to be the useful person she was well capable of being in her wider family, or in her loan club or in one case as a key figure in a twenty-two-storey block of flats. A committee would organise and run their own group and feel responsible for members when they needed help.

EXPERIMENTS

THERE have been many attempts to break out from the patterns of traditional church life. Today, many ministers and laymen press upon church congregations the need to put church maintenance second to the call of mission. Various experiments have produced groups which have perhaps never come fully into the organised church or have not stayed there. Others stay and act as more or less effective irritants. At times the temptation is to over-react. There has been reaction against the ineffectiveness of many churches in serving the community because they seem to be so taken up with church life; against the over confidence of some Christians who have come into a culture they don't understand, yet claim to know the answers.

The anxiety to serve the community and not to 'ram religion down people's throats' has led some to a position where there seems to be no distinctively Christian conviction. It has also led to a somewhat feverish search for the right role for the minister and for the church. There is the temptation to leap from one band-wagon to another; to acknowledge that the minister is not called to be an amateur social worker just in time to see community development as his all-absorbing task. A church which simply fills in the gaps which other agencies do not yet deal with is always likely to be overtaken by events and find that it no longer has any reason to exist.

The Best Experiments

The best experiments take seriously both the community as it is and the Church as it is. Their leaders stand up to church members who seem only to want traditional church life, but do not write them off. The best experiments need to be taken seriously and supported by the institutional Church. Our day is a day of projects, many of which last three years or less. It takes time for people of a district who have seen many college boys come and college boys go to take us seriously. When we'd been in Canning Town two or three years, a local man asked my wife, 'Have you come here to do some survey?'

A number of examples come to mind of clergy and ministers learning with great sensitivity to listen to the district, to help local people to interpret what their frustrations and their hopes really are. The priest or minister is often better placed than almost any other professional worker. He lives in the district. He can stay a long time. He is a 'generalist'; that is to say he is not obliged to concern himself with a particular category of needs. Often he can bring to community groups a sense of proportion and humour. The pattern of his work may sometimes be unrecognisable as church life to orthodox Christians. His priorities may be to enable local groups, through a community newspaper or through constant pressure on the Town Hall, to get their complaints heard. He may build friendships and make discoveries about life with many people who would never come near the Church as an institution. It will take years to see if this approach to proclaiming the gospel in secular terms brings about changed lives and new allegiance to Christ.

We need to persevere long enough with experiments to build relationships with people and to see them take confidence and accept responsibility. If you accept that mission is more important than maintenance, then you will want to insist that Christ's love is brought to people through personal relationships and the sharing of a common life.

THE PENTECOSTALS

ANY world picture of churches in the big cities should include an account of Pentecostalism in South America. There has been a very fast rate of growth among Pentecostals. Their members are most likely to be from the poorest groups in Brazil, including those of mixed race and Indians. The strongholds of Communism in Chile, mining districts in the provinces of Arauco and Concepcion were also the bastions of Pentecostalists, who in many cases in South America are reported to vote for the Communists, because they claim to express the aspirations of the poor.

Many Pentecostalists are to be found among the millions who have been swept by poverty into great cities like Sao Paulo and Santiago. Their preachers are likely to be men who live in the midst of their problems and belong to the same social groups.

One commentator, Christian D'Epinay, sees the Pentecostal Churches in Chile as a haven for the masses.[20] For people without status here is somewhere where they are valued; because of the gift of tongues all can participate, and because of varied gifts possessed by different members of the population, they can feel of equal standing there. A large majority of members in Santiago in 1960 had themselves migrated from the country to the big city. A high percentage were out of work; only one third of people in Santiago in 1960 had jobs at all. They found in the Pentecostal Church something like the large extended family they had left behind in the country. The pastor has great authority; he plays an important part in problem solving, and provides a kind of fatherly protection. This perhaps fits the protection which the ideal *patron* would have given in the *hacienda* in the dreams of those used to feudal-style rural life.

No Worldly Involvements

The Pentecostal Churches studied in Chile produce membership whose personal honesty and reliability is admired. They follow the frequent Pentecostal attitude of withdrawal from worldly involvements. D'Epinay listened to a pastor preaching from the Book of Amos without once mentioning the prophet's message of social justice. He tackled him about it. The pastor replied, 'I know that there is a social message, even a political and revolutionary message in the Bible. Not only in the Old Testament; there is also the Epistle of James. And this message, which is a part of the Gospel, attacks the rich who exploit the poor. There would be a great deal to say on this subject in Chile. But for the time being we cannot do it. Our people are too weak, they lack maturity . . . they would not understand . . . In the Pentecostal Churches there is a very great fear of anything political . . . A ring of spiritual ideas has been created to prevent all contact with the political world . . . People have the idea that each church forms a privileged people, the people of God, which should live without contact with the rest, who are called "gentiles". It is a bit like the Jewish idea at the time of Jesus and the Samaritans.'[21]

In Brazil the largest Pentecostal Church is the Assembleias de Deus.[22] Based on their own resources, they had grown by 1967 to a membership of 1,400,000 and 5,200 congregations. There are some striking differences in attitudes from what D'Epinay observed among Pentecostalists in Chile. There is much less acceptance of being a dependent group ('too weak . . . lack maturity . . . would not understand'). There is an aggressive programme of education among their members, teaching those who are illiterate, building community libraries and day nurseries. Part of the roots of the Assembleias de Deus lie in the Waldensian Church with its tradition of co-operative help and a high degree of responsibility towards fellow men. A number of industrial undertakings, such as a tile factory, are formed to help deal with unemployment. In these only a small proportion of those involved (6%) are to come from its own church community. Its building work in Sao Paulo also includes a hospital, an old people's home, a secondary school and a Bible school.

The Assemblies do not withdraw from the life of the

community. They have a very high opinion of Martin Luther King, and the belief is expressed that political and social engagement go hand in hand with evangelism. Communion does not arise, they say, by alien infiltration, but in the 'trough of misery'. It is 'nourished by poverty and injustice'. 'Communism denies God, but laissez faire denies one's neighbour. Both are equally unjust.'

'The Low and the Least'

Pentecostalism in London has its membership almost entirely among lower middle class, working class and poorer people. In one local Elim church, for example, there was no one among the sixty members who could be described as of the professional classes or of independent means. Principally they were factory workers and labourers with a few office workers among them. They often refer to themselves as the 'low and the least', and rejoice in the many promises in the Bible to such people. There is strong emphasis on the Second Coming and the era of justice after the millennium. This world is expected to have unfair distribution of opportunities. An Elim member's lack of this world's goods allows him to be indifferent to this world and its goods.[23] There are strict rules about not taking part in a series of worldly activities. The Elim movement expects its members to spend the greater part of their leisure time within the church circle, frequently visiting one another's homes for prayer and hymn singing. There is a strong family spirit in each congregation, which is generally small enough for everyone to know each other well. I went to the Elim church in Canning Town for a crusade which was led by a well-known preacher within the movement. This was supported by other Elim churches in the east London area. About 100 were present. The great majority seemed to know each other well.

The Elim church was born in east London through the preaching of the brothers Jeffreys in the mid-1920s. It was consciously a working man's church, and in a sense has remained such. Sadly its days of growth seem to have given way to a static or declining situation. For example the crusade meeting to which I went did not seem to me to have more than half a dozen non-Elim members present.

Perhaps two suggestions should be made about why the movement has not found new momentum. There has always been in it (and in many mission halls) a strong, and very understandable, distrust of learning. It was a natural reaction of a working man's church against religion whose leaders invariably seemed to have come from university backgrounds. But it has led to a faith centred almost exclusively on personal experience. Instead of the gospel stretching men's minds, it has been allowed to ask no more than that they should repeat spiritual experiences to one another. The other comment is that, unlike the Assembleias de Deus in Brazil, it has seen the church community as something totally apart from the world and from other Christian denominations. Its pastors would be very likely to feel as the Chilean pastor did in his comments about the Book of Amos.

BLACK CHURCHES

SEVERAL factors have led West Indians and Africans in London and elsewhere to form their own churches. There is a massive culture shock in being brought from rural life to urban. There is widespread disillusionment with English society, where they expected to be welcomed, and with English churches. Stories are regularly told about black people being rejected if they go to white churches. Some of the stories are true. In fact it no longer matters if they are true or not, for they are widely felt to be true. They feel that English churches are run by white people and the place offered them is not as equal partners. Most West Indians live in the worst parts of English cities where English churches are at their weakest. Asian young people on the whole make it easier for themselves by moving within their own community, and have their own aspirations. West Indian young people, on the contrary are more likely themselves to come from a labouring background, live largely in the inner city and have been anxious to conform to what English young people around them want to do. One part of that pattern is that the great majority do not go to church.

All these factors add up to the astonishing drop from sixty-nine per cent going every Sunday to the six 'main line' denominations (Church of England, Roman Catholics, Methodists, Baptists, Presbyterians and Congregationalists) in the British West Indies to four per cent of West Indians going every Sunday to the same denominations in London.[24] It's still worth commenting that four per cent church-going is undoubtedly much higher than the figures of white people in the same areas. Those churches where there is something of a mixed congregation should not 'despise the day of small things'. They should make sure that West Indians have a full opportunity to share in leadership and decision making.

Humiliating

Many West Indians have turned to black churches. One Black Pentecostal pastor's experience suggests the process which led to their formation. When they first came to England they went to an English Pentecostal church. They did not feel altogether accepted. He was asked to preach in another church; a letter confirmed the invitation, but said that the minister had to be away. When he arrived, with the letter in his pocket, the church officers said his name was not on the list. 'It was very humiliating. A number of us decided we would not go again.' Next he set about hunting for rooms. At one door he said, 'We would like to go into this area because we are ministers. It's a good area. We'd like to live here.' The woman slammed the door. Another day they went room hunting for four hours. In one house there was a notice in the window advertising a room; on enquiry the answer was 'Sorry. The room was taken ten minutes ago.' It was with this background that such men felt that they could reach their fellow men better than native Englishmen could; black people would have more confidence to come and tell them their problems and secrets. In 1962 it was estimated that there were seventy-seven West Indian congregations in Britain. By 1966 the number was estimated at 390. Since then it has been impossible to offer further estimates. Some may be small, independent congregations meeting in a house. Most are Pentecostal in doctrine and practice. The largest group is the New Testament Church of God. In 1970 this had seventy-four congregations in Britain with a total membership of 20,600.

There is no one pattern of worship; much is spontaneous. Singing, participation and interruption is frequently uninhibited. Many congregations allow anyone to bring a musical instrument (a reminder of English villages before the nineteenth century and its organs replaced the village band in the gallery). There is a strong emphasis on the full participation of the whole congregation. When the leader says 'Praise the Lord', everyone present is expected to say 'Praise the Lord'. This is often repeated time after time. Often there is foot washing before the celebration of Holy Communion.

There is a high degree of 'togetherness'. There is also generally a strongly authoritarian leadership from the minister or the elders. High standards of personal morality are demanded. Tobacco, alcohol and cosmetics are generally banned. Members give a tithe of their income to their church, and often make great efforts to raise sums of money for the purchase and maintenance of buildings. There is some evidence to show that the more established black churches have the bulk of their members not from the lowest classes but from the immigrant 'new middle class'.[25] Most sermons are about the wickedness of the world, the sufferings of the people of God, the coming great day of deliverance, the future judgment and suffering of the present evil-doers, and the final vindication and joy of the faithful. Social issues are not dealt with directly, though in describing the present sufferings of God's people, allusions are often made to difficult living conditions and discrimination. Pastor Oliver Lyseight, National Overseer of the New Testament Church of God said, 'It's good to talk about social things, but spiritual things have got left out. They're even more important than social things.'

Lively Songs

One group joined a parish congregation I was visiting in Peckham. The singing was lively and repetitive, and everyone joined in. The songs were all about devotion to Christ or about the promise of heaven. The content of worship of groups of those who have been described as the 'disinherited' has often been limited to that of personal spiritual experience and of the promise of justice in another world. The black churches provide a place where black men can exercise leadership and make their own decisions. But it is in a separate community, too totally sealed off from the whole community in which they must live out their lives. I have heard another West Indian Christian challenge some leaders of black churches about whether they can expect to win the support of thoughtful young black people who are asking sharp questions about the society in which they live.

The black churches do not really like the title; they claim that English people have come to faith in Christ through their witness. With their love of music, their spontaneity and unique approach to worship, they have something very special to offer in our cities. They find their worship a more satisfying and joyful experience than the average English church-goer.

In some working class areas of London, West Indian churches stand at the same point at which churches like Elim and the Mission Halls once stood. It is healthy that black churches should develop their own distinctive church life. It would be tragic if they and we stay in isolation from one another. For the possibilities of mutual benefit are great.

A DISTRICT CHURCH

BRINGING clergy from outside does not contradict the possibility that local initiative and leadership will emerge. The teams which have failed to produce strong local leadership have often assumed that people in working class neighbourhoods fall into one of two categories. The first are those thought of as the leader type (generally measured by success at school or at work) who always move out of the area. The second are thought to be the poor and needy. They have failed to identify the third, and probably the largest group, that have been called the 'proletariat'. Where Christians really believe that local leadership can emerge, and have the faith and patience to work for this, there are a number of examples of churches where such leadership has appeared. The examples are not restricted to one kind of church-manship or to one denomination.

Five attitudes seem to be common ground among 'enabling leaders' who come from outside the district: enjoyment of living in the district; listening to what God has to say through the district; personal conviction of the truth and relevance of the Christian gospel; trusting local people and making them know you believe in them; refusing to allow the Church to forget its calling to be the Church of and for the district.

Enjoy Life

Enjoyment of life in the district leads some at times to defend characteristics of a neighbourhood which are bad. Perhaps, though, we have to love uncritically, before we are able to criticise intelligently. Along with enjoyment of the life of a district goes a wanting to be involved in it. The minister is often in a position to encourage people to stand up and be proud of their own district; if he stays there long enough, he will be able to join in offering good criticism of it.

Listen to God

Often a clergyman or minister goes to serve in a church which is so full of meetings, even if the congregation is no bigger than forty or fifty, that it demands all his thought and energy. Because there was no church life at the Mayflower Family Centre when I first went there, there was no round of church activity to shield me from our non-church neigh-

bours. I had to learn to meet and to listen to the district. I
dare to believe that over several years I began to learn some
of the things which Christ was trying to say to me through
the district. It happened through listening, arguing, trying
out ideas about issues in the district's life with local people,
those who professed no Christian faith and those who were
trying to work out a faith which felt very new. It included
trying to explain what my faith in Christ meant to those
same people and listening to their come-back. The priest or
minister who goes to a busy church will do well to give some
priority to some secular involvement in the neighbourhood.
In this way he meets adults of the neighbourhood, and not in
some meeting which he is running on his terms.

Personal Conviction

Listening to what God has to say through the district can
lead to supposing that He speaks in no other way; then it is
sometimes believed that to bring anything explicitly Christian, or to hope that people will be baptised and join the
Christian Church is to bring a foreign concept into the area.
What is foreign is a church taken mass-produced from a
blueprint designed in middle class European communities
and imposed on every other sort of community. We must be
willing for the patterns of church life to vary greatly from
district to district. But Christ is not a foreigner to any district, and men will only believe that He can make a
difference to adult life, if they meet men and women who
themselves have deep personal conviction and experience of
Christ.

Trusting People

Local people will take time to assess whether we really mean
it when we say that we want them to take responsibility, or

whether we shall snatch the reins back as soon as we think a mistake is being made. They will not feel trusted, until they know they are expected to make decisions about all areas of church life, and to speak out with their understanding of the Christian faith and of God's activity in the world. To encourage this is not an abdication of leadership by a clergyman. Indeed he mustn't abdicate. He has got knowledge and skills which are not to be held in contempt. He should argue the case when he believes something important is at stake. But he may be voted down. All this most clergy know and accept in a parish where laymen are directors, managers and generals. It only sounds remotely surprising when we talk about dockers, drivers and labourers.

The Church's Calling

Most individuals, especially in working class areas, need a group with which to identify. That group can easily become a refuge to which people escape from the tension of the community they live in. We mustn't be afraid of encouraging local church life. But the activities the church promotes should be appropriate for those who readily affirm that they belong to their own community.

The call to be the Church for the district involves corporately taking the trouble to find out the needs and the issues of an area. It means encouraging Christians to join as partners with other agencies and individuals in tackling those needs and issues. Being the Church for the district doesn't imply that Christians should always go along with the majority opinion. It does mean that they must not try to escape the tensions and hard brain work of wrestling with the issues of the district. It means they must be willing to take sides and not be neutral, when they are clear that justice demands it.

A friend of mine asked me, 'Why are so many Christian

books written about the first few years of a Christian work?'
Parish churches, Baptist churches, settlements, the Primitive
Methodists, the Elim churches have at different times made
a very significant impact on working class districts. The un-
answered question seems to be how a group of new working
class Christians can grow in the faith and at the same time
be a Church of and for their own district. We must not say
that they are not mature enough to think about the issues of
work and life in the big city. God wants Christians to increase their vision of Christ and His purpose for themselves,
for their district and for the world.

Having looked at some of the characteristics of church
life we must move now into 'the inheritance' that makes up
the city as we know it and experience it today. This will take
us into many areas, for there are many factors at work in the
creation of the here and now.

In Part Three we shall look at some of the influences that
make up 'the inheritance' — we take West Ham as the
microcosm of the city for this purpose. This means taking a
quick look at poor relief, the Temperance movement, the
Labour movement, and tracing to some extent the churches'
relationship — or non-relationship — to politics. Later, in
Part Four, we must give considerable attention to education
and its aims, and in Part Five deal with some areas of priority about which Christians should have concern.

Three

OUR INHERITANCE:
URBANISATION

WEST HAM

CHRISTIANS tend to speak of bringing people back to Christ or back into the churches. The assumption is made that there was a time, perhaps a hundred years ago or fifty years ago when Englishmen belonged to the Church on an altogether different scale from today. That is substantially true of middle class and rural England. It is a great misunderstanding to assume that this holds good for urban and industrial areas of big cities. It is difficult to understand the present situation without examining carefully something of the history both of the city and of the churches. So I turn now to one area I know from experience — the West Ham area of London.

Big cities are made up of a vast and complex network of forces. I have chosen to focus on one area in order to present a bold picture of what has gone to make up our inheritance. When certain issues arise I shall call on wider evidence. I have chosen West Ham for three reasons.

First I worked in West Ham for twelve years and therefore know it from personal experience. I was in that part of the area known as Canning Town. Secondly what happened to the mass of humanity which poured into the big cities can be seen more starkly in West Ham than in older districts, for example like Lambeth and Stepney. This may, of course, lead to simplifications which we should treat with caution.

Thirdly my friend and former neighbour Colin Marchant, minister of the Baptist West Ham Central Mission, has allowed me to see the large amount of original material which he has researched for a thesis on the history of West Ham and of the churches in West Ham.[1]

POPULATION EXPLOSION

TED LYONS, a Christian young man, who was a leader at the Mayflower, wrote to me when he knew I was attempting this book; 'When my own grandfather and especially my great grandfather knew what losing one's dignity and self respect meant, what was the Church doing? That's what I want to know.'

In 1855 the Royal Victoria Dock was opened. Two new towns, Hallsville and Canning Town which were quickly to join up with all the overspill to the east of Poplar, were built on the marsh. They were seven feet below high water mark. There were no roads when Charles Dickens went there in 1857. His brother Alfred who was Inspector for the General Board of Health had already made adverse comments. The houses were built at £80 a time. All backed on to marsh ditches. The vicar of West Ham told Charles Dickens that he once lost his shoes while visiting in Hallsville and didn't know they were gone until much later, because his legs were so thickly encrusted with mud.

The stench was unmitigated on Dickens's second visit. On the first, the local Board of Health had scattered about a ton of deodorising matter on the stagnant pools and ditches. 'The steadier class of mechanics' wouldn't live there. Hallsville was described in the second edition of the newspaper, the *Stratford Express* in 1858. There were 8,000 to

10,000 persons, twenty beer houses and fifteen houses licensed for the sale of spirituous liquors . . . no less than two hundred prostitutes.

The Victorian church's main response was to be schools and Sunday schools for children, temperance campaigns and charitable relief. F.D. Maurice, Charles Kingsley and a few other Christians were already joining the voices which asked that the structure of the society which created these conditions should be changed, but their influence was not felt in Canning Town in the 1850s or for a long time to come.

Partnership

A church meeting of clergy and laity in 1859 in east London spoke of partnership between clergy and laity, and about the problems of population migration and density. They agreed to send more clergy, to build more schools, and 'to endeavour to remedy the evils which have grown up around them almost unperceived'. The remedy needed would have been so drastic and the forces which drove the evils were so complex that most Christians continued helplessly to watch them grow up — and then tried to relieve the worst misery which resulted.

The 1859 East London Church meeting was reported in the *Stratford Express*. Next week, an anonymous writer from Victoria Docks wrote what might be the foundation text for community development:

'If those kindly disposed gentlemen who are trying to civilise us barbarians by means of schools and missionaries will assist us to get the drainage to which we are entitled, I think we could almost civilise ourselves.'

Growth had only just begun. An act of 1844 had barred some of the more offensive trades from London. They rapidly came over the border, across the River Lea, into West Ham. No lobby against pollution existed there to stop the smells and dirt which new industry brought to Stratford, West Ham, Plaistow, Canning Town, Custom House, North Woolwich and Silvertown. The population swept in.

In 1871 it had reached	62,000.
In 1901	267,000.
In 1925	318,500.

That was the peak year. It was to drop away gradually until 1939, then drastically with the bombing from 1940–45, and to level off at 165,000 by 1964 when West Ham joined with East Ham to form the London Borough of Newham.

Whenever industry boomed, more labour flooded in. Whenever there was a recession more and more men were out of work. Insecurity, unemployment and widespread distress was a regular and increasing feature of West Ham's life. Wages for labourers fell from 7d. an hour in 1876 to 5d. or 4d. in 1884. The *Daily Chronicle* pointed out that few men could count on being fully employed. In 1904 an outraged West Ham discovered that it was excluded from the Lord Mayor's Mansion House Fund for relief because it was on the other side of the River Lea. In 1906 the figures of applicants under the Unemployed Workmen Act showed that West Ham had by far the worst record in England. That unenviable honour was to pass to smaller industrial towns in Wales, Scotland and the North in the 1920s and 1930s. But some willing workmen remained out of work for perhaps fifteen years in West Ham too during those years.

Only in the post-war years from 1945 did the Welfare State take away the worst fears and distress of poverty. Jobs seemed more secure, but the strong reaction to recent fears of redundancy in the docks shows that they have reopened deep scars of the insecurity of many years.

URBAN SHOCK

THE shock of being suddenly projected from the slow moving life of the country to the big city was by far the biggest factor in breaking the links between working men and the churches. It often broke men's links with the extended family and with every experience of the past which had connected good feelings with creation. This is not to romance about rural life. It was rural poverty which drove men to the cities, and it still is. But it was infinitely harder to feel the reality and beneficence of a Creator God if you were trapped in the world of exhausting, dangerous and erratic labour, shortage of money and ill health, than in the slow but sure seasonal changes and events of the country.

One of the most perceptive interpreters of what urbanisation and industrialisation were doing to people was C. F. G. Masterman. Later to be a Liberal cabinet minister, he was living in Albany Road in Camberwell when he wrote about south London in 1904. He described the working men he knew as 'A race passing in bulk through the greatest change in the life of humanity'.[2] Millions are now passing through this same change as they are sucked into Calcutta, Jakarta, Mexico City, Sao Paulo. In the same year 1904, W. W. Hough compared the quick, intelligent faces in the day schools, the eagerness to learn, the spirit alive, with the same faces after two or three years' experience of 'the drudgery of mechanical labour and the burning fiery furnace of street life' around the Old Kent Road in south east London. The keenness to learn was gone, the intelligence seemed dulled, the spirit quenched.[3] Bishop Lightfoot, in the same vein, had spoken in 1885 of the widening gulf separating class from class and threatening the total disruption of society.[4]

The Victorian church responded with great energy to the needs of the big cities which Dickens and others shocked them into facing. Yet 'it was as if the spirit of history had said to the churches what the Red Queen said to Alice, "It takes all the running *you* can do to stay in the same place." '[5] Christians cannot deny that a great number of people felt and understood something of the warmth of Christ's love as a result of this activity, and statistics could never show how many responded in their own way to that love. When however we ask what was handed on to future generations in urban working class areas by all the Victorian church's effort and love, the truthful, if sad, answer is very little.

There were three major areas of activity by which the church left a lasting impact: relief to the poor; the Temperance Movement; and settlements, Sunday schools and clubs for children and young people. Part of the inheritance is that the majority of adults in urban and industrial areas have always thought of the Church as a kindly body that has nothing serious to say to them unless they are in trouble.

POOR RELIEF

APPEALS for help stressed the poverty of the area in order to touch the heart strings of the more affluent. Masterman distinguished between the poor who received 'a continuous vast river of charitable help' and the working men, 'the matrix of which the great mass in South London is composed'. In West Ham, Given-Wilson, the vicar of St. Mary's, Plaistow raised money on a very large scale, not only for halls and institutions in his parish, but for hospitals. Local people resented the disparaging remarks he made about them and their district in order to raise the money. Fund raisers have often caused the same resentment into our own time.

Church spokesmen have sometimes exaggerated the roughness and poverty of an area in their zeal to recruit helpers. In 1923 the Bishop of Southwark, Cyril Garbett, asked George Potter if he would be ready to take on the most derelict parish in the diocese, St. Chrysostom's, Peckham. The 'feel' of George Potter's book is of church people coming to a very poor parish. It is full of humour and faith and dramatic stories about boys in trouble and needy families.[6] This was typical of how the life of inner London parishes was often presented. We've all been tempted to play 'Bet you my parish is tougher than yours'. The descriptions were perhaps true, but they weren't the whole truth. They by-passed the mainstream of independent-minded working class people. For them it was often as though the Church came from outside to serve the poor, offering beneficent help, when its real purpose should have been to ask them to commit themselves to working for Christ's kingdom which would have included their serving the poor.

The needs of the very poor were great. *The Bitter Cry of Outcast London*, a penny pamphlet, stirred the emotions of Christian people in 1883. It resulted in a conference called by the London Congregational Union with the other Free Churches. A 'forward movement' was agreed on, rather than any combined approach. Some would move forward by way of the missions, in traditional or adapted ways. Congregationalists opened 'halls' for the homeless. Methodists

founded Central Halls with carefully planned social services. Baptists concentrated on strengthening their churches
in poorer areas. Kathleen Heasman declares that the social
work of the Salvation Army and the Church Army was a
distinctive response to the *Bitter Cry*.[7] Both began in 1886
to employ sisters who visited, nursed and generally helped
the very poor. Both set out to provide for the 'down and out'.

Social Concern

The nineteenth century Evangelicals had an important place
in social concern. They got things done. Wilberforce and
Shaftesbury showed that by influencing the influential it was
possible to make the lot of the poor better. Largely they
were not in sympathy with those who wanted to change
society, so that inequalities should be removed.

Hannah More around 1800 had identified the social
change Tom Paine and William Cobbett called for with
their 'godless' ideas. She was genuinely anxious that it was
impossible to teach the poor to read the Bible without also
making it possible for them to read godless radical tracts.
Many Evangelicals could not make their mind up whether
God would use secular processes to bring about progress.
They were not in fact sure if they believed in progress. They
couldn't live comfortably with ideas about the evolution of
society, if they were connected with the theory of
evolution which they believed to have attacked the Bible.
They rejected 'the Social Gospel' because it seemed to take
peoples' concern away from 'the Gospel'. Their reforms and
relief alone would have left the structures of society as they
were. But given the poverty which stared them in the face,
no one did more to alleviate suffering than this group of
Christians. No one did more than they did to bring the personal approach and the human touch, to social work.

CHARITY RESENTED

INDEPENDENT-MINDED working men in West Ham bitterly resented having to accept charity. Percy Alder, a Congregational minister who was Warden of Mansfield House in Plaistow and later a Labour M.P., described a visit from such a man in 1895. He was a hard working man, a sturdy Trade Union and Friendly Society member, whom he knew quite well, who had probably never asked for help in his life before. He was a stevedore, had broken his leg in an accident at work, had been off work for nine months with the break and a subsequent illness. Six weeks of frost had driven him to ask for help for the first time in his life. Alder said that he was not to consider himself under any obligation to him; it was merely a case of one brother helping another; he was sure that if he was ever in such a position the man would help him. 'Up to this point his face had been hard and stern, and his lips were very tightly pressed together .... Suddenly, he covered his face with his hands, and sobbed like a little child.'[8]

It was bitterly resented when the world of better off people showed that they did not trust working class people to manage relief themselves. In the week before Christmas 1904, newspapers competed to see how much they could raise to provide money for the unemployed poor in West Ham. Over £15,000 was raised by the *Daily News* and the *Daily Telegraph*. The *Daily News* distributed money through a 'Central Committee', chaired by a councillor. It appointed ward committees of all shades of political opinion and religious belief. The *Daily Telegraph* decided to distribute its funds through those it had carefully selected as being most likely to exercise discretion in their allocation of money. They were largely clergy and ministers.

Blocked with Crowds

Canning Town Public Hall took in a thousand men, shut the doors, and allowed the next thousand in when the first had received their tickets. The pavement on both sides of the road and the margins of the tram lines were blocked with crowds. But you could get help also through the Socialist committee rooms, through the *Daily Telegraph*'s trusted agents, and through many more individuals. The Salvation Army, the London City Mission and the Church Army (who alone had sixty workers in the district at one time) joined in. The whole degrading process encouraged adults and children to beg and to lie, and cumulatively helped to make the poor believe there was nothing they could do to affect their destiny. They could make no choices, only stand in queues.

In 1910 the same thing happened. Two national papers, the *Morning Leader* and *Standard* began to raise money. The papers appointed a committee to handle financial affairs — eight clergy, two councillors and the two sec-retaries of the local Distress Committee and Charity Organ-isation. There was an immediate outcry against a committee of 'them'. West Ham had been a Municipal Authority since 1886, but it seemed as though the newspapers would not trust them.

Mass unemployment was only dealt with *temporarily* by the 1914–18 war and perhaps more permanently by the 1939–45 war. In 1920 special committees started to appear again. When the Stratford Unemployment Aid Committee tried to help, West Ham's Board of Guardians reacted strongly: 'We think it very much better that, whatever is done for those unfortunate people who are unemployed at the present time, it should be done with some system rather than by these self constituted committees.'

The scale of the problem was far beyond what either charitable relief or the current statutory organisation could bear. The Board of Guardians found themselves ploughing deeper and deeper into debt. In 1926 Neville Chamberlain, then Minister of Health, carried the Board of Guardians (Default) Act which empowered him to replace the elected Guardians by nominees of his own. This was enforced in only three cases, one of which was West Ham. The new Guardians were sent with the specific object of reducing expenditure on Poor Law administration, and of stemming the financial chaos that had come about. The numbers in West Ham who received 'out relief' dropped from 74,999 on April 1st, 1926, to 56,027 (still nearly one in five of the population) on October 30th. The burden on tax payers was reduced but greater hardship resulted. The Local Government Act of 1929 abolished the Poor Law Unions and made public assistance the responsibility of local authorities. Even then West Ham was found to have special needs. Perhaps the older inner city areas had greater ancient charities to help cushion them from the worst pressures which hit West Ham, but dependence on aid from someone else was very widespread in urban and industrial areas.

Burning Issue

A principle, which is still a burning issue, was slowly and grudgingly acknowledged. It was that the inner city's scale of problems are not only of its own making. Those who moved out of West Ham and those who took their living from working in West Ham were as much responsible for what it became as were those who still lived there. Inner city boroughs need to acknowledge that they do not possess the resources to meet their needs; national resources are needed. Equally, national government (which means all tax payers) needs to acknowledge that the scale of problems in relation to limited resources cannot be compared with those of a town or small city. The inner city is the responsibility of the whole country.

In 1945 the concept of National Insurance put the matter of how to offer help without pauperising people on a healthier footing. 'The Welfare State' has often been blamed for turning people into scroungers. This brief glimpse at the effect of haphazard charitable relief ought to show what had gone before the Welfare State. The scrounger spirit had long been encouraged by these erratic attempts to help.

In older urban areas there had been a much longer history of pauperisation. Picking up the casualties of society and refusing to look at the roots of working and living conditions had meant that in 1800 *paupers* were, on average likely to live much longer than *workers*.[9] National Insurance put the matter of relief on the basis that when you are strong and able to work, you insure yourself against ill health or unemployment. On that basis you can receive help when you need it without damaging self respect. As with all the major problems of urban living this needs to be seen as corporate insurance and not simply individuals being pressed to stand on their own feet. They may have been robbed of the precious and fragile commodities of self confidence and self respect by the corporate process of urbanisation. It was the steady denial of duties to one another which corporate living demands which caused so many casualties to occur, who then 'couldn't cope' and 'gave up'.

THE CHURCHES HELP

THROUGH the long years of insecurity and unemployment churches and settlements made efforts which from one point of view seemed massive, yet from another seemed only a drop in the ocean. William Booth founded the Salvation Army in order to reach the masses which he felt the ordinary churches were failing to do. There is disagreement about how many people responded in the early years in areas like east London. In 1890 William Booth wrote *In Darkest England*, focusing on the poverty which existed in the cities. Consciously or unconsciously the movement turned its main attention to the poor rather than to the working classes.[10] Help for the destitute was provided on a very considerable scale. Booth had asked as late as 1886 in the *War Cry*, 'What is the fruitful source of poverty? Is it not sin?' He now challenged working and living conditions very sharply. It was necessary to 'change the circumstances of the individual when they are the cause of his wretched condition, and lie beyond his control'. Labour yards, an emigration scheme, the missing persons bureau, lodging houses, a legal aid scheme and for nine years a model factory were established to show that matches could be manufactured in safety without the use of yellow phosphorus. The main body of the working classes in the big cities approved strongly of what the Salvation Army was doing for the poor, put some coppers in the collection boxes in the pubs on Saturday night, but never seriously considered joining the movement.

The Methodists never rooted themselves strongly in the working class areas of London. Their policy from the late nineteenth century was likely to be the building of large Central Halls. All seats were free and like one another (in reaction against the appalling social divisiveness of pew rents). The architectural style was intended to help the non-church-goer feel more at ease when he came inside. Preaching tried to hold the balance between evangelistic and social challenge. The Central Halls provided outings, holidays, houses and hostels. Sometimes there were soup kitchens and labour yards for the unemployed.[11]

The Church Army built hostels, and mounted a building programme of improved housing. In West Ham, the Church Army opened twelve houses in 1933. There were two hundred applicants. In 1937 they built thirty-six flats and eight cottages. The St. Pancras Housing Association operated on quite a large scale between the wars, foreshadowing the present movement of housing associations which can provide a third arm to housing provision between owner-occupied property and council-owned housing.

Human Needs

Whatever needed to be changed in the structure of society, human needs stared the churches of West Ham in the face. A great deal of their time and energy was taken in trying to make some response. In 1925, 650 people came in one day to a church hall. They received seven shillings each, most were given 'a useful woollen garment' and the men an ounce of tobacco each. In 1929 the Victoria Dock Mission entertained 4,000 people at Christmas. In 1933 there was a traffic jam in Balaam Street, Plaistow, caused by prams, barrows and go-karts as 250 of the poorest people of the district queued up to receive coal and wood from the Church Army. The same year free hot dinners were being provided for one hundred people on Mondays, Wednesdays and Fridays. West Ham Church, the Dockland Settlement, Plaistow Congregational Church, Canning Town Settlement and others organised unemployed work centres, doing tasks like boot and shoe repairing. Churches were exhorted to find work on their premises and to open centres for recreation.

Churches never solved the dilemma of how to give relief without patronising and without encouraging dependence. This dependence was accepted by some too easily and bitterly resented by others. The numbers of the poor who came for what the churches could give obscured the churches' failure to stimulate responsible local growth. It led greatly to wrong assessments of the real needs of the district. Charles Booth in his historic study of the *Life and Labour of the People of London* between 1890 and 1900 frequently commented unfavourably on the many churches where the poor were gathered in by the liberal granting of relief.

Gradually, churches and borough came to see each other as partners and not rivals. Talk about the Church's role in recent years has often concentrated on the 'servant Church'. It no longer expects to run all the welfare projects, but can offer its help in partnership with the vastly greater resources of local authorities which are properly answerable to the local community. Many local authorities now see that the churches have much to offer in partnership and that clergy and laity may even on occasions have a better 'grass roots' understanding than authorities administering social services in a borough of 250,000 or 300,000 people.

NEVER ON A SUNDAY

THE gospel which was heard most clearly in the nineteenth century in urban and industrial areas was that of the Temperance movement. The Band of Hope, the pledge, teetotalism — even a teetotal public house — came to West Ham. To working class people it all gave the strong impression that the Church's main hope was to make them behave respectably. This was strongly reinforced by their experience as children when Sunday school and Bible class seemed little more than a running battle for the maintenance of discipline. The motives behind temperance preaching seemed to its intended recipients to be nothing more than an effort to prevent urban people from enjoying themselves in the only ways open to them. Insistence on Sunday observance seemed to be part of the same attitude.

In West Ham antagonism between the churches and a large section of the population flared into a battle when the Council voted to allow Sunday cinemas in 1911. The churches nominated candidates to oppose Labour councillors in the municipal elections of November 1911 on this issue. The clergy and ministers addressed an appeal to the electors. For a variety of reasons, Labour was no longer the dominant party after this election. Labour councillors refused to attend the Council's annual church service. The Labour party held a great open air meeting in Beckton Road, Canning Town to celebrate their victory locally over the churches.

In 1922 the new London County Council agreed to allow

organised Sunday games in the parks. Independent-minded
West Ham had refused to be part of the L.C.C. But on this
issue there was no difference from them. In 1923 West Ham
voted by a majority to allow Sunday football in the parks.
Anglican and Free Churches united in opposition against
the decision. The Bishop of Chelmsford devoted the whole
of his August pastoral letter in 1922 to the subject. The Free
Churches sent a deputation to the Council. The Council's
decision was reversed after a free vote against the background of bitter correspondence and local feelings. It is
even likely that local men felt that the churches' insistence on no football on Sunday was an attack on football
itself.

The extension of drinking hours from 10.0 p.m. to 10.30
p.m. moved the Bishop of Barking to appear, on behalf of
the Anglican and Free Churches, at the West Ham licensing
justices in 1935. When a greyhound racing track was proposed in Custom House in 1927, the members of the West
Ham Central Mission registered their protest. Little prom-
inence was given to their arguments about the needs of
space for housing, playing fields and allotments. All these
church protests suggested that the church people couldn't
understand or sympathise with the ways in which people in
the inner city chose to enjoy themselves.

Sabbath Breakers

In the mid-nineteenth century, Sunday Observance had been
one of the issues which convinced many people in London
that the churches were against them. At the beginning of
Victoria's reign, Sunday in east and south London was a
noisy and sometimes exuberant day. Street markets flourished like fairs. Steamers carried to Richmond or Margate
noisy crowds of what Bishop Blomfield called 'gaily dressed
Sabbath breakers'.

There were two different problems. One was to see that everyone had a day of rest from work. This battle needed to be fought. More barges with cargo sailed on the Thames on Sundays than on any other day for example. Cattle were herded into Smithfield market on Sundays. The other problem was whether people should be free to enjoy their leisure on Sundays. Evangelicals in particular regarded these two problems as one. They were offended by seeing drunkards being ejected from bars as they drove with their children to church. This happened because the law said that public houses should close at service times. Church people attacked Sunday steamers, railways, buses, newspapers. The well off had leisure time to read on other days, could drive out in their own carriage, could walk in their own garden. The poor couldn't. Passions were stirred over whether the Crystal Palace should open on Sundays and, in 1856, whether military bands should be stopped from playing in the London parks (at a time when on one Sunday 250,000 people listened to the bands in Hyde Park, Regent's Park and Victoria Park).

The Sunday Observance campaign was seen to be an attack by the country and the suburbs on the urban poor. Devout Christians would have been appalled to see it in these terms. They could not bear to face the fact that towns, suburbs and country held an overwhelming majority in every Christian committee, conference or rally.

The London poor protested noisily. 150,000 people assembled in Hyde Park in June 1855 to protest against proposed Sunday legislation. Forty-nine police were hurt, seventy-one arrests made.[12]

When it came to the matter of drink, there is no argument that thousands of homes were ruined by drunkenness. When we criticise the Victorians for their concentration on particular evils like drink, we should remember just how terrifying the wolves at the door seemed to be. It was as necessary as it was natural for all the 'educators' to underline the virtues of temperance and thrift.

Dividing Line

One of the results was to accentuate segregation in the big city. Jobs, housing, environment and schools have all had an interlocking effect. The division of labour puts a line between labour and management. But from the beginning there has been more than one dividing line. 'The steadier class of mechanic' wouldn't live in Canning Town when it was first built. Schools, clubs and churches generally assumed that salvation involved being taken out of areas like this. It was soon possible for the skilled artisan or the boy who obtained a job in an office to buy a small house. By 1870 there were 2,000 building societies with a membership of 800,000 people.[13] The typical 'success story' of a club boy was one who came from the poorest family, had worked hard and now owned his own business and lived in the suburbs. 'Winning a scholarship' was seen as a road to another style of life and, inevitably, to another district. The testimony of a man converted through a Mission Hall would usually have included the fact that he no longer wasted his money on drink, and that he had learned to improve himself. Improving the district by staying in it was not a likely view to be taken by those who had been educated by those who came from outside.

The 'decanting' in the 1920s and 1930s of large numbers from the inner city on to the great L.C.C. estates such as Dagenham, Downham and St. Helier accentuated the process of 'streaming' as surely as any schools did. They provided only one type of housing. One age group of council tenants moved in en masse. When children of Becontree Estate in Dagenham grew up, the one place they couldn't find a house was in their own district. The population of such an estate were cut off from their roots and also from their next generation. Nothing could have more effectively destroyed what was left of the extended family after the original shock of urbanisation. Another stream of east Londoners were attracted by advertisements such as this one in the *Stratford Express* in 1937: 'Where do you live? How do you live?' Photographs showed terraced houses in West Ham compared with detached suburban houses. 'Three rented rooms in a street cost the same as five rooms of your own placed between two spacious gardens. Working men earning from £3 5s 0d. weekly have turned from rent paying to ownership . . .'

The development of New Towns and 'overspill' since 1945 has had a rather different effect, around London. The 1920–39 estates often took those in the worst housing. Because new towns have meant moving further away and paying higher rents, it has largely been the more adventurous couples who have moved to them. Only 25% of those who are living in new towns and Greater London Council overspill developments were on the housing list of the G.L.C. or a London borough.[14]

HOPE THROUGH LABOUR

IN West Ham, working class people's hopes for a more just society became increasingly pinned to the Labour movement. In 1884 120,000 people gathered in Hyde Park to support the Liberal government when its reform proposals were being approved in the House of Lords. This was still in the tradition of Liberalism with upper or middle class

leadership. Quite different were the marches from the East
End to Trafalgar Square. These were organised and led by
working class men. They led to Bloody Monday in 1886 and
Bloody Sunday in 1887. In forty-eight hours after Bloody
Monday, the Lord Mayor's Relief Fund for the unemployed
jumped from £3,000 to £80,000.

In August 1889 began the strike for the Docker's Tanner.
Wages for dock labourers were 5d. an hour (6d. overtime).
They claimed 6d. an hour (8d. overtime). Labourers and
skilled men joined together and 40,000 were soon on strike.
Those who believed that working class men were unable to
organise, to lead and to speak began to see otherwise. The
strike lasted nearly three months. Great daily marches were
organised. Up to 100,000 people took part. No trouble was
ever reported and outstanding self control and organisation
were shown. Lady Ashburton's Mission, later Canning
Town Women's Settlement, provided room for the strikers'
headquarters. Church of England and Free Churches, especially the Salvation Army, provided meals. In the fourth
week a small committee of six was set up to try to reconcile
the directors and the Union. It included the Lord Mayor,
Frederick Temple, Bishop of London and Cardinal Manning. Negotiations broke down. It seemed nothing else could
be done. Temple went away on holiday to Wales. But Manning went on and on, and at last secured a compromise.[15]

Free Churches and Roman Catholics had for long lined
up with the Liberal Party, the Church of England with the
Conservatives. The Labour movement presented a new set
of choices. In 1888 Mr. Gladstone had been heard by over a
thousand men in Canning Town (two Roman Catholic
priests giving the vote of thanks). But later that year the
Liberals split on choice of candidate. The traditional support of shop keepers, office workers, often members of the
Congregational and Baptist churches, stood by the orthodox
Liberal candidate. His inaugural meeting was held in the

Baptist Barking Road Tabernacle. Meanwhile down at the
Methodist church, with the Roman Catholic priest taking
part, the more radical candidate was adopted. The newly
articulate working class leaders supported him.

Church Support

In 1890 Keir Hardie was adopted as the Labour candidate
for south West Ham. He was elected in 1892 as the first
Labour M.P. in the country. From then on the majority
attached its hopes to the Labour movement. Among church
leaders a few Free Church ministers, with Percy Alder at
Mansfield House and some Roman Catholic priests, made
their support known from the beginning. Robert Rowntree
Clifford, minister of Barking Road Tabernacle (which was
to become the West Ham Central Mission) held back for
some years. Then in 1906, surrounded by destitution, he said
the distress was the 'outcome of the barbarous economic
conditions under which they lived . . . the sooner there was
an uprising of the working classes the better'.

It was some time before there were Church of England
clergy who would offer their support to Labour. In the
Church of England at large the influence of F. D. Maurice
and those who took his thought further gradually meant that
there were many clergy who were eager to see a radical
change in society. But the working classes could not see the
Church as an agency sympathetic to radical change. George
Lansbury, one of Labour's most respected and radical
leaders and himself an Anglican from Poplar, would have
expressed the view of most of his colleagues, when he told
the Chelmsford Diocesan Conference in 1919, 'Most people
in the Labour and Socialist movement regarded it as rather a
waste of time and effort trying to convert what they called
"that hoary Conservative institution" the Church of England.'[16]

After the 1914–18 war the Mond-Turner talks in which a number of industrialists invited Trade Union leaders to talk with them held out hopes of a more co-operative future. But prices and wages dropped. In 1921 there was a long and bitter dock strike. Ernest Bevin, later to be a famous Minister of Labour representing the Union as the 'Dockers' K.C.' was told in the court of enquiry that a docker could certainly feed his family on 2s. 10d. a day. Bevin went to Rathbone Street Market in Canning Town bought 2s. 10d. worth of food and took it into court to prove it couldn't be done. Unions were fighting a rearguard action in the 1920s. Bevin was not altogether accepted in the Royal Docks. It was one of two or three dock areas where he failed to bring all dock workers within his giant Transport and General Workers' Union. The much smaller 'Blue Stevedores' Union continued a separate existence. Part of the folk lore of some families in Canning Town, repeated to me in the 1960s, was 'Bevin sold out to the bosses. All our fathers believed this.'

Armoured Cars

In the General Strike of 1926 armoured cars escorted food lorries from the docks. Troops and police lined the streets and large crowds watched. Churchill was for 'taking on' the Unions. But on the government side Baldwin spoke softly, gave a little, a very little. And on the Labour side both parliamentary party and the main T.U.C. leadership had firmly rejected International Communism. The hope was still that a Labour government would come to power and put things right. The disillusionment following the Ramsay MacDonald government and the slump and mass unemployment, and then the terrible experience of 1939–45 left many believing that no real change for good could come. In the bombing 14,000 out of 50,000 dwellings were destroyed in West Ham. In the southern end of the borough near the docks it was one house in every two.

The 1945 Labour government began to turn into legislation what working class people had fought for. National Insurance, the National Health Service, a limited programme of nationalisation of industry meant the achievement of some of the goals. Large scale housing programmes by a Labour government and a Labour council were tackling on as big a scale as possible the obvious and massive needs of rebuilding a devastated area.

In the 1960s and 1970s fatalism became the more typical attitude. Obvious political goals which had a hope of being achieved were no longer clear. Labour in office did not seem to have a markedly different policy from the Conservatives. Redundancy in docks and industry brought back a great sense of insecurity. Some turn away from corporate hopes for the community into a private and comparatively affluent family life, confining their ambitions to a motor car, a caravan on a seaside site and a colour television set. Others feel frustration that the city still confronts them with educational and cultural blocks which prevent them and their children sharing in the full life. The way through it all is by long term detailed work, which doesn't necessarily rouse passions.

POLITICS AND THE CHURCHES

In West Ham there were moments of sharp antagonism between the churches and the Labour party. In wider circles relationships between the churches and politics were interpreted differently. The most typical Church attitude was contained in the Bishop of Chelmsford's letter to his clergy in 1923. He told them 'never to introduce anything like the party element into the House of God or into your service'.

A hundred years earlier Methodism had officially taken up the position that it was politically neutral. Neutrality, however, generally amounts to keeping the *status quo*. This means that those Christians who have argued for a radical change in the structures of society have been acccused of introducing politics into religion. Those who have stood for laissez faire have not. But many nineteenth century governments were elected after a campaign whose specific programme was laissez faire. It is as decisively a political stance as is a programme of change.

Relief, temperance and provision of clubs and settlements did not change the society which caused the wounds. They only put ointment on them. Arnold Toynbee made a Confession to the Poor just before his death in 1883; 'We — the middle classes I mean, not just the very rich — we have neglected you; instead of justice we have offered you charity, and instead of sympathy we have offered you hard and unreal advice.'[17] The same crucial words were used in an argument in the 1890s between two French Roman Catholics about work in the big city; 'We come in the name of charity,' said one. 'No — in the name of justice,' said the other.[18] Masterman in 1904 spoke of the Christians in the strong churches of south London. They lived decent family lives with much individual personal piety. They were generous in charity, 'But no appeal for justice in the name of the forgotten poor goes forth with united voice from the churches of south London.' The suburban Church, he said, was content to cultivate its own garden, to save its own soul; it was loth to identify its interests with those of its less successful neighbours.[19] Masterman saw that it was impossible for the better off part of society to argue for justice without surrendering some of its power and sectional interests. In other words, justice involves sacrificial political change.

Fear

Fear has prevented the Christian Church from supporting the aspirations of the poor or of working class people. It still does. At key moments in Church history bogeys have appeared which have frightened men off when they have started to believe that the Christian gospel challenges inequality of opportunity. Instead of asking whether there is real injustice to be tackled and what the seed bed is which breeds revolution, men have fixed their eyes on the bogey. In Luther's day it was the Peasants' Revolt. For the early Methodists it was the French Revolution. In our day it is Communism. A brief look at the two earlier moments in history may lead us to learn something useful for our day. One of the main planks of the Protestant Reformation was 'the priesthood of all believers'. This meant that all believers were to be responsible for reading the Bible and thinking out their faith for themselves rather than depending on what the priestly élite taught them. They were all to be responsible for spreading the faith. All were to be conscious of the calling of God to whatever trade or profession it might be. Neither they, nor the Protestants who have followed them really meant *all* believers. We've settled for the priesthood of all *educated* believers. We couldn't conceive that leadership and responsibility in the Church might fall into the hands of men who have not been through the educational processes recognised by society as it is.

The phrase in the New Testament from which the priesthood of all believers was coined spoke of all Christians being kings and priests. It would have helped to have kept the whole phrase. The priesthood idea by itself too often limited their thoughts to spiritual or Church matters. To have spoken of the kingship of all believers would have challenged the idea of a ruling élite which knows best in State as well as in Church.

Peasants' Revolt

The bogey which terrified most of the leaders of the Reformation was the Peasants' Revolt which broke out in 1525. (only eight years after Martin Luther had nailed his theses to the church door at Wittenberg). Luther spoke firmly to the princes about righting some of the injustices the peasants complained of. But he condemned the resort to violent rebellion, and spoke in extreme terms against the revolt. He said that it was God's service to stab and kill the peasants. At least three influences were at work in Luther. He gave great weight to the injunction in Romans chapter 13 to be obedient to the powers that be. He did not read that verse as some Christians have done more recently in in the light of the verses which immediately follow it;[20] this has led others to say that government can expect obedience only as long as it is 'working for the good' of the people. (The Nazi government in Germany, for example, was thought by some Christians to have lost the right to be obeyed.) Then Luther feared that the whole Reformation movement which had overturned the settled Church establishment of centuries would now fall into the hands of wild fanatics who would break up the whole framework of secular society. He saw Thomas Müntzer, a Reformation leader who joined the Peasants' Revolt, as one such. In addition there had been genuine fear for his own death ever since he stood before the Emperor at Worms in 1521. Only the protection of the Elector Frederick the Wise seemed to stand between him and martyrdom.

There was a long background to the Peasants' Revolt in 1525 in Germany. France, the Low Countries, England and

Germany — the Mediterranean countries as well — had seen repeated outbreaks of violence from those who felt that they were the disinherited. The soil in which such revolutionary causes flourished was the result of the first steps in industrialisation. It was not on the scale of the Industrial Revolution. But it might produce, for example, in Flanders or in the Rhine valley a cluster of towns, each with a population of perhaps 20,000 to 50,000.

In the newly developing towns artisans drew strength from craft guilds, though even their position was sometimes precarious. But the increasing number of unskilled, casual labourers possessed no equipment, had no guild to support them, and were entirely at the mercy of the market. Men like this moved about. They could obtain only a small amount of living space. The high death rate meant that fresh labour was constantly being recruited.

From this section of the population, cut off from the settled life of the land, came the armies of mercenaries, the beggars, the *pauperes* in the Crusades, the flagellant bands, who made up the religious underworld of the Middle Ages. Sometimes their leaders and preachers were ex priests or ex monks. Sometimes they were unlettered weavers. Professor Norman Cohn[21] has shown how susceptible they were to millenarian hopes. The millennium was the thousand years in the Book of Revelation when Christ would reign on earth with His saints.

Millenarian movements took one of two directions. Both appealed to the dispossessed poor then, as they do now in the cities of Africa, South America and North America. One was peaceful, spiritualising the millennium which Christ would establish by His own intervention in history. The other proclaimed that the day of the Lord had come now, and that Christ would establish His reign through His saints. Violence was a feature of many such movements and accounts partly for the reason why the powers that be reacted so violently to movements like the Peasants' Revolt.

The Levellers

More peaceful, and more carefully worked out on Christian grounds were the demands of the Levellers in Cromwell's army in the Putney debates after the English Civil War. The argument (it is an argument that is part of the 'problem' of Rhodesia in our day) was about whether the right to vote was to remain only with those who had 'a local and permanent interest' — in other words, those who owned land — or whether, as Colonel Rainborough argued, 'Every man that is to live under a government ought first by his own consent to put himself under that government.' 'By natural birth,' said Richard Overton, 'all men are equal ... even so we are to live, everyone equally ... to enjoy his birthright and privilege ... every man by nature being a king, priest and prophet in his own natural circuit and compass.'[22]

The Early Methodists

The bogey the early Methodists faced was formidable enough. The French Revolution had at first seemed to be indeed the beacon light for liberty, brotherhood, equality. Everything happened at breakneck speed as far as the Methodist Conference was concerned. It was forced to take up its official stance about politics under great pressures which were more felt than understood.

In 1791 John Wesley died, and was carried to his grave by six poor men. By a deed of Wesley the government of Methodism was vested on his death in the Conference, which was in effect made up of the hundred senior ministers meeting once a year.[23] A hundred senior ministers are always likely to err on the side of caution. No doubt many wanted to stand for the cause of the poor and the unrepresented. But would the new ideas work? And which movements should be supported? The French Revolution changed in English eyes between 1789 and 1793 from the standard bearer for Liberty to the Terror and then to Bonaparte threatening English interests and invasion of England itself. From other sources came a whole welter of pressures which lumped together on the one hand King, Constitution, Church, Christianity, Law and Order, and on the other 'those who want change like Tom Paine', the Guillotine, the enemies of England, atheism. Tom Paine didn't help Christians who argued for change by publishing in 1793 and 1796 *The Age of Reason* with its attacks on the Bible and revealed religion. Methodism understandably framed the 'no politics' rule and affirmed its allegiance to King and Constitution.

John Wesley is the only figure in English Church history who, on any scale, captured the poor and the working classes. The exception, perhaps very significant, was that he never established that sort of following in London, which was the only city in England then of any size. Wesley not only reached the masses, he provided a structure in the local organisation of Methodism which gave an utterly new set of opportunities for men and women to know themselves valued and useful. The class meeting was the basis of every Methodist society; every member was expected to belong, to speak freely and plainly about every subject for their own temptations to plans for establishing a new cottage meeting or visiting the distressed. A class might number five, ten or twelve. Leaders were appointed, not elected, and had to be members of the Church leaders' meeting. Nevertheless, working men became leaders of classes, collected the weekly contribution of a penny from each member; they might become stewards, visitors, trustees, local preachers, possibly travelling preachers. Women might take these responsibilities in leadership, except that of travelling preacher and were sometimes in a position of such strength that they could outvote men in a leaders' meeting.

Under this scheme working class men and women, who had no vote, no say in fixing wages and nothing to do with making decisions in society, found that they were now expected to take responsible leadership. They learned self confidence and the ability to organise and to speak in public.

It was a revolutionary step to take at that moment in English society. Authorities always suspected the early Methodists of disloyalty. Field preaching, local preachers and, perhaps more than anything, the class meeting seemed a deep threat to ordered society. You couldn't keep control of what they might do. They might put into the hands of 'seditious persons' opportunities of raising riots or tumults. Secret plotting might be going on in those class meetings.[24]

The Methodists' 'no politics' rule was significant in the early nineteenth century, as it would have been for no other Church. Men who had learned self confidence in the class meetings became leaders among the Luddites and the Chartists.

Efficient Manager

After John Wesley himself the most influential Methodist — and he was not neutral in politics whatever he might publicly proclaim — was Jabez Bunting. He was its extremely efficient manager from 1814, when he became secretary of the Conference, for forty years. He came from being superintendent at Halifax. In 1812 a Luddite had been shot dead trying to break into a mill at Cleckheaton. Bunting refused to conduct the funeral. He was always thereafter regarded with hostility by the working class. His life was threatened. 'No politics' for him meant unswerving opposition to the changes which many wished to introduce. An address was sent to the societies warning Methodists against attending tumultuous assemblies. 'Fear the Lord and the King; and meddle not with them that are given to change.'

The Luddites, the Chartists and the early Trade Unions called for the support of working class Methodists. Central Methodism said 'no politics'. This was a major cause in the splits in Methodism. The New Connection never grew very large (17,000 members in 1849 compared with 358,000 Wesleyan Methodists). It insisted on the right of laymen to representation in district meetings, in the Annual Conference and in decisions about expulsion of members, the choice of local officers and the calling of candidates for the ministry. They were sometimes called the Tom Paine Methodists.

In 1812 the most successful of all the Methodist offshoots was established, the Primitive Methodists (104,000 members in 1850). The Primitive Methodists could be justly described as a working class association. Their rules of church government were drawn up during the years of political agitation and anti-clerical feeling of 1819–20. Their principle was that in every church court laymen should outnumber ministers by two to one. In 1821 their conference very nearly affirmed official sanction for a connection with Radical politics. This move seems to have been defeated by the intervention of Hugh Bourne who was not a member of the Conference, but who personally owned the chapel in which they were meeting.[25]

Methodism was strong in many of the new industrial areas where distress was greatest. They were the only Christians that Durham miners or Manchester mill hands felt might be allies in their struggles. O'Connor, the editor of the *Northern Star*, steadily campaigned for Chartism to adopt small class meetings on the Methodist model. Further, he believed that the Chartist principles were religious. He wanted to declare Chartism to be in the same category as the Methodists. Then prohibition of Chartist propaganda by the Government would lead to similar action against the Methodists.[26] This was exactly what the Methodist Conference feared.

'No Politics'

Conference's 'no politics' in effect meant laissez faire. Its effect was to keep many Methodist labourers out of the political movements. Many others left the Wesleyan connection. The first drop in numbers in Wesleyan history was in 1819. This was the year of Peterloo, when the yeomanry charged a crowd in Manchester. Thomas Jackson was a minister in Manchester in 1818–21. He warned Methodists to 'stand apart from those who feared not to speak evil of dignities'. He distributed 20,000 tracts, visiting house to house, to counteract 'the dangerous nature of radical politics'. In 1819 several Sunday school scholars were expelled from the Wesleyan Sunday School in Manchester for wearing Radical badges. Their teachers were warned that they would be expelled too if they didn't discard their colours.[27]

In 1835 the Primitive Methodist Conference requested travelling preachers not to make speeches at political meetings. Further, chapels and meeting rooms were not to be lent on any account for either political or religious controversy. They checked up on it too. Next year two or three confessions had to be made with expressions of regret. They had to promise to show more firmness in refusing.

In spite of what Conferences might say many Methodists did support Chartism. At least seventeen chapels were opened for Chartist meetings in Yorkshire, Lancashire,

Northumberland and Durham. A Government commissioner blamed Methodist local preachers for the violence in Northumberland in 1839. Several Methodists were imprisoned for their association with the disturbances around Manchester in 1842.

The miners of Northumberland and Durham made desperate attempts to improve their pay and working conditions in 1810, 1831—2 and in the 1840s. Methodism had brought education and self respect. It was bound to lead people to ask searching questions about the appalling conditions in which they and their children were expected to work. Sydney Webb declared that Methodists provided an astonishingly large proportion of Union leaders from the beginning of the Trade Union Movement, and in forming Friendly Societies and later in attempts at adult education.[28] Tommy Hepburn was the leader of the miners in the 1831 dispute. When the struggle began he was a Primitive Methodist, though later he ceased to be one. It was claimed that he could be heard at one time by 40,000 people. He insisted on praying openly for God's guidance before conferences, including one with the Marquis of Londonderry, the chief coal owner and Lord Lieutenant of Durham, who was said to have joined in the act of prayer.

Spokesmen

Evidence from the coal owners' side said that 'these educated persons, or Methodists, are most decidedly the hardest to deal with'. They were put forward as spokesmen in disputes, and were often among the first to be dismissed by the masters as soon as the strike was over. Many were put in jail. To be sacked as a ringleader often meant that a man's family was put out of its company-owned home. They had to see blacklegs brought in from other districts, not only taking their jobs, but their homes too. The scale of these evictions was such that, for example, the Durham Primitive Methodist circuit was reduced from 1,500 members in 1843 to 520 in 1844. Frequent prayer meetings helped support men and women through this bitter experience. Picketing had its distinct character; 100 or 400 men might assemble beside the road praying for the success of the strike and, as the Psalmist might have done, that blacklegs might be injured, lamed or killed. Generally they seem to have left vengeance to the Lord, though they were accused of inciting violence. But, considering the bitterness of the dispute and the hopelessness of their position, the miners were extremely restrained, and undoubtedly their Christian beliefs were an influence against violence. Tommy Hepburn always argued for patience, peace and order.[29]

R. F. Wearmouth the historian of early Methodism defended the no politics rule; 'Self preservation demanded neutrality.'[30] He said that aloofness from political agitation undoubtedly saved Methodism. An alliance with Radical movements would have brought all the forces of Government against it. My own view is that while it is easy to pass judgments a century or more later, neutrality is not the proper attitude of Christians when people are oppressed and their cause is basically right. The Durham Primitive Methodist circuit was nearest to the issues, and it did not believe that it was right to be neutral.

Official Methodist neutrality may have saved Methodism as a denomination; it did much to break the strongest link which a Christian Church ever had with working class hopes in this country. If Methodism had risked death as a respectable denomination there might have been a resurrection of a Christian body which working class people could have respected and joined whole-heartedly. No doubt the Luddites and the Chartists acted wrongly on occasions. Methodists should not have joined the movements uncritically. But the

injustices they faced were real, and only those who stood up
to be counted as their allies could have expected members of
those movements to listen seriously to their criticisms.

Towards Conservatism

The Primitive Methodist Conference also moved towards
conservatism. It was admired by the upper classes for ele-
vating the morals of the poor. In the 1820s and 1840s much
energy began to be directed towards the Temperance Movement. The Conference of 1848 (the year when Europe was
boiling with its revolutions) pressed Methodists not to
attack the Constitution, and asked them not to travel by
train on Sundays nor take Sunday newspapers nor share in
the Sunday promenade.[31] Working men once took Methodism as a serious adult proposition which reflected the indignation of Christ against injustice and His call to men to take
responsible decisions. They now saw it as but one more religious body which told the poor to behave and be patient
and keep their place. They turned away.

The subjects which were most likely to bring church
leaders into the political ring were Sunday observance, drink,
church schools and removal of civil disabilities for Roman
Catholics and dissenters. Somehow they regarded these as
non-political issues. It is hard to escape the conclusion that
these were the issues they believed to be most important.
Those who were most influential in the churches did not feel
the pressures of urban and industrial life. All the issues
which were most important to working class people fell into
the category where most Christians felt they must stay neutral.

In 1848 F. D. Maurice, J. M. Ludlow and Charles Kingsley were brought together in the year of ·Europe's
revolutions, when some of the Chartists were threatening
violence in England. Maurice and Ludlow edited a penny

journal, *Politics for the People*, which first appeared in 1848.
Cautiously it said that Liberty, Fraternity and *Unity* are
intended for every people under heaven. Most of its writers
believed that inequality and a class society were inescapable
facts of life. Its most outspoken writing came from 'Parson
Lot', who was Charles Kingsley; he said his only quarrel
with the Chartists was that they did not go far enough.
'Instead of being a book to keep the poor in order, it (the
Bible) is a book, from beginning to end, written to keep the
rich in order.'

F. D. Maurice, 'this confusing and struggling prophet',[32]
opened his mind to the socialism in which Ludlow believed.
Maurice always regarded himself as being first and foremost
a clergyman and as a servant of the Church. At the root of
his beliefs was Christ's sacrificial death. 'Every year and day
convinces me that our preaching will be good for nothing if
the main subject for it is not the atonement of God with man
in Christ . . . if we stop short of the Eucharistic proclamation
that God has given us His Son to be a full, perfect and
sufficient sacrifice, oblation and satisfaction for the sins of
the whole world.' To say less than this, Maurice believed,
was to deprive men of 'the only effectual foundation for
social and individual reformation'.[33] He emphasised texts
about the cross which claimed its effectiveness to reconcile
all men, indeed the whole universe to God.[34] So he went on
to speak of the whole world's being in Christ. He spoke
also of the possibility that men could consciously turn
away from Christ and shut themselves out from His Kingdom.

If the whole world was in Christ, it followed for Maurice
that the whole world was Christ's concern. There was no
possibility of one set of values being right in the Church and
a different set being right in the world. It followed too that
Christ was at work in the world, Himself bringing about
changes. What was needed was not simply individual re-

sponse to Christ, but changes of the way the world was ordered towards the way a world in Christ should be.

Maurice's Influence

F. D. Maurice was very influential among both Anglicans and Free Churchmen. In the Church of England, Stewart Headlam founded the Guild of St. Matthew in 1877. He fiercely attacked E. W. Benson, the Archbishop of Canterbury for implying that sin caused poverty. Headlam said that if this were true, it was the sin of the rich, not the poor. Society produced poverty and society must be changed. Claims were made for the Guild of St. Matthew in the 1890s that there were seven and seventy socialist priests in it. The Christian Socialists, as they were called, were always under fire from both ends. Hensley Henson was debunking it from the Church side; some churchmen said its members didn't preach the gospel any more. On the other hand Samuel Barnett felt uncomfortable in its circle.[35] He did not want anything explicitly Christian to be said.

In the Church of England, much larger than the Guild of St. Matthew was the Christian Social Union founded by Henry Scott Holland in 1889. By 1897 it had 2,600 members and Westcott as its president. Headlam attacked the C.S.U. for being lukewarm. But its moderation allowed many to study social issues without making a commitment to socialism for which they were not willing. Years later in 1924 a National Conference on Politics, Economics and Citizenship was formed. A three day meeting of C.O.P.E.C. was run by the churches in West Ham. This tried to hold together personal faith and social concern. It discussed among other things the relationship of Christianity to commerce and industry, education, home and international politics, a Christian order of society and the Church's social function.

In some European Countries the Young Christian Workers movement was to be a much more militant force from within the Roman Catholic Church. Cardinal Cardijn came as a young Belgian priest to meet some of the leaders of the English dockers and other workers. He believed that they had shown the way by which workers could have a say and the power to bring about change. He said, 'A talk with Ben Tillett and Tom Mann did me more good than a retreat.'[36] He believed firmly afterwards that workers must be those who helped workers. Joseph Cardijn formed the Young Christian Workers in 1920; he wanted to form groups of really militant leaders, searching the Gospels, looking at issues at work, providing an educational programme.

Theological party differences in England lent a hand in polarising Conservatives and Liberals. Anglo-Catholics had been an unpopular group within the Church. They were not acceptable in many of the strongly established parishes. Many of the very best Anglo-Catholics were ready to go and work for a lifetime in the parishes of east London where at that time no one wanted to go. There they were confronted with what their parishioners had to face. Many took sides uncompromisingly. John Groser in Stepney saw his part as enabling working class men to develop their own gifts and leadership. He worked locally with the Workers' Educational Association with which William Temple was strongly connected nationally. Father Groser disagreed sharply with his bishop and insisted on taking sides quite openly during the General Strike of 1926.

Another Gospel?

More Conservative clergy feared this involvement in politics In addition, Conservative Evangelicals wouldn't join a body which they felt was dominated by Anglo-Catholics. Nor would they join hands with those who went along with *Lux Mundi*, a collection of essays by Anglo-Catholic scholars who accepted Biblical criticism and the theory of evolution. The emphasis on personal conversion 'first' made them suspicious that what men then called the 'social gospel' might be 'another gospel' which was untrue to Christ. They felt that others should tackle the social needs of the nation and that, if they didn't press the claims of Christ on men, nobody else would. One group seemed always to emphasise the need to change the structures of society, the others to emphasise personal commitment to Christ. Neither was prepared to allow that the other had a real concern to do both, so they moved further away from each other without hearing what the others were saying. The separateness meant that each side ignored insights God had given to their opposite numbers. Both sides suffered loss accordingly — as did the Christian mission.

Still others, neither Anglo-Catholics nor Evangelicals, nor followers of Maurice reacted against these arguments. There was so much to be done. Councillor Jones, visiting the Canning Town Women's Settlement in 1919, voiced the attitude of many local men. He said he wouldn't have come if it was an ordinary religious meeting, but felt the settlement stood for religion in fact and not in theory. They got on with the work of helping people wherever they could. In another compartment of their life they led worship for such people as wanted to come. Often they did not work out the connections between 'religion in fact and in theory'. It was assumed, and it is still assumed, that all that was needed for the best possible ministry in such areas was a great pastoral heart. Clergy and others assumed, and many still assume, that they knew what to do if only they could double the staff and the money. So they worked and worked, harder and harder. They were too busy to go away for what we now call 'in-service training'. The trouble was that the problem didn't just require organisation, money, enthusiasm and hard work. Above all it needed thought and fresh vision — together with the sensitive love of a pastoral heart.

Scott Lidgett

Among Free Churchmen who learned from F. D. Maurice was Scott Lidgett, by some accounts the biggest figure in Methodism after Wesley. Scott Lidgett spent more than most men's lifetime in Bermondsey, staying on until he was over ninety. He came to Bermondsey, he said, 'Because of Cambridge,' after being already eleven years in the ministry. 'Because of Cambridge' meant both his awareness of his inequality of opportunity in England, and also that Cambridge men could both learn and give something through association with south London. He started the Bermondsey Settlement in 1891. He faced the question whether to be involved in politics; when he asked W. F. Moulton, the president of the Methodist Conference, about this he was told: 'We sent you to Bermondsey to take risks.'[37]

Dr. Salter came to the Bermondsey Settlement as a student. He was a brilliant bacteriologist and a militant agnostic. He used ostentatiously to avoid going to Scott Lidgett's Sunday evening lectures. Eventually he went in. As a result of the lectures he came to strong Christian convictions, though they didn't quite fit with any denomination. Dr. Salter helped found a medical practice which has served Bermondsey consistently until today. He was a member of the London School Board. He persuaded Bermondsey to plant trees along many of its streets. He was Labour M.P. for Bermondsey from 1922–45.

Scott Lidgett was himself a great academic, was involved in the beginnings of London University and established a large educational programme at the Settlement. It was intended to cover the widest possible field in night schools from art to book keeping. In 1892 there were over 900 students enrolled. That number was maintained in 1912. By 1938 it was 400. After the war this collapsed. The local education authority now provided all that was needed in this field by its adult education programme.

Scott Lidgett stayed too long. He made it harder for the Bermondsey Settlement to review its purpose and to find a new line while it was still strong. It is a very proper function of churches and settlements to pioneer tasks which the state then takes over. But if this becomes their *only* function, there is no possiblity of any continuing local based life. A settlement's purpose is then limited to filling in the gaps which no one else has filled.

With this degree of analysis of history and development, we can now return to look at the way the churches have responded to the fact of urbanisation. How have the churches coped with the human flood that has poured into the big cities, and what can be learned from history to help us respond better now?

MEETING THE FLOOD

THE churches were slow starters in responding to the flood of urbanisation. It was in fact fear of revolution after Waterloo which jolted many into some kind of action. Six hundred new churches were built in urban and industrial areas between 1824 and 1884. For example, St. George's Camberwell was built out of the Million Pound Fund. Even so, ancient parishes were swamped with numbers. St. George's in the East in Stepney had 38,000 parishioners in 1842. St. Mary's Lambeth had 139,000 in 1853.[38] Slow response by the Churches to large new arrivals could mean missing the opportunity of establishing contact altogether. Those who were pouring into the city from the rural areas had only slender church attachments. If the church-going habit was totally lost for five or ten years, it might never return.

Sir Robert Peel wanted the Church to thrive in the new urban areas. He was a realistic politician, though, who knew that parliament would not vote money for church building in the 1840s as easily as it had been done in 1824. The last attempt to give state money to the Church was when Peel tried, in the Factory Bill of 1843, to include money for Church schools in factory areas. He was unsuccessful.

From then on the Church of England was on its own if it was to produce new resources. It had never had to raise money before. Pew rents, glebe rents and money from ancient tithes and endowments had produced what was necessary. The first Church census in 1851 shocked Victorian England by showing that just about half the nation did not go regularly to church. The largest sections to stay away were the urban working class and the urban poor.

Numbers of clergy increased from 17,320 in 1851 to 21,663 in 1881. Church schools provided places for a million and a half children at the time of the 1870 Education Act. The bishop who perhaps was most committed to trying to understand what cities were doing to people, James Fraser, bishop of Manchester from 1870–85, saw to it that there was an energetic Church school programme. Church schools rooted a Church in the people of its own parish. It was claimed in 1888 that the Church of England had collected in voluntary contributions £80,500,000 in the years 1860–1885. £35 million of this was spent on Church building programmes. The Free Churches spent even more in those years on buildings. The Baptists founded more churches in London in the 1860s than at any other time. There was an evangelical revival in Britain in 1859. No great city was among those areas where some kind of revival was reported, but a strong tide was running in many parts of British society. The great preacher, C. H. Spurgeon, came to the Elephant and Castle in south London in 1854. Mass evangelistic meetings were organised in the Exeter Hall by Lord Shaftesbury and his friends from 1856. Services were conducted in 'low theatres in the poorest parts of London'.

Nineteen Day Mission

Moody and Sankey came to Britain first in 1873. In 1883–4 they spent ten months in London. A typical part of this was a nineteen day mission in West Ham. The Salvation Army was established in 1865, the Church Army in 1882. Hymns reached working class people's minds more than most Christian activities. if we criticise middle class Christians of the Victorian era for not learning to respect the culture of other nations or classes, it is perhaps unfair to criticise in the next breath the words and music of hymns which attempted to respond to contemporary taste. But the content of the Victorian hymns was heavily loaded in the direction of man's need and dependence on God, rather than of God's call to all men to responsible service.

Tait became Bishop of London in 1856. He preached in the docks to emigrants leaving England, in Islington to bus drivers, in Covent Garden to costermongers, to railway porters from the platform of a locomotive, and on Shepherd's Bush Common to gypsies. His predecessors hadn't acted like that. The first public school mission was established in North Woolwich by Thring, headmaster of Uppingham, in 1870. Settlements and missions from universities and schools followed to every working class district in London.

The Church of England generally attempted to treat the big cities as though they were made up of a series of villages. Bishop Blomfield argued for a parish church and two clergy for every 2,000 souls. He set out to build twelve churches, named after the twelve apostles, to serve Bethnal Green. In Liverpool, in one stretch of half a mile, there were seven parish churches and fifteen Free Churches. J. C. Ryle, Bishop of Liverpool, was one of those who blamed absentee rural vicars in the eighteenth century and the identification of the clergy with the interests of the squires for the aliena-tion of working men from the Church. So he went on to argue that the parochial system had never been properly worked *before* men came into the cities. Ryle exaggerated the gap between rural labourers and the Church, but there was some truth in what he said. Joseph Arch, a Primitive Methodist preacher, who founded the National Agricultural Labourers' Union in 1872, would tell a crowd on a Norfolk village green that 'The Church belongs to the rich man'.[39] But the real break came with the shock of urbanisation. Ryle and others did not understand just how massive a change of life urbanisation brought. The policy of treating the city as a series of villages and creating as many small parishes as possible was challenged at the time.[40] But, as far as funds allowed, this policy generally carried the day until in the mid 1920s and 1930s new housing estates were more suit-ably serviced by larger parishes. The Roman Catholics never built so many churches, even among large Irish popu-lations, partly no doubt because they were then a much poorer Church, but partly too because it was their policy to try to establish centres of strength rather than spread their manpower as widely and as thinly as possible.

Energetic Work

The *Record* published a supplement on the Church of England in south London in 1888. It joined those who argued that the parochial system had never been worked properly. This comment was made in the context of describing the energetic work of Canon Pelham at St. Mary's Lambeth, now a parish of only 12,000. He was 'able to secure an unusual amount of outside help'. But what was the parochial system? Was it the system at All Saints, Hatcham Park in the Old Kent Road where a parish of 20,000 'attracts but very little outside attention'? The staff there was a vicar and a scripture reader. Or was it the system at St. John the Divine, Kennington, where Charles Edward Brooke had a staff of nine other clergy, a band of Sisters, and an earnest and devoted army of voluntary helpers to serve a parish of 17,000? Was it the energetic visiting, the clubs and the activities of such a parish? Or was it more like this:

> You see on the notice board of a church 'weekly service in mission room' ... The room is in a back street, where in the daytime children scream and play, and in the evening men lounge and smoke. The doors are opened. A little bell goes ting, ting, ting. A few women glide in quietly to service and then disperse as quietly. The doors are shut, and the children go on screaming and playing, and the men go on lounging and smoking, and that means of influencing the parish is over until next time, when it will be repeated again.

The author says that he nearly drew his pen through what he had written lest he be thought to be sneering at such work. But he rightly allowed it to stand, and made the important point that clergy and lay people would be much less discouraged if we faced the facts honestly.

Very Erratic

The parochial system of south London described in the Supplement to the *Record* was very erratic. It depended greatly
on whether the vicar could attract help from outside or not.
If all parishes were to be staffed on the scale of those where
the Supplement and others suggested that the parochial
system was working, either there would have to be a vastly
increased force of clergy, or there would have had to be
fewer parishes so that strong teams could work together.

If Bishop Blomfield's proportions were followed everywhere:

Population	800,000
Parishes	400
Clergy	800

It may be of interest to compare the proportions for the
three south London boroughs of Southwark, Lewisham and
Greenwich in 1973.

Population	732,360[41]
Parishes	111
Clergy	152

Charles Booth, in his mammoth survey made between 1890
and 1900 of the *Life and Labour of the People of London*,
said that, with the exception of the Roman Catholics, the
regular working classes did not go to church. Of those who
did join any church, he said that they became almost indis-
tinguishable from the class into which they then mixed, so
that 'the change that has really come about is not so much *of*
as *out* of the class to which they have belonged ... The bulk
of this regular wage-earning class still remains untouched,
except that their children attend Sunday School.'[42]

True Figure

Masterman used the figures from a survey made on one Sunday in 1903 of adults attending all churches including Mission Halls; he compared Walworth, an Inner London area, with Dulwich and Sydenham, a suburban area. He calculated that the true figure of adult church attendance in Walworth by working class people and the poor was two per cent, compared with the suburban figure of 30%.[43] The strongest churches in Walworth were the Baptists; Charles Booth was impressed by the fact that working class people seemed at home in the Baptist churches more than elsewhere. But C. H. Spurgeon said of Walworth (a few hundred yards from his Tabernacle at the Elephant and Castle) that it was breaking his heart. The peak of Baptist numerical strength in London was in 1907, and they found it hard to maintain their momentum after that.

A survey of West Ham on the same Sunday in 1903 showed a comparatively high church attendance. But the prediction was made (and came true) that, as the middle class population, which still lived in Forest Gate, Stratford and West Ham itself, moved out to the outer suburbs, church-going would be seen to drop to the average inner city level. In Canning Town, where there was never any substantial number of privately owned houses, regular, adult church-going was never strong. On great occasions a larger number might be in church (stocking memories which would recall that 'it always used to be packed'). For example, at the Watch Night service 1901—2, 1,400 were in the church at St. Luke's, Victoria Dock. 'It was not a congregation of even occasional church-goers. Quite a large proportion had never entered a place of worship since the corresponding date last year, and comparatively few of the regular congregation were present ...'

In 1911, twenty parishes united to conduct a borough-wide mission. Six months careful preparation by clergy and laity went into it. They said the mission had good effects in the churches themselves, but were disappointed that a large number of those outside the church had not been touched. It began with a Church of England Men's Society march of 400 men of the twenty parishes from St. Cedd's church in Canning Town.

Love-Hate Reaction

West Ham had a love-hate reaction to the idea of establishing a new diocese (eventually of Chelmsford) in 1907–8. Without being consulted, it had found itself part of London Diocese, then Rochester, then St. Albans. The question now was, where should the centre of a new diocese be? It might be supposed that at that time many councillors would have regarded themselves well rid of the Church. But the Mayor urged citizens to attend public meetings and to sign petitions. It was argued that the centre of the Church should be where the largest population was. In the end, West Ham (population 280,000) ran third to Chelmsford (population 13,000) and Colchester. Angry local reactions included the Mayor's blaming the undue influence of wealthy county families. The Roman Catholic Church followed suit in 1917 by establishing its diocesan centre at Brentwood. Ripon and Southwell are both modern Anglican dioceses. In each the centre was again placed in a small town rather than in the heart of the city of Leeds or Nottingham.

Few Victorian bishops understood or lined themselves up with the needs and aspirations of the urban poor and working classes. Fraser of Manchester was an exception. Thomson, who became Archbishop of York in 1862, was sometimes called the working men's bishop. It was said that 'He had a way with' the men of Sheffield. Walsham How in east London and Maclagan of York might have been described in the same way. But of the 104 bishops who led the Church between 1783 and 1852 only seventeen had ever held an urban living.[44]

That situation is different today, yet not so very different. The structures of Church life do not easily allow a bishop to appreciate the realities of life from the working class point of view. The first Bishop of Chelmsford was in fact Watts-Ditchfield from St. James the Less, Bethnal Green. But it would have been hard for him to keep the priority needs of areas like West Ham before him. He had the work of establishing a new diocese. The most influential laymen would have been the church people of Essex and of the outer suburbs.

Then and now, there is great good will towards anything which speaks of reaching the working classes. If a man with a cockney voice or a Yorkshire accent speaks up in the Church's General Synod, he is quite likely to be given twice as long as he merits? But when it comes to hard decisions about money and manpower and to thought about what the Church should be saying and doing, there is a built in majority in the Church's Synod for the towns, the suburbs and rural England rather than for the cities. Inevitably this majority, fairly elected on the basis of electoral rolls, comes from the areas where Church membership is strong.

The two World Wars both damaged such church life as had been painstakingly built up — the sheer carnage of the 1914–18 war; the bombing of 1939–45 which altered the whole landscape; the questions about the goodness of God which experience of both wars raised; the change of social habits which wartime brought — all these had their effect on religious belief and on men's relationship with the churches.

The period between the wars was a time when relatively large staffs served in some churches. The Methodist Central Halls were busy — 1,000 was a regular congregation at

Bermondsey Central Hall up until the first Sunday of September 1939. The congregation the following Sunday was 300, and it never rose again. The huge West Ham Central Mission church was built in 1919. Over 1,000 children were on the Sunday School roll. Mrs. Rowntree Clifford's women meetings had a membership counted in four figures rather than three. 1,500 women went on an excursion to Southend in forty-seven charabancs in 1926.

Like other centres of strength the West Ham Central Mission was well staffed. In the 1930s there were fifteen clergy and twenty paid lay workers at St. Luke's, Victoria Dock. At the Dockland No. 1 Settlement, which was later to become the Mayflower Family Centre, nearby there were forty paid lay workers. Some of them were only paid five shillings a week. Some would have been students staying in the Settlement. When considering such large staffs, it should be remembered that they attempted in amateur fashion much of what professional social workers tackle today. Often the pattern was that everyone on the staff had to be out of the house with the doors locked behind them every afternoon. If doubling the staff and hard work could have done the trick, it would have been done in the 1920s and 1930s.

Those who believe that Church life was strong in inner London between the wars might weigh up C. F. Garbett's words in 1929 about the riverside parishes, when he was Bishop of Southwark. 'It is quite impossible for me to stress too strongly either the weakness of the Church in these parishes or the difficulties under which its work is carried on'.[45]

Memories

Canning Town adults, like most working class Londoners, would have some memories of discussing Christianity in schools and youth clubs. They very likely experienced worship or prayers between the wars when they were taken out of London to camp, or when they went 'hopping'. Hopping was in a sense typical of kindly society's response to the evils of life in east London. Families went down to the hop fields in Kent where seasonal labour was needed. They lived in huts and were paid a small wage. It gave families a chance to have country air all together. Missioners would come for the weeks they were there. It all seemed great fun with cockney songs and the atmosphere of a great party. Perhaps it also helped to develop awareness of God. There was a romantic and good side to it, but it could never have happened if men had been in steady work. Casual work left its legacy. In the 1960s some boys and young men would pick up enough money hopping or fruit picking to see them through till Christmas without finding a steady job. Then they could borrow or fiddle enough with a casual job or two to tide them over till the summer came. It was a typical 'spin off' from the vicious casual labour system of the docks which dominated the life of the area. It meant that boys would not bother to learn a trade, in the hope that they would be taken on at the docks when they were twenty-one.

Since 1919 the Churches have had the challenge of providing staff and buildings for the huge numbers who moved from overcrowded Inner London to the large estates further out. The Bishop of Chelmsford launched a crusade in 1919 to raise £400,000 to erect buildings and put in staff. The population of the diocese has increased by nearly a million since then. Anglican communicants on Easter Day 1919 in Essex numbered about 5% of the population. In West Ham the figure was 2·3%.[46] Those who moved to estates like Dagenham were from the areas where fewest went to church. Often, as today, the move to a new estate broke the habit of church-going. The church's way of worshipping might be different from that which the new arrivals had known at home — and the ways of home were the only ways they knew. One of the most disheartening experiences which clergy on new estates have had to face is that of discovering those who have been active workers, even church-wardens or deacons, in inner city churches, who have no links at all now with the Church. You also find some are happier to travel back to church in the district from which they come. The demands made upon laymen in a small congregation in the inner city, their over-commitment to many organisations and large buildings, are such that, having moved, they do not intend to be trapped by the church again!

No Glamour

Clergy on housing estates served areas which did not have the glamour of slums or poverty issues. They rarely knew the reinforcement of such allies as settlements. They set out to serve a section of the urban population which had been cut off from its roots for the second time. The support which young couples in Bethnal Green found from family and friends just round the corner was deeply missed at Dagenham and Debden —as they are now in the newer towns of Basildon and Thamesmead. Frequently, men and women find that they have much further to travel to work. The increased travelling time has to be added to the longer working hours which people on housing estates feel they must do in order to pay the high rents and the costs of a new standard of living to which a new home often leads. Leisure time is shorter for evening activities.

If fatalism is a distinctive feature of the old inner city streets, it is often even more so of new estates. People often have unrealistically high hopes of an instant better life when they move to a new house on a new estate. The growing pains and the slow development of community awareness often mean that those who looked for quick results lose heart. Communities take years to develop their own distinctive quality of life. Ten or twelve years is a short time in the life of a community. But it is often long enough to breed again a sense of powerlessness and fatalism.

Lessons from History

There are lessons to be learned from history. The churches and other educators have done a great deal *for* people in urban and industrial areas. They have not done so much *with* them. They have been slow and half-hearted in believing that local responsibility and leadership can develop here. Much compassion has been shown, but the churches as a whole have not been seen to stand for justice. The churches which have been concerned about the whole life of the community have sometimes been trapped into filling in the gaps without finding a continuing local purpose for their life. Theological divisions have caused different groups of Christians to react against each other, so that each has offered an unbalanced insight. The Christian gospel has only been believed when it has been lived out and spoken out by those who really believe it themselves. There is no 'spiritual' gospel for the city in isolation from a gospel which proclaims the reign of God over every part of life in it.

So much for the factors that make up 'the inheritance'. It is necessary now to look at how we learn and so to try and set out our aims in education, especially as they are related to the purpose of this book which is to find God's purpose for the city. What do we expect of working class people in this area? How can we develop the latent intelligence of those for whom, despite all our ideals and theories, there has not been equal opportunity? These questions of intelligence levels, language and learning we must look at now.

Four

LEVELS, LANGUAGE AND LEARNING: THE AIMS OF EDUCATION

EXPECTATIONS

WHO expects what of working class people? When Plato wrote in *The Republic* of the ideal state, he assumed that there would always be separate categories in it. The rulers were made of gold, the warriors of silver. The traders and work people were made of brass and iron. He did not expect the men of brass and iron to be able to take responsibility within the community. That belonged to the Guardians. His main preoccupation in education was with those men of gold. He expected their lives to be marked by 'high spirits' — enterprise, indignation — along with austerity and responsibility.[1] Plato did not expect the children of the men of brass and iron to develop these characteristics.

In Britain the ideal of equality of opportunity has been generally accepted as a goal for many years. Those who have achieved well in schools or in jobs often say, 'Surely everyone has a chance to get to the top nowadays, if he has the ability?' The answer is, 'No, he hasn't the chance.' There are many success stories of those who have 'made it to the top', whether 'the top' be in politics, in business or in the entertainment world. But surveys repeatedly show that the right proportions of able children of manual workers do not achieve as well as they should in our educational system.

A research project, which follows a representative sample of over 5,000 children from birth, showed in 1968 that middle class pupils had retained, almost intact, their historical advantage. Nearly half the lower manual, working class pupils of high ability had left school before they were sixteen and a half.[2] A study of educational priority areas in 1972 took the view that equality of opportunity in schools without equality of conditions in the home and environment was a sham.[3] Provision of schools is only one factor, and one of limited influence, in children's lives. What achievements are expected of children by teachers, parents, employers and by the children themselves and their friends has a massive influence on whether they achieve well or not.

Gold or Iron?

The factor which more than any other has prevented the churches from rooting strong local Christian communities in urban working class communities is that we, along with other 'educators', have accepted Plato's divisions of men into gold, silver, brass and iron. It has been too often assumed that leaders come from certain social groups with certain educational experience. The abilities of working class people have been under-valued, and are often wasted. The division of the great city into one class zones of housing heightens the force of the question whether we believe that the world is to become permanently divided into those who are within its system of privileges and those who are excluded by lack of opportunity.

No one can calculate how much potential is latent, but hemmed in and wasted. I find something more is at stake. I believe as a Christian that man is made in the image of God. Part of what I understand by this is that men should not be just creatures who react to the forces of the universe. They should be able to make decisions which alter their own (and other people's) destiny. We have allowed urban conditions to make people despair — and with good reason — of making significant decisions about anything. We mustn't be surprised that they have turned away from the Christian challenge to make decisions about the whole of life and about eternity. It is highly relevant for Christians to try to understand the pressures which limit people's development of ability and to search after ways of removing such barriers. That means that we must look at housing, jobs, schools, planning and the total environment of the city.

When I went as a new curate to Islington in north London I was infected by the attitudes of a very large number of educators, both in the teaching profession and elsewhere. For example, I gave away the prizes at a primary school in Islington very near where Risinghill School was later to be built. On the duplicated slip of paper which was given to us (us prizegivers, managers, parents and teachers), we were informed that, of thirty-nine leavers one had passed the eleven-plus. 'With the material available,' it said, 'this was a very creditable result.' I've been learning steadily since that it was a disgraceful result, not to that school alone, but to the whole of society which had put so many barriers in the way of God-given intelligence.

Having lived and worked now for eighteen years in similar districts of inner London and for ten years in Liverpool, I am aware how wrong that attitude was. If we have a proper Christian doctrine of man, made in God's image, made to be part of a royal priesthood, we must believe that there are leaders within every district. They may not measure up to the definitions we have made of 'leader'. I know from my experience for twelve years in Canning Town that there is intelligence and ability within that community to provide the responsible leadership needed.

'Talking Groups'

An academic surgeon came to the Mayflower Family Centre to talk to forty or so adults about the ethics of transplants. I reckoned that perhaps three had in their time passed the eleven-plus. They pushed him for over two hours' keen questioning. He said, 'I was as exhausted as I am by my brightest students.' They had learned to discuss and to 'think on their feet' by joining a variety of 'talking groups' — some while they were teenagers, more when they were already adults. On other occasions I made notes of comments made about a talking group by its members. Here are some of them:

'Nobody made you feel silly.'

'You learned to talk to others.'

'In an argument you let yourself go.'

'It's all part of your training, though you don't know it.'

'You learn to respect other people's point of view.'

'Your mind's working all the time.'

The most crucial hurdle to surmount is the matter of self-confidence. To make matters harder from this point of view, we had, in the traditional style of a settlement, some thirty residents who were 'the college type'. It was made plain to them all before they agreed to come to the Mayflower that they were not being asked to come as leaders. They were asked to join a community which was undergirding a young local church as it came into being. Whenever local leaders emerged, the settlement residents would be asked to step back.

A local housewife in her forties was asked to take over the youngest part of the children's church. She compared herself with a teacher who had run it previously. At regular intervals she would say, 'I'm no good at it. You should get someone like Jean.' I would reassure her that she was in some respects much better equipped than the teacher, because she understood the children, their home life and the neighbourhood in ways a teacher from outside would take years to learn. In fact the same housewife was the adult that the roughest teenagers in the open youth club talked with and listened to most in the years that I was there. Once her self-confidence grew, her ability grew.

One of the most dangerous remarks that can be made is that 'working class people like things simple'. The remark is dangerous because it easily leads on to the untrue statement, so often implied, that 'working class people *are* simple'. When we try to assess how intelligently someone is able to discuss a subject, the context is all important. For instance, if I am taken round a factory making highly sensitive electronic equipment, my intelligence would be rated very low in the context of a discussion on the latest developments in computers. It might be rated higher if the context were personal relationships and how decisions are made within the firm. At the time when the Devlin Report on the future of the docks came out, it would have been impossible to listen, as I did, to dockers discussing it, and then to say that they were unable to handle abstract ideas. They were speaking in a context where they were involved and which they understood.

Concrete to Abstract

The suggestion has been made that in urban and industrial areas we should be using concrete thought rather than abstract. This distinction is one which is made in the way children learn. It has been widely assumed that their thinking develops in three stages: an *intuitive* stage; a *concrete* stage and *abstract thinking*.

The theory has been that children move from the *intuitive* stage to the *concrete* at about seven to eight years of age; and from the *concrete* to the *abstract* at about thirteen to fourteen years of age. It has been held that if children have never grown used to handling abstract ideas, they will often grow up to be adults who only think in concrete terms.

This theory about moving, or failing to move, from stage one to stage two and on to stage three at expected ages has a limited truth. But it should be treated with great caution.

For one thing different children develop at different speeds. For another, there is a sense in which children are using all three stages of thinking at a very early age. Adults ought to be using all three stages in their thinking.

Perhaps my own experience in inner London which I have been describing, may serve as an illustration. When I arrived, my *intuition* (stage one) said, 'I don't expect to find leaders here. I expect I must provide ideas and leadership.' I expressed this in *concrete* terms (stage two), 'We can't get local people to take responsibility in church life.' This led me to an *abstract* thought (stage three), 'Leaders can only be expected from those who've had certain definable educational experiences.'

Gradually my experience has widened and *an interplay of intuitive, concrete and abstract thinking* has brought about a wholesale change in my attitudes. The concrete idea perhaps came first: 'Many working class people do take a very intelligent and responsible lead in trade unions and politics,' and I began to be able to list men and women whom I came to know. Intuitive thinking played a part, 'Jim has it in him to be a very able leader, though in school he was "D" stream.' I began to understand abstract ideas and to try out some more; 'If you expect little of people, they will probably achieve little. Perhaps providing all the leadership from outsiders helps to create the problem by making people more dependent — and only brings dependent people into the Church. If I didn't take all the decisions, perhaps local people would accept responsibility and grow in what they themselves expect they can achieve.' Abstract ideas need constantly to be tested against references of concrete 'for instances' and intuitive feelings.

Many adults do not use abstract ideas. But that is not to say that they *could* not use them. Many adults in Canning Town learned to handle abstract ideas when they became members of some talking group where they felt accepted.

Gradually they tried to think on their feet. Some got very hung up on one idea or another perhaps beause they had not been used to tossing ideas around, or sometimes because their ability to handle ideas was in fact very limited.

Many people have been brought up to understand that everything was right or wrong, that the teacher knew the answer and that you must learn it and remember it. Church teachers have been too ready to encourage this way of learning. So we've often produced the kind of Christian who says, 'I did know the answer to the problem of suffering in the world, but I can't for the moment remember it.' Jesus's method seems to have been very different. For example: 'What is written in the Law? What is your reading of it?' 'Which of these three do you think was neighbour to the man?' 'My good man, who set me over you to judge or arbitrate?' 'Why can you not judge for yourself what is the right course?'[4]

Painful Experience

It is a painful experience for both when the clergyman bounces back the question a layman asks, when the layman has been brought up to expect clergy to provide all the answers. My most unpopular moments have generally been when I have refused to be the kind of clergyman-teacher that is expected; moments when I have refused to take on responsibility for a matter which I believe belongs to local people; moments when I have asked a question in return instead of giving the immediate answer. (I believe there are moments also when we can betray each other by refusing to say what we really believe at the right moment. And, when we don't know the answer ourselves, we need to admit it.) A group picks up quickly enough from its leader what he expects of them.

In the first confirmation class I ran at the Mayflower

Family Centre there were six adults. Quite early in the life of the group, one young man, Joe, said that he hadn't understood a word of what I had said on the Sunday in my sermon. An elderly woman came rushing to my defence, 'If some people don't like your preaching, I'm sure I do.' On the way out at the end of the evening Joe said to me, 'I hope I didn't speak out of turn.' I said, 'Joe, how can I possibly know if I'm on the right wavelength unless people tell me. I hope you always will.'

One of the most important of the comments I listed about the life of a talking group was, 'In an argument you let yourself go.' Few people can learn to think on their feet unless they feel free to try ideas on other people, to 'lash out', to get angry at times. Again, they quickly grasp what is expected by the leader. His attitude can say as clearly as words, 'We don't want people who rock the boat here', and the members of the group will respond accordingly or withdraw. The opposite is also true. If members of a group get over the hurdle of coming out with the question which might make them look stupid or with challenging the orthodox viewpoint or with getting angry — and are not rejected by the leader or the group — they begin to think with freedom. Once this has happened, I have frequently been astonished by the way adults of forty years of age, or seventy, have shown far greater intelligence than they thought they possessed. The younger that people come into the atmosphere of such a group, the further their intelligence is likely to develop.

There remains a place for teaching facts or providing access to facts. Neither children nor adults can 'buy' new ideas unless they are provided with the necessary 'change'.

THE SELF-PICTURE

WHAT is expected of you is clearly very important in developing your intelligence. What follows is even more important, namely, what you expect of yourself. This *self picture* can be the most crushing and crippling factor in a man's development. Everyone has said at some time of someone else, 'He's got an inferiority complex.' We realise the effect it has on his achievements. To speak of a self picture helps us to realise that every one of us has one, and that every one of us is influencing the self picture which others have. It is particularly relevant to urban and industrial areas. A whole district can get the picture that people who achieve things in life 'don't live round here'. Those who were selected for grammar school or who were labelled 'A' stream have moved out of the district to buy their own house in the suburbs. Those who make the decisions at work travel in from somewhere else. So do the teachers.

I discussed the effect of the one class area with three men who lived in such areas in Leeds, Liverpool and London. They described the low expectations which young people become used to, because of what teachers, parents and their mates expect of them. They affect the level of educational success which children picture themselves achieving, the level of job on which they set their sights, and also their view of what they can be in the community. George from Liverpool started at work in the 1930s: 'My two brothers were both out of work. My horizon was to get a job. The Post Office offered a steady job as an engineer. I wasn't unhappy.

But I was limited.' Ted from London said, 'Parents would be content if their son became a foreman. They wouldn't look beyond that.'

Damaging Factor

In a Canning Town discussion a group of adults was discussing education. 'Now I think of it,' said Jack, 'the teacher always noticed the bright ones in our class, and we illiterates sat at the back and mucked about.' Jack in my view is a highly intelligent man who would run rings round many university graduates, if he was familiar with the context of the subject they were discussing. But his self picture was that he was illiterate. It is the most influential single factor in damaging his life. He has rarely kept a job as long as a year. If you press him to accept responsibility, he will generally throw it back at you. The picture which parents, friends, teachers built up by what they expected of him had come to be his own self picture.

It is very important for Christians to ask what should happen to the self picture when men face up to Christ. It has often been assumed that the first result of a confrontation with Christ will be that our pride must be shattered. What, then, if men already have too low an opinion of themselves? It is not a true meeting with Christ if the result is that they say, 'I'm useless. I'm even worse than I thought.'

Consider Jesus and Simon Peter. He looked at him at their first meeting: 'You're Simon Son of John. You shall be called Cephas,' (that is Peter, the rock).[5] Jesus let him know that he expected a great deal of him. Going with Christ was a stretching experience. The temptation to Peter as he saw how much Christ expected of him was to run away: 'Go, Lord, leave me, sinner that I am.'[6] However much he failed, he found that Christ still wanted to know him, still expected him to grow up into what He called him — the rock man.

Those who went around with Jesus in the Gospels might be said to have gone through three stages: they met someone who really wanted to know them and made them feel valued; if they went around with Him for a while, they were stretched to their capacity, and began to feel deeply ashamed of how far short they came of His standards; and they found that He still wanted to know them and to help them.

Intelligence and Ability

The Biblical doctrine of man claims that all men have intelligence and ability. The way Jesus Christ treated men challenged them to enlarge their view of what they were capable of achieving. My experience has made me believe that we undervalue the intelligence of many men and women. This experience has led me to ask more questions about the nature of intelligence and about the failures of schools, clubs and churches to develop that intelligence. For if what I suspect from my experience is true there is a shameful waste of ability and 'a mutilation of God's creation'.[7]

I am not asserting that all men are equally intelligent. There are indeed different levels of intelligence. It is not loving or helpful to encourage a boy with lesser abilities to suppose that he can achieve the same as his friend who has greater talents. He will spend the rest of his life trying to live up to it — and failing. Nevertheless, in what I've described of my experience several factors have begun to emerge: the self picture influences a man's intelligence and achievements; what others (parents, friends, employers and teachers) expect of him strengthens, or weakens, the self picture; the context in which we try to assess a man's intelligence will alter how intelligent we think him; there are different kinds of intelligence; intelligence is not a static factor, as though we carry an unalterable IQ around with us like a birthmark ('he's five feet eight; he's got brown eyes; his IQ is 98').

So far I've deliberately talked largely about adults. Clearly behind this discussion lie many questions about children and their education. But we have to ask first what we are educating children for. It has been necessary therefore to ask what place we expect working class adults to have in our society. It should not be simply to fill certain jobs in the industrial machine. It should be to know that they have a full stake in the community as responsible people. This means that education must be as much for leisure as for the jobs that will be available.

Six Aims of Education

In the light of those beliefs I hope that education will offer children — through schools and youth organisations: equipment with basic tools and techniques to go on learning; a vision of greatness, leading to ideals of personal and corporate behaviour; awareness of the whole community and the wider world; confidence in the gifts they possess and ambition to use them for the good of the community; respect for reasoned authority; creative discontent with society as it is and experience of bringing about changes for good.

Under Fire

When I have listed these objectives to adults, the last one has been the most frequently under fire. To stimulate discontent by itself is destructive. But to pose problems to young people, to enable them to identify issues which should be tackled, and to experience some effecting of change is deeply creative. Education has too often been the means by which society has simply put its stamp on children, so that they 'fit in' to its jobs and values.

Education ought not to be about a static and closed world which has to be accepted and to which children must learn to adjust. It ought to be about enabling people made in the image of God to be 'transforming rather than adaptive beings',[8] in relation to the world as it is. Many children will live out their lives in educational priority areas. They must learn to be realistic about what life in such communities is like. But education in schools and youth organisations should inspire them to 'think boldly about it rather than lapse into resigned apathy'.[9]

All six aims should be maintained in education for any children. No doubt in a very poor country some hard choices have to be made about offering a limited education very widely or a full education to a selected few. A country like Tanzania was determined to take the risk of not concentrating so decisively on the selected few. A country like Britain has the resources to offer a full education to all. It does not at present have the will to give priority to those who are at a disadvantage because of the environment in which they grow up.

INTELLIGENCE

A CRITIC may fairly say, 'cut out the humbug and the patronising. May it not be true that if the more successful have been moving out of working class areas for so long, middle and upper class children *are* more intelligent than working class children?' I give two answers to that: first, we don't know, because we've never given working class children the opportunity to develop to their capacity; secondly, yes, middle class children are probably on average more intelligent, but not by the margin which our educational system shows. An attempt at a comparison was made by Basil Bernstein in 1958. The sample consisted of sixty-one working class boys of fifteen to eighteen years and forty-five public school boys of the same age. In IQ terms the public school boys were eight to ten points superior on the non-verbal test and twenty-three to twenty-four points superior on the verbal test.[10] I do not dispute that inheritance is a major factor in intelligence. However, no one has ever been able to measure 'innate intelligence' reliably, and the difference environment makes is too great to ignore. A child who has difficulty in expressing himself and who comes from a home where conversation is limited will be likely to score low in intelligence tests.[11]

Selection automatically hangs a label round a child's neck — 'selected' or 'not selected'. To know yourself not selected adds powerfully to a self picture which does not expect to achieve much. That will be reflected in both verbal and non-verbal tests. 'We're not intelligent', a class of school leavers told a visiting lecturer at their Nottingham secondary modern school. They were the bottom stream. 'The intelligent ones go to grammar school. The next to the bilaterals — and then there's us. We're the dustbin, sir.'[12]

It is going to be difficult ever to make those young people believe that they are valued. The dream which produced the tripartite system of grammar, secondary modern and technical schools was not unworthy. It hoped to offer appropriate opportunities. Success in exams is often not the best yardstick of whether children are developing their potential as well as they might. But the tripartite system underestimated the effect on both children and teachers of expecting low achievements, from those who are not selected. And secondary modern schools, especially in urban and industrial areas, never succeeded in attracting a fair share, let alone a priority share of the ablest teachers.[13]

Less Complaint

If we could be confident that intelligence tests could place children reliably at eleven years of age in the school where their abilities would be best developed, there would be less complaint. Even then we noticed earlier how other people's expectations affect the self picture we have. And we noticed how devastating the self picture, 'us illiterates', was to an intelligent man's life. So the prophecy of intelligence tests becomes self-fulfilling. Children often perform according to the low expectations we have. Success to a great degree breeds success. And the opposite is true.

Since comprehensive schools came into existence, their success has been measured by many according to whether they match the exam results of fee-paying schools. Comprehensive schools in Inner London are not fully comprehensive as they do not receive all Inner London children of secondary school age. In 1983 13% of children of above average ability (Band 1) went to fee-paying schools. The others are going to grammar, direct grant and public schools. In a sense the title comprehensive school should not be used as long as selective schools continue to exist alongside them. They are often better described as large secondary schools. Nevertheless, enough evidence has emerged from the years in which some comprehensives have been operating to add to the doubts about the reliability of deciding appropriate selective schools on the basis of intelligence tests. It shows that children who would not have been selected for grammar school at eleven years of age have, for example, won university places because comprehensive schools gave them the opportunity.[14]

The concept of one ladder, called intelligence, with rungs on which each of us can be properly placed, needs to be dropped. Instead we need to realise that there are several ladders and that each of us would be placed on different rungs on different ladders. There is a variety of intelligences. For example, Richard Hauser speaks of four kinds of intelligences — academic, technical, creative, social.

Even then, the placing on the ladder is very hazardous because it makes the false assumption that intelligence is a static, unchanging factor. Lord Boyle rightly spoke of 'the acquisition of intelligence'. Intelligence will increase given the right stimulus. It will decrease if the stimulus is missing. This is what I sensed among adults in Canning Town. If the stimulus is there much earlier in life the intelligence — certainly the measured intelligence — will increase much more.

THE USE OF LANGUAGE

BERNSTEIN spoke of a restricted code and an elaborated code of language. The 'restricted code' of language will tend to contain a high proportion of short commands, simple statements and questions. The symbolism is descriptive, tangible, concrete, visual:

'Come round my house tonight.'

'We're decorating indoors.'

'I've had to tell two lies at work today. If I didn't, I'd lose my job, or my mates would never speak to me again.'

The 'elaborated code' will make qualifications of what is said and will include advanced logical operations. Children in professional families' homes would generally be used to hearing and taking part in conversation which uses both restricted and elaborated codes. Children in working class homes tend to know only the restricted code.

More recently, Bernstein has regretted the use which has been made of his phrase 'restricted code' of language.[15] It has been taken to mean that working class children are deprived in their use of language. There is such a thing as language deprivation. That is another issue and an important one. The frustration of being unable to express yourself in words often is a direct cause of violence.

However it is not right to assume that the majority of working class children are linguistically deprived or culturally deprived and therefore need 'compensatory education'. To talk about compensatory education implies that something is lacking in the family and in the child. It returns to the notion that educators will lift them up to their standards — and will expect them to do less well than their own children. Working class children are expected to leave the culture of their home and community behind at the school gate, and compete on terms laid down by another social group within the school community. It is not surprising if, having to adapt to a different culture, they achieve less educationally than the children from middle class homes who experience the same culture and variety of language which they meet at home. We expect working class children to understand at a deep level the culture of the teacher. We have no right to expect this to happen, unless the teacher first understands at a deep level the culture of the child, and respects it. Children will learn better if they are at home with the context in which they are learning. A lecturer was amazed, and somewhat shocked, in listening to some tapes of a colleague teaching social studies with pupils who were in their extra year at school, following the raising of the school leaving age to sixteen. The teacher's own use of language changed to something much nearer the pupils'.

Partly because of this respect for their culture and interests, the amazement was also at the amount of theoretical material absorbed in the discussions.

Wide Range

To be able to use both the restricted and the elaborated code helps people to have a wide range of language forms. But we don't rely on words to learn and to communicate with each other. Knowing and feeling come to us by other routes also. Music, art, movement, drama, mime or role playing all help people to express themselves.

I watched a group of disturbed children using masks and puppets. They were able to express themselves in ways they could never have done if they themselves were speaking without the mask. Drama can enable the player to have insights and emotional involvement in situations which might not be possible through other media.

Looking at my hopes for what children will be offered by education, high on the list I put A. N. Whitehead's phrase 'the vision of greatness'. Enduring love is part of my vision of greatness. I hope my child will know and feel something of what it means. 'Ideals of personal behaviour' would include her learning how to deal with her own anger. Learning about enduring love and about dealing with anger is less likely to be achieved if all our educational hopes are pinned on verbalised forms of learning.

The child who is rich in language ability may turn out to be a poor little rich boy. Language is the way we organise and then represent the world we experience. If we fear other ways of communicating and rely on words alone, we may be less sensitive to extra verbal communication. A definition of language is 'the reduction of experience to a familiar form'. To reduce the experience of being in love to words is clearly a *reduction* — unless you are a poet. Words reduce the impact of feelings upon us. We have organised our defences by putting things into words. If we have always to reduce our feelings to words, we don't learn as much as we could from continuing to experience through our feelings.

Protestant Christians often fear ceremonial, drama and emotion. If we reduce our experience of God to words only, there is certainly a reduction. If we try to communicate our faith by words only, we shall certainly not see the vision of greatness, and we shall not communicate with those who are not familiar with the context of religious life or with our elaborated, organised language about God.

Into Words

All this should not lead us to turn old values on their head, and insist that non-verbal communication is *better* than verbalising. It is an essentially human capacity to be able to put things into words. We help people to grow when we help them to be more articulate (which doesn't necessarily involve elaborated codes of language). To have the ability, which verbalising gives, to be a spectator, to evaluate past experience, to share one's experiences with others and to interpret them together — all these deliver us from being victims of our environment.

Experience is the greatest teacher, we say. But that statement is manifestly untrue. There are many who have a mass of experience and have learned nothing from it. The greatest teacher is experience plus interpretation. Language helps us to go back as a spectator to an experience.

A small boy comes home from school and tells his mother what happened today. Putting it into words makes an experience last. The boy may turn over in his mind a school visit to the swimming baths in order to savour the enjoyment again of his walk with his friend and his achievement in swimming a length for the first time. His mother's responses of interest and pleasure will increase his understanding.

Language is representing the world in words. It allows us to work on our experience as the small boy did, and it allows others to work on our experience too, as his mother did. There is a need for gossip — such as a child ought to have with a teacher at the end of a class — when knowing and feeling are very close. Then the role of language is often that of a spectator, reflective, meditative, going over the past and reworking old experience with the new experience of gossip with a friend.

HOME AND SCHOOL

IT is sometimes said that the achievement of middle class children in school is because their parents care passionately about their children's education. The inference has often been drawn that other parents did not care. This is quite untrue of most working class parents. They care deeply, and are profoundly interested in their children's educational development. What is often true is that such parents feel unable to help their children with school work, and are over-awed by the professional standing of teachers.

The Halsey Report argued that, in the pre-school years, the need was to develop educationally informed families. After that the problem was to create socially informed schools.[16] Nursery schools now rightly come high on the list of priorities. If there is truth in the prime importance of developing spoken language, the years before five will be very important. Some of the hopes and achievements of one nursery school were: to offer space. One child from a tall block of flats ran every day for half an hour before doing anything else; to aim at a wide variety of experiences — with adults around to help verbalise; and to teach children to be intelligent — as we teach reading.

One of the movements which has gathered greatest momentum in London is that of pre-school playgroups. Their existence should not be a reason for holding back the provision of nursery schools. One of the solid gains from playgroups, which must not be lost when more nursery schools are opened, is the number of local mothers who have taken a major role in their child's learning. A growing number have received training. They will not easily be prevented from sharing in their children's education at later stages.

One of the many major issues which runs through Leila Berg's passionate account of the events which led to the closure of Risinghill comprehensive school in Islington is the different attitudes of teachers to the culture of the neighbourhood. Some were ready to learn about the district and to respect its way. Others would say 'For most of these children school is a waste of time. They come from a rotten home. They will be rotten people.' They said of a parent, 'This little market stall holder thinks he can have his opinion.'[17] A vicar said to me of the people who lived in his parish, 'Their behaviour disgusts me.' And another, 'There isn't a single decent boy left around here.' The tension in the staff room at Risinghill is common in working class neighbourhoods. Some teachers are critical of the community and only wish to 'raise its standards'.

Teachers Discouraged

Teachers can easily be discouraged by the small number of parents who come to functions which are put on for them in urban and industrial areas. Clergy and others who have organised institutional occasions will tell them that such occasions on their own will be unlikely to bring parents. Many head teachers prefer not to have a parent teacher association, because they feel that such an institutional body is liable to be dominated by middle class parents. Many parents won't come to 'an authority thing'. For the majority, it isn't that they aren't interested in their children or grateful to teachers for helping them. The idea that parents know something and have a right to be heard about the education of their children is comparatively new in working class areas.

One pattern proposed for primary schools suggested four ways of meeting parents:[18]

(a) An open meeting early in the term for all parents.

(b) Private talks between parents and class teachers. This means teachers welcoming parents at all times of the day. Diary appointments are not the normal pattern, but parents are reasonable people and will arrange to come back if a particular moment is not convenient.

(c) Meetings on teaching methods in particular subjects.

(d) Home visits to parents who don't come to the school.

Research in educational priority areas showed that the appointment of a home school liaison officer gave a human touch to the links between home and school which duplicated notes and forms failed to do.[19]

One comprehensive school head tried to set up occasions in as informal a way as possible; for example, Harvest Festival was the climax of integrated studies work for the first half of the term. Parents were asked to come in to see the work their children had done. On another occasion, a family evening was run, again devoted to children's work, and included a dance, stalls, with parents bringing small children, granny and the rest of the family. More important than the events was the exhausting business of being available for face to face conversations.

Some parents' way of getting over the sense of being over-awed by teachers is to be aggressive. If the teachers want there to be genuine participation, they mustn't lay down as a first rule of all meetings, 'This isn't a staff bashing meeting.' There is unlikely to be real communication across this divide without some conflict. A wise teacher will not avoid it, even though it's painful. It depends on what the objectives are. If they are 'to help parents understand the new teaching methods we're using nowadays', that's one thing — and an important one. But it's not participation. If the objectives are that teachers want to learn from the adults of the community, hoping that this learning will be a two way process, they will think some painful conflict worth accepting on the way.

Foreigners

At a college of education I was asked by a student if clergy were not regarded very much as foreigners in a working class community. I said that a bigger divide than clergy/laity in these areas is local people/professionals. 'My school turned me against my home', said an able young leader in Canning Town. The underlying truth was probably, 'My experience of school led me to turn away from my home.' It took a deliberate change of attitudes for her to start thinking positively of her home and district, after she had left school. Other teachers want to build a socially in-formed school which does not ask children to break faith with their own loyalties and traditions, and which at the same time is in no sense academically second-rate. Clergy certainly feel strange if they come from a different social back-ground; but no more so than other professionals, and the clergy may have the advantage of living in the district.

It is the feeling of confusion created by the pressures of the district in which they live that has caused more and more clergymen to seek in-service training on some urban training course. We need to understand how the city and communities within it function. Teachers need this sort of understanding no less. They would benefit from urban training courses, and even more from getting to know adults in the area where they teach. I doubt if a teacher should attempt to teach children good manners, for example, unless he knows some adults from the community to which the children belong and their style of life at home. Good manners are what put people at ease. They vary from country to country and community to community. We no longer believe in some fixed book of etiquette. Few things would do more good to a teacher than making friends with half a dozen adults from the area where he teaches. He or she would then begin to discover, in a context of mutual acceptability and understanding, the kind of issues with which education deals if it takes the concept of the community seriously.

One of the best ways of understanding the life of a community is to live in it. Colleges have frequently taught teachers that it is better not to live in the area where the children live. Sometimes the reason given is that discipline might suffer if the children know their teachers out of school. Such discipline seems to me to be a brittle thing if it is going to be damaged by meeting in informal ways. Some teachers, very reasonably, find it too demanding to live in the district. They believe they can teach better by withdrawing. Others find it impossible to obtain housing in the district. An increasing number of local authorities provide housing for teachers and others who serve in their area. More teachers make a point of living in the district in urban and industrial areas today; they give themselves a better chance of understanding the 'feel' of the district. It might encourage them to commit themselves for a longer time to the area and the school. For another handicap which schools in working class urban areas have to carry is the short time that teachers stay. The turnover of teachers is appreciably quicker in areas where teachers are less likely to live.[20]

I have set out these aims of education because I believe they are aims related to Biblical insights that are highly relevant to the masses who live in areas 'built as a city'. Such aims now compel us to take up the question of 'priority' areas in that field and in other fields (housing, jobs, etc.,) that are inseparable from human needs. To share scarce resources may be part of the Christian obligation that is highly relevant to our times. But this and other responses to industrial life must wait until we have looked at these priority areas and also delved deeply, as we are now committed to do, into the basic issues by which we are faced — those of power and, even more so, powerlessness.

Five

PRIORITY AREAS

SHARING SCARCE RESOURCES

THERE are certain scarce resources in a big city. The scarcest of these are: land, good jobs, and good teachers.

It is frequently assumed that, if only the whole country can become more wealthy, there will be some fall-out and the most disadvantaged will receive their share of the benefit. The weakness of this assumption can be seen by considering the three scarce resources I have listed. More national wealth does not increase the amount of land. It may actually decrease the number of appropriate good jobs. It should increase the number of good teachers — though there still remains a limit, because the number who are highly gifted is limited.

In all three cases the *share* which different groups in the country receive decides where advantages and disadvantages lie. In a just society it should be the aim that, if one group receives less than its fair share in one set of good things, it should receive more than its fair share in another. The unjust society is one in which one group always wins in the share-out of the land, the good jobs and the good teachers while another group always loses in these areas. Christian comment should recall that a distinctive mark of the mission of the Christ was that good news was announced to the poor.[1] Jesus seems to have given priority to the poor and calls us to do so too.

I shall discuss what *real poverty* and *real wealth* are today in the next section. Plainly they cannot be defined simply in terms of wages, but they will include that share which people receive of the good things the city has to offer.

Positive Discrimination

The concept of priority areas has been acknowledged. Certain urban districts have been designated as educational priority areas. This means that primary schools in those areas receive 'positive discrimination' for staffing, buildings and materials. It means too that, in the new programme for nursery school education, these areas will come first. The factors which were considered in designating an education priority area[2] show that disadvantage is the result of interlocking factors which are by no means all in schools:

> *Jobs. (A high proportion of men in unskilled or semi-*
> *skilled jobs.)*
> *Supplements in cash from the state.*
> *Overcrowding of houses.*
> *Lack of basic housing amenities.*
> *Poor attendance.*
> *Proportions of handicapped pupils.*
> *Immigrant children.*
> *Teacher turnover.*
> *Pupil turnover.*

An effective programme for priority areas cannot stop short at a little extra for primary schools and nursery schools. A review of attempts at compensatory education in the United States saw that it was necessary to go further and further outside the educational system, as the ramifications of the initial problem were uncovered. Poor achievements in school were seen to be merely one factor in a series of social and economic inequalities experienced by disadvantaged groups.[3] We must not expect education to solve all our problems. Nevertheless, education is one of the areas in which positive discrimination on a very large scale is most needed if there is to be any serious movement towards equality of opportunity.

Priority means coming first in the queue. A nation cannot afford everything at once. References to priority areas should mean that these areas actually receive the first share of available land, of appropriate jobs, of good teachers, and of the finance to make these possible.

Priorities and Values

For example, everyone would have agreed in the 1960s that we should implement both the Robbins Report on Higher Education and the Newsom Report on the secondary education of the less academically successful half of our children. Massive finance was put towards higher education (which only a tiny proportion of children from priority areas ever receives), but very small amounts, proportionately, to the Newsom children. *The priorities displayed what our values are*. It was assumed that it was absolutely essential to educate the academically 'more able'. It was regarded as a luxury that could not be afforded to give an equal opportunity to the children who had been labelled as 'less able'. These priorities were the wrong way round — as the Bible confirms. Serious priority in education would take into account what is spent on each child in nursery, primary, secondary and higher education. It would mean that more money should be spent on children from priority areas than on any other children in the country. It would mean that the more wealthy must be restrained from spending more on their children. If people buy an advantage for *their* children, they also buy a disadvantage for *other* children. If they pay to have a higher ratio of teachers to children, fewer teachers will be available for other children.

Serious priority given to housing in disadvantaged areas

would mean that these areas received first claim on the scarce resources of land and of money. When we look at attempts at urban redevelopment after slum clearance, we see it forced by restrictions on land and money to produce very high densities with very limited facilities. It does not receive priority.

THE QUESTION OF SCHOOLS

THE influence of *parental* support cannot be over-emphasised in a discussion of education. Part of what that means is parents' insistence on good standards and values in the school which their children attend. A minority of parents know how to bring effective influence to bear. They are the same minority who are most likely to send their children to fee-paying or selective schools. If there were no choice for them but comprehensive schools, they would very quickly bring powerful influence to bear to see that the £15,000 million a year spent on the state system was better used. However much compassion these parents may have for other children, they will not have the sense of urgency about educational reform which would come if their own children had to face the inadequate buildings, the tension about 'whether I'll be grammar', and the large classes of many state schools.

Many of us who argue for what we conceive to be a better system are in a personal dilemma. We believe in comprehensive education. But we believe there can be no truly comprehensive schools, so long as selective schools exist. In the meantime do we send our children to the large secondary schools which do not have a comprehensive intake? Is it fair to ask a few children to take on the system until we all take it on together? Or do we send our children to a grammar school or fee-paying school, when we don't believe in separate development? On the one hand we are accused of using our children as pawns in the game, and on the other hand of being untrue to our convictions. We cannot win.

My view of London is a very privileged one. I see a very wide range of institutions and bodies which serve people. A high proportion of men and women whom I find giving valuable and creative service, are the products of the grammar and direct grant schools in the Inner London area. I realise very keenly the force of the argument that says, 'Why destroy well-established schools in pursuit of the most unresearched leap into the dark in history?' By definition, a fully comprehensive system must always be 'unresearched' until it comes into being, though there is good evidence in existence from twenty years of some of the 'comprehensive' schools which do exist. 'A leap into the dark' has often been a description of faith. The priority of most church people and of many educators has been to guard our base in the well-established schools, and to inch our way forward from it. I believe the advantage of the minority in these schools has contributed steadily to the disadvantage of the majority of the country's children.

Life Through Death

The demand of Christian obedience seems to me to give priority to those children who are most disadvantaged rather than first guarding our base. It asks us to take Jesus seriously when he says: 'Unless a grain of wheat falls into the ground and dies, it remains a solitary grain; but if it dies it bears a rich harvest.'[4] The law by which new life only comes through death cannot be related only to 'spiritual' matters. If we have the faith to demonstrate in our schools that we are called to be members one of another, we may find fuller life for the well established schools rather than their destruction. And we may give richer life to the majority.

Excellence is something for which every school should strive. But there can be an idolatry of excellence which wrongly restricts the number of those who have access to what it offers. There is an illustration of this from a children's hospital in Africa. Every child who came to the hospital received the best treatment. Then a new paediatrician came. He discovered that the infant mortality rate in the areas served by the hospital had not altered over many years. It was 282 per 1,000. He concluded that it would stay that way as long as excellent medicine was practised in the hospital.

Solving the problems of the neighbourhood was, in this case, not too difficult when there was acceptance of the possibility of diagnostic mistakes. This paediatrician had been taught at home that individual excellence in diagnosis is the mark of a good doctor. But he had to produce first in himself and then in other doctors a new personal excellence suitable to the job required. He taught a few girls of fifteen from the local mission school and sent them into the villages. They made many mistakes. It was fortunate that there wasn't a legal system where they could sue for wrong diagnosis. But in five years' time the infant mortality rate dropped from 282 to seventy-eight per thousand. What was killing all those children before was 'a sacred, stereotyped view of excellence. That is a graven image of excellence, tempting us to idolatry.'[5] Excellence is a good aim for a school. But it must be excellence which is suitable to the job required among the children in the area it serves.

Social Engineering

Am I using education for 'social engineering'? So far I have
argued that we can only increase the excellence of comprehensive schools, if all the children and all their parents
are involved in them. I do not want to avoid the charge of
social engineering. It urgently needs to be done, if segregated big cities are not to explode in violence or to die of
apathy. Those who think 'social engineering' is a dirty word
must answer some questions too: Do you believe that our
society is as God intends it to be? If not, what is your programme towards a more just society?

Any policy which may be described as egalitarian is accused of making for mediocre sameness, whereas human
beings are different and should be expected to produce
different achievements. That for which I am arguing is not
that this should be equality of achievement, but that all
people should be valued equally, and given equal opportunity to develop their own varied gifts. R. H. Tawney
pointed out that equality of provision is not identity of provision. Indeed, it can be claimed that equality of opportunity is likely to produce greater variety of human
achievement. I look forward to a diversity of comprehensive
schools, offering courses which will meet the specific needs
of their children.

It has been said that compelling the independent schools
to come fully into the state system is an interference with the
freedom of parental choice. If this is true, there are two
questions which have to be asked in return. First, which
parents have freedom of choice now? The answer is those
who can afford independent schools or those whose children
are being successful on the academic ladder at eleven years
of age. The second question is this. What choice do the
parents of the 70% or so of children who don't fit those

categories now have? The answer is that they now have very much less freedom of choice than they would have, if all schools in their area were comprehensive. Freedom is made up of different freedoms, some of which must be defended at all costs, some of which may rightly have to be surrendered for the good of others. We do not permit the strong man to do what he likes with his own physical strength. We limit his freedom so that the weaker man may experience freedom. We do not allow the rich man or the clever man to do as he likes, because the freedom of the poorer and the less clever depends upon the restraint of the sharper.[6]

World Setting

Place this whole discussion in a world setting. Many responsible parents, who care deeply about the Third World, about the overseas mission of the Church and about causes like Shelter in our own country, send their children to independent schools at considerable financial cost, and argue for their continued separate existence. They see that aid must not prevent the growth of indigenous leadership and responsibility in the Third World; that trade must not make poorer countries even more dependent on the rich; that it is easy and dangerous in developing countries to produce an educated class hopelessly out of touch with the uneducated majority; that development should not mean simply the increase of a country's gross national product, but a more equal distribution of the world's wealth and opportunities. How can we feel those objectives to be so important in the Third World, without seeing their relevance to the kind of society we are building here? Is it that we see more clearly what happens in the Third World because we are detached from it by distance? In the situation here, our personal interests are involved, and the same detachment is not easy.

Set this discussion in a racial context. A politician, whose courage in standing for racial justice I admire greatly, said to me: 'We have to accept that there is a class structure in this country. If we do, we shall much more quickly be able to establish a black middle class.' So what have we then achieved? Instead of a structure which goes like this: white professional and intellectual classes — white middle classes — white working classes — blacks, we achieve instead: white and black professional and intellectual classes — white and black middle classes — white and black working classes. And the black working classes will inevitably be at the bottom of the heap in a society which continues to accept that the layers in the cake cannot be challenged.

Philip Mason shows in his major study, *Patterns of Dominance*, that racial dominance and class dominance are closely related subjects. We cannot claim to have solved one without having seriously tackled the other. For example, Brazil can claim that the races are remarkably integrated. But no country has greater class barriers or divisions between rich and poor. Philip Mason writes:

'For those democracies in which white people are in a majority, there is no easy solution. They can solve the problem of their coloured minorities only by solving their own, that is to say by creating a more just society.'[7]

Public Schools

Consider the discussion in the setting of the history of the public schools. The great era of their founding or revival was 1860 to 1880. They set out to extend education from being the preserve of a few in the private schools. They claimed that hundreds went to school who would not previously have done so. They determined to be *public* schools.

The man who most determined the pattern of the public schools was Edward Thring who was headmaster of Uppingham from 1853 to 1887. His own background was that of the excessive discipline of a harsh, unsympathetic father and a miserable private school 'penal both in respect and character'; then he went to Eton in the worst days of Dr. Keate. He totally rejected Dr. Arnold's principle that 'the first, second and third duty of a schoolmaster was to get rid of unpromising subjects'.

Thring did not expect children of the labouring classes to share in the opportunities of education any more than the first freedom-seeking Americans expected the Indians to share in their society of equal opportunities. Indeed, he reassured his parents that it was not possible that a class which was compelled to leave off education at ten years of age could oust by superior intelligence a class which was able to spend more years in acquiring skill.

Few men of his age believed that opportunity should be given to all. But within what to him seemed a given framework, Thring sounds like an advocate for comprehensive schools. He always declared that it was unfair to gear the school system in favour of the bright intellects. It was not only unfair, it was blind, he felt. Thring believed that every boy, however unpromising he might appear, could do something well. It was the school's duty to discover the ability and to develop it for the service of the community. Therefore, there must be a wide curriculum with opportunities for cultural pursuits, workshops for those whose ability lay in working with their hands, games in which many a dull boy might win self respect.[8] Indeed, he was accused of undervaluing the intellect.

Since then, the public schools have perhaps learned to prize academic learning rather more highly. But many of them would hope to keep Thring's goals as their goals. We may fairly claim them as the aims of comprehensive schools.

The public schools grew strong at a moment when resources were thought to be too limited to offer such education to more than a limited section of the population. If they continue separately now, when resources are clearly much greater, they defeat the objectives which Thring set them; they become the very thing many of their best teachers would abhor — private schools for the few.

Much to Give

The public schools and direct grants schools would have to change greatly if they came into the state system. They would also have much to give to the state system. They can only make that contribution once they are fully within it.

The role of those church schools which come fully within the state system may be a pattern in some ways to follow. At their best, church schools do make the contribution which springs from their particular values and their measure of independence. Sometimes, by giving priority to children of church members over a wide catchment area they may unwittingly (or wittingly?) become schools for 'the better type of child'. But this need not happen.

Primary schools particularly, where there are enough schools for them to be *local*, can make a very positive contribution to the state system. Church secondary schools, because there are fewer of them, have to make a more decisive choice about which children they are to serve. There are many natural processes which could make Church of England secondary schools offer education which appealed to the socially aspiring. Indeed this can only be avoided by deliberate policies. The Joint Board of Education for London and Southwark decided in 1973 to recommend that church schools in the Inner London Education Authority's area should plan to become comprehensive, accepting the same proportions of children from each ability band which other comprehensive schools are allotted.

It has often been argued that the continued separate existence of a private sector, only taking five per cent of school children cannot damage the development of the state system. But the influence of the five per cent is far more dominant in our educational scheme than the numbers reflect. A small number are brought up to see themselves as leaders; other parents, teachers and children see the independent school boys and girls as demonstrably receiving a head start in the hunt for the best jobs. If the top layer of the educational cake continues to exist, then the other layers will be compelled to fight harder to guard their position. Grammar school children from working class areas have often seen their education as the means to a good job. Frequently, it has made them see their working class parents and neighbours as those who 'can't get on', who 'lack abilities'.[9]

Margaret Thatcher said in 1970 that schools like Manchester Grammar School had never deprived any poor boy in Manchester of opportunities, but had most certainly given many a chance they would otherwise never have been given. If you accept that there must be layers of top leaders, middle leaders and a very large layer of those who are led; and if you think about *individuals* who've broken through rather than the good of the *community* from which they come, then this makes good sense. But the values which I see Christianity to stand for challenge the whole basis of such thinking. The object of education which takes the whole neighbourhood into consideration must be to help the majority in the community to increase in confidence, not to strengthen that damning self picture of disadvantaged children which says, 'We're not the intelligent ones like John who's "grammar".'

In any discussion on equality of opportunity the

objection is raised that whatever policies have been pursued, and in whatever country, some sort of ranking order has always remained. Inequality has not been abolished. That is quite true. Neither has crime been abolished, nor sin. But we are against them! So must we be against inequality. If we cannot attain their ideals, we must still try to make as much progress as we can in our time.

THE STRUCTURE OF THE 'COMPREHENSIVE'

FIVE brief comments arise from the view of urban and industrial areas which I hold on issues which relate to the structure of the comprehensive school: smaller classes; streaming; size; sixth form colleges and neighbourhood schools.

Smaller Classes

No reorganisation of structures alters the need for more teachers. Modern methods of learning and less streaming of classes require the teacher to give more attention to each individual. Teachers should be more ready to welcome help from unqualified staff who may understand the neighbourhood better than they do. The teaching profession is sometimes over-conscious of its need for status. This is won much more by arguing for teachers to have a greater say in how decisions are made than in the wrong sort of assertion of professionalism. Such assertions reject the part that parents should play, that other adults of the neighbourhood could play and what more mature students from a less academic background could bring, with appropriate training, to the profession. There should be a cost of living bonus to encourage teachers to work in all schools in urban areas where it is difficult for them to find housing.

Streaming

If a comprehensive school streams all its pupils rigidly for all subjects, it is not likely to alter very materially what was done in grammar, technical and secondary modern schools. Children's expectations about their achievements at school and the status of the job they will do may be as heavily influenced by being labelled 'A' stream or 'C' stream as if the labels were 'grammar' or 'secondary' modern. At home with our own children, parents know the importance of building up confidence; it is the greatest single hurdle which has to be surmounted if working class children in particular are to learn according to their capacity. Therefore, though streaming will be needed for a number of subjects, it should be used as little as possible.

A survey of eighty-one comprehensive schools outside London in 1968–9, all established long enough to see one comprehensive intake right through the school, showed that thirty-one were unstreamed to a greater or lesser extent.[10] Where streaming continues, it is usually in broad bands, A, B and C, rather than in the fine distinction between one class and another. De-streaming cannot be accomplished in a moment. Many teachers have not been trained for non-streamed classes. In-service training courses — and smaller classes — will give an increasing number of teachers the confidence for them.

Size

One of the major objections to comprehensive schools is that of size. Indeed the debate often supposes that 'comprehensive' must mean huge. The Joint Boards of Education for London and Southwark Dioceses, in recommending church schools to become fully comprehensive, challenge the need to have very big schools. To offer a variety of teachers for sixth form subjects, a sixth form of 120 or more is regarded as necessary. This is what dictated the creation of schools of 1,800–2,000 children. School leaving at sixteen reduces the size needed for a sixth form of 120 to 1,000–1,200 pupils. If some schools passed their sixth formers on to a sixth form college — or were prepared to share sixth form facilities with other schools — the need for schools to be so large would go.

A huge school can bewilder a child who comes at eleven from a small primary school. He has to find his way to perhaps twelve different teachers in twelve different rooms during the week. The same factor can too easily destroy the relationship of chat and gossip which the child had with his class teacher in primary school. Some large comprehensive schools have deliberately reduced the number of teachers a child has to meet in the first year to six. Schools break numbers down perhaps to thirty in a tutor group.

The appointment of a pastoral counsellor provides the right sort of relaxed adult support for some, but the counsellor is often likely to have a great deal of time taken up by those with the greatest problems. A housemaster will have responsibility for contacts with parents. Others dislike the competitive feeling which houses cause and divide a large school horizontally (by ages). This means that children come to the top of their age group three times in the source of a school career and are given their share in the responsibilities that go with being the seniors at each stage.

The problem of bigness is one which much of modern society faces. It has one advantage. It shouts for all the world to hear that there is a problem of making relationships personal and human. One teacher, moving from a grammar school of six hundred to a comprehensive school of two thousand said that without doubt there was better pastoral care in the school of two thousand. This was because they had recognised that they had a problem on their hands, and had broken the school down into houses and small tutor groups.

Sixth Form Colleges

There is a case for more experiments when children move on from one school to another in rural areas. The three tier system may be particularly suitable. This has first stage schools (up to eight or nine), involving limited travel; middle schools from eight or nine to twelve or thirteen, involving perhaps rather more travel; and secondary schools from twelve or thirteen to eighteen. In urban areas it seems more likely that the change from primary to secondary will remain at eleven. A sixth form college would take on from sixteen to eighteen. Either the middle school or the sixth form college would help reduce the size of the comprehensive school.[11]

Some teachers object that sixth form colleges would mean losing their oldest and ablest children at sixteen — and in turn that many of their ablest teachers would go to the sixth form college. They believe that sixth formers can give much to the morale and tone to the whole school. In working class areas this effectively says yet again: 'We must have the academically able boys and girls to give a lead.' It might be positively helpful to the comprehensive school if all left at sixteen. Boys and girls of all kinds of intelligence would then have the opportunity of taking responsible leadership in the school. This is denied to those who leave at sixteen in a comprehensive school — or in a secondary modern school which builds up a fifth form. Our anxiety about what to do with sixteen year old school leavers in their last year might be less if they plainly had to take responsibility as the senior year in the school.

Sixth form colleges could continue the comprehensive principle. They could become comprehensive colleges of further education to which those also come who do day release courses from work. It would save the country from the expensive item of having to provide separate colleges and staff for part-timers in every area. Those who have left school at sixteen should still be able to use educational facilities. Whether through industrial training or through youth organisations, they should be able to use the playing fields and other facilities now available almost only to those who remain at school.

Neighbourhood Schools

There are great advantages to be had if a good school is clearly *the* school of the neighbourhood. There can be a two-way flow of interest and service between the school and the community, as, for example, in the village colleges of Cambridgeshire. But suppose that a neighbourhood is a 'one class' neighbourhood. In a real sense it will be impossible for a neighbourhood school to have an intake comprehensive in social groupings and certainly in academic abilities. And what about allowing parents their choice of school?

There are three principles, all of which are good, in conflict here — the neighbourhood principle, the comprehensive intake principle and the principle of parental choice.[12] None can be followed fully. The more parents can be free to choose the better. But some schools are bound to be in greater demand than others. It will then have to be either the neighbourhood principle which decides or some sort of banding such as the Inner London Education Authority has used. This sees that the right proportions of children from each of three broad ability bands enter the school. This system may mean that two children who live next door to each other may have to go to different schools. In a big city it may be best to encourage children to criss-cross to schools across quite a large district — perhaps of two London boroughs. This makes for criticism about 'bussing' and needless travel. But this is the normal pattern of working life in a big city.

Some London parents have for years encouraged their children to travel for up to an hour on public transport to reach the school they thought most appropriate. It would be unnecessary for any children to travel as far as these do now in order to provide a wide choice in a district. Travelling is a disadvantage, but the greater disadvantage seems to be that, if neighbourhood is the decisive factor, parents will literally move house, as many do in the United States, in order to be in the catchment area of the schools they want. The one class quarter has so many limiting effects that we should not add to the factors that create it. I would therefore choose 'banding'.

HOUSING NEEDS

THE housing problem is massive. Politicians and officials all alike genuinely want to deal with it, yet we seem to stand still. The Greve Report on Homelessness in·London said that their most striking finding was the similarity between the situation in 1971 and what it was when the London County Council made a study in 1962, except that the problem had grown larger.[13] The hard core of all housing problems is located in the inner city areas of our major cities. The population of London is in fact gradually decreasing. But at the same time the number of households is increasing. This is happily the result of a higher standard of living. Instead of older people living with their children, they want a dwelling of their own. Young executives as well as young students in very large numbers want a flat instead of staying at home.

National resources are needed for an emergency housing programme. This must not be instead of, but in addition to the regular programme for those waiting their turn on housing lists. A determination to abolish poverty demands that housing receives the first priority. The community is wasting money on social services maintaining people in poverty. The longer they stay in bad housing, the less able are they ever to pick themselves up. Those in greatest need are frequently far down the housing waiting lists, or are not on them at all. Therefore normal housing redevelopment programmes generally will not help them. Indeed redevelopment means that next door twilight areas of old houses, each occupied by several families, are reduced in space, while more people crowd into them.

Emergency Programme

An emergency programme would begin at the bottom, regarding housing as a service which is provided for all. Only that way can discrimination against tenants who are unpopular with council or landlord be ended, whether they are immigrants, families with children, single homeless or old people. It should be nationally financed. Families who are under stress in all parts of the country, whether in areas of high unemployment or in Northern Ireland, or immigrants coming to the country, make for districts which are already under stress in big cities. Local authorities resent putting them on housing lists because they have their own responsibilities to cope with. National resources are needed.

Private landlords find it very difficult to afford to keep flats and rooms in good repair without pushing the rent up beyond the means of those who need the housing most. It would be better now if local authorities took over private rented accommodation, except where it is, for example, a flat or a room in the owner's own house. The laws of the market are too uncontrollable to allow them to work freely in urban areas where housing is so limited. But there is a need for a 'third force' in housing in between private and public ownership.

Some housing associations are already making a greater contribution than bare numbers suggest; they can take families and single homeless who are not at the top of the housing list in a way which local authorities cannot. They can also offer housing to teachers, social workers and others who can bring a special contribution to the area. Some housing associations simply operate on the basis of first come, first served. But they can be made accountable, if they want to receive grants, in a way which private companies and landlords cannot.

Housing associations claim to have provided many thousands of homes in Britain. Given more resources, they could make a greater contribution to the problems of those groups in greater need.

New Building

Beyond such an emergency programme must stretch the much larger-scale programme of redevelopment of urban areas. As long as each Inner London borough looks at this on its own, it is likely to repeat many of the old mistakes. The reaction to a massive problem is naturally to mount a massive programme. But it is not simply a matter of constructing or improving as many housing units as possible. There is not one objective but many. The environment, the style of community which will develop, is an equally important objective. If the programme continues to be to demolish whole areas and build vast council estate after vast council estate, we shall create 'new one-class ghettos' in the inner boroughs of a city like London.[14] In the past I have been told that the policy of at least one Labour council was to wipe out the private housing sector. This may have had a political motive, to establish a solid base of council owned property. Such motives may not be unknown in influencing housing policies in inner or outer London today. Whether it is an outer borough's determination to keep a belt of owner-occupied property, or an inner borough's wish to have a zone of council-owned estates, the segregation of the big city is increased.

Two pressures drive Inner London borough councils to feel that only great rolling programmes of new building can solve the problem. The first is the waiting list for housing. I have worked in three London boroughs. I have a helpless feeling that there is always a list of 10,000 families in each borough waiting for rehousing. Side by side with the pressure of the waiting list is the shortage of land. No Inner London borough has enough land to solve its own problems. It is not always in the interests of the outer London boroughs and the counties round London to have yet more people come to live in them. But unless this does happen, the inner boroughs will have to continue to house a higher density of population than will allow the development of a good environment.

There is a Biblical comment which is hard to avoid at this point. In the Old Testament you were not allowed to buy freehold land from anyone. You could buy leasehold property, the ownership reverting to the original owner at the Year of Jubilee (which came round every fifty years).[15] It was to guard the poor against those 'who add house to house and field to field until not an acre remains'.[16] This was a rural system, and it did not apply in a walled town. There you could buy freehold property.[17] The principle behind guarding a secure patrimony for the rural poor had not yet been worked out for the urban poor, for society was predominantly rural. But there is a principle, and it challenges some basic English beliefs.

Many Englishmen think of their rights to their property, to build it up and to hand over the increased property to their children. The first part of the Biblical teaching about land is that God said, 'No land shall be sold outright, because the land is Mine.'[18] The Israelites were to remember that they came as aliens and settlers. In the same way the responsibility Deuteronomy teaches about caring for the alien, the widow and the man who's grown poor and sold himself as a slave is based on the repeated reminder, 'Remember that you were slaves in Egypt.' We can carry the principle over into urban life. It is surely that every man should have a home, and that the powerful should not be allowed to increase his holding at the expense of the less powerful.

Precious Land

In our day land is precious. Many who live outside the densely populated inner ring of big cities are concerned about housing. They care about slums; they say they would hate to have to live in a tall block of flats. What perhaps they don't understand is that the defence of their own interests has a direct influence on forcing very high densities of housing (not necessarily tower blocks) in Inner London. Their local authority is likely to be under pressure from its electors not to allow council housing estates to be built. At least two outer boroughs refused requests from inner boroughs in

1972 to release land for new council housing estates. Some inner boroughs have given up asking, resigned to having to reproduce over populated, one-class quarters.

In an ideal world there would be close co-operation between inner and outer London boroughs with the common interest of those in greatest need throughout the city. The Secretary of State for the Environment has already asked the outer boroughs to give land to help provide for the inner boroughs' housing needs. He has appointed an action group 'to review regularly and at frequent intervals the progress of the drive to eliminate the London housing shortage, and to take any action necessary to keep up this momentum'. We have to face the real possibility that such co-operative efforts will fail in many cases. The sectional interests competing for this scarcest of scarce resources, land, are not equal. In the case of land, 'what we have we hold' is by far the strongest principle, and many outer boroughs or outer metropolitan areas, are most unlikely voluntarily to take the densities which are needed if a balanced development of Inner London is ever to materialise.

Many people in the inner city do not want to move out. When a questionnaire was put to the whole population in the Golborne Ward of North Kensington, seventy per cent said they wanted to stay in the district. Plans are therefore being made to house them in the district even though it means a rather higher density of population than is generally planned in redevelopments. But there has to be room for the thirty per cent somewhere else. National or Metropolitan bodies with powers to act and willingness to use the powers are needed if scarce land is to be allocated in ways which the greatest need dictates.

I have dealt with these matters in the context of London which I know and with which I have had to do. The details may differ elsewhere, but fundamental human issues are the same, especially where land is a vital problem.

A MORE MIXED COMMUNITY

INNER London is to a serious degree becoming more and more a community of the left-behind. The movement of professional classes into some inner areas adds to the problem by increasing housing stress in the limited land available. One family from outside the area often buys a house which may have housed three or four families before. It produces an illusion of a better mixed community. But the skilled worker and those who, having done well at school in Inner London want to buy their own house at a modest price, are forced out. The leader of Southwark Borough Council said, 'Most of us have friends and relatives who would willingly have stayed in the borough had housing been available, but because they were not eligible for council housing and because they could not afford to buy property within the borough they have been forced to move some distance away.'[19]

In the country as a whole the gap between the rich and poor has narrowed and is narrowing. London is the one place where there has been a tendency over the last few years for the income gap to widen.[20] The middle income groups are moving out. The lower incomes do not grow. In fact they decrease in terms of real income. The upper incomes go on growing. Sadly, instead of a cross section of community, the process of 'gentrification' means simply that the two 'poles' of society are brought together. The professional classes move in and the lower income groups have to squash in a bit more tightly in the housing that is left. Given the right housing stock, the return of professional people to the inner city would be a good development. As it is, it only sharpens the housing problems.

Sometimes planners have decided to demolish a whole district, when they believe that the better answer would have been to make it an improvement area. What has forced them to choose to demolish has been the fear that private owners would buy their way in from outside. This would mean that the local authority would have those who were displaced to house, and fewer properties in which to house them. So they demolish. A better way might be to apply a compulsory purchase order to such an area, and sell accommodation which was not occupied by the owner to housing associations.

Luxury Housing

If the Inner London boroughs could feel that the pressure on land was less, they would be more able to consider releasing some for private development in order to produce a more mixed community. There is immediately another problem. The price of land is so high in Inner London that it would probably only be profitable for a developer to buy land if he developed it for luxury housing. The more mixed community I have in mind is one where a young couple who have grown up in a neighbourhood may buy their own place. Those who do better in school will often have the ambition to buy their own house. Generally, the lack of private housing in the inner city and on large council estates forces them to move a long way from their area. Segregated housing probably has an even greater effect than selection in schools in dividing the community. It is not possible to have a complete 'social mix' among every 50,000 people. But we should work towards the possibility of young couples buying a house reasonably near their own home if they want to in every district in England. Some boroughs, like Newham, build for sale to young couples from the area. Or a local authority could sell land at subsidised rates to private builders, however much that may offend traditional Labour Party dogmas. It should not be impossible to attach conditions that properties built on such land should be sold within stated price ranges, or else be sold back to the local authority.

In visiting a parish in Walworth I was delighted to notice that local people who had lived in the district for a long time were taking responsibility for every part of the church's life. I asked the vicar about this, for in most parishes in that neighbourhood there is the cry that the young people have always moved away. He said: 'It's something good the Ecclesiastical Commissioners have done.' The estate, which they administer, dates back to the days of Octavia Hill. She said that the right management of the houses was the greatest need.[21] The policy has been that if a young couple from the estate got married and wanted to live on it, they must be offered a dwelling there.

I met such a couple living on the estate in 1972, who had been married the month before. The policy has been that, when children are born, a larger home should be offered; when they marry and leave home a small dwelling must be found again. I noticed the difference in the life of the church sixty-five years later, as I believe I should do in the life of the whole community.

One-class Quarter

A major aim of housing should be to produce a more mixed community. Housing policies can be a major instrument of segregation. For instance, one aim of the Housing Finance Bill's 'fair rents' was avowedly to push the better paid council tenants off council housing estates. It was felt that if tenants could afford to buy their own house, they should do so. It is logical enough to argue that subsidies should go to the person rather than to the house. It would be a wise proposal, if there was the right stock of housing in existence, so that the former council tenants could buy reasonably priced housing in their own area. Given the stock of housing we have now, the effect would be to drive the better paid council tenants out of the area altogether into the owner-occupied suburbs. This would increase the segregation which makes so much of Inner London what Willmott and Young called a 'vast one-class quarter'.[22]

If Government, national and local, acknowledged that housing policies perpetuate divisiveness much more drastic development plans might emerge.

JOBS

JOBS are crucial to the kind of community we produce. Occupation is the most significant way in which a man can change his status, class or power.[23] Several pressures are limiting the kind of jobs available to those who grow up in Inner London. In the London region the most rapidly expanding area of industry is in the outer metropolitan region, immediately beyond the Green Belt.[24] New towns demand a high proportion of highly skilled workers. They attract the more successful and adventurous. Americans usually won't use the term working class. I was intrigued, listening to Dick Luecke from the Chicago Urban Training Centre, to realise that he had a description of what might be called in English terms lower working class. It was 'relatively less mobile'.

It has long been generally assumed that London and the south east have been highly favoured when it comes to jobs. Government policies have set out to encourage firms to move out of London to the new towns or to regional development areas. It came as a shock to Woolwich when the old established AEI works, employing some 5,500 men and women, announced in 1968 that it would close. In four south east London boroughs thirty-one closures or part closures resulting in major redundancies took place during 1968–9. The Greater London Development Plan had already expressed fears that too much industrial blood was being taken from London to the new towns and to the regions. The reduction of jobs forecast by 1981 by the Plan had already taken place by 1972.[25]

To set the situation in a national context, London, as compared with the south east region as a whole, had about the average unemployment figure in 1972. Unemployment in the inner ring of boroughs stood above that average at 7%. But this has to be set against 20% unemployment in some regions of the country. Naturally, Government policies have to be directed especially to those regions; but the sheer complexity of London should mean that very serious attention should be given to the warning lights which are flashing about the dangers of industry running out. There are strong indications that Inner London does not share the overall prosperity of the south east.

Galloping Redundancy

An enquiry was made in 1971[26] to see what had happened to 537 workers made redundant at five south east London factories, of which AEI was the largest, about two years after closures. On the surface the dire results forecast at the time had not taken place, 7% (largely among the over fifty-fives) of those wishing to work again were not able to find jobs at all. The majority found a job. But there has been a cost to pay. First is the deep sense of insecurity reflected in the answer that half now put security first in their hopes from a new job, and in industrial unrest in other industries nearby. The review discovered that there is increasingly a 'galloping redundancy'. Those who have been made redundant once are more likely to be made redundant again than those who have been longer at work in their new firms: 'last in, first out'. This was a relatively old, long-service group of workers, who had felt that they were in good, secure jobs. They hadn't wanted change, and they hadn't expected it. It is in the nature of closures that younger, short-service workers will not have been taken on for a while before the closure took place. Those who are displaced are therefore just those who, first and foremost because of age, will find it hardest to discover other jobs.

The national trend is of a movement from manufacturing to service industry. This is what has happened as a result of these closures. Older men suffered most, particularly supervisory staff (such as foremen) and the semi-skilled. Among skilled workers, where British economy has had a shortage for years, a rather disappointing figure of 64% found skilled jobs. There has been a loss in real earnings — 15% less than they would have been receiving if their earnings had kept pace with average increases. Supervisory, semiskilled and unskilled workers did worst. While their real earnings were reduced, the distance they had to travel to work (and the cost of travel) increased by a quarter. A crucial factor in finding new employment is whether men are willing to move house or not. Three quarters said they had never seriously considered it. White collar and managerial workers were the most likely to have considered moving. No unskilled worker did.

The Left-Behind

The community of the left-behind increases, hemmed in by middle class suburbs. The jobs available for those who grow up in it are either in the old-established, and sometimes declining, manufacturing industries or in the service sectors, serving the needs of the city centre for transport, public services and the lower level of jobs in the central business district. There is likely to be less opportunity for social mobility (in its best sense) through jobs for the children of the inner city. This trend would increase the feeling that there are barriers to the realisation of hopes which education has raised in young people's minds. It makes the deprivation of these areas more explosive.

There follows a series of questions: Must we abandon any idea that in the big city we can be 'members one of another'? Should inner city boroughs like Southwark and Tower Hamlets feel they must use precious land now available in the docks to increase their rateable value in order to finance their social services and amenities? This tends to lead to hotel and luxury flat development, rather than guarding every acre of land for the priority of housing and appropriate jobs for the people who live in the most overcrowded and least favoured parts of the city.

Do borough councils understand that London is not a chain of provincial cities, each able to find its own land and finance? Ought not inner boroughs concertedly to demand more central Government resources to tackle the greatest housing stress in the country and the provision of the right kind of jobs for those who live in the inner city?

Must we accept that Inner London comes low on the Government's priorities for stimulating jobs? Are borough councils making serious attempts to encourage industry to stay or return?

Alternatively, is it realistic to provide very cheap or free travel from inner to outer London (commuting in reverse)? Are there enough jobs in Outer London for this to be effective?

Should outer Boroughs be required by statute to provide housing for a larger proportion of those who work in them?

Does anyone know the number and the type of jobs which are required? Until they do, our planning is largely tinkering in the dark. The problems of the great city are an interlocking mesh of housing, jobs, schools, facilities. The Department of the Environment's Six Towns Study of the inner city needs to look seriously at all that makes up its life. This must include a careful look at jobs and schools as well as housing and facilities.

And there is this crucial question. Ought all land, or at least all development land, now to come under public ownership? The shortage and the price of land are the greatest barriers in the way of balanced housing and industrial developments.

So we turn now to the big issues of power and powerlessness. For it is especially the latter that is felt to be the end-result of the tremendous pressures of urbanisation. What can the city-dweller do to make his presence felt? How can he be enabled to have sufficient power to change life in that which is built as a city?

Six

POWER AND POWERLESSNESS

Introduction

A programme for changing the whole environment of those who are at a disadvantage will be a very expensive one. It will affect the better-off in terms of cash, real wealth and the relative influence and power they possess. The cost of doing nothing is even higher. It is higher in cash terms. For example, in 1973 there were 360 children in public care for every 50,000 people in Tower Hamlets. That was more than the *total* in care in seventeen out of the twenty outer London boroughs.[1]

It is higher in terms of the real well-being of the nation. If a community, who increasingly realise that they have been left behind, feel that they cannot gain fair access to the nation's scarce resources, there will be increasing militancy. This will appear wherever opportunity affords, and particularly in industry, where an assertion of power is more easily made. It is higher in terms of wasted resources. No nation can afford to waste the abilities and intelligence of any considerable proportion of the population.

THE WORLD OF WORK

INDUSTRY is the primary force in dividing society into men of gold, silver, brass and iron. Marx saw a clear cut division according to men's relation to the means of production; on the one hand those with access to power, sharing in making decisions; on the other hand those without access to power, reacting to the decisions — human reactors. If we want to deny Marx's theories that untold evil springs from the division of labour, we must set ourselves to remove the gap between the decision makers and the human reactors. It is often said by professional or middle class people, 'We don't regard people differently in our village (or suburb). Why do we have to have all this talk about class?' But management *does* regard people differently at work. According to whether men are directors, managers, office staff, laboratory technicians or manual workers, a whole range of differences will be apparent to the boy arriving at his first job — different hours of arrival, some groups having to clock on and off, others trusted not to do so.

A multiplicity of entry places must be understood, and at meals there may be a *works'* canteen, a *staff* dining-room, a *senior staff* dining-room and a *directors'* lunch club.

The change from school to work is often the period when flickering hopes and ambitions are snuffed out. At a good school a boy has been expected to learn to use increasing freedom, to think for himself, to question the way things are, to make choices which will effect change. When he starts his first job, unless he is a management trainee or an apprentice, the emphasis will be on conformity, on fitting in, on doing what he is told. That way he will come to be regarded as a good worker. Good teachers may have encouraged those who did not produce great achievements; the employer, with reason, is generally not over-interested in, for instance, their artistic ability. He wants to know if they can do a task reliably.

Hopes Dashed?

There are points to be learnt both by schools and by industry. Schools must beware of raising hopes about work which will be swiftly dashed. The temptation then is to settle for the notion that work will be a necessary bore, and that life starts with leisure time. Work and leisure cannot be so sharply divided. The world of work influences the kind of functions we accept and the kind of relationships we make in our total life much more pervasively and subtly than we like to believe. Schools must continue to plant hope and determination to change society, including the work situation. Industry must increasingly wake up to the potential which may be hidden by a sleepy and sullen face. One of the yardsticks by which good industry judges its managers and foremen is by 'human asset accounting'. This will want to know how the abilities are developing of employees for whom the manager is responsible.

Before a boy gets to work, the streaming process, which may have been carefully reduced at his school, has begun again. A separate careers advisory service offers specialist advice for boys and girls with 'A' levels. They and their parents do not have to go to the youth employment office with the lower expectations of jobs which it suggests. They might insist on a better service if they did.

Training programmes show what managements expect in the future. The same group who have achieved poorly at school often now find that two days' or a week's induction is the sum of the training that may be expected. The Industrial Training Act of 1964 set up training boards for each industry. They make a levy on employers who do not provide approved training. The Act therefore makes it worthwhile for an employer to do so. But it does not say who the training is to be for. Firms will generally offer it to those whom they see as potential managers, foremen and skilled workers. The grant/levy system was regarded as 'shock treatment' for employers. There is a danger that it may be withdrawn before there has been a fundamental change of heart about training. The purpose of the Act was to enable individuals to develop their abilities to the full, as well as to ensure that enough workers are available to do efficiently the jobs needing to be done.[2]

In Germany, virtually 100% of young workers are sent on day release courses. Six years after the passing of the Industrial Training Act the figure in Britain of the numbers of those sent on day release courses (a decreasing number) was just over 30% of boys at work and 70% of girls at work. Moreover the number of apprenticeships in some areas at least has decreased. In one large firm in east London six apprenticeships a year are offered where ten years ago there were twenty. On one strip of riverside industry in east London it is asserted that there are twenty-four apprenticeships where there were once some hundreds. Perhaps the better way forward in order to see that everyone has some opportunity of continuing to learn is to make part-time further education compulsory.

Unskilled Labour at Twelve

In 1911 Alec Paterson, later a great prison reformer and the initiator of Borstal training, wrote a book much read in its time, *Across the Bridges.* He was currently teaching in an elementary school in Bermondsey. It is interesting to observe how much an enlightened Christian man was limited by the thinking of his generation. Alec Paterson said that each school class roughly divided itself into two main divisions of 'hopefuls' and 'very doubtfuls'. If a boy couldn't write legibly and read in a rough way, schools should be 'content to relinquish him to the claims of unskilled labour at the age of twelve'.[3]

Our generation rejects a belief that many boys will have learned all that schools can give them by twelve years of age. But the often expressed view, that the raising of the school leaving age to sixteen is a waste of time, is sometimes an echo of the same attitude. It suggests to boys and girls that their function in life is to get on with manual work, rather than to do too much dreaming and thinking. Some people do have to do the less interesting jobs. It is all the more important that they should know that they are valued, and that they see the importance of their job in the corporate scheme of a company.

Industry generally still consigns the 'very doubtfuls' to no participation in the decision-making process. Again it is true that there are many who do not want to participate. But it is often assumed that these 'higher' reasons why men and women should want to work do not motivate less skilled workers. It is expected that the opportunity for sharing in policy making and for continued self-development will be an important motivation for those at management level but not for the semi-skilled and unskilled workers.

A. H. Maslow, one of the great names in studies of motivation at work, speculated in 1965 that the principles of participative management were primarily applicable in the more highly developed countries.[4] Why should he make such a speculation? Who knows that people made in the image of God, in developing countries, or anywhere among less skilled workers, would not respond to a genuine share in decision making? The developing countries are frequently treated by western technology and aid in the same way as western countries have been. So the same conditions of working are set up in which it can be asserted that 'they wouldn't want a share in making decisions'.

Difficult Workers

Philips at Eindhoven in Holland observed that some of their dull and difficult workers were doing very creative things in their leisure time. They broke up their production line, and formed self-supervising working groups of twelve. Production and human results supported the experiment. I know many men to whom industry has given no share in making decisions who in community life take responsible decisions and think widely and positively about corporate living. 'Unimagined resources of creative human energy' could be released within industrial organisations, given the right expectations.[5] People need to know that someone believes in their potential if it is to be developed. Those who dare to hope that such participation can be developed need to persevere over a long time. 'Participation' is no magic wand which can be waved over a situation soured by years of mistrust. It can only become real on a basis of continuing hard work for good and trusting relationships. Those who offer a greater share in decision making must expect that at first it is very likely to be thrown back in their teeth. They must stick to a dogged belief in the potential of human beings.

Some of that potential develops late in most families. The early school leaver has much less chance of doing well as a 'late developer' than, for example, the son of professional parents. The latter is very likely to have exam qualifications from higher education of some kind. He goes through a stage of being unsure what he wants to do. He does voluntary service overseas or works on a building site. At twenty-five he decides to settle down to a steady job. It's not too late.

It was too late for Ron when he decided he wanted to settle down to a steady job at *nineteen*. He had drifted from one dead end job to another. Now he had a steady girl friend and there was a strong motivation to learn a trade so that he would have a good wage in the future. Ron wanted a job in engineering. By bus and by foot he had presented himself to a variety of firms. The frustration of first finding the place in the confused jumble of streets which make up east London's ancient and modern industrial areas, then finding the right man to see, and then being told he was too old to learn a trade had made him almost give up. I offered to see if I could help. I had resources Ron hadn't. I had a telephone, a lot of contacts, a motor car. Sometimes I got no further than a telephone conversation; sometimes I got him to the gate of a factory. Everywhere in the end the answer was the same, 'He's nineteen, so I'm afraid it's too late for him to learn a trade.' Trade unions have helped to keep the Rons semi-skilled, because they have believed that they must prevent too many craftsmen from having to fight for too few jobs.

Massive Difference

The difference in treatment of apprentices and non-apprentices is generally massive; for example, a light engineering firm employed over a thousand men of whom two hundred were youths between fifteen and twenty-one. Fifty of the two hundred were apprentices on a four year training scheme. This allowed first block release and later day release to the local technical college. The apprentices had other 'perks'. They had their own meeting room with a very active social club, sports team, newspaper. At the company's ex-

pense they could attend outside courses to broaden their
general outlook and to make visits to other factories.

Here was an enlightened firm, taking training very
seriously. But none of these opportunities was available to
non-apprentices. The apprentices were treated as if they
were capable of developing themselves and establishing
their own youthful identity within the firm. The non-apprentices (one hundred and fifty of them) apart from not
having so many amenities and concessions, were merged
into the mass of the adult labour force, and had little opportunity to establish a separate identity.[6]

The first few years in industry are going to settle most
young people's expectations both of what work will mean
for them and of what they are capable of contributing to
work and also to society as a whole. For the self-picture
which is built up — or undermined — at work goes with you
outside the factory gates.

Christians and others who care about making industry
more human frequently wonder what positive role they can
play at work. Their ambition is to be a loyal company man,
to give full value for their pay, an honest day's work, to
develop their own potential to the full. With this goes the
sense of having to stand against the tide in matters like ma-
licious gossip, theft, dishonesty in time-keeping and ob-
scenity. They would hope to give a lead to youngsters
starting at work in these directions. So far so good. At the
same time a man, responding to God's plan to change the
world for good, cannot limit his ambitions at work in such
an individualistic way.

In a discussion of the name of God, John Macquarrie
wrote that it is of the nature of God to 'let be' — to create
the right conditions in which others can develop their full
potential.[7] If all Christians are called to reflect God's
character, here is a positive role for all Christians in industry. It is to 'let be'. The last thing that this means is laissez

faire. It is not a case of simply fitting in with things as they are. It means creating the right conditions in which others can develop their full potential. It means the 'dynamic enabling' of others to grow.

The Paste Boy

Consider the story of the paste boy told by Elizabeth Pepperell of the Industrial Society. The paste boy was at the bottom of the whole hierarchy in a cigarette factory. He had to mix the paste for cigarette papers. This boy was so small that he had to have an upturned crate to stand on in order to work at the bench. The training officer asked him if he would like to go on a day release course. Politely he said it was quite impossible. If you mixed the paste too thin the cigarettes wouldn't hold together. If you mixed it too thick ... It was plain that the whole work of the factory could not continue without him. 'Well, think about it', said the training officer. Next day the paste boy came and said he'd worked out how he could manage it. If he came early on his bicycle, he could mix up the paste before he went off to the college. And he could look in again on his way home to make sure everything was all right.

The point of the story is to learn who had given this boy the sense of the value of his job. No regular induction, no work of the training officer, was responsible. Eventually they discovered that it was an old retired man who had been kept on and given the job of sweeping up. He had given the boy time, and an attitude to work which was likely to last a lifetime.

Sometimes other workers see younger men as rivals who may displace them. A young panel beater complained that he could get no help from older men because they were jealous of their skills and would not pass them on. An insurance company decided that all its employees could clock in and out at the time they themselves chose, provided they were within wider hours which were laid down. One manager said at a conference that you couldn't trust the workers. Later he said privately that the right to decide exactly when to come in was a dividing line, holding that group back. He feared that, given the chance, they might take his job.

Lack of training, lack of job prospects, lack of any effective participation, lead a large number of workers to settle down to a low expectation of what their job will offer them. Boredom follows. A shop steward told me that he believed the frequent trouble in the car industry was directly related to the production line nature of the job, though he acknowledged other factors. Car workers were trapped into continuing to earn the high wages their industry offered by high mortgage and hire purchase payments. Being unable to escape from the monotony, their frustration erupts like a volcano from time to time. Other workers disagree. They are content with repetitive jobs and can find their satisfaction in factors which don't belong to the actual work they do.

Boredom

The process of coming to terms with boredom may be seen in a group of girls working in factories in the north east of England. Work for them meant boredom, fatigue and being bossed about. Yet work offered some positive compensations; it gave the chance of feeling accepted in a work friendship group. The mere fact of having and holding a job boosted the ego of one of the most erratic girls.[8]

The self respect which flows from having and holding a job should not be underrated. Unemployment makes a man feel impotent and angry that he cannot 'play the man' and provide for his family. School leavers who cannot find a job hang about streets and pin tables. They are an easy prey for petty crime or perhaps for 'mugging', to show their manliness. The destruction of self respect which unemployment brings sometimes leaves deep and lasting scars.

One such scar from the unemployment years of the 1930s still damaged a marriage relationship thirty years later. The husband had punched his wife and left her when she was carrying their first baby. She told me all those years later how she remembered a child bringing her a note from a man who was standing at the end of the street. It asked if he could come back. At the biggest moment of his life, when his wife was bearing his child, this man who grew up in an orphanage was unable to do anything significant for them, because he was unemployed. The punch, the running away, the inability to come to the door to ask for forgiveness, the pathetic note, can all be seen in context. He was wrong, but many of us would have felt the same turmoil and anger he did, if we had been denied the self respect of being able to earn a living.

Social Centre

For many mothers the factory or the office is a social centre. For many men it is the most significant social centre in their lives. Part of the dread of retirement is that it will cut a man off from the web of relationships which is part of the world of work. So if we ask what manual workers expect from work, there is an important and healthy series of answers to put alongside the frustrations; industry provides:

an earned wage,
self respect,
a work friendship group,
recognition and respect by your fellows, and . . .
you're the paste boy,
you're the joker,
you're the counsellor they turn to in trouble,
you're the secretary of the photographic club,
you're somebody.

The 'higher needs' someone may want fulfilled at work only become a strong motivation when the more basic needs of personal security have been met. If a man is still anxious about having an adequate wage, he is not likely to be stirred by the chance of being creative or of increasing his knowledge of his industry. If a worker and his fellows have spent all their time fighting for basic needs, like an adequate wage, they may come to feel that these are the only needs that have to be met. The failure, for example, of production line work to meet 'higher level' needs of personal fulfilment may sometimes be the actual cause of frustration. But workers who've been preoccupied with the struggle for basic needs may not identify what has now gone wrong. They may very well react to their general feelings of resentment against life in the big city as a whole, not just at work, by asking for more money. 'Wage demands are a barometer of industrial frustration',[9] and sometimes of social frustration.

Nothing is solved by paying out more in wages, unless the actual problems are attended to. In the motor car industry higher and higher wages have been paid without bringing industrial peace. What was necessary first was to tackle problems like the wage structure, redundancy and trade union relations. I believe there are deliberate 'wreckers' at work in industry, but they need to have grievances and frustrations to work on if they are to persuade others to follow them.

It has often been asserted that manual workers simply want higher wages. If that has sometimes been true, it may be retorted that they learned their values from the initiative of managements and shareholders, whose only goal was higher profits. It may also simply demonstrate that anxiety has persisted about 'lower level' needs. Some quite sophisticated researchers reported their findings that among directors and managers personal fulfilment in their work was more important than pay. But no one ever asked them whether money was important to them or not.

Security

It is impossible to tell if personal fulfilment is something manual workers want from work until two matters are clarified. First they need a deeply felt security. Secondly, a man needs to be persuaded of the real possibility of personal achievement and also that he will be taken seriously when he is asked to participate in decision making.

It is right that there should be different functions in the working process of a firm. Different men have different capabilities; everyone is not capable of carrying the burdens of decision-making that the managing director bears. The Christian model of a society is that of a body. Each part has a different function. Its achievements are co-operative achievements. Every part is valued, 'special honour given to the humbler parts, so that there might be no sense of division in the body, but that all its organs might feel the same concern for one another. If one organ suffers, they all suffer together. If one flourishes, they all flourish together.'[10] The sense of partnership is destroyed when honour is not given to the humbler parts, and when the power to make decisions is held by a few without their being answerable to the wider community.

Some decisions have to be taken ultimately by one or two people. But participation in decision-making is possible at many more levels than most firms have dreamed of. One large firm has believed that the encouragement of participation is important enough to have devoted in the last three years over 2,000 man days to what might be called totally non-productive conferences. They believed that in the long term such conferences, bringing together men from every level, would be highly productive. Another firm has

recently built into their annual budget 1% to be spent on
stimulating participation. They have recognised the need to
give time and money as a basic part of business operations
towards developing mutual trust.

Frustration

'The working class feel they're never completely trusted',
said one Christian manual worker to me. Another spoke
about the root of the industrial disputes which happened at
his place of work; 'They were mostly over matters of detail
. . . their real cause was that we wanted to have some say in
the running of our own lives, and Mr. A wanted to feel that
he was boss in his own factory.' Behind the frequent cry
from workers to management, 'Open the books' (to see
the details of their company's finances) lies not simply
greed — though that may be there — but the frustration that
you can never see the total picture.

   The dignity and worth of a craftsman's work have always
been recognised. It has never been difficult for him to want
to do his work as well as he can. H. V. Morton met an old
craftsman making beautiful wooden bowls, and said to
him: 'You could make a lot of money out of those bowls.'
The old man replied, 'I don't want to make money; I want
to make bowls.' Such an attitude to work is not so easily
developed in a large factory. Yet there should be more dignity — not less — in recognising yourself to be a member of
a great team which is corporately producing a useful product,
rather than simply 'working for yourself'. Time and money
are well spent, both in helping men understand their contribution to the whole task of a factory, and in giving them a
genuine say in matters. In industry special honour is too
rarely given to the humbler parts of the organisation. Arguments about status are generally covering up an urgent need
for a man to be assured that he counts. To feel that you have

no status, that you are never expected to take the initiative, that your opinion will never change any decision, all these increase a man's sense of powerlessness.

THE CAUSES OF POWERLESSNESS

THE function a man has in the world of work influences the function he expects to have in society. Industry has a primary influence in settling whether people expect to have a say in how life is ordered or not. Schools also have a primary influence; so does housing and the neighbourhood you live in. The fact that there is such a subject as 'social geography' which can be drawn on the map of a big city shows the segregation which builds up the picture of 'us' and 'them'.

In a big city, directors make off to their zone where they meet other directors, managers to their zone, office staff to theirs, skilled workers to theirs, semi-skilled and unskilled to theirs. These zones in a big city do not have easy communications with the others as they can in an industrial town or even in a small city of half a million.[11]

In towns or suburbs it is generally not too difficult to have some contact with those who make decisions about schools, recreational facilities, housing, provision of family and social services. In the poorest neighbourhoods or in solidly working class quarters of the big city it is often unclear whom to go to in order to influence decisions. Many residents are unlikely to know decision makers personally, for borough officers are likely to live some way away in the suburbs. Nor are they likely to feel confident about filling in forms or what to say, when they reach the right counter in the right office. Those who are new to the life of a big city feel particularly bewildered.[12]

A sense of powerlessness in the face of the bigness of society is felt by people in all areas of industry and society. But, like all deprivation, this powerlessness is relative. Power has to do with having access to those who make decisions, 'knowing the right people', understanding how to bring influence to bear. Those who have least access to the decision-making process at work are likely to go home to council estates. There they are sometimes not even allowed to paint their own front door the colour they want; often there is no garden, no shed where a man can work out some of his own creative urges.

Decision Makers

People take what is expected of them home from work too. Those who are decision makers at work assume that they are expected to take on that function in the community; they feel able to be a magistrate, a member of the regional hospital board, joint chairman of the parochial church council, a member of an action group against the siting of London's third airport. Those whose opinion is never asked at work are much less likely to feel able to respond, even if they are asked, to an invitation to act in such ways in community or church. They will probably say 'Me? No I'm not sticking my neck out', if asked to go and see the social services department about the old man downstairs, or to serve on the youth club management committee or the parochial church council.

One of the lessons industry has taught working class men who are determined to have a say in what is decided is that they only have power if they organise themselves for corporate action. This often leads men in industry and in the local community to expect confrontation rather than partnership. Differences of function in industry as it stands lead to very different attitudes to society. Professor Tom Burns contrasts the managers' view of the social world as 'a graduated pyramid of status positions' with the workers' view of 'Them, the management, the controllers, the middle class, and us, the labour force, the managed, the workers'.[13]

Those who feel that they, their children and their neighbours receive less than their share of good jobs, good schools and space for housing are bound to feel relatively powerless. The big city is such a confusing web of forces that it is very difficult to pinpoint the source of our frustrations. Trying to come to grips with the pressures of Inner London sometimes feels like wrestling with a ghost. People feel blocked, deprived. But they cannot trace who is responsible for the deprivation. Is it: the management? their parents? the landlord? the social security? poor schools? low paid jobs? fatalism of the neighbours? the council? the politicians? affluent society which doesn't care?

It is not surprising that when some perceivable target appears out of the fog — a threat to jobs in your industry, an urban motorway coming past your window, black people moving into your street — you lash out. Strikes are often an expression of pent up frustration with a total, vague but very real, sense of deprivation and powerlessness. Setting up scapegoats often comes from the same source.

RELATIVE DEPRIVATION

PEOPLE do not starve to death in Britain today. Families do not have to sleep on the pavement, or rent half a day's occupation of a space on the landing. There isn't poverty of the order which may be found in Calcutta, but there is serious deprivation; it is all the more hurtful because affluence is so common in families who live so near. Deprivation is relative. Housing which would be tolerated in Rwanda is not acceptable in London, because less than a mile away there is obvious affluence. We are talking about inequality. Every society has some sort of differentials. We have to ask if the differentials which exist between different social groupings in the same city are just and tolerable.

Real wealth and real poverty cannot only be measured by wages. Wages are important, because in a cash economy money offers the opportunity to make choices. But any debate about real wealth must ask far deeper questions about what we possess and about the relative wealth or poverty others have. A questionnaire about real wealth might include these questions:

In my job

> What wages am I earning now?
> Am I on a scale of increments?
> Do I have security?
> What non-money rewards do I receive?
> What recognition am I given?
> What personal fulfilment do I find?
> What power to make choices do I have?
> What holidays can I take?

At Home

> Do I own my own house (with the power to sell and move)?

> Can I buy a house within the neighbourhood where I want to live?

What space do I have for my family? (136 or 10 persons to the acre?)

Do I have a garden? A shed?

Can I afford to take the family out once a week? Abroad for our holidays?

Can I have silence when I want it?

Do I own a car? A television set?

In the Community

What commercial facilities (shops, theatres, pubs, restaurants, sports clubs) are within easy access?

What public amenities are in the neighbourhood?

What quality of hospital treatment can I expect to receive?

What kind of schools can my children go to?

What transport is available?

Can I get in touch with the people who make decisions?

Personal Resources

What self-confidence do I have?

How many years of education did I receive?

What recognised qualifications do I possess?

Do I enjoy the world of books? Of music?

Is my wife, or am I, a good manager of our resources?

Do I know how to use and have access to the expert knowledge of others?

A comparison based on this questionnaire between families who live in a 'professional' district and those who live on a council estate would reveal very great differences in real wealth. Clearly there will be differences between individuals according to their ability or personal development. Whole social groupings also have a widely different chance of access to opportunity and power.

The phrase 'real wealth' makes one stop and think. Christians have sometimes said that poverty is blessed. If poverty is blessed, why should we want to abolish it? A distinction needs to be made. St. Francis chose poverty. An increasing number of affluent families choose some measure of 'voluntary austerity'. That sort of poverty is open to us to choose. Some people have no choice but are trapped by lack of opportunity and by a sense of powerlessness.

There is no simple answer to the question, Who are the poor today? I believe a reasonable shorthand answer is, Those groups and individuals who are relatively deprived of opportunity and relatively powerless. Christian mission must always take seriously the special relationship which Jesus had to the poor. We must try to work out the contemporary meaning of His terms of reference for His own mission. They were: 'to announce good news to the poor, to proclaim release for prisoners and recovery of sight to the blind, to let the broken victims go free, to proclaim the year of the Lord's favour'.[14]

These words must not be 'spiritualised' away. His healing ministry, for instance, shows that He wanted there to be actual changes in people's present situation.

Idolatry

Christianity challenges many accepted values of our society. Covetousness for possessions or status — whether to get what Mr. and Mrs. Jones have or to cling on to what you already have — is described as idolatry.[15] Perhaps the poor are blessed[16] because they are less likely to worship Mammon.[17] Good news for the powerless is not simply to offer them what the powerful already have. The idea that material affluence by itself would set men free is exploded by a look at any 'advanced' urban and industrial society, whether we look at the suburbs or the inner city. More wealth by itself may only reinforce the false values of our society. Real wealth must include wealth in ideas, in consciousness of having a stake in society, of belonging and of mutual responsibility. Therefore, access to good education and participation in the way decisions are made at work and in the community must be part of the good news we announce to the poor. There is a difficult question which should be asked in any human situation; By what right do we educate? People should be free to reject our education, but they won't know what choices there are to make unless their potential has been given opportunity to develop.

False aspirations must be challenged, but human beings in a just society should be given the wherewithal to make their own choices. There is nothing blessed in the poverty of opportunity which blocks the development of a child's gifts or in the sense of powerlessness which makes a man feel that he has no control over his destiny or over anyone else's.

THE SPECIALLY HANDICAPPED

I HAVE made the distinction already between the main stream of working class families who live in the inner city and those whom in one obvious sense we may call the poor. In fact, working class people can be very harsh in their judgments on minority groups, or on those who are labelled 'problem' families. This is not least because they too feel some deprivation, and resent the apparent fact that others do not seem to make the same effort as they do to keep up in the race.

The specially handicapped or, as one might say 'disadvantaged', will very likely be rather inarticulate. They will also possibly be unpopular. For example, unmarried mothers, single alcoholics who are homeless, black teenagers looking for work, are likely to feel rejected by the institutions of society. Perhaps they expect trouble, but there is truth that social security officials, employers, landlords and police sometimes make judgments as though they have to decide if they are dealing with deserving or undeserving poor. The sense that the system is judging them and is against them leads some to withdraw into total apathy, other to respond by violence.

Some assume that there is a culture of poverty, in the sense that there are cultural patterns which keep people poor even when the opportunity to stop being poor is offered them. Certainly some poor people have given up. They cannot or will not fight to regain their self respect. There are others who are physically or emotionally too ill. But there are many more who can respond if they are given the opportunity of good housing, a good job, a wage or allowance which removes anxiety. The help the state offers depends on what we want to achieve.[18] I want to help families and individuals who can do so, to break the poverty circle. Therefore I would rather spend more money in giving a genuine opportunity to the poor, and particularly their children, rather than the bare minimum for survival. This means that taxpayers should not resent seeing people on social security being able to afford cigarettes or the chance to take the family out to the pictures. The basis of social security is that all pay national insurance when they can. Free schools may be thought of as a massive form of social insurance and development of our assets. By the same token appropriate housing as a service for all would be a wise form of social insurance.

The Difficulty of Access

When it comes to receiving grants from the state, some groups find more difficulty than others in gaining access to resources.[19] The first distinction is that state resources are more readily given to those who may produce wealth for the state in return; for example, grants to farmers or to school children and students are given, because it is hoped that they in turn will be productive. Such grants are not widely regarded as destroying self reliance. The second distinction is that state resources are more easily given to those whom we regard with respect than to those we are disposed to blame. Widows and old age pensioners are without power, and therefore do badly. But others are more likely to take up the cudgels for them than they are for groups like, for example, unmarried mothers, who are often fighting against great odds to keep up in the race.

The emergence of rather aggressive bodies like claimants' unions is a banding together for strength by people who feel they are being pushed around by officials. Such people are often repeatedly referred by one department to another, they do not know how their grants are calculated, or what legal rights of appeal they may have. Both such as self help housing groups have shown that people who have been written off as irresponsible can often act very responsibly, if they are given some real opportunity to make their own choices and to help themselves.

In the street where I lived in Peckham a woman was rehoused in a large house which had been done up for short term occupation. She had seven children. She had previously lived in a house in generally bad condition where the plaster had fallen down from the kitchen ceiling. She informed the council. After a long delay the ceiling was repaired. The family took this as a sign that they were to remain there for some time, and redecorated the living room. Soon afterwards families started to be moved from the far end of the street. Mrs. P. could not get any satisfactory reply about how long it would be before she moved. She asked a friend who had a telephone, and knew government departments and their methods, to see if he could find out when she was due to be rehoused. He telephoned the housing department. Between long waits he spoke to five voices. The fifth said authoritatively that there were no plans for her to be moved yet and, when the time came, she would be told in the usual way the same as everyone else. Within the next four weeks she was moved to our street.

Unsatisfactory Tenants

The house was clean, had a bathroom and toilet. The signs of what are naturally thought of as unsatisfactory tenants soon began to appear. Pieces of string nailed across windows to support the curtains; bikes blocked the newly decorated hall way; the dog bounded up and down the carpetless stairs. In the first few days the large glass pane which covered the entire top half of the front door was smashed as one of the boys slammed the door. It remained broken, the wind blowing in. The wood of the door was rotten, and had so much movement in its frame that only the glass would have previously kept it rigid. Mrs. P. told the rent collector. He said that he had reported it to the maintenance department. Months had passed, the second winter was approaching and the wallpaper was lifting off the wall where the rain had come in. Their friend agreed to write to the housing manager, pointing out the long delay and inconvenience to the family. There was an official acknowledgment to the letter. They waited. After the second winter a man came to repair the door. In a few days it slammed shut, and the entire glass was broken. In due course a door was taken from the derelict house next door and put in its place.

Mrs. P. stayed in that house for three years. She often complained of the damp, and said that it was the house which was getting her down. She obtained a doctor's letter to say she needed rehousing, and asked their friend to try to find out when she was moving. One evening he arrived to find the big stone steps leading up to the front door all broken and wedged up by wooden boards. Mrs. P. said the third boy had nearly had a very nasty accident. 'He was just going down the steps, when they all collapsed. I always said they were dangerous.' She had reported it, the council had come to prop them up, and were coming back the next day. The next evening he found the steps in a far worse condition. Mrs. P. was standing, arms folded, in the kitchen. 'We're moving', she announced defiantly. She said her older boy was just going down the steps, when they collapsed. 'He nearly had a nasty accident. I always said they were dangerous.' She was moved before the end of the week. Privately, her eldest boy said that after dark he went out to the front with a pick axe and knocked down the front steps.

As far as the family was concerned, the moral of the story was that using the right channels of communication and appealing to reason achieved nothing. Violence got them moved.

Mrs. P. believed that it was the house that was getting her down. It is hard to exaggerate the demoralising effect of uncertainty. Mrs. W. lived in a house without electricity. Because it was difficult to get mantles for the very old-fashioned gas light, she and her three children generally sat by the light of the open fire. Four years later, in 1970, when a visitor raised the matter with her, she said that it was not worth bothering about. The houses would soon be coming down.

Mrs. W. spoke to the rent collector. A man came round to estimate. He said the Council would also redecorate the two main rooms which had not been done since before 1939. Hopes were raised. Then months passed and nothing happened. Mrs. W. was now very dissatisfied. Approaches were made on her behalf to the housing manager and the maintenance section. Mrs. W. threatened to write to the *People* newspaper — the *Sunday People*, as it is now known. It so happened that within a few days the decorators arrived and wall-papered the two rooms. The electricians did not come for some further weeks. They bored holes through the new paint and wall-paper and black wires went over white walls. They told her it didn't matter as she would be moving soon. In fact, she was still living there in 1972.

Low Morale

Low morale can spread quickly to a whole district which faces redevelopment. No plans can be made. Pessimism and apathy, frustration and dissatisfaction abound. The effect on children is likely to be deep and lasting. What seems a temporary period of necessary uncertainty to the planners may be five years at a crucial period of a child's development. Those years can train a child to accept the poverty to which his parents have resigned themselves. Of course there are personal failures which contribute to the picture. One woman, badly housed, said, 'even if I had a bathroom, it wouldn't stop the quarrelling'. It wouldn't, but if families who are struggling to make new opportunities are to make some kind of positive response they must do it from the firm base of a good house.

Appropriate housing and a basic wage or allowance should be a service for all people. No doubt some people will sponge on the state, as they do now. But such a principle would prevent many of those who are most severely disadvantaged becoming chronically dependent on state aid. It will be argued that people will then not want to work. Other factors will have much greater influence on whether someone wants to work or not. It is a risk we must take if we are serious about wanting to break the vicious circle of poverty. The assumption that there will always be a great army of the poor leads to the opposite policy. This is to be obsessively worried that 'scroungers' may be taking advantage of the tax payer (though 'scrounging' never costs the state a fraction of what tax evasion does). It will lead to paying as little as possible — so that the recipients survive, but remain as a sort of under class who can never pull themselves up. If the welfare state is administered in this way, it does nothing to abolish poverty. It merely salves our consciences that we care for the poor. It soothes the worst wounds of poverty. But it keeps poor people poor.

Unpopular groups and minority groups who are not likely to speak up for themselves need to be the responsibility of national Government departments rather than of local authorities. Local people often feel that gypsies, for example, and 'dossers' who sleep rough should simply be moved on. Some boroughs in London are alleged to give single homeless men their bus fare to leave the borough. Some boroughs in the inner city receive more than their full share of those who are the casualties of the whole nation. The upgrading of property in the inner city, the development of the City Centre, and the cost of land means that common lodging houses and very cheap rooms are fewer.[20] This is at a time when, because of advances in mental health, many people who would have spent all their lives in a mental institution are encouraged to cope as far as they are able with ordinary life. In addition to day centres and sheltered jobs, there is a great need for small hostels.

Responsibility for the whole field of homeless single persons and their needs should rest not with local authorities but with one Government department, the Department of Health and Social Security.

THE RACIAL DISADVANTAGE

THERE is one quite distinctive set of groups in the big city, namely those distinguished by the colour of their skin. The subject of race is one which needs attention in its own right rather than as a small section of a book like this. Black people and Asians face particular disadvantages in addition to those which other disadvantaged groups have. However, many of the principles which apply to other forms of inequality of opportunity and powerlessness are relevant.

The reaction to the sense of powerlessness follows perhaps three main patterns. Asians, with a long tradition of community self help, are inclined to develop a quite separate and self-reliant life. First generation black immigrants are inclined to accept that they will have to do the lowest paid jobs and live in the worst housing. But young black men and women have been taught in schools that there is equal opportunity. When it comes to the search for jobs and for housing, they find that they are at the end of the queue. Many do not even bother to register at the youth employment office. As far as the careers advisory service (for young people with 'A' level exams) is concerned, there was early in 1973 only one black careers officer in all the Inner London boroughs. It helps to build up the picture that black people cannot gain access to the best jobs and the best housing.

There were those who argued against the need for a Race Relations Act in 1964 by pointing to cities like Liverpool and Cardiff as examples of peacefully integrated communities, where for many years there had been a black community. It was integration at the cost of the self respect of black people in those two cities. Their attitude had been that it was no use trying to get a good post, because you could only expect the lowest paid jobs if you were black.

A strong assertion of black consciousness is not a denial of true integration. Community development has to go through a stage where a community, which has felt itself powerless, has to develop consciousness of its own culture and life. This cannot be in organisations which are indefinitely controlled by white men. It means that the leaders of such a community will speak aggressively at times, before true dialogue can be established on equal terms. But this must not be the last word. Leaders of community groups of any kind have to assert that any community which exists simply for its own sake denies our solidarity as human beings. As powerless groups find power in themselves they need to find occasions when they can meet with other communities.

It is on the basis of such community bridge building that individual friendships can develop.

COMMUNITY DEVELOPMENT

POWERLESSNESS and dependence have been major ingredients in the vicious circle which has perpetuated deprivation. Community development is an attempt to tackle them at root. In some circles it has become a bandwaggon on to which every progressively-minded citizen must climb. In other circles, notably in some town halls, 'participation' has become something of a dirty word. It takes time of over-worked staff away from 'getting things done'.

To take community development seriously will be costly. But it is not just the latest bandwaggon. Its affirmations, some of which are not entirely new, correct some of the fundamental mistakes which have been made in great cities. There has been too much dominant leadership from outside the local community providing facilities *for* people. There remains a role which professionals from other social group-ings can play. Their contribution should not be swept con-temptuously aside. But the principle holds good. There is ability in every human community. Where some groups have been disadvantaged and undervalued, and have lost confidence in themselves, it is the task of society at large to provide the resources, human and material, to enable those groups to stand up and take confidence in their own ab-ilities.

Different agencies and individuals have different hopes from community development. Generally they have one of two purposes. The first approach would believe that par-ticipation in neighbourhood groups or self help schemes can contribute to social health by restoring a lost sense of com-munity involvement and belonging. It combats power-lessness, creates self-confidence in people's ability to help themselves. The second approach assumes that deprived communities are ultimately the product of the competition between different interest groups in society for shares of scarce resources — space, houses, jobs, education, social ser-vices. It sets out to mobilise power in the local community, so that their claims will have to be heard.[21]

Human Warmth

Both approaches are valid and necessary. Instead of simply employing professional social workers to pick up the casualties of society, it is right to stimulate human warmth and responsibility in a neighbourhood so that fewer people become casualties. Apparently trivial social occasions may be the beginnings (and the maintenance) of significant growth in community life. Often tenants' associations and the like have been formed to express some grievance. Frequently they have run out of steam as the source of grievance was removed, or as their attempts to remove it failed. They then continue, supported by those who like committees and are often unrepresentative.

The community development officer, or the project team, has a crucial role in stimulating people in a community to put into words what they themselves feel its needs are, what specific changes would help and what action they themselves might take. A professional 'outsider' can give just the encouragement which is needed to help people over the hurdle of self-confidence. He can give the undergirding of continuing support when projects don't go well or are not appreciated. If some organisation is appropriate, he can stimulate people to consider how best they can set it up; he can again provide the right sort of undergirding and stimulate review of what has been done and of current needs.[22] He asks questions, he provides information, he enables the people of the district to develop their own resources.

A debate emerges about whether the community development worker should ever impose his own values and beliefs. Some say that he must never do so, but that his task is simply to draw out the aspirations of the community itself and enable it to attain them. This is certainly a necessary reaction to the kind of dominant leadership which has 'run things for the people' so often. But what matters is respect for people's ability to think for themselves and their right to choose for themselves. If he maintains this respect the worker does not have to be a kind of enabling eunuch with no convictions of his own. Indeed it would be showing lack of respect if at times he was unwilling to enter the cut and thrust of hard debate.

Lavish Party

For instance, a neighbourhood worker wondered about the amount of money a group he served was raising to spend on a very lavish party for its own members. It seemed to him that they were taking on the false values of the more affluent. He held back from commenting. It was their right to make their choices. But if he stays a number of years in that situation, he would not show respect to that group if he did not express his opinions. He would have to be very careful about when and how he spoke. But to keep silent indefinitely would certainly be to deny that in any sense he regarded them as his friends. For you tell your friends what your convictions are, while at the same time you respect their right to differ from you.

This debate about 'enabling' leadership expresses different approaches. The worker who does not live in the neighbourhood or who takes an appointment for two or three years is less likely to feel able to express his convictions than the worker who deliberately tries to put down his roots in the area and to belong to it. There is real danger of offering a very 'professional' but impersonal service for a short period of time. There is perhaps something to learn here from the experience of clergy and ministers; they have generally felt that longer ministries give them confidence to challenge local presuppositions which they would not have understood sufficiently in the first two or three years.

Churches, settlements and other voluntary bodies need to learn the same lessons about enabling local people to express their understanding of their needs and to play the major roles in leadership. Because they are independent of local authority management, they are well placed to offer support to neighbourhood groups which may want to be critical of the council. There will be times when this is the right role to play if justice is at stake. They may also find themselves pushed into being the spokesmen for unpopular, minority groups. Clergy and staff of voluntary agencies will be in a better position to make social comment if there is strong local membership in the church or settlement which is representative of the main grouping of the area. Otherwise they run into the tensions that 'white Liberals' or 'middle class Liberals' face everywhere.

In a south London borough a West Indian family was on the G.L.C. housing list for rehousing. By a bureaucratic decision that list was transferred to the local borough. Instead of the good housing which had been promised, they found themselves offered very poor housing. They turned to the vicar. He managed to get the officials to put the matter right. He saw it as an issue of helping the individual to stand up to the system. I'm glad he intervened. But in a sense he's part of the system. Officials are often ready to co-operate with those who have headed notepaper, know the right way to approach, speak with the right accent. The system remains unchanged by that sort of intervention. Whole groups of people remain unable to gain a hearing unless they can organise themselves to be powerful enough to be heard.

Minority Causes

Raising minority causes can present some great dilemmas. A clergyman was a member of a tenants' association on a large housing estate. He found it very hard to know if he should speak up for the rights of gypsies whom the majority felt strongly should be moved out. He knew he did not have the same pressures on him. He had only lived there a few years. In a 'twilight' area some able clergy supported a squatters' group who were using houses which were standing empty while they waited for demolition. The head teacher of a school said that he had never known his parents, black and white, so united over an issue as in their hostility to the squatters who they feared might be 'jumping the queue'. This is not saying that the majority group of an area is always right. Unpopular minority groups should be able to voice their needs too.

Other local leaders will emerge as neighbourhood groups grow stronger. Among these and among community development workers some will be what are referred to in secular terms as 'charismatic leaders', who have that magic touch which makes others respond to their leadership. It is right to beware of the strong personality, particularly if a new community group is offering him a status he finds nowhere else. But strong personalities — and erratic personalities — are to be expected in such movements. The danger is that the instability of authority in a new movement seems to require that the leader constantly proves himself by fresh successes. He makes more promises, and must go on producing greater successes. Competitors for leadership are likely to make still more militant claims.[23]

Such leaders need to develop the maturity which can ride disappointments and stand up to the group when it is right to press needs beyond its own self interest. Training of the character to be able to wield power responsibly is often a long process. Sometimes it takes several generations. On the other hand too many safeguards can crush initiative. The spark of many lively movements has been put out by bringing the forces of routine and committee decisions to bear with too heavy a hand. If the leader emerges out of a group who learned to talk and plan together, he is likely to be held to account by them.

Sectional Interests

Much deprivation has continued because of the fatalism which has led people to accept that they were without power and should withdraw from the contest. Those who have bemoaned apathy must not be too quick to condemn the conflict which lively community development groups often produce. Anger is a healthier reaction than withdrawal, and it can be channelled into a determination to bring about change for good.

Democracy does not deny that there are sectional interests. What it requires is that the sectional interests which are weaker in economic or political power should be heard. When the Enquiry into the Greater London Development Plan began in 1970, individual London Boroughs engaged Counsel to argue for more resources. The longest and most elaborate case was made by the institution which already had most — the City of London.[24] The poorest areas have less resources. It is not to be wondered at, or regretted over much, that when under-represented groups, for example, black people, at last find their own voice, it should be rather an angry one. If enduring change is to take place, there needs to be persistent external pressure on institutions.

One of the difficult decisions here is to know when it is right for community groups to join in the consultative process, and when it is better to retain the position of standing outside. Some American observers hold the pessimistic view that participation reduces the commitment to social change.[25] In Britain, a community group feared their teeth were being drawn when they were asked to join in the planning the next stage of a housing development. But the history of good labour relations should encourage us. It is possible for trade unionists to participate in joint consultation and, at the same time, to make it clear that on some issues they maintain their position to bargain. In the same way management participates, but retains its right to manage.

In the Golborne ward of North Kensington a neighbourhood council which grew out of protests against a motorway has joined in planning for the area. The Greater London Council took responsibility for redeveloping a housing stress area. It invited representatives of the neighbourhood council to join the steering group. This group consists of four representatives from the G.L.C., two from the borough council, four from the neighbourhood council, one from the West London Fair Housing Group. Officers and advisers are in attendance. The neighbourhood council representatives report back to public meetings. It is claimed that making information and the timetable public has not delayed matters, but has in fact kept them moving. If local groups are to be able to take part on equal terms, public resources of advice need to be put at their disposal. Taking participation seriously means that local residents should be represented, and not only by one or two token representatives on management of schools and neighbourhood projects.

It is frequently said that people won't come forward; the question then, is how seriously authority tried to find local people, and equally how serious a share in the making of decisions they were offering. School governors in London are too often largely comprised of local councillors of the majority party who sometimes are governors of as many as ten schools. Community development is showing that more people than were expected will come forward, if the offer of participation is not just a token. Many institutions like trade unions and political parties, which we now recognise as part of our democratic process, were 'invented in this arena of informal and potentially subversive political action. Urban society has not exhausted its capacity for invention of that kind.'[26]

Conflict Issues

There is a danger on the other side that all the life of a community action group should be centred round 'issues' — in the sense of conflict issues — so that, like the Sorcerer's Apprentice, we become trapped by the spell we have cast ourselves. Then community action appears to proceed from one controversy to another. It can deny the significance of the ordinary. In fact, changes for the good are brought about by process as well as crisis — and some parts of life need preserving, not changing. Perhaps it is of the nature of journalism that community newpapers are often centred on controversy. It is good when they also point up the steady influences for good, even among public servants. If we rightly reject the attitude of so-called reconciliation, summed up in the words 'pouring oil on troubled waters', we can also forget the importance of a call to true reconciliation which means that people and groups do not deny or waste the assets each can bring.

How Powerful?

Within limits, community development can be very powerful. This may create an illusion of power, because its neighbourhood is not the whole borough, nor the whole city, nor the whole country. Some issues are more subject to pressure from demonstrations than others. David Donnison rightly says that it is easier to squat in the unoccupied house or private park that you want to capture for the people than in the school which you believe should be built or the jobs which do not yet exist. It would be possible to be drawn up a byway if those who work for change put all their energies

into pressure for more participation. We must also acknowledge the present realities of institutional power, and work
through the institutions wherever that is possible.

Only some of the problems of the poor can be solved
through neighbourhood action. Others, especially if a re-
distribution of resources, power and status is needed, can
only be brought about by national action. A neighbourhood
is local. A borough is local. A city is local. How local is
local? Borough councillors, Greater London councillors
and Members of Parliament are elected locally and represent localities. The recent development of 'grass roots
politics' in neighbourhoods suggests that local government
has become regarded by many as too remote. But that does
not mean that neighbourhood councils can claim that they
are the only legitimate representatives of the local community. A Church such as the Church of England can demonstrate from long experience both the strengths and
weaknesses of parochialism. In Church terms I should want
to affirm the value both of the Congregational (local) principle and the Catholic (universal) principle.

One of the false expectations which participation should
not raise in local groups is that they can influence all planning decisions. Many issues for London should be planned
for by the Greater London Council, or by a nationally appointed group looking at the whole picture. It should properly be subjected to pressures from different interests, and
should weigh their validity one against the other.

Neighbourhood councils must acknowledge that other
sectional interests have a right to be heard. They need to
search for an over-arching principle of justice. A group who
are conscious of representing the majority group of an area
may be very hostile to unpopular minority groups. One of
the destructive effects of any system of dominant groups is
that those who feel themselves relatively deprived are likely
to feel hostile towards other groups below them in the

system. A coloured South African from Cape Province said that one of the evils apartheid caused was that coloured people, feeling relatively deprived, had great hostility towards black Africans who were lower than themselves in the ranking order. Working class people are more likely to be hostile to West Indian, Irish or Asian immigrants than those who feel more secure in jobs, status and class. Because they feel relatively deprived, they also feel more keenly the threat of newcomers.

Weaker Groups

One of the objectives of good community development should be to identify the needs of other groups in the area, and in particular of those with less power to speak for themselves. As a neighbourhood group becomes more powerful and articulate, it should face its responsibility for such groups. They will also be wise to try to produce a lobby on the scale of London and on the national scale where appropriate.

Community groups who have become newly aware of their own identity and of their power throw up leaders who often find it very hard to work harmoniously with other leaders. Dog eats dog. The ideology is not right in the next group, so we cannot work together at all. It is inclined to be the same in the world of voluntary organisations and charities. It throws an interesting sidelight on the long history of Christian disunity. At first sight it is shameful that people working for good causes should not be able to show unjudging attitudes to others in the same field. A Saturday night group in a pub seems to be better at unjudging attitudes. On second thoughts it is worth noting that it is easy to be tolerant if you do not have any strong convictions yourself. It is harder to tolerate others if you care passionately that change is brought about, and if you have agonised your way through to ideas which you believe are important. On third reflection it is important to learn both to hold strong convictions and to respect others who may be seen as potential rivals. If community development is to be as effective as it could be, its leaders need to learn to talk to each other and to learn from each other.

The object of community action is to enable groups which have been deprived of power to be heard. The hope will often be that there will then be a national dialogue, continued because pressure is continued. For change to be achieved there needs to be an interplay between all these levels from grass roots groups to national politics. It must include local and national government departments. Grass roots politics by itself cannot succeed in bringing about large scale change. There is no reason for supposing that confrontation by such groups will succeed more often than rival operators working for more privileged people who have lawyers, journalist-friends, cars, telephones, typewriters and organising skills. 'If the game is to be played with guns and bombs, past experience shows that the Right is more likely to win than the Left.'[27]

There are many channels which have not been exhausted through which we can work for change before any case for violence can be made out.

LOCAL AUTHORITY ATTITUDES

NEIGHBOURHOOD groups must not treat local government and its officers with contempt. They may argue with them;

that is to take them seriously. If they simply attack them, any sense of partnership is likely to be lost. From across the counter local authorities should not resent the pressures and the awkward questioning which come from such groups.

The attitude of local councillors and officers is crucial to creative participation. Confrontation can put both sides on the defensive. One community worker wrote that in the predominantly working class borough where he works many of the officials have little understanding of the subculture of the people they are dealing with. They are often surprised at public meetings by the lack of order and bluntness of speaking which is often characteristic of working class communities.[28] Once people start talking, they cannot be confined to the agenda of the department which called the meeting. The official who really wants to serve the community will be glad that communication is happening, however untidily, and that he is learning something of what people really want. Officials will be tempted to resent the demand for participation as simply another burden to prevent their over-worked staff from getting things done until participation is regarded as a necessary part of the process and is budgeted for.

Local authority officials, more than most, are tempted to label people and problems. After all, it is only if the right label is put on someone that he reaches the right department! Having labelled a family as a 'problem family', the social worker or officer may not realise that he himself may also be part of the problem. For example, an educational psychologist is asked to visit a school to see a disturbed child. He pauses. He knows that there is a *disturbing* child, or he wouldn't have been sent for. Before he is prepared to accept the label *disturbed*, he needs the opportunity of considering the whole disturbing situation. The child is part of that. So are his parents. So is the teacher. So are the other children. So is he as a visitor. Sometimes by helping the teacher to look at the child in a new way, he may alter the whole disturbing situation. He may, for example, ask the teacher to tell him three things which have surprised him about the child. Instead of having a fixed 'map' of the problems of the child the teacher may begin to revise his map and to go on doing so.

Problem Family

Officials at the Ministry of Social Security may be appalled when a 'problem family' comes supported by the local claimants' union. If they could see things from the other side of the counter they might understand that they themselves represent part of the problem. A man who is a regular prison visitor asked a senior probation officer if he had ever gone to a particular prison on a Saturday afternoon without his brief case and its crown stamp. He had not. He agreed that he didn't know what it was like to visit a friend as any other member of the public would have to. The prison visitor did it, and said that he saw that it involved a two hour wait in a queue, in dark, cold corridors with toddlers and babies, not knowing when you were allowed to give in your gifts, coming away feeling that you also had been classed as a criminal because you had chosen to visit one.

Social workers, council officers, policemen and warders are tempted to make people fit the bed of Procrustes which their categories allot to them. Procrustes was the man who lived by a mountain pass, and had one bed for visitors. He insisted that they should all fit the bed exactly. If they were too short, he stretched them. If they were too long, he chopped their legs off at the end of the bed. Human beings don't fit our social work categories or our social security rule book any more than they fitted the bed of Procrustes. This means that, for example, the staff of the Social Security must be willing to use the discretion they are allowed and to take responsibility for doing so, in order that awkward human needs may be met.

Labelling

The labelling can be of groups as well as of individuals. In one London Borough councillors spoke in damning terms of the people who lived in The Buildings. It was a 'problem' area. The tenants' association which had talked aggressively to the local press were 'Communists'. There was a disturbing situation there. But the council was part of it, for their policies of allotting tenancies in past years had helped make the district what it was.

Let me tell you a story about a very large new estate in another borough — the account has been given me by a community worker in close touch with the tenants' association. No doubt the story would be told differently by different officers and councillors of the local authority, and in varied ways again by various tenants.

The estate was extremely large, housing 8,000 people on sixty acres. During a period of about three years, while the building was taking place, and as the tenants moved in, about £200,000 worth of damage was done, mostly by eight to twelve year olds. Vandalism on the estate was heavily publicised in the local press. This encouraged youngsters from other areas to come and join in; and it seriously affected the morale of families coming to terms with living in an unfamiliar style on a new estate for it to be so widely attacked in the press.

Many families moved to the estate from appalling housing conditions. The block where the worst vandalism happened housed those who came from the very worst slums.

Some explanations were that they could not be expected to look after good flats, because they were not used to them. When such explanations were expressed widely, they added to the vicious circle; families living in that block felt that they were even less welcome. Perhaps it was also a part of the vicious circle that this was the one high rise block on the estate where large families were housed. The generalisation about people from slums not looking after good flats needs to be challenged.

There is much evidence that those who move from appalling housing conditions become, in their delight with their new home, almost excessively house-proud. One woman went to see some neighbours in their new maisonette; they, like her, had moved from a very drab set of Buildings. She took her shoes off before going upstairs in her neighbours' house. Indeed, some children and teenagers found themselves under new pressures from their parents which they had never met in the ever open door style of life of the Buildings or the terraced streets. As with most new estates higher rents and considerable hire purchase commitments for appropriate furniture for the new flats meant that additional income was needed. This meant that many mothers started going out to work. So, at a time of transition, confusion and dislocation for children, the central person necessary for the child's emotional security was in many cases removed from the scene during the day.

Some observers in the housing department commented that it always takes an estate three years to settle down. In fact, damage is still continuing at an alarming rate. Even if it were not, it would be a mistake to concentrate only on the problem of vandalism. This may avoid the question whether it was a symptom of anything. It would be wrong to assume that, once damage has declined, then everyone is contented. During the three years tenants made many attempts to protest, and to have a say in how their estate developed. Many

who came with high hopes of a better life on a new estate felt
that they were not listened to, and that they were powerless
to alter conditions. The fact that people have an astonishing
ability to adapt to a new environment may be at the price of
growing the protective skin of a massive fatalism.

Peace and quiet can sometimes be less healthy symptoms
than protest and anger. The tenants' association, feeling
rightly or wrongly that their efforts had been very
ineffective, worked out some of their frustration in internal
bickerings and resignations.

Frustration led different groups and departments to
blame one another. It would have been better if they had
been able to acknowledge the scale of the problems which
would come with bringing large numbers of people together
from areas where they had already been subject to disadvantages all their lives. Add to that the difficulties of establishing any new housing estate, and in this case a very
large one. The over-riding pressure was for as many housing
units to be built as soon as possible in order to get people
out of terrible housing. What is most needed in planning is
vision of how to enable a warm, human community to develop. That is why participation of people with a variety of
insights makes sense. Co-operation with every available ally
was needed. In this case, partnership seemed to be knocked
on the head at every turn.

Advocates

The community workers realised that, from the beginning,
they had been seen by the housing department as advocates
for the tenants. One of the community workers had almost
too low an opinion of most council officials to make any
sense of partnership with them a congenial experience. The
council departments, perhaps because of other experiences
in meeting community action, quickly regarded the com-

munity workers as hostile. Confrontation seemed to be the order of the day. It may have established some solidarity among tenants which will help strengthen community life. But it was at the cost of preventing effective co-operation which was essential if the environment was actually to be changed.

From the community workers' view point planning of facilities, especially for young people, was badly co-ordinated between departments. At crucial moments in planning, the architects' department and the planning officers did not appear to communicate well. The youth service officers were not consulted at the decisive moments. It was not accepted as essential that facilities for children, including youth workers and adventure play leaders, should have been available as soon as the first families moved in. The borough engineer favoured fixed play equipment and unattended playgrounds. His department had to work within a strict budget. But such a policy ignores the human environment which adults, who have time and are interested, can provide.

Some attempts were made to inform and consult the families who were going to live on the estate. Plainly it is very difficult to find ways of consulting so that people understand something of what their new environment is going to be. It will take time. It will need the planners to believe that local people's participation will help significantly in the ultimate building of a community. Borough councillors and officers largely believed that inviting such participation would lead to a confusion of comments and a waste of time for hard-pressed departments. The sense of confrontation pushed councillors and officials into a very defensive attitude, resenting the demands or offers of other people to share in the decision-making process. If they had shared with them the constraints within which they had to work because of a tight budget laid down by the Government, they might have found a much more positive sense of partnership instead of confrontation.

A look back at history suggests that the worst terraced streets and tenements would never have been built if there had then been a serious attempt to offer those who were to live in them a share in their planning.

INDUSTRIAL PARTICIPATION

BIGNESS is one of the great bogeys people fear in modern industry, as well as on vast housing estates. Nostalgic dreams long for the day of the small family firm. Very large firms can make for the destruction of any sense of personal commitment to other persons; sometimes they lead to a helpless resentment of some distant management which is never seen. However, the truth is that some small firms have extremely bad relations and working conditions, and some very large firms have very good relations and working conditions. There are good and bad results from large size in a firm. It has been claimed that the arrival of the very big public companies set off a chain of events: scientific management; study of what makes men want to work; attention to inter-personal relations; rediscovery of the worker as a human being; development of consultation and awareness of a firm's responsibility in its neighbourhood and nationally and internationally.

There has been great progress from the beginnings of scientific management. 'Time and motion studies' were often deeply resented by workers. Even more, they gave them the feeling that 'the working class aren't completely trusted'. They seemed to threaten jobs, because the object of the exercise was to see if fewer workers could do the same work. The next stage must be to strengthen mutual trust rather than to study men's deficiencies. There is all the difference in the world between the worst forms of 'breathing down your neck' and the best attempts by joint consultation to help a worker set personal goals for his work. This is quite often done now at management levels. If we value every worker as a thinking person, we should argue for some such joint work consultations between every worker and his immediate superior. I've seen the notes of such consultations on a building site. The sort of questions which can be asked right along the line to the most junior paste boy are: What have I achieved of significance during the past twelve months? What do I hope to achieve in my job during the next twelve months? Which part of my job do I do best? In which part of my job would I most value help? How can I best develop my skills during the next twelve months?

There need to be agreed notes, and they need to be reviewed and new goals set — by the worker himself — twelve months later. The best ideals of capitalism are that it should give the greatest possible opportunities for individual choice. Management which defends these ideals has an obligation to make some sort of choosing possible for all workers.

Management Skills

That will mean not only some sort of personal consultation but joint consultation which is seen to be taken seriously when decisions are taken. This calls for a very high order of management skills. It means: not coming with a settled solution; putting the problem on the table; listening to the group explaining the obstacles; planning for enough time to have 'feed-back'; making clear that management has to make the decision and communicating intelligibly what the decision is.

All this demands that management does its homework very thoroughly; the hardest resistance to such methods comes from foremen and junior management in the 30s and early 40s — not altogether surprisingly because there is the fear that they won't be able to cope intellectually with the demands this form of management makes. As in some town halls, participation is seen by some managers as preventing them from getting things done. But the prize of developing a firm in which every worker has a real chance to feel that he has a stake is worth a great deal of time and money.

Particularly where industrial relations have been sour, men on the factory floor may reject overtures to share in joint decision-making. If they have settled for no other goals than the most money for the shortest working week, they may prefer simply to keep their bargaining position. The same is true of profit sharing and co-partnership schemes. The General Congress of the T.U.C. in 1957 said that clumsily handled schemes might threaten union rights. But its advice to unions was not to condemn co-partnership but to take each case on its merits.[29]

Impracticable

Co-ownership and profit sharing have often been regarded as impracticable. Men have not been slow to discredit the idea when particular schemes have failed. What worked for Robert Owen in the Lanarkshire Village of Co-operation did not seem so practical when he produced a nation-wide dream in the Grand National Consolidated Trades Union. He believed the unions could take over the whole economy and run it co-operatively.[30] There were strong motives for self interested men to dub all Owen's ideas — and present day schemes for co-ownership — as 'visionary' and 'unrealistic'. This has helped to keep progress slow. Yet it would be hard to deny that such enterprises can and do work.[31]

An example of profit sharing and co-partnership is the Scott Bader Commonwealth. Ernest Bader began by believing powerfully as a Christian in the prime virtue of individual enterprise in business. His attempts to relate a growing Christian understanding of the corporate nature of life led him to share and eventually to hand over a very considerable measure of power to the three hundred employees of the business.[32] Workers' representation on the board of directors, which happens in several European countries, can be significant, but only if it is built on hard work towards participation at every level. Otherwise it is no more than a token.

A Social Audit

The concept of a 'social audit' was put forward by George Goyder as long ago as 1961.[33] Very large companies, whose headquarters are often in another country, drastically affect the well-being of the whole community by their operations. They are accountable to no one except their shareholders and the law. When an extreme case occurs, like a large office block such as Centre Point standing empty for years, or a shipyard's closure creating large-scale unemployment, the mass media can bring pressure to bear and governments may intervene. A social audit, which a revision of the Companies' Act could require every three or five years, would make every firm accountable to society as a whole in the regular order of its life and not just at crisis moments. Such an audit would have to be conducted by an independent body who would need skills in: finance, technology, organisation, urban planning, overseas development,

sociology, communications and perhaps theology and inter-
personal relations.

A social audit introduces other factors beyond profits and
wages. It asks what is the effect of the firm's operation on
society and on the environment. What has the result of the
last three years' operations been, for example, on: the development of the 'human assets' of all its employees? unemployment in the area where it operates or in an area from
which it has withdrawn? the environment in the immediate
neighbourhood? the whole community, by advertising products which people don't need? countries in the Third World
who need trade which is now going to a safer market?

An example of a responsible link between industry and
society as a whole is found in West Germany. Industry has
been given great incentives to help solve the housing problem. If it builds a factory, a firm must invest a proportionate
amount of capital with a developer or with the municipal
authority for housing. That capital sum is free of tax. An
example of the most difficult sort of question Western industry may have to ask, if overseas development is taken into
account, is how the sugar beet industry affects the economy
of countries like the West Indies where so much depends on
the price of cane sugar.

The 'overmighty barons' of today, regarding their sectional interest rather than the interest of all, are sometimes
international companies. They are sometimes property developers. They are sometimes trade unions in key positions
of power in the economy. Any attack on the pursuit of 'sectional interests' by such unions must admit that all of us
have sectional interests. Private house owners in the more
'desirable' areas of the big city want to keep factories and
council estates away from their district. That is their sectional interest. Parents defend their freedom to buy smaller
classes and more teachers for their children's education.
That is their sectional interest.

It can be argued that in both cases their action is against the best interests of the whole. When powerful trade unions are attacked for pressing their sectional interests against that of the whole, other powerful groups should admit that in more subtle ways they may do the same thing.

Key Positions

The more powerful trade unions are sometimes guilty of hindering the advance of those who are less powerful. The strongest force against the unskilled labour pool in the earliest days of industry was often the guilds of skilled artisans; the greatest influence against black advancement in the United States or in Southern Africa will most often be the blue collar white workers of a Chicago suburb or the white African or Rhodesian workers who jealously cling to the key jobs. Those in key positions in industry can name their price if they ask at the right moment. When a motor car manufacturer is 'all tooled up' for a new model, they know that his capital is committed and he cannot afford a prolonged dispute. They have him over a barrel. But if the wage demand is given, to keep them in their high place in the wages league, the sufferers will often be the weakest group in society, the occasional labour force who have no key position to bargain with. A union which bans overtime while there is unemployment is standing by the principle of working class solidarity. The most powerful unions who know that they can wreck an industry in order to stay at the top of the wages league are undermining working class solidarity. They are out for themselves, no less than the property developers they accuse of being robber barons.

The Trade Union Movement will not have sufficient power to control its most powerful members unless there is a national wages policy which goes right through society. Difficult though it may be to establish, it would express our mutual dependence, that we are members one of another. Every wage or salary should have some reference to a standard wage for everyone willing to work. If we believe in differentials, they should be justified. If we believe that one man is worth ten times what another is paid, let the case be made openly and negotiated.

No restraint by the key workers in one sector of a nation's life is likely to be exercised if another group of key workers in Stock Exchange, finance, commerce and consultancy is allowed to stretch the market as far as it will go.

In an industrial society where the ability to accept change is of vital importance, security is crucial. Otherwise, insecurity breeds irrational opposition to changes which are for the common good. Only if there is a sense that everyone is in it together, and only if the relationship of each group of workers to one another is clearly seen, can voluntary restraint seriously be expected. As long as chairmen and directors say that their first objective is to produce the greatest profits for their shareholders, trade unions must be expected to try to produce the greatest wages for their members.

Tender Plant

Participation is a tender plant.[34] It has to be patiently worked for. It needs management to take great care over good communications, and to come out from behind the desk to be involved in personal relations. It requires trade unions to be willing to take part in the decision-making process and therefore accept a share of responsibility for the decisions made. It is easier for both management and unions to stay in the negotiating situation where there are two sides, each trying to achieve its goals with as little compromise as possible. A great deal of continuing pressure is often needed to bring about change. But the honesty of the claim to want change is often tested by whether those who demand it are willing to join in the hard and complex process of bringing it about.

In industry there are 'wreckers'. Their intention is to destroy society as it is in the belief that a good society can only come about when the present structure has vanished. The history of those countries which have had their revolution shows that there are no short cuts to the long process of building a society in which all are able to have a stake. In our generation Christians have debated the rights and wrongs of revolution and violence. The solid values of a stable society need to be reasserted. Stable government is a fragile thing.[35] It is a necessary framework within which people may be valued and can develop their abilities. On the one hand there are huge dangers of complacency in a country like Britain. It is when a group within the population feel that they do not have a fair deal and that their voice cannot be heard that finally they resort to violence. It is impossible to condemn men who have taken the violent way in situations where every peaceful way of putting their case has been denied. On the other hand, such peaceful and reasonable ways have not been sufficiently pressed in this country to argue now for a resort to violence.

It is not right to say, 'Violence is reasonable in South America, therefore violence is reasonable in Britain.' A great many ways of reason and protest have to be exhausted before a responsible man can seriously start thinking about violence, whether it is by strike action as a political weapon, by civil disobedience or by urban guerillas with guns and bombs.

Gradualism

This should not encourage gradualism to go even slower. Progress towards a fuller share for all employees in all the processes of production needs to be a great deal faster.

Before we pride ourselves on having a just society, one of the questions we must press is how those who do not sit in the industrial seats of power can make their voice heard. Idealism must be kept in front of those who have power. They must not be allowed to get away with, 'This isn't a Sunday school. We're running a business now.'

When asked if his objection to a particular deal was on business or ethical grounds, a Christian business man said, 'There can, of course, be no difference.' Those who hold ideals have the responsibility to do the hard grind of making the ideals work. No one will be convinced by any other means. Eric James in a university sermon said that he wanted to say to students demanding power, 'You want power. By God you shall have it. But don't drop it. And don't tire when you realise it involves minute particulars.'[36]

Power still corrupts. Good management has humanised industry in many details; but in as much as it attaches employees more closely to the company and its future, it increases the power of the company. It may also therefore add to the powerlessness of those who remain outside the limited circle of those who participate at present.

This book is primarily about those who society leaves relatively without a say and without power. A comparison of the modern non-apprenticed, unskilled urban workers with the unskilled workers in the weaving industry of the Middle Ages shows depressingly little advantage except for welfare. A comparison with the Indians and the blacks in the early days of 'freedom' in the United States is a reminder that the assertion that all were free, provided they were within the charmed circle, makes the lack of freedom of those outside it hurt all the more. The serious offer of participation must be for all, if we are not to increase the sense felt by those outside of being excluded.

Just below the surface there is often a deep despair among

those who have worked for participation in industry and in the community. They feel they have seen such small progress. Little attempts at co-operation have been quickly abandoned when something goes wrong in favour of confrontation or withdrawal into apathy. Men of good will are then tempted to sink into an even deeper fatalism, and to withdraw to individual good works at home.

Such withdrawal is the greatest sin of our times. Grappling with the big city demands hard work to understand its interlocking forces. It needs the willingness to set limited objectives, and to know that it will take years to achieve them. It means that those who have power and those who are without it must be willing to move on from confrontation. It prizes very highly every group which takes those with other insights seriously. It refuses to abandon the dream of partnership in which everyone feels that he has a stake and that the big city is *his* community.

Seven

RESPONSES TO INDUSTRIAL LIFE

Introduction

WE have travelled a long road through history in our efforts
to lay bare the heart of the urban problem as it faces us
today. This has meant extended sociological analysis of the
nature of and background to the big city and some detailed
assessment of the multiplicity of factors — historical, educational, social and religious — that create the modern problems that arise where life is 'built as a city'.

What then is there to say as we turn to the effort to relate
religious, Biblical and Christian concepts to modern industrial life in the urban situation?

This again will take us into deep water, without any as-
surance that we remain afloat in it. But the effort to swim
must be made. Merely to sink in it will add to the sense of
hopelessness and helplessness that is always threatening to
engulf the life of the Church today. We must look first then
at various responses that have been made or are being made
to the facts of modern industrial living. After that we must
attempt to describe the Church's task in the situation, and
finally we must try to think out what the Gospel for the city-
dweller is.

We begin then by looking at some responses to industrial
life that can be identified. The first is the so-called 'Protestant ethic'.

THE 'PROTESTANT ETHIC'

In the Middle Ages men accepted without question their station in the regular ranks of society. It was regarded as part of the natural order. The Reformation emphasised God's calling to each individual to secular tasks as well as to religious ones. The seventeenth century Puritan, Richard Baxter, believed that God called men to rational labour in a particular calling. The Puritans were against privilege and monopoly; they were for rational, legal acquisition by virtue of one's own ability and initiative.[1] Next to the saving of his soul, (the tradesman's) care and business is to serve God in his calling and to drive it as far as it will go', wrote Richard Steele in 1684.[2]

The direct link between Puritan religion and the rise of capitalism has been challenged. It is a mistake to exaggerate the extent to which theories were ever consciously worked out. In fact the Puritans did not invent capitalism. Two factors in Reformation thinking did however have direct and far reaching effects. First, the reformers were less committed to the traditional order and adjusted themselves more rapidly to the new economy. Secondly, other things being equal, 'those who practised thrift, temperance, honesty, consideration for others and who believed in active life as a layman in society to be a vocation from God, were more likely to be successful merchants than those without these qualities'.[3] Refusal to accept things as they are, plus a strong sense of personal responsibility, drive and initiative, stem from a sense of God's calling to the individual. It is a more godly attitude than that of fitting into the *status quo* without asking questions.

Sir Frederick Catherwood in a modern restatement of the 'Protestant ethic' says that it is the duty of the Christian to use his gifts to the limit of his physical and mental ability. It is wrong for him to relax as soon as he has got enough money or as soon as he has mastered his job. He has a duty to train himself and to develop his abilities to the full. When he has mastered one job, he should go on to another. He should not be content to administer, but should try to improve and innovate. 'He should not stop until it is quite clear that he has reached his ceiling.' As long as he thinks only of his development as an individual and through his own family, he will not think of asking how his personal growth affects the development of the community to which he belongs. 'The Christian need not live between the gasworks and the linoleum factory if he can afford to live somewhere more salubrious.'[4]

New Standards

Here is a philosophy which we meet at many less developed levels. It expects a Christian to develop new standards of behaviour, to improve himself, to want something better for his children, to take promotion to a job where he would have greater influence. In isolation there is nothing wrong with any of these developments. The trouble is that for a working class Christian they so often mean rejection of the culture of his neighbours, and removal to a 'better' district. The assumption is that 'better' is measurable by some set of values which hold good for everyone. The truth is that different groups at work would hold different values about the job where the best influence may be wielded. Different social groupings would have different values about what is 'better' for their children.

We discussed this complex subject on numerous occasions in Canning Town. When I had been there two or three years, the whisper came back: 'Mr. Sheppard doesn't hold with going up in the world.' This made me think furiously what I did 'hold with'. Christianity never says that you should hate yourself. On the contrary, you should love yourself and develop the God-given gifts you possess. You should certainly love your children, and want the best for them. But you should also love your neighbour as yourself. This means that when there are decisions to be made about whether you move house from near the gasworks, or whether you accept promotion, *your neighbours will go into the scales along with you and yours.* Christ talked about letting yourself be lost, 'for My sake and for the Gospel'.[5] It is a relevant comment here.

A number of working class Christian couples have put aside some of their personal ambitions in order to stay in the area where they have grown up. Seeing that not only social geography but Church members' geography is a subject which can be drawn on a map of the city, they have felt called to stay, *for the sake of the gospel.* This is not saying that all working class Christians should stay as they are. It is saying that each Christian must open his mind to the questions, Who is my neighbour? and in the light of that, At what level does Christ call me to work? and, Where does He want our home to be? And crucial personal questions these are.

Educators in schools, clubs and churches often turn their ablest young people against the culture of their own neighbourhood. This is likely to happen if education and development as a Christian is seen essentially as an individual experience. Among our aims for education should be helping people to have an awareness of the whole community and the wider world and the ambition to use the gifts they possess for the good of the community.

SOLIDARITY

Now let us turn to a crucial word in the history of the working classes — the word 'solidarity'. It began with a sense that you had no strength by yourself. A friend wrote to me of finding the attitude 'You can't win' both in a middle-sized Lancashire town and in the east end of London. He felt that it was said with a greater sense of despair in the Lancashire town than in London where there was a much stronger sense of belonging to the working classes. A worker's self-confidence, the ability to stand and answer back has often stemmed from seeing himself as a member of the working class.

Ernest Bevin, when he was Secretary of the Transport and General Workers' Union, said that there would have to be an assertion of trade union power 'before a recast of values would be accomplished'.[6] The values he spoke of were not only about money but just as much about the relationship between employers and employed. They were about power, and who had a share in wielding it.

It has been widely asserted that traditional working class solidarity is rapidly breaking down. Ferdynand Zweig found in interviews with 672 workers in Sheffield, and in big firms like Vauxhall, Dunlop and Mullard, that they no longer cherished fierce solidarity.[7] He believed that there was a general 'move towards new middle class values and middle class existence'.

Zweig's conclusions have been sharply criticised in a more recent study of Luton. Goldthorpe and Lockwood saw a move not towards a 'middle class worker', but towards a more individualistic worker, interested most of all in home and family life. They saw also what they described as a 'convergence' towards a 'new worker'. Among white collar workers there was a shift towards greater reliance on collective means of pursuing their economic objectives.[8]

Visiting Mullard's electronics factory in Mitcham, I met an entirely skilled work force facing the threat of redundancy. Over 300 out of 1,800 employees were made redundant that year. A recession in the computer business in the United States meant that American computers were being offloaded on to Europe at prices which no British firm could match. Impersonal forces like this spread the fear and experience of unemployment right through the work force, graduates included.

The workers questioned in Luton, Sheffield and Mullard's of Mitcham do not lack qualifications or have the same sense of being left behind as do many people in the inner city or on the vast council estates of a very big city. Solidarity remains a much more real concept among those who feel shut out from the common future of a more prosperous nation.

Temporary Alliances

It must not be assumed that solidarity is always an enriching experience. Often it is built on temporary and self-serving alliances. In a printing works the 'chapel' voted by eighty-seven to thirteen in favour of a serious questioning of major pay differentials. The very next day one whole group of twenty-five refused to go by it. They had discovered a new kind of solidarity when their self interest was threatened. A group of dockers said publicly that they would support the interests of black people. The next week, after a report had appeared which made them feel that their jobs were threatened, many of the same dockers were expressing strong hostility towards 'blacks'. They realised that they might be interested in jobs on the buses which black people were doing.

When all this has been said, there remains a powerful feeling of belonging to a common culture and of having a common view of life with other working class people in each of the areas where I have worked. Christianity should not ask a man to abandon all that culture and fellow feeling. It should challenge some of the limitations solidarity can impose. It should enlarge understanding within the community to which a man belongs, and lead him to work with others for the enhancing of its whole quality of life. A Christian should not simply have a 'vertical' sense of responsibility as an individual to God. He must also have a 'horizontal' sense of corporate responsibility.

An enthusiastic young Christian worked as fast as he possibly could on the assembly line at Ford's. He was very conscious that he must work to the glory of God. Next to him on the assembly line was an elderly man who had known unemployment days. He had long ago worked out how fast he was going to work, and he was not going to change in order to keep up with this young man. A large number of components piled up between them. The young Christian told me years later, 'I wouldn't do it now.' He had not learned then that his faith should lead him to think out complex horizontal loyalties too. For his neighbour was at the same time the old man, the employer and the customer.

Trade unions, like Community Action, force Christians to work out their attitude to conflict. 'Reconciliation' has been the word which has dominated our thought. But it has often been taken to mean: shrinking from conflict; pouring oil on troubled waters; trying to calm people down; the stage clergyman persuading two men who are violently disagreeing that really it is an unfortunate misunderstanding and actually they agree in principle . . .

Clash of Interests

The disputes which matter are not necessarily caused by a misunderstanding of interests, but by a clearer understanding of a clash of interests. The kind of reconciliation which Jesus brought was not peace at any price. It demanded that first men must face truth. 'You are mistaken,' He told the Sadducees, '. . . you are greatly mistaken.'⁹

There are times when a Christian must take sides; he will still criticise the side he believes to be right if they act unjustly. He will still want to know those whom he believes to be wrong. But he will not pretend that he agrees with them. He will want reconciliation with justice, between grown ups and not as between fathers and children.

A Christian shop steward from Dagenham, Frank Deeks, says that you may be a better neighbour to your boss by forcing him to concede to a just demand. 'Equally, you may need to be a good neighbour to your fellow worker by opposing an excessive pay rise that will damage the enterprise you work for, the economy of the country and those who have not the power to demand increases.'¹⁰

Georges Velten visited Paul and his wife in their three-roomed prefab in St. Nazaire. Paul had been on strike for over a week. A neighbour came in and after a while asked Paul if he would like a better paid job than the one he had in the ship yards. It was in a garage and he could start straight away. The neighbour was a good friend who clearly knew them and wanted to help. After a glance at his wife who clearly understood and supported him, Paul firmly and swiftly showed his neighbour the door. Velten said that he couldn't understand why he had turned the offer down so flatly. Paul said with a sad smile, 'Mr. Velten, you are still bourgeois.' Velten agreed that he was, but remarked, 'That doesn't explain anything.' Paul sat down, poured out glasses of wine for both of them. He went on in the tone of a good Sunday school teacher trying to explain things to a rather stupid child. 'Didn't the Lord tell us to love our neighbours as ourselves? Who are my neighbours, if they aren't mates on strike with me? How could my wife and I dream of letting them down for the benefit of our own family, and still think that I could witness for Christ to them? It would all be up with me ... Mr. Velten, you are a minister, you are here to preach the gospel, but not the gospel wrapped up in a middle class ethic.'[11]

The gospel will not destroy working class Christians' sense of belonging to their own class. But loyalty to Christ will sometimes mean falling foul of people on either side. A Christian who was convener of shop stewards in a ship yard on the Clyde won a good reputation for being fair. When a new method of work on a ship was being discussed, it became clear that a critical precedent of piece-rate payments was at stake and this would have repercussions in the industry as a whole. He was asked by the management to take responsibility for fixing the payments so that in everyone's interest a dispute could be avoided. He agreed and worked out a scheme which was generally thought to be very fair. But his union wrote to him that the scheme was unconstitutional and should be terminated forthwith. The men on the job stood by him, maintaining that it was a good scheme. He reported their verdict to the union. The reply he received was the withdrawal of his credentials. Thirty years spent working for the union came to an end abruptly. He had to take another job with less pay. The incident contributed to breaking his health.[12]

ONE WORLD

'BRIDGE people' frequently get themselves hurt. They can never allow the development of their group to be the last word, whether the group is a trade union, or a neighbourhood council or a black community group, or a developing country, or a tribe. Christ is not described as 'the last Abraham', the father figure of the tribe or the nation of the class. He is described as 'the last Adam'.[13] For example, tribal Africans have built their security on their own solidarity; it is as though they were saying, 'Abraham is our father.'[14]

The first figure in all primitive African religions is the counterpart of Abraham. But when African villagers discover the figure of Adam and of Christ as the last Adam they find a 'Charter for a human solidarity which can outlast the breakdown of tribal and kinship ties'.[15] This isn't to attack their loyalty to their tribe or family; rather it is the challenge to lead their tribe on to the enriching experience of acknowledging and meeting other people on level terms.

Nothing has brought home more clearly the sense of our being one world than the strongly-supported arguments that there are limits to growth. If some sort of social audit isn't taken into account voluntarily, it will soon be brought home to roost by forces and by people who don't sit in boardrooms or at international conferences. For instance, it was black people's pressure on the company in the United States which made Polaroid conduct a social audit on the wages they were paying black people in South Africa.

The debate about Britain's entry into the European Economic Community has been conducted by both supporters and opponents on the basis of the need for our economy to grow. But suppose growth has to stop. Suppose it is true that the resources of the world have limits, and that there is no chance of the countries of the Third World coming up to our living standards if we go on growing. Suppose there is only so much wealth for us all to have.[16]

Unequal sharing out in the world or in a nation is obscured, as long as the promise of more growth for all can be held in front of everybody. If we have to stop growing, then we have to face in acute form the questions about why one man or one nation should have a higher standard of living than another. Max Weber said that when economic development slows down, people's status becomes much more important to them. They cling fiercely to their rung on the ladder, and frustrations and inequalities become much more explosive. He wrote before the Nazi era. But the cause and effect can be traced: low productivity; loss of status; resentment against the scapegoat, the Jews; demand for room to live from neighbouring countries and blind allegiance to a saviour.

Voluntary Austerity

The conclusion that has been drawn from this German experience which led up to Hitler's rise to power is that a steady rise in productivity and a corresponding increase in levels of income is always necessary.[17] But the social audit demanded by the developing countries. and by new knowledge about the urgency of world conservation, question whether we can any longer have such growth. A call for 'degrowth' in standards of living — 'consume less, enjoy it more' — must begin with those with more than average income. This may be voluntary austerity now; but there will

need to be Government action to achieve any effective trans-
fer of scarce resources from those who have more than their
share. There can be no policy which begins by demanding
that those further down the ladder start the process of
asking for less.[18] It is significant that it is from among the
students who see themselves as children of privilege that
many of the sharpest criticisms of the values of our society
come. They could lead the next generation to want fewer
consumer goods.

The Old Testament writers had what has been described
as 'a theology of enough'. The farmer was not to glean over-
thoroughly or to beat his olive boughs a second time. He
was not to over-exploit the land. The first fruits of harvest,
which might have brought the go-getting trader the highest
prices, were to be offered to God in a great thanksgiving
celebration. They were to leave opportunity for the widow
and the foreigner. Such moderation was encouraged by re-
membering their own dependence. They were not self made
men. They had been slaves in Egypt and they were never to
forget it.[19] In the New Testament, Jesus warned men
against ruthless greed; 'for even when a man has more than
enough, his wealth does not give him life'.[20] As soon as a
nation considers saying 'enough is enough', it is bound to
ask how one country can possibly act alone. These are issues
that matter to the world. If the world is in any sense one,
they have to be faced.

The issues which must be considered in one big city turn
up when we talk about one world. Poverty, powerlessness,
share of scarce resources can only be effectively dealt with
by corporate planning and action. The lead must be given by
wealthier nations acknowledging that they have enough and
do not need more, or may want more but have decided not
to have it. This has its immediate implications for those who
are relatively deprived within a wealthy nation like Britain.
Those who are concerned about world poverty and inequality

must be concerned to tackle the same issues in their own country at the same time. There must be determined policies to produce a more equal distribution of real wealth. Those who feel they have less than their share in their own country often find it hard to accept that people in other countries face poverty and lack of opportunity on a much greater scale.

More Urgent

If there is less growth, all the needs of priority areas within our cities become more urgent. The questions which an industrial society was always likely to pose have to be faced now. There is now no escape route by means of fresh sources of cheap labour or mass emigration to a new Empire. We must face up to the co-operative nature of work. The need to bring everyone within the circle of those who belong and are consulted at work and in the community becomes greater. Only those who can see the whole picture, who know that the accounts are not being hidden from them, will co-operate with trust, rather than resist threatening changes. It is no longer possible to allow a blind market and private decisions to control industry. Its decisions must be open and accountable to the public. Harder still, a contracting economy would need fewer workers or fewer hours of work. There would have to be co-operation of a very high order, if work needed to be shared around.

The need for appropriate technology for the needs of a particular community is becoming plain in developing countries. Western and eastern blocs sell or give highly sophisticated machinery which may have disastrous effects on the societies it influences. For example, a European government as part of its aid built a textile factory in a rural town in an east African country at the request of its government, because there was great unemployment in the region. It was so highly automated that it needed to employ only five hundred workers. The capital value of that plant was about £1½ million, so each work place had cost £3,000. Part of the result was that armed guards had to protect the factory gates from the crowd of young men outside who were desperate for jobs.[21] In many areas of the world intermediate technology is what is needed, not the most sophisticated machines. Zambia's poultry farmers needed one million egg trays a year. The sophisticated machinery which they could have bought would have had to produce one million egg trays per month in order to be economic. The Intermediate Technology Development Group with the help of Reading University designed a machine that can be operated by local labour to manufacture strong, convenient egg trays by pulping ordinary waste paper. It was appropriate for the needs of Zambia.[22]

Appropriate technology is also needed in a developed country like Britain. Those who have expressed fears of redundancy because of the introduction of automation have sometimes been dismissed as new Luddites, wanting again to smash the machines which bring wealth and growth. Perhaps the Luddites weren't so foolish after all. If there had been participation in planning in those days, and they had been encouraged to take part in making decisions, industrial development might have been slower but have brought more well being. Perhaps economics would have started not with markets and machines, but 'with people and their education, organisation and discipline'.[23]

A shop steward in Liverpool asked the chairman of a huge international enterprise why they had such sophisticated trucks. The chairman said, 'I really don't know. But why do you ask?' The shop steward said, 'We have sophisticated trucks, but we haven't got sophisticated drivers, and you've got to do something about it.'[24] Wide participation might mean slower growth — or

degrowth — but it would be more likely to produce appropriate technology and more well-being in the community at
large. Trust and co-operation cannot be expected without
it.

WORK — IN BIBLICAL TERMS

INDUSTRY as it is often leaves men with a low or twisted
expectation of work. A Biblical review might make five ob-
servations:

It is part of the proper nature of man to work.

The harmony of man's working life has been spoiled by
human selfishness.

Work should offer rewards in terms of real wealth.

There is a place for leisure.

Work should be a co-operative enterprise.

Man Must Work

It is part of the proper nature of man to work. Some an-
xieties about work arise from a romantic view of it. This
demands that all work should be 'creative'. Certainly a man
should be able to see his work as a part of his response to
God, Who wants to change the world for good. But this
does not mean that every man is frustrated if he cannot
achieve the same kind of creativity in his job as can an artist,
a research scientist, a craftsman or a mother. To be made in
the image of God has its implications for work, but creativity in this sense is not one of them.

Work is often presented by Old Testament writers as part

of the regular order of life.[25] They wouldn't have criticised people who said, 'We're in business to stay in business; otherwise people will be out of a job.' 'You work to live.' 'You've got to earn the money.' In his place in nature's cycle 'Man comes out to his work and to his labours until evening.'[26] Manual work is honoured.

Shalom — Peace — is one of the most important of Hebrew words. It means wholeness, right relationships with God and with men. Work has its proper place in life when there is *Shalom*. It is wrong to think of work itself as a curse. The great promise of restoration to Jerusalem in Zechariah might stand for all that *Shalom* means. Jerusalem will be called the City of Truth. 'They shall be My people, and I will be their God in truth and justice.' Old men and women will sit in the streets, each leaning on a stick because of their great age; the streets of the city will be full of boys and girls playing in the streets. Man and beast will be hired again; men will go safely about their business; no longer will all be set one against another. They will sow in safety; the vine will yield its fruit and the soil its produce. Men will speak the truth to one another, and administer true and sound justice in the city gate. Four times a year there will be festivals of joy and gladness. They will love truth and peace.[27]

The son of a line of rabbis, Karl Marx depicts something very like *Shalom* in his ideological, almost theological, description of the relationship man is meant to have to matter. His description could be set out in a continuing circle. The worker goes to work on matter; productive life leads to 'life engendering life'; from the act of production emerges the product of labour and from it comes wealth. Marx said that if this circle remained unbroken and wealth flowed back to the workers, man going to work on matter would engender life and wealth beyond our dreams.

Breakdown of Harmony

The harmony of man's working life has been spoiled by human selfishness. Somehow in the mystery of evil the whole material universe is affected by the breakdown of a world in harmony. Marxists and Christians find some common ground in explaining the breakdown, but they also diverge in their analysis of it. I shall attempt to look more deeply at this in the last section of the book. Whatever its causes, the mystery of evil in the world affects work; 'You shall gain your bread by the sweat of your brow.'[28] 'The whole created universe groans in all its parts as if in the pangs of childbirth', waiting to be freed from frustration and from the 'shackles of mortality, and enter upon the liberty and splendour of the children of God.'[29]

One of the French worker priests, 'Lucien', was deeply aware of his relationship to the material universe. He would stop on the night shift at Renault's and look across at men working and at the machines. He saw the result of thousands of years of interaction of man upon matter, and of shaped and humanised matter upon man: sweat of the brow; comradeship; anger; pride in fine engineering; taking the family out in a Renault car; living in crowded streets; solidarity and hostility to those for whom it meant wealth. All these and more spring from the association of those workers and that machinery. He was aware of the groaning of the whole creation. 'Our function is surely to prepare, through blood and tears, the great festival of the freedom of the universe.' This wasn't based on an optimistic dogma about the triumph of labour, but 'By the gathering together in the same faith, around the Man-God, of men, of those labourers who change the shape of the world and are themselves changed in return by their work.'[30]

Real Rewards

Work should offer rewards in terms of real wealth. The idea of reward for work well done is firmly built into the Biblical writings. 'The worker earns his pay.'[31] There are strong hints, though, that part of the reward should involve what happens in the work situation; the worker who proves trustworthy in a small way is put in charge of something big. His real wealth is not to be measured simply by his capacity to amass possessions.[32]

Modern studies of workers who are well rewarded in cash terms have often concentrated on them as consumers rather than as producers. When highly paid manual workers have been questioned about their jobs, a very large proportion have expressed strong dissatisfaction with the job. They have seen it simply as a means to the end of earning a large wage which increases their capacity as a consumer. Part of what Marx complained of in 1844 was that the worker felt at home only during his leisure time, whereas at work he felt homeless.[33] Che Guevara said that man should not have to try to liberate himself through art and culture in order to compensate for eight hours a day of dying because of his alienation at work.[34] Behind this statement lies the suggestion of a belief that when the means of production belong to the workers, dull work will become 'creative'. The truth is that in whatever way industry is organised, some jobs, seen in isolation, will always be relatively dull.

Being regarded as a 'cog in a machine' can be utterly dehumanising. On the other hand, some people are willing to be cogs, because they believe that good reliable cogs are necessary. They have been helped to see themselves as a significant part of a corporate enterprise which is producing something valuable. Part of the reward they receive is intrinsic to the job itself. If a man is not consulted about the task he is doing, and if no one helps him set himself some objectives, he will do what he is paid for, but no more. He is a machine-minder. He will not care for the customers, because no one cares for him. A worker in a great firm cannot expect to have the same kind of satisfaction that a writer has in stamping his own personality on a book. He can be made to understand that the organisation is providing something useful for its customers and that it is acting responsibly towards its employees and the neighbourhood where it is situated. This means showing him the fullest possible picture, *in work time* (not arranging that workers can see a propaganda film about the company after working hours). No doubt many workers would at first laugh at the idea of taking part in a social audit about the effect of their work on society as a whole. That is because they have been left to work without any conscious responsibility. Such a public review would make many ask questions for themselves about the values they place on having more material possessions or on quality of life.

The Puritans learned the great incentive of regarding daily work as a grateful response to a loving creator and sustainer. They found in work itself a major part of the reward. This bred a wish to care responsibly for the material world, and a sense of partnership with the Creator.

The Place of Leisure

The Biblical concept of work is not confined to what, in a money economy is thought of as productive work. It includes much that we think of under the heading of leisure. It includes all attempts to co-operate with the Creator in developing the world for the good of all. This concept cannot allow us to divide leisure as sharply as we tend to do into a different category from work. Man made in the image of the Creator has a responsibility to care for the world entrusted to him and to develop it for the good of all. He may do this because he is paid to do it, or because he chooses to do it.

Leisure is not necessarily the same as rest. Leisure is 'choosing time'.[35] In it a man may choose for his own satisfaction to do what another is paid to do. The Catechism in the Book of Common Prayer contains an unexpected 'find' on the connection between work and leisure. Given the question, What is thy duty towards God? (in other words, Explain the first four commandments), the answer as it relates to the fourth commandment (six days labour, the seventh day rest) is, To serve Him truly all the days of my life. The Puritans argued that the commandment was about the use of the Sabbath. Those who defended the Catechism replied that the commandment was about the way we use *all* our time. There is to be a rhythmic relationship of work and rest. If education is to be for the whole of life, it will aim to equip children not only for a job on six, five or four days a week, but also for leisure on one, two or three days a week. Man is to develop not only as a worker and a churchman, but as a husband, a father, an admirer of God's creation and responsible member of the community.

Such a view of work and leisure may help us towards a right attitude to the painful subjects of retirement and redundancy. As well as a weekly rhythm of work and leisure, there is a lifetime's cycle. The thought of longer years lived in retirement fill many people with dread. This is partly the fault of our community attitudes. We do not value the elderly as the commandment about honouring parents suggests we should. We ought to restore ideas of old people's value to the community as: givers of wisdom; unhurried observers; learners from mistakes and story tellers of a community's history (perhaps being available in a public library or visiting schools). If the community valued old people more highly, perhaps fewer would move away to a totally different district, and it would perhaps become easier for them to give way to others. One able business man said: 'Posterity for me is my son and no one else.' If he had a more corporate attitude to life it might help him to see younger men whom he had enabled to develop within the firm as his heirs.

There are some even harder questions to answer, if it is likely that there will never be full employment in a productive sense again. Automation — or 'degrowth' — probably means that a limited number can earn all the wealth that a country needs. What happens to the other 10% or 25% who no longer need to work? As our society thinks at present, to be 'out of work' would cut the ground from under a man's feet. Part of his self respect is to be able to support his own family and help carry some other people's burdens. A man made in the image of God should be assured that his abilities are needed — by society. He must see that he can make a useful contribution. This demands that society provides more than simply an allowance made to him because he exists. He needs to be paid for doing something useful, and something which others will recognise as useful. It is therefore right either for some jobs to be shared (half a week's work each) or for more 'non-productive' jobs in the community to be created (which will mean more taxes).

Co-operation

Work should be a co-operative enterprise. A friend was staying with us. In the way these conversations often begin, he threw off a vast question at 11 p.m.; 'Why don't men come to church?' We settled down to a late night. My wife and I both made our attempts at answers, then asked him the question in return. 'It's something to do with the culture', he said. 'Men spend their working hours immersed in the culture of the working world, maximising profits, pushing the next man out of the way to win promotion. "If you don't look after yourself nobody else will." "He's in the

money." "I'm all right, Jack." All these express the dominant culture at work. On Sunday, if they come to church,
they hear about a quite different culture; it's about loving
your neighbour, turning the other cheek, not being able to
serve God and money. The tension between the two cultures
is so great that most men cut the knot and keep away from
church.'

I find nothing in the Bible that says specifically that competition is wrong. There is no simple Christian directive on
this issue. When the man asked Jesus to tell his brother to
divide the family property with him, in the end His answer
was, 'Why can't you judge for yourselves what is the right
course?'[36] God-given intelligence challenges us to work our
system and see how it can be improved.

On the other hand the Bible holds up certain values which
clearly bear on modern industry. The first part of Jesus's
answer to the whining brother was unmistakably that
money, profits, productivity and growth are not to be regarded as ends in themselves. First He said, 'Be on your
guard against greed of all kinds.' Then He told the story of
the rich man who ploughed back his profits into his
business, and made provision for himself to enjoy his
leisure. It is called the story of the rich fool, because in the
light of eternity he had built up no treasure. James applies
this story: 'Next a word to you who have great possessions
... Your riches have rotted; your fine clothes are moth-
eaten; your silver and gold have rusted away ... You have
piled up wealth in an age which is near its close. The wages
you never paid the men who mowed your fields are loud
against you, and the outcry of the reapers has reached the
ears of the Lord of Hosts.'[37]

The culture which the Sermon on the Mount breathes,
cuts across the whole atmosphere of a society for whom
increased productivity and growth are the first goal. Western
Christians have not believed the Sermon on the Mount can

be practised; we have not attempted to relate its values to working life. We are like Solzhenitsyn's character Yefrem in *Cancer Ward*; all his life he pushed other people around, believing that no one else would look after him unless he did. Then he read a little blue book by Tolstoy, talking about love as the controlling influence in life. That little blue book had some good ideas, he thought. But everyone would have to agree to start living by them at the same moment, or it wouldn't work.[38]

Engels contemptuously rejected the possibility of a society built on love. Wilfully misunderstanding what Christianity means by love, he saw it as proceeding simply from the emotions. C. F. Andrews's definition is better and more relevant: 'Love is the accurate estimate and supply of another's need.' The understanding Andrews had of Christian love drove him to spend much of his time helping Indians to found trade unions in Africa and in India itself. And the essence of love as we see it in Christ is that He didn't wait for everyone to agree to start living by His ideals at the same moment. He made the first move.

No Clear Dogma

There will be no clear dogma which declares either sheer competitiveness or sheer co-operation to be the guiding star for industry. If we abolish private property, we shall not have removed clinging to status and lust for power from the scene. The bourgeois are quickly replaced by the bureaucrats. The rulers of eastern Europe regard participation and use of personal initiative by individuals as anarchy. Czechoslovakia attempted to live by the principle 'the development of each for the free development of all'. Their experiment was brutally crushed because centralised power might be threatened.

The tension between the principles of competition and co-operation reflects a tension between two truths. On the one hand the world is God's world and works best, in every part, if we live as near to His way as we can. On the other hand it is a spoiled world in which evil principalities and powers are at work. The New Testament acknowledges the presence of powers of good and evil. It does not, however, settle for a dualism (believing the good and evil powers to be equal). It does not believe that the world has been bound and gagged and handed over to the devil. It says that on the cross Christ defeated the cosmic principalities and powers,[39] and that one day He will make all things new. Though it may lead us through experiences which feel like crucifixion, we are to believe in His victory over evil in industry and commerce too. Therefore we must not abandon attempts at participation and co-operation, however fragile they sometimes seem against harsh competition.

The tension remains however. The sheep are safe enough in Luther's ideal picture, where he imagined all animals herded together and charged voluntarily to co-operate and live at peace. But soon, as he pointed out, there wouldn't be any sheep left, because the wolves will not voluntarily keep the rules. We rightly fear absolute power because we rightly distrust the selfish ambition which is present in human nature. We reject private monopolies because they give absolute power in a particular field to a small group of men who are not accountable to anyone except those who also stand to benefit from the profits. A nationalised industry also holds a monopoly but is accountable, at least in theory, to Parliament. Both with nationalised industries and with public companies, we need to make sure that checks and balances are constructed which can prevent irresponsible use of power.

Safeguards

The danger of too many safeguards is that decision-making becomes almost impossible. Study of interpersonal relations has helped us to understand some of the drives which God has planted in human personality. For example, we try to look at the drives of sexuality and anger within ourselves, and to learn what to do with them, rather than repress them. One of the God-implanted drives in human beings is the ambition to get things done, to achieve and to change. We need to acknowledge that ambition is there, recognise its dangers and try to direct it to the glory of God. The Puritans were right to see this. The story, for example, about the bags of gold (the talents) makes the point that all are to use the varied gifts they possess to the utmost of their ability.[40] The reason why 'the Protestant Ethic' has sometimes become unbalanced is that *it has not sufficiently stressed the Bible's concern for the development of the community and for the protection of the less powerful.* As far as the building up of private property and private capital is concerned, the Old Testament Law of Jubilee, as we have already noted, made all land which had been acquired revert to its original owner every fifty years. This was to keep a fair distribution of land (and wealth) by preventing the building up of great estates.[41] Our nearest parallel is contained in death duties which in a modest way put checks on the perpetuation of private fortunes. Death duties do not deal with the re-distribution of wealth as radically as the Law of Jubilee would have done in a rural community. This does not add up to saying that the possession of private capital is wrong, but only that there should be much stronger checks and balances. For capital spells power.

The moral basis which is claimed for capitalism rests upon the argument that freedom to choose is good. 'Every time I choose for myself I grow'; 'every time I am deprived of an opportunity to choose I am deprived of an opportunity to grow.'[42] This is not the same as laissez faire economics, in which only the very few strongest are free to choose. Interference with their power is needed if a reasonable number of people are to be free to make choices for themselves.

The goal of co-operation includes the ambition to develop all the human assets of the firm and the community to the full. It needs all the variety of gifts which can only emerge if personal initiative is encouraged.

INDUSTRIAL MISSION

MANY responsible people, at every level of work, long for help in finding a way through its complex, interlocking web of responsibilities. It is assumed, too lightly, that because Christian laymen are at work in industry they will know how to witness to Christ's cause there. Because of the complexity of industrial life Christians often withdraw from hard debates about the most difficult issues at work. They are afraid of speaking without sufficient knowledge. This will be particularly true if they have grown up in a church where there is generally an unchallenged agreement about what the Christian line is on any question. Such Christians need a new kind of confidence to raise questions to which answers are not known, or to realise that answers which made sense a year ago have to be modified this year. Because they have not been helped to develop this kind of confidence, they are afraid of entering the sort of arguments about common interests which arise at work. Some withdraw, and become 'very private people', respected by their fellows, but not consulted. 'You can be a monk at work', retorted a Christian shop steward, when another Christian asserted that there was an effective Christian presence at work, just because Christian laymen were present. Others go into the thick of it, and sometimes become very critical of other Christians because they won't get involved in matters which seem to them so transparently what God cares about.

An efficient factory doesn't give over much time for gossiping at work. Therefore the natural points of contact will very likely be to do with working conditions, how decisions are made, redundancy ... It is just here that Christians should dare to speak up, 'in fear and trembling'. Surely they would if they really believed that the living God was present and cared about these issues which affect their lives and the lives of their fellow-workers; if they had been encouraged to think such issues through in a company of Christians where each member's ideas were listened to with respect; if they had the confidence that they wouldn't make fools of themselves; if they weren't kept so busy running church organisations, that they didn't have time either to belong to such a thinking group or to risk getting involved at work. I suspect that most Christians who keep silent do so because of the last three points.

Deep Division

Approaches to industrial mission reflect one of the deepest divisions within the ranks of the Christian Church. Christian fellowships of laymen at work often have a programme for their meetings which seems unrelated to issues in the work situation. Many of them would not believe that their friends can understand Christian insights into life and work, unless they have first responded to Christ's challenge to repent and believe. 'If they're not born again,' one man expressed it, 'they won't know nothing.' If the interest of the group is primarily to say 'repent and believe' to those who don't belong, and to deepen the 'personal' and 'spiritual' life of the members, it will not be the kind of support group which gives its members the confidence of having thought work issues through with other Christians. So the objection, 'They won't know nothing', often hides another objection, 'I wouldn't know what to say.'

Other Christians react sharply against this kind of approach. For them it bypasses all the real issues, and is simply concerned with 'souls with ears' and not with the whole man. If 'preaching the Gospel' means ignoring these issues, then they believe God wants none of that preaching in their factory. For them repentance means a change of heart in matters to do with pay, promotion, disputes, the life of the trade union. The first group in turn reacts by saying that this is all social gospel which leaves out Christ, and that Christians shouldn't involve themselves in politics. So the two groups collide, and bounce off, hardly understanding or listening to one another.

Few Visible Results

Industrial chaplains have generally become deeply involved in trying to understand issues in the world of work. They have produced few results, measured in terms of newly-committed Christians who come to church. Some of them do not see it as part of their task to name the name of Christ. Most of them see the role of industrial mission as holding up the mirror to industry, to make it ask the right questions, to draw attention to values which otherwise are ignored. I believe that God is present in every factory, in sustaining, life giving, reason giving power; in love and in judgment. If He is present, then I believe too that it is a proper Christian task to stimulate management and workers to think about the way He values people.

In one very big firm I was taken by the chaplain to lunch with a number of directors. Instead of chit-chat about old Tommy who was a chaplain in the navy, the chaplain asked the senior director over the meal table, 'What are you in business for?' 'To stay in business,' came the reply. For an hour we talked hard about the burning issues of that company. It included the agonising problem of one department where what they felt to be the right decision would make seventeen men redundant. One man tried to persuade me to give them the answer. I said that they knew I couldn't do that. I could help by asking some of the questions about people in the light of the way I believe Christ treats us. So we were talking, not round the fringe of life, with the organised Church and the chaplain providing a sort of extra welfare service, but at the centre of daily bread problems.

We talked seriously. We didn't always agree. We talked about God and Christ. I don't doubt that, with some of those men, a right moment comes in their meeting with the chaplain when they would want to talk about what being a disciple of Christ means. Disclosing the values of the Kingdom of God includes living out life at work, pressing God's questions on men about work, and naming the name of Christ, if the right moment arises.

There is a man-sized task for full-time and part-time chaplains in industry. Theological skills are needed to help Christian laymen have the confidence to wrestle with complex issues. Courage as well as tact is often needed for a chaplain to use the independent position he has to raise thought-provoking questions with those who make decisions on both the management and the labour sides; sometimes as an observer he can bring a wider perspective than those whose own self interest is at stake.

If we rely simply on the presence of Christian laymen in

industry, there will be whole sections, particularly of working class life at work which are not aware of that presence. I spent six months in a steady effort to lead a mission in a factory employing 4,000 people in east London in 1959. I visited throughout the factory for half a day a week (the absolute minimum which could make a contact significant). At the end of that period together with an able layman who had spent many years as a shop steward, and with a team of theological college students, I spent a fortnight in the factory. There was an exhibition open day and night; we had a film and a sportsmen's meeting during the first week, and a meeting each day during the second week. During the first week we reckoned that three people came to each meeting who did not belong to the Christian Fellowship. At the last meeting there were some thirty who didn't already belong. No one came to these meetings from the factory floor, where the majority of the work force was employed, except for one young man, who belonged to the Mayflower Family Centre where I worked, and one woman, for whom the meetings proved a great help.

The first problem was that the Christian Fellowship was entirely made up of office workers. However devoted and prayerful they might be, they could not prevent the strong sense that this Christianity was for 'them' and not for 'us'. More deeply it meant that there was no connection being lived out between what might be said in a meeting and what happened on the factory floor. The contacts which were made with manual workers were in visiting around the factory, and being invited occasionally to meet small groups over their tea break. If I had been able to go on visiting over a period of years, I believe we would have developed some of the good conversations we had about work and life, and occasionally about the Christian faith. And it should have been possible in time to help bring into being some lay groups on the factory floor with lay leadership. They would include any committed Christians and all who were prepared to meet and do some serious thinking about life, the community and what God might say about it. But these lay leaders need a lot of encouragement, and themselves need some group where they can think through work issues and their Christian understanding of them.

Support

A group of factory floor workers was established over a long period of time with a member of the South London Industrial Mission Team, Cecilia Goodenough, providing support and theological resources. On one occasion they were working very unwillingly at studying a chapter from the Bible. It was from Ezekiel all about the shepherds of Israel. 'We don't see many sheep around here'; 'I did see a sheep once on holiday . . .' One man who knew his Bible well and was the secretary of the local branch of the Electrical Trades Union started to talk, apparently at a tangent; 'We had our annual meeting last week. We've got 1,000 members and only three turned up.' 'Where were the 997, do you suppose?' asked Cecilia. 'Straying on the mountain tops,' he said, 'and it says it's our fault. We've not made them realise that the union is significant. We've allowed them to be bored by our meetings.' He understood that the shepherds of Israel are the rulers, and rightly applied the chapter to himself as a responsible leader.

The group looked at the Bible with new eyes. The shepherds care only for themselves — they ought to care for the sheep — they drink the milk, wear the wool, slaughter the fat beasts — do not feed the sheep — haven't stopped the fat sheep from butting the lean sheep and from polluting the drinking water — haven't encouraged the weary, tended the sick, bandaged the hurt, recovered the straggler, or searched for the lost — even the strong they have driven with ruthless severity — God's sheep go straying over the mountains.[43] It had much to say to government, management, supervisors and shop stewards.

Reflections on that Mission

Thinking back about my attempt to lead a mission in that factory over a period of six months brought some reflections on industrial mission:

1. It is most unlikely that there will be many visibly committed Christians on the factory floor in an unchurched area in a big city.

2. Special meetings are most unlikely to attract men from the factory floor.

3. The only basis on which factory floor workers are likely to be encouraged to think about God's concern for their life at work is through working alongside a thoughtful Christian (which statistically is a very remote possibility) or through the regular visits of a chaplain set apart for the task.

4. The 'way in' to discussions about God is going to be through listening, 'Picking up' the matters which are important to a group, asking questions in return, and having the courage at the right moment to challenge some of the assumptions which are made. It is then going to be possible at the timely moment to speak explicitly about Christ and His claims.

5. A group of fellow workers will be the most natural context in which men will be set free to think, rather than a series of personal conversations. Personal talks may very well happen, once a man belongs to a group where questions are opened up.

6. It is not possible to 'tack on' a small group of factory floor workers to a Christian group which is largely composed of office workers — without the character of the group being dominated by the viewpoint of the office workers.

7. Factory floor workers who are prepared to engage in a very serious discussion at work about Christ and His claims are probably still a very long distance from considering church-going in their own neighbourhood.

8. There is a need for support groups for laymen to stimulate Christian reflection. Support groups may well be for men and women who work in several factories. In turn they may promote a 'lay project' or group in their own factory.[44] The eight full-time chaplains of the South London Industrial Mission support twenty-seven groups, including a number of factory floor groups.

9. The Church should set apart some men and women with theological training to help establish such groups, offer their resources to lay projects and give regular time to becoming part of the life of a factory.

10. Such work cannot be assessed by surface measurement, such as how many new church members have resulted.

Making the connections with local churches for those who have started hard thinking through contacts with industrial mission is always difficult. It is even more so in a big city. The factory floor workers at the factory I have quoted travelled in to work from a radius of twenty-five miles in all directions (some managers travelled fifty-five miles). Coherent industrial mission is more difficult in a big city than in an industrial town or city where one major industry predominates and there is a limited number of factories. The South London Industrial Mission, for example, regularly visits some sixty firms through its full-time and part-time chaplains. But this is a drop in the ocean compared with the number of firms in south London.

The Logic of Influence

There is a logic to the argument that the first priority of the industrial mission should be that of influencing the 'influencers' of society.[45] If management is encouraged to value the worker as a human being, efficient personnel officers will humanise jobs more effectively than any clergyman from outside could do if he saw his task as a welfare officer. The role of the chaplain with the influencers is much more to be a free man, independent of sectional interests in the firm; a long term supporter of those who bear heavy responsibilities; an observer who can make honest comments and a perspective-giver keeping certain values in front of them.

Indeed the prophets of the Old Testament generally delivered their messages about justice and concern for people to the rulers and the full citizens of Israel, not to the foreigners or the landless man or the widow.[46] But if the argument of this book is followed, we shall beware of always identifying the 'influencers' in industry with those whom society regards as 'influential' or 'strategic'. The question of who is significant in the Kingdom of God is one of the many upside down things of the coming of Christ. The first shall be last; whoever wants to be first must be the willing slave of all;[47] the humble have been lifted high, the rich sent empty away.[48] Many of the crucial influences in industry can only be influenced by patient beavering away at the factory floor level.

This means that a key task of industrial mission should be to find and support those laymen on the factory floor who see a primary calling from God to act for Him in their work situation. To bring supportive groups into being would be to challenge a number of working class Christians to think more deeply about their work and their relation to their fellows at work. It is easy to criticise laymen for withdrawing into a private shell at work and finding their Christian service in their leisure time. Many such laymen feel terribly alone at work, and the Church has offered them no support in 'taking on' the immensely complex web of relationships which confront, for example, a shop steward. If men were helped to face some of these painful 'work' issues together with others who understand how life on the shop floor feels, they would grow immeasurably as Christians.

One man in Sheffield hadn't much time for the Church. First through a friendship with a chaplain and then through industrial mission groups and weekend conferences his attitudes to people and to his work changed. He used to be a 'little rabbit'. Gradually he grew tougher, not afraid to stand up for what he believed right, to get involved in union affairs, and sometimes to 'play merry hell' both with his colleagues and with the management. 'People come to me with their problems, as they might to a friend or a priest. And they watch me to see what I will do.' He said that the size of the task of the Christian appalled him; prayer became natural, 'Because I feel the job I'm on is too big for me.' He was very critical of the churches and of many Christians at work, 'They are people with their minds made up.'[49] Christians are called to face life at work and not to withdraw into a world where home and family and church are the only places where the gospel 'bites'.

Involvement at work means opening the mind to questions which have no ready-made Christian answers. It means the risky and stretching experience of believing that the living Christ goes with us into the thick of it and that we learn from Him as we go.

WORKER PRIESTS

THE most dramatic attempt to 'take the Church over to the other side' of the class line has been the worker priest movement in France. The background was a much more acute consciousness of the class struggle than in Britain. Anticlericalism of a kind unknown in Britain had emerged in France, particularly in 1848 and 1871, and had continued. The crucial years after the end of the European war in 1945 saw very bad conditions in France. Their involvement in colonial wars continued in Indo-China and in Algeria. The country was near bankruptcy. There had been comparatively little destruction in the big cities, so there was no immediate urgency to rebuild the slums. A quarter of France's voters was firmly committed to the Communist Party. In big cities like Paris whole zones could properly be described as a 'red belt'.

The worker priests were sent to make contact with the working classes and to preach the gospel in what were seen as de-Christianised areas. In order to do this they believed they must live in and with the world of the proletariat, 'renouncing all strategy and scheming'.[50]

They went to work in the first place to prove visibly that they were earning their own bread, and that they were not financially dependent on unknown backers who manipulated them from behind.[51] They quickly felt the blast of workers' hostility to the Church. They saw from within it an industrial system which they believed was degrading millions of human beings. Henri Perrin said that it was

impossible to keep in with the employers and at the same
time serve the course of justice. The Church and most of its
members saw Communism as its greatest enemy. In 1949 all
members of the Communist Party were excommunicated.
The priests of the Mission de Paris, in a Green Paper, asked
why the dangers of working class life were feared when no
question was raised concerning the faith of the employers.
They saw the Church defending a system against which 'we,
together with the working class, will fight with all our might
because it is unjust and oppressive.'[52]

Naïve

The worker priests were accused of being naïve, of being
exploited by Communists, that instead of working for co-
operation between the classes they had slipped into Marxist
conflict. Perhaps they were naïve. One of their number said
that if the worker priest has to become involved in a secular
liberation of men, he must learn to do it with freedom.[53]
Perhaps they were not given long enough to learn how to
hold an attitude of *critical* solidarity with the group they
wanted to serve. But events moved very swiftly. In a demon-
stration against the handing over of the N.A.T.O. headquarters to General Ridgway in 1952 two worker priests
were arrested. The question of their whole mission became
headlines in the popular press. It was widely felt within the
Church that, instead of winning the working classes 'back'
to the Church, they themselves were being won over to false
political action. The leaders of the French Communist Party
in fact consistently attacked the two dozen priests of the
Mission de Paris. After the General Ridgway incident Jea-
nette Vermeersch who was wife of Maurice Thorez and a
member of the Politbureau wrote that worker priests 'under
cover of demagogic workers' slogans, try to keep the
workers submissive'.[54]

The worker priests were trapped between crossfire from several sides. But how could they back out? It would seem to those they came to serve as though it had all been a trick or a milieu study.[55] They didn't see their purpose as 'bringing the working class back to the Church'. Rather, the Church must live 'in this new world coming to birth, a world in which the poor and the exploited should assume their role of responsible producers'.[56] So they must discover afresh the meaning of their faith in a new context; 'The Church would rather have seen us as teachers of labour, but we were pupils, mere children in the school of life, with no teachers,[57] They felt themselves introduced into a new world, 'whose laws, language, sufferings, aspirations and even structure were alien to the Church'. At the heart of the working man's world, a *new man* was trying to come to birth, who upset the *old man* created by their education. They belonged first to this working man's world, torn as they were by the fact that they belonged also to the Church.

Suspended

Cardinal Suhard, Archbishop of Paris, who had founded the Mission de Paris during the war years, died in 1949. In 1951 the Holy See said that this form of apostolate involved more dangers than advantages, and forbade any increase beyond the eighty-five worker priests there then were. In 1954 they were suspended and in 1959 Pope John, who had been papal nuncio in Paris during the years of their greatest activity, ordered the end of the experiment. Some continued to work and broke with the Church. Others refused to stop working but kept some links. No ecclesiastical sanctions were used against them. A third group obeyed the order in 1954 but kept on pressing for the experiment to be restarted. These have more recently been allowed to start work again. They now avoid positions such as foremen or trade union leaders.

The first official reason for stopping the experiment was that it compromised the nature of the priesthood. In addition it was said that they were taking away the laity's place. Lurking behind was almost certainly the biggest reason that, living in a 'Marxicised' environment they were being won over, in the eyes of those in authority, to false political action. The worker-priests felt that the majority of Church members were only perturbed by the obvious tensions which had been revealed by men trying to live as priests within a working class community. They felt they were not stirred to any action.

E. R. Wickham argued in 1961 that the worker priests experiment was not right for Britain.[58] His first reason was that he believed it would displace positive lay activity. That is a question to which I shall return in the next section. Partly it was on the ground that the cleavage between the classes is much more subtle, less obvious in Britain — 'much grumbling, no barricades'. He also said that the case for the informal Church in a milieu of its own with a priest who is one of themselves was relevant in a truly missionary situation, but not in working class Britain (would he have said that if he had then been working in London?). Yet one of the very few in Britain (not as many as ten) who regard themselves as worker priests said that he believed the class divisions in Britain, being much less easy to define and to tackle, would persist longer and more pervasively than the divisions of race.

In Britain there is a growing number of men in the Supplementary Ministry or Auxiliary Pastoral Ministry who see their main reason for being ordained in relation to their neighbourhood. There is also an increasing number of priest workers. They are most likely to be found in education, medicine or another profession; in social work, the civil service or in business. The direction that this movement has taken owes much to the history of the Southwark Ordination Course, which started in 1960. S.O.C. was brought under pressure to run a course measured by academic standards comparable to those of residential theological colleges. The course which has developed has largely shut out the possibility of those, whose intelligence cannot be measured in academic terms, taking part. But the S.O.C. course has helped another concept of the ordained ministry to re-emerge, which had almost been forgotten in the Church of England.

The work required by S.O.C. is spare-time and in the context of regular secular employment. 'Because the student is continually running the second mile, he is encouraged to see himself (not just his spare-time self) in terms of ministry.' This often leads him to see the job, which takes up most of his time, as a sphere of ministry. So he sees the gap not between the Church, including himself, and some other world as the worker priests do, but inside himself. This attempt to hold together his Church commitment and his commitment to his job is not something other than what the Christian laymen should be doing. To ask, 'Exactly what does he do which a layman doesn't?' is a rather unfair question which produces misleading answers. The priest worker would want to answer less in terms of what he does than of what he is. Nevertheless, it is not really enough to say that he brings with him a 'Christian presence'.

The Christian Presence

It is important to ask the reason for the presence. Beginnings of an answer may be that his presence is a sign of God's attitude to the situation where he is; stands for something which might otherwise be ignored; provides a 'theologian' in the sense of a practitioner of a working theology such as arises in living situations and is applied to them; offers the help of an interpreter to Christian laymen.

The debate about worker priests can perhaps be continued with less drama than it was in the post-war years in France. Belgian worker priests in a report to their bishops and superiors in 1970,[59] describe each of the great urban zones of Anvers and Liège, Ghent, Charleroi and Brussels as profoundly de-christianised regions. The report says that the manner in which the Christian faith is generally practised is incompatible with living in working class conditions. They feel they must espouse those conditions themselves, and not play at being tourists in the working world. The description they prefer is worker priests, not priests at work. They often feel pulled in opposite directions by the working class world and the Church. There is astonishment that so many Christians are indifferent to the fact that the working classes have been for so long de-christianised. Yet in spite of the gap and what they see as compromises in it, the Church remains one body and they must maintain fidelity to it.[60]

Priest workers are said to be justified in Britain, because it is healthy for the Christian mission that they should feel the tension within themselves between their commitment to Christ in His Church and to Christ in the world, largely in the professions. If that tension needs to be felt and interpreted, how much more is it needed in the world of manual work. Massive indifference rather than hostility confronts the Church in Britain. But the gap remains real and massive. So we must now look at the Church's task in this complex and challenging situation.

Eight

THE CHURCH'S TASK

AN INSTITUTIONAL CHURCH?

LET us dig as deeply as we can into the task the Church faces now. It is a task in which the basic problem is not hostility but apathy and indifference. The gap between Church and world, and especially the world of industry and manual work, is historically wide and contemporaneously massive. Where do we start in all this?

We have to start with a question basic to the life of the Church. It is the question: should there be an institutional Church at all? From our standpoint within the Church, we assume an affirmative answer to that question as a matter of course. But we must, because of the questions we have raised so far, make no such assumption. We have to face the question.

As one institution to be compared with other institutions in working class areas, the Church probably does better than our harshest judgments suggest. It has survived long after other bodies have collapsed which predicted its early death. The hard fact is that *all* institutions are ignored by the majority in such areas and the Church often falls into the same traps that ensnare other tidy organisations. There are many who admire Jesus Christ, but reject the Christian Church, in working class circles, not least among younger people.

Two men who believe passionately in Jesus Christ, and equally passionately that the Church is a dreadful mistake, argued through a long night with my wife and myself. As an illustration of a spontaneous development, one of them described how a group of mothers of handicapped children had found common interest. 'What did they do next?' asked my wife. He laughed. 'They organised themselves,' he said.

Groups which arise spontaneously often collapse when one or two leaders move house, or take another job. Tenants' associations often spring up because of an explosion of indignation, but lose steam when the particular issue is settled. Youth clubs often begin because a particular leader appears on the scene. Many collapse for want of some organised body to continue nurturing work which is still needed. Unattached workers, in youth, community or Church work, sometimes find the strain too great and are broken, because there is no person or organisation in support to help them know clearly what is expected of them.

In one sense we need to be wide open to experiments, yet not in the sense that we are always chopping and changing — and disappearing. A youth club member came into the club for the first time for two years; 'Where's Pam?' she demanded. Pam was a voluntary helper who came one night a week. Happily she was there that evening. A young mother came to the Church for help. It made all the difference that the Church worker was the same woman she had known there when she was a teenager. Continuity is a vital factor if the Christian community is going to be available when it is needed.

I believe that Jesus Christ intended there to be a visible, organised, world-wide Church. That belief doesn't mean defending the visible Church as it is organised now. But the evidence suggests that the Churches which are best placed to serve 'unchurched' areas are those which are organised on a universal basis. Those Churches which are organised on a congregationalist or independent basis might be expected best to express spontaneity, but when their congregations move out to the suburbs, it is logical enough that Churches so organised tend to close down in the areas they have left.

The Church of England, and, for rather different reasons, the Roman Catholics have the opportunity to serve unchurched areas, because they have never abandoned the parochial dream (which is not the same as the parochial system). This dream means that we commit ourselves to putting resources to serve an area, whether there is response in terms of church-going or not.

'Institution' may describe a good body or a bad one. It's unhelpful to hate all institutions. The lesson for the Church to learn is how to maintain continuity of life, and at the same time be ready to change when new needs appear. The organised Church must encourage spur of the moment 'happenings'. It must risk giving erratic leaders their head. It must take non-Church groups of Christians seriously, be willing to learn from them and give them a say in how things should be, when they join up on a very occasional basis. This will mean that the Church leadership is not able to keep control of events. Things may get out of hand. But that may allow the Holy Spirit to intervene.

The Church which will make Jesus Christ and His claims a serious adult proposition will need to have at least four characteristics: a Church of and for the area; a believing and worshipping Church; a common life providing unjudging and thought-provoking fellowship and local leaders and decision-makers.

A LOCAL CHURCH

A CHURCH of and for the area implies that it is a truly local Church. When the Mayflower Family Centre was first established in 1957, there were long discussions in its Council about the style of community which we should try to establish. One view was that, if a warm and obviously harmonious community of Christians from other parts of the country could be established, this would of itself attract the people of Canning Town to want to know about Christ. The other view which carried the day was that we needed above all to appoint staff who would listen to the district, serve it and shape our community and Church life, as best we could understand it, to match its culture. Those who came to live in the community must understand that they were there to undergird a local work and that, wherever local leadership emerged, they must be willing to step back. The decision meant that we appointed staff who did not always make for the most harmonious community life in the short term, but who were concerned to learn from and to serve the district.

An imported team or community will often be necessary to give the necessary strength for getting a work off the ground. But one of the lessons from history is that from the beginning there must be a deep conviction that locally based Church and community life can develop. The imported community may provide a 'Christian presence'. It may run beautiful services; it may provide for children and dependent elderly people; it may establish good liaison with social workers and teachers. But such a presence will not disturb local people enough to encourage them to believe that Christianity is a serious adult proposition for them. That will only happen if they meet local Christians and realise that they experience a new quality of life in the Christian fellowship.

There is no problem in establishing first contacts. An ecumenical experiment on a new housing estate listed the following meeting points: the schools, the senior citizens' clubhouse, the clinic, the doctor's surgery, the rent office, the corner shop, the shopping centre, the mobile library, the youth centre, the park, the bus, the launderette, and the various organisations which come together in any of the public meeting places. To come were the community centre and library, the pub, the health centre and further schools. There was hardly a lack of opportunity to meet neighbours for someone who was interested in the life of the community.[1]

The trouble with so much Church endeavour is that it goes on and on making first contacts. A vicar and curate visited their parish faithfully year after year. To the question, 'What do you do next, after you've had a good visit?' the answer was, 'I wouldn't want to ask them to church.' I wouldn't have expected a church service to be the next step either. What worried me was that they seemed to go on visiting almost for the sake of it!

A Voice

Bare words alone spoken by a stranger will not present such a challenge. I quoted something I had heard a preacher say to Len, a Canning Town Christian. The preacher had said, 'What we want in this country is a voice.' I asked Len what his comments were. 'You'd have to have lips and a mouth and a body as well, wouldn't you?' he said.

He had learned what the Incarnation teaches better than the author of an article which described two visits to an old man in east London. It said that he had rejected Christ. I read the article again carefully, for that is a solemn thing to say about any man. The only evidence the writer had was that after two doorstep visits he had been sent away with a flea in his ear. I have no idea if the old man rejected Christ or not, for I do not know if he had ever experienced the warmth of genuine Christian fellowship among people of his own kind. The visitor was paid to visit, came from another part of the country, spoke words which possibly rang no bells for the old man.

The difficulty of the 'professional Christian's' communicating with those from a different social grouping is highlighted by the experience of a minister and his wife who lived in lodgings in another part of London, sharing a house with a young working class couple. They said they had tried sometimes to speak with them about the Christian faith but they felt they would get no further unless they were able to share in common life with people whom they recognised as belonging to 'us' and not 'them'.

Meeting needs to grow into friendship. Friendship needs to develop into discovery.[2] We must think it important enough to give priority in our time to join together with other people in the community. The growth of friendship takes time. It takes time too to think out our attitudes to common matters, and to tackle some of the issues which we discover. Issues which bring adults together might be: the need of an adventure play-ground; helping promote a local festival; bringing up children; schools and discipline; local attitudes to unpopular minority groups (black people, 'problem families', gypsies); the rights and wrongs of a current industrial dispute and attending to the dehumanising effect of a large new estate.

Bridge-building

If Christians give priority to indentifying such issues, thinking them through and, if need be, joining hands in action, *bridges* will be built on which there can be the meeting of equals. A bridge in this sense is no gimmick — 'we must run a youth organisation in order to get them in'. It is the response of the servant Church to a genuine need. On such a bridge friendship will develop; a small group will often come into being; there will be mutual support and shared discovery of what is valuable and what is not. Christians will not set out to dominate such a group; but, because it is based on friendship they will be willing to explain why they have the attitudes they do. A discussion about: why they value youngsters whom others call 'yobs' or 'hooligans', enabling other people to develop their potential at work, or how to 'forgive and forget' often leads on to the disclosure of Christian values and beliefs. These can then be discussed on level terms.

Working class people are more likely to relax and to make discoveries in a group than if they are alone, face to face with a vicar. In 1960 my wife and I set aside every Thursday evening as a couple to meet couples who did not come to church, but with whom we had good links. One local couple, then engaged, strongly committed Christians, joined us. One Thursday each couple would go visiting one home or at the most two, regarding the television as a friend which provided common ground, rather than the enemy of a good visit. We would invite them to an evening in our flat the following week. We said in the invitation that there was a discussion at the end of the evening. In our flat there was always background music, for a visit to a vicar's home is a nerve-racking adventure for non-church people and sitting on the edge of chairs in silence is to be avoided. A cup of tea, gossip, sometimes a noisy game called Pit, another cup of tea and some sandwiches and half an hour's discussion.

Late at Night

On evenings like these after some had gone home, and in visits to homes, a high proportion of the best conversations started at 10.30 p.m. To be available for people late at night, when their children are settled and when they feel relaxed, is often in conflict with the kind of spiritual discipline which demands very early rising. This is not to reject the need for

Christians to guard and nourish their own souls. It is to question what the appropriate form of spiritual discipline in urban life may be. It is likely to be different from what is tried and valued in religious communities and among older groups whose children have grown up. Working a 'late shift' also makes demands on a vicar's wife. It is important for a clergyman to organise other time to be in the home. The fact that many men do shift work and other members of the family are in and out at erratic hours is part of the rhythm of life of urban and industrial areas. Often there will be no regular evenings free or regular weekly day of rest. We must not expect people who are yoked to this rhythm to fit into the times which suit us best.[3]

I kept a log book of our Thursday evenings for two and a half years. We visited just seventeen couples. Meetings gradually turned into friendship, not only with us, but with other local couples they met on these Thursdays. Together we made some discoveries, and my wife and I certainly learnt a great deal by having to test our values with our contemporaries, who knew the feel of east London so much better than we did.

After eighteen months I went to a number of the couples, and asked if they would consider joining a 'searching group' for six evenings. Five couples came. They already had the self-confidence that they would not be thought foolish whatever ideas they expressed. I learned then just how powerful a learning weapon has been created when a 'talking group' has come into being, whose members sense that the others feel the same way about life. Such a group may explore deeply into the Bible and into worship. Some of the searching group members joined a confirmation group after a gap.

After two and a half years, my wife and I 'retired' from running these home meetings. By now a number of local couples were convinced Christians, and we felt that our continuing might well inhibit them from taking over. Nothing now happened with the regularity of our Thursday evenings. Few wanted to have a set piece discussion; they preferred subjects to arise from a friendly evening together. In terms of home meetings the number over a period of years was perhaps disappointing. But the experience helped a number of couples over the hurdle of feeling able to invite others into their home. This had not been part of the tradition of the neighbourhood except for parties. A lot of 'dropping in' on each other and of occasional informal evenings resulted. Other groups met, formed friendships and made discoveries by finding common interests through social events or over community issues.

Critical Comments

It is perhaps worth making some critical comments on this one small-scale attempt to build bridges. The 'searching group' became a regular part of the year's programme at the Mayflower. In September we would make a list of perhaps forty adults (always as couples if possible) with whom we had strong links and who might consider joining the searching group. It might be said that, unwittingly, we institutionalised it. The lesson of the first searching group which we sometimes ignored was the eighteen months of working for meeting, friendship and discovery in the bridge groups. By taking a short cut to establishing a searching group we tended to limit its membership to those who were ready to accept an invitation to what sounded like an institutionalised church group.

The second criticism is that we then knew very little of how to offer the continuing support which 'enabling' leadership can give. We saw two opposites: either we ran a group, or we left local people to get on with it by themselves. In fact we did offer support, including a tape recorded 'starter' for a discussion. We made sure someone was always invited who had the ability to spark off a lively conversation. But we were perhaps too dogmatic insisting that the man of the house should always be chairman. We were afraid of producing just a small circle of trained leaders. We insisted that members of the staff should not be present for fear that they would dominate the group. There was much to be learned about the role of the enabler who is in the background to nurture and support the group and helps to provide the resources it needs to keep interest at a high level.

Thirdly, perhaps two different kinds of leadership are required. We needed the 'catalyst' who stimulates a group to come into being. His gift may be to break fresh ground outside the continuing life of a local Church. If it is, he should be set free from most other Church commitments. The gift of pastoral support which helps the continuing life of largely Christian groups is a different gift. One man may not have both. Even if he does, he will not have the time to nurture both kinds of groups properly. When a priest or minister is the only full-time member of the team, he needs to acknowledge that he cannot provide all the kinds of leadership required. He will look for help from among his lay people; clergy or laymen from other Churches (perhaps of other denominations); from diocesan training staff; and from clergy or laymen who are specialists in one field or another.

The Servant Church

The fourth criticism is that we lim.ted our thinking about such bridge groups to those which we could run ourselves. The debate about the servant Church has highlighted this issue. The Christian Church is 'to proclaim the triumphs of Him who has called you out of darkness into His marvellous light'.[4] This does not mean believing that a non-Christian has no light of any kind or that he is unable to understand or do any good. In the servant songs in Isaiah the remarkable

statement is made that God regards Cyrus as His shepherd
and as His anointed even though he has not known Him.[5]
Cyrus is a wise and good ruler who delivers God's people.

This is not to believe that people are Christians who, like
Cyrus, do not profess to know God, yet do His will. To say
that a friend is a Christian, when he says that he isn't, is
extremely patronising. Nor do I regard it as particularly
helpful to describe community-minded people as the 'latent
Church'. But I am very ready to join hands with them, and
learn from them as those who possess intelligence and abilities, which I believe come from the Creator who made us
both.

To 'proclaim the triumphs' of Christ does not mean that
His Church should be *triumphalist*, believing that only we
can run things properly. Once the Church ran hospitals,
schools, clubs, hostels. Increasingly, the state or voluntary
bodies, which are not exclusively Christian, promote such
agencies today. Christians can play a major part in these, if
we come as servants in partnership with others whom we
acknowledge to have God-given abilities too. We do not
have to proclaim, 'Anything you can do I can do better',
with every secular organisation matched by a Church one.
Often, rather than start an open youth club at a Church,
Christians decide to go and join the team running a secular
club.

The philosophy of community development, encouraging
the community to discover and develop its own resources
rather than be dependent on outside leadership is very close
to Christian understanding of God-given potential in all
human beings. Christians as individuals can play the servant
role in neighbourhood groups; the Church as an organisation will sometimes be the one independent body which
can support such a development.

Community groups ought sometimes to be critical of the
borough council. It is often difficult for a community de-

velopment officer not to be in the pocket either of the council
if they pay him, or alternatively, of the most militant group
among his members. An independent voice can bring an
important perspective which stands back a little.

Monopoly of Halls

Often the need is quite simply of premises, and in many
over-crowded areas the Church has a near-monopoly of
halls. In Liverpool, Paddy's Market moved into a district of
Everton in 1968 bringing rubbish and chaos with it. A protest meeting was organised in Shrewsbury House Youth Club
by a member of the local Church.[6] A community association
sprang out of this, though it is entirely independent of the
Church. The critical support of the Church as an organisation, or the lack of support, can sometimes be very
significant.

Christians should not simply climb on the bandwaggon of
community development without bringing a critical mind to
it. In one London district neighbourhood groups came to
represent simply one political position against another.
Christians who worship God rather than a cause, the 'Creator rather than created things',[7] ought to help such groups
to see themselves within a wider perspective. Neighbourhood groups can quickly forget their original purpose and
develop such a rigid ideology that fresh development
becomes very difficult. Like all institutions they need to re-
hearse their past and at the same time be open to the future.
There will be moments at which the Christian has an obligation to say, 'This is something of what the Church is
always talking about when it says . . .'[8] He can never fully
identify with the aspirations of one group against all others.
He must be willing to put his shoulder firmly to the community development wheel without believing that this is the
be-all and end-all of existence.

Dilemma

One clergyman on a large housing estate found himself in a great dilemma when the tenants' association to which he belonged expressed great hostility to the gypsies who were encamped there. His Christian conviction made him concerned for the gypsies' cause, yet he had to admit that he did not feel the same pressures from their presence as those who were bringing up their children on the estate. The Church, not just the clergyman, ought to feel the tension between on the one hand the aspirations of the majority group in the local population and on the other the needs of the poorest (and most unpopular) groups. Part of the proclamation of the Kingdom of God to the working classes involves challenging what is often a contempt for 'problem families' and a bland statement that charity begins at home when subjects like world poverty are mentioned.

But concern for the more dramatic needs of the homeless or the drug addict or the unmarried mother — and groups which have been called 'the interesting poor'[9] — can blind us to the needs of the majority in districts in the inner city and urban housing estates. This will be more difficult in some districts to which those with particular needs gravitate; 'I came to Whitechapel to serve east Londoners. Instead I spend all my time serving Scotsmen, Irishmen and northerners.' 'I've never yet seen a cockney alcoholic; I can't get to the people of the parish in Spitalfields, because the poor won't let me get out of the door.' Perhaps the cockney alcoholics are surrounding missions in Glasgow and Leeds! The servant Church rightly mounts special projects to serve the poor who congregate in the inner city. As I have argued about national government, the Church should acknowledge that these are the casualties of the whole nation and it should make sure that Churches in such areas are given special resources to serve them. Otherwise, the majority who live in such districts and who are not 'casualties' will not be served at all.

A BELIEVING AND WORSHIPPING CHURCH

THE emphasis on the servant Church has often highlighted the care not to 'break the bruised reed' or 'snuff out the smouldering wick', the silent ministry of 'footwashing'; he 'will not make himself heard in the open street'. He will persevere in bringing 'justice to every race'. But the Servant of the Lord in the Servant Songs is not always silent; God makes his 'tongue His sharp sword'.[10] He has given him the 'tongue of a teacher'. If we have had the patience and the interest in people, so that meeting has led to friendship and to discovery, we shall have the sensitivity to know when it is right to name the name of Christ. It may mean waiting for years. But if we are willing to be discovered as well as to discover — which is part of what friendship means — we must be ready to explain what our beliefs are.

The majority of urban dwellers will never come near the institutional Church and will never meet a clergyman. They will only hear the name of Christ and be able to argue themselves straight about what He stands for, if they know workmates or neighbours who carry conviction by the way they live, and who are willing to talk about it. They will not expect to meet someone who knows every answer and has no doubts of his own; they will expect to see the right kind of difference in the lives and attitudes of Christians, if they are to believe that what they say is true.[11] Nothing is more powerful in proclaiming the gospel than the perhaps stumbling words of Christians who, without pretending to any experience which they don't have, try to express what Christ means to them.

There is a dangerous half-truth in suggesting that our experience is all-important. Young people especially demand instant feeling; experience is all. In response to this, the Christian is tempted to say, 'Turn on to Jesus, because our experience is more exciting than drugs or sex.' That is the half-truth. Along with it must go the costly demand that this experience is never for our own sake. We are to be followers of the Suffering Servant, who is the Servant of the Lord and the Servant of others. There is truth and experience which comes from other centuries. Our understandings and feelings have to be tested against these.

Good Preaching

There is an important place for preaching and teaching; this may be in a formal situation in a Church service or a special meeting. It may be that in a discussion the questioning and probing has set up the situation where someone should unashamedly hold forth for ten minutes or more. We should argue for good preaching; if the only sort of learning we tolerate is from the hurried remarks in a television argument ranging between every possible point of view, or from a spontaneous discussion, our understanding of Christian issues will be skin deep. We must welcome a carefully prepared attempt to bring together the Christian revelation and the human situation in which we find ourselves.

Good preaching will take the Bible seriously. It will be expository, trying to set out what the Biblical writers were really getting at. Good preaching will also be existential; it will begin from the pressures of life which people feel. The

bite of the gospel generally comes not when we stop at ex-
pounding Christian belief or principles, but when we go on
to show that a change is needed in attitudes and actions.
Paul was given a hearing in Jerusalem as long as he ex-
pounded his spiritual experiences. It was when he said that
God sent him to the Gentiles that they shouted him down.
He was touching then on the raw nerve of racial prejudice
and the threat to their privileged position.

The Roman Governor Felix let Paul talk about faith in
Christ Jesus. But, when he turned to questions of morals,
self-control and the coming judgment, he would have no
more.[12]

Alongside His earthly demands for daily obedience,
Christ asks us to lift up our hearts, to worship, to dream of
how things might be. In a sense this was the point of His
teaching about the Kingdom of God. It was a dream of how
life would be when God reigned fully. As partners in working for His Kingdom we are to take this dream seriously; we
are to try to work out its implications in every day practice.

For instance, there was the story about a dinner party.
The Kingdom of God was like a banquet at which guests
were the poor, the crippled, the blind and the lame. God
valued people because they were people, not because of any
rank or what they could do for you. The successful, respectable, charity-begins-at-home men were too busy, and sent
their excuses. The story was told because of the existential
situation in which Jesus found Himself in a 'real' dinner
party; it was aimed at people who wanted the best seats and
who valued those who could give them something in
return.[13]

A Piece of Dreaming

Every act of worship is in a sense a piece of dreaming. We see life through God's eyes. We must in due course make the difficult effort to translate the dream into daily obedience, or we shall deserve it when our dreams are brushed aside as vague idealism. The men who do the world's work and the dreamers must take each other seriously. Working men are inclined to undervalue dreamers and to want down to earth answers too quickly. We must encourage one another to dream a little longer. We need to celebrate, to soar above the 'real' world, to indulge in a little holy fantasy. Our dreams and our prayers and our aspirations are part of God's real world too. But the festivity is not to be just a celebration of celebrations, excitement for excitement's sake. It has particular content. Christian worship celebrates the mighty acts of God in Christ, and looks forward with hope to the resurrection of the body.[14] Therefore it must relate to the way we live in the material, physical world this week. If we celebrate the love of Christ in which He makes the first move, we must be ready to make the first move in industrial or family matters. We celebrate His dying in order that we might live. Sometimes He calls us to risk the death of the security we cling on to for ourselves or our children in education or in the community, in order that new life and new opportunities may be possible for others.

The greatest sin in worship is to make it dull. It should have excitement. At the same time it needs to have content. I value a set Liturgy because I am no poet. Especially when it comes to praising God, I am thankful that I can use some of the treasures other men of God with greater abilities have given us both in prayers, in psalms and hymns. Liturgy, rightly used, can help to draw a congregation more fully to participate in worship than an entirely free service where so much depends on one man, unless he has spent long hours with others in planning and rehearsal. But we need not have 'total liturgy'. Assuming that the rebellions of at least some of the Free Churches have been movements of the spirit, we should learn that the Holy Spirit does not wish to be bound within the straitjacket of uniform services.

For example, the Church of England's Alternative Service Book 1980 has taken a first, rather tentative step by allowing alternatives which can be included or omitted and intercessions which can be taken in a variety of ways. Frequently laymen and women take these from the body of the church, and read the Epistle and Gospel. There is a great value, especially in a highly mobile generation, in finding that the framework and the heart of the service is the same wherever we go. But around the central core we should encourage local experiment to go on. Many Christians have discovered what worship is about, because they have shared in a group who have tried to 'make worship' around a theme which has mattered to them. Often (because it takes a lot of time) this will have been during a weekend away together, or it may have been in a service in someone's home, where everyone in the group knows each other well.

Healthy Experiments

It is healthy for experiments to happen in the main services from time to time. To have nothing but experiment would destroy the possibility of participation, because members of the congregation wouldn't know where they were. Many Churches, instead of just having an angry explosion by the young people — or the old people — once a year, set up a worship workshop with representatives of different viewpoints, so that they have to work out a plan which takes each group seriously.

It is unlikely that experimental services can be passed on to another Church, any more than that the songs that most local guitar groups write can become universal. They spring naturally out of a local community and are right there. As soon as they ask to be used universally, they are judged by the standards of professional groups, or of liturgical committees.

Concern about new forms of worship is not only for the sake of those who come to church for the first time. It will certainly help them if Christian worship is seen to be colourful, related to life and celebrating something of the corporate experience and belief of the Christian fellowship. Even more important than this evangelistic reason is the need of new Christians of whatever age. I used to defend the 1662 Prayer Book Communion Service on the ground that it was primarily a service for convinced Christians who had been carefully prepared before confirmation. I was dismayed when they spoke honestly to me, and I realised that they felt it was rigid, wordy and wholly unrelated to their attempt to follow Christ in everyday life. When the Series II Communion Service appeared and we started to use it, one of the most perceptive of our members said, 'It isn't any different from the old one.' This fairly represented the viewpoint of a group to whom all forms of worship were new.

Colour and Ceremonial

Protestants have looked with a suspicious eye at colour and ceremonial, because ceremonial has often expressed untruths. But it can be good or bad, depending on what it is signifying. Outward things are certainly very influential. For instance, a holy table or altar far away from the congregation beyond a screen and choir communicates to many people something about God being far away beyond choir and clergy. Move it to the nave so that the congregation is all around it, and it suggests that God is in the midst of His people.

We all have our ceremonials. An onlooker who could speak no English might suppose from many services that the climax of the whole event is when the collection is brought forward after the sermon and just before the last hymn. The question that should be asked is not, Is ceremonial to be avoided? but, What does it signify? Many Churches work hard for children's services, at finding visual aids and ways of encouraging participation. They know how important 'eye gate' is — and the way the service 'feels'. All the same needs are there for adults, especially in areas where communication is not often done by means of lectures and books.

To make worship interesting, colourful and truth bearing needs hard work. That means giving priority of time to thinking, planning and getting others to take part. This is very difficult if it all falls on one pair of shoulders. I tried hard and rather unsuccessfully to 'change gear' during my years at the Mayflower. At the beginning of my ministry there I had decided that it was right not to give too great an amount of time to plan and prepare for worship. It seemed to me that I must make time for people, no more than twenty of whom ever came to church. As the congregation grew, so I tried to give more time to prepare and plan. I would have done better if I had asked for help from someone elsewhere who would have been willing to give us a day or an evening occasionally to help us think and plan our worship, of if I had appointed to the staff someone who had particular flair and interest in that direction.

The Pentecostal experience and the spontaneity in many West Indian and African Churches in London brings excitement to worship. Other Christians must be interested in an experience which enables all believers to express themselves in worship, including those least able to put feelings into words. Speaking in tongues, repetitive singing and clapping, or forms of dancing allow the whole congregation to participate on equal terms. But many working class Englishmen feel that there is something 'white hot', 'unnatural' about this. They fear 'showing themselves up'. There is a very illogical situation. The same Mayflower members, adults and young people, who would sing their heads off in a coach coming back from a holiday party or a day out, would hardly make a sound when asked to sing some of the same songs or hymns in church.

Establishing that it was possible to wander in and out during the course of the service at the Mayflower gradually helped people to feel relaxed and at home. A 'Sunday special' service was established one Sunday evening a month, when local people ran the service entirely and the clergy sat in the congregation. This seemed to help overcome many inhibitions about 'letting yourself go' in worship.

Informal Worship

It need be no denial of spontaneity to say that we need careful preparation of services. The opposite of formal is informal, not casual. An unrelieved diet of casual, unplanned services will quickly produce a very barren land, though we should encourage quite spontaneous moments in our services. Worship should make our picture of Jesus Christ grow bigger. The danger of concentrating on excitement is that it becomes a celebration of celebrations and can turn those who enjoy it inwards to concentrate on their own experience.

I commented on the history of some Mission Halls and Elim Churches that their very understandable hostility to intellectualism had caused their worship to go round in smaller and smaller circles of personal experience. Instead, worship should stretch our minds. We should find the Holy Spirit giving us fresh insight for the world of work and community. The prophets were the classic Old Testament example of spirit-filled men. They might have stayed no more than 'seers' who could tell Saul where his father's asses were to be found.[15] Then they would have been like the diviners of other religions, with their trances and non-rational words for the initiated.[16] The prophets of Israel had at the heart of their experience a growing relationship with the living God who cared about injustice, false weights in the market and oppression both among the Jewish people and in other nations. The prophet became a *seer* in a new sense. He was to go into the city and *see*.[17] The city today urgently needs insight and vision. He also became a *nabi*, a bubbler-up, a weller-up, in a new sense. He bubbled up about what he saw. The spirit-filled man today ought to be as concerned about such issues of justice in the community as the prophets were. Dr. Leslie Davison, a distinguished Methodist, long to see the charismatic movement producing great scientists, skilled technicians, fine artists and teachers who value knowledge and use it as a charisma, a gift of God.[18]

One spirit-filled man (if a highly erratic one) bubbled up about justice during the German Reformation. His name was Thomas Müntzer. He was executed in 1925 for taking part in the Peasants' Revolt. East German writers have claimed him as an early Marxist — wrongly, for his concerns sprang from the Bible and from Christian worship. He was the preacher in the artisan weavers' guild church in the important industrial town of Zwickau. Today, on the wall of the town hall in huge blue lettered facsimile are reproduced the words with which he once signed the receipt for his stipend, 'Thomas Müntzer qui pro veritate militat in mundo' (who for the sake of truth fights in the world).

At the root of Müntzer's belief was his sense of wonder at the work of the hands of God. God's work is first to be seen in people, he said, Christians, Turks, Jews and unbelievers. From the mystical tradition he drew on the doctrine of the uncreated Logos, 'the light which enlightens every man'. He didn't say that this light was the same thing as human reason, but that by it God may speak directly to all men. Müntzer believed that the preacher must explain Christ's forgiveness, 'But the Work of the Hands of God must have first shown a man reverence (*Verwanderung*) before God, otherwise all preaching and writing is vain.'

Müntzer saw much suffering and inequality; the world did not consistently breathe purpose and goodness to him any more than to us. What he saw written in the universe and in the mind of man is 'the suffering Christ — in head and members'. From his worship grew the attitude which would have eyes to see the changes which God was wanting to bring about in the world, and which should dominate the Christian man's thinking — and attitude of 'ceaseless wonderment'.[19]

Something Beyond

In our age there is much instinctive feeling after 'something beyond'. It appears in folk songs, pop songs, plays like *Godspell* and *Jesus Christ Superstar*. But in the work-a-day world the spirit of our age will have no surprises, no wonder. It believes that, having explained something, it has explained it away. We should strengthen those flickers of wonder, of religious awareness, wherever we meet them.

A German pastor said that he felt he must continue to work in an unchurched area, 'so that the rumour of God should not altogether die out'. The clergyman who insists that church services are only for committed Church members would cut our links with many families at those points of birth, marriage and death where they feel religious awareness. We ought to meet such people where they are, gently questioning superstition, and perhaps helping them on towards an awareness of God in the centre of life and its decisions.

Like other clergy, I worry at asking people to make great

promises in the Baptism service, when they have perhaps never thought about what they mean. I am strongly in favour of offering people the choice between baptism or a service of blessing. The meaning of both services can be explained, and copies given to the parents. The vicar visits a few days later to ask which they have chosen. It prevents him from being put in the position of judge, and enables them to make a responsible decision — whichever way they decide.

Christians are influenced by the spirit of the age. We need to nurture our own sense of awareness of God. Worship, personal and corporate, is life-blood for us. We should expect to feel and understand something about the greatness and goodness of God. We need to develop an attitude of ceaseless wonderment, of being open to surprises. If we strengthen this attitude in our prayers and worship, it will gradually influence our whole attitude to life.

An elderly vicar's wife told me that a woman who was homeless came to the door one morning. She took her to a housing advice centre. Her heart sank when she saw that the young man who was to deal with the problem was wearing jeans, a T-shirt and had an enormous mop of hair. She is a very traditional sort of person, and her instinct felt that a young man like that would be of no use. 'He was marvellous', she said, and told me of his patient day-long search.

The vicar's wife was open to the surprise of seeing such patience and care in a young man dressed like that. I think I know why she was open to that surprise, because I have several times been with them at their prayers. They are always thanking God for what He's meant to them today, and done for them today. Their prayers make them open to surprises.

Significant Occasions

Special occasions are particularly significant in areas where regular commitment to an institution is not part of people's background. We too often measure 'success' by the increase or otherwise of regular attendance. Many Churches of different traditions try to make a few great occasions and visit their members to remind them. At the Mayflower, more came on Sunday evenings to a fairly informal service at 6.30 p.m. than to the Communion service at 10.0 a.m. Once a quarter we put out a 'three line whip' and invited all Church members to a meal followed by a Communion service at 6.30 p.m. One of those four Sundays would be Easter Day. Not everyone came. Often they were not able, sometimes they were not willing, to fit in to the rhythms of life which the Church suggested. We also made the most, as many Churches do, of the days when people's more primitive religious awareness was likely to be touched, Mothering Sunday and Harvest.

For the Harvest Thanksgiving on the Downham Estate at St. Barnabas' Church, a great deal of imagination is put into involving every group who express the life of the estate and who serve its community. Dozens of people of all ages bring symbols of their work or leisure pursuits. They have included a coalman bringing a sack of coal, a youth club member his motor bike, Red Cross members their equipment. It becomes an occasion when the community realises something of the great variety of life on an estate, which can easily think of itself as rows of little boxes, and to acknowledge that God cares about that variety.

St. Paul's Deptford makes big occasions of the great Church festivals and also of an evening service to launch the autumn programme; then, during the Festival of Deptford, there is a special service together with cannon and fireworks on the roof and a 'knees up' afterwards in the crypt. Thanksgiving to God finds a central place in the middle of the community's special effort. Big occasions can encourage a false sense of 'success' measured by counting heads in church. On the other hand there is a genuine value in encouraging Christians, who often feel very few and defensive, by sharing in a Christian celebration in a crowd.

The Claims of Christ

Special evangelistic efforts have the genuinely important effect of keeping in front of Christians our calling to present the claims of Christ. But the special effort must not ignore what we have said about the patient building of bridges; we should not take short cuts from the long journey of meeting, friendship and discovery. At the same time we need to present people at the right moment with the challenge to get off the fence and decide to become followers of Christ. When we felt it was timely to have a special evangelistic effort at the Mayflower, our programme was to have a month in which we attempted to cancel as many meetings as possible at the Centre. This was to set people free to invite groups to their homes during that month. I believe the idea was right. It might have carried people further forward if we had brought from outside someone who could have been free of regular pastoral cares to be an evangelist.

Soon after this, another east London parish invited the Mayflower to conduct a mission. They were thinking of a team of local Christians. Eventually it was agreed that one Canning Town man, Jim Gosling, who had become a Reader, should be set free from all his involvement at the Mayflower for six months. He would go over to the other parish for two evenings a week to meet groups in various houses. Often he took two or three other local people with him.

A NON-JUDGMENTAL FELLOWSHIP

A COMMON life providing unjudging and thought provoking fellowship is essential to make Christ's claims an adult proposition. If there is to be a distinctively Christian contribution to the needs of people within the community, there needs to be a distinctively Christian fellowship. This calls for a common life of the Christians in which that fellow feeling of belonging is nurtured. At once we face the danger that we shall give all our time to maintenance of the Christian company and its common life rather than to mission in the world. But, unless there is a strong common life from which the Christians draw inspiration and thought, they will not have the confidence to bring any distinctively Christian contribution to their community.

A good industrial concern must keep three needs in balance:

> *the task* (actually providing the service which is needed);
> *family feeling* — maintaining good relationships and communications within the organisation;
> *care* for individual members of the organisation.

If any one of the three is neglected, the whole firm and its effectiveness will suffer. If, for example, industrial relations are neglected, the whole of production may cease. If all the emphasis is placed on maintaining a kindly family firm to the neglect of the task it may find that it is producing goods which are no longer wanted by the public.

The Church needs to keep the same balance between its

task of mission, its maintenance of family feeling and its concern to value individual members. And the same processes are needed as in an industrial concern: identifying needs of groups of people; analysing what the real needs are; planning how they can best be met; enabling the gifts of its members to develop and carrying through projects to meet the needs.

Many Organisations

In working class areas, Church membership is generally small. Often there are large buildings to maintain, and there is the sense that 'live' Churches must have the usual round of organisations. This means that it is very difficult to keep the right balance between mission and maintenance. There are only a few to attend to the maintenance which seems so overwhelmingly important that mission slides into a very poor second place.

A small group of Christians working in urban and industrial areas spent three training weekends away together. In the two months between weekends, one home project was to read a book which raised a number of great issues in the world which Christians ought to be concerned about. One woman said, 'Any Christian would agree with that book.' 'They wouldn't, you know', said a shop steward. A clergyman said, 'I think they would agree, but they wouldn't do anything about them.' We then discussed for the rest of that evening what factors stop Christians doing anything about issues in the community. From all round the room came the same story of the time demanded by all the activities 'round at the Church'. One man was deeply involved in a community development project in the immediate area of the Church where he belonged. No one else from the Church was willing to get involved. Further, he felt that Church members were wondering if he was wasting his time. 'What results are you seeing?', they asked him repeatedly. He felt that they could only measure 'results' in terms of people coming to Church activities.

Our priorities in the time we give ought to show what we believe to be most important. I have listed from the Gospels some of those things which Jesus said were not very important to God and some of those which He said were very important:

Not very important to God.

Tradition for tradition's sake.
Ritual washing of cups, jugs, copper bowls.
Sabbath rules.
Keeping respectable company.
Safeguarding earthly possessions.
Tithes of mint, dill, cummin.

Very important to God.

Prayer. Learning what God is like.
Justice, mercy and good faith.
Forgiving and accepting forgiveness.
Caring about people who were hungry, strangers, sick or in prison.
Helping bad characters.
Caring about elderly parents.

I nearly made another list of a Church's weekly or monthly programme. What the Church hall is used for and the way loyal Church members divide their time should reflect their priorities. It ought to show what they think is most important. You might make such a list yourself. A comparison with the priorities of Jesus shows that the Church has often led its members, and its neighbours, to suppose that matters are very important to God which are actually trivial. Often this will be because of the sheer pressures of maintaining the buildings and organisations of the Church, rather than because careful thought has been given to the matter. Membership of any organisation means that we have to give some time to doing things for its maintenance which we might not choose to do.

Some of the engagements in my diary as a bishop fall into this category. There is no escaping some commitments of this kind, and we should not resent fulfilling them. But we each need to ask some sharp questions about our priorities.

Important Things

Another measure of what Church people count important is the correspondence columns of a Church newspaper. Suggest a new translation of the Lord's Prayer, discuss which hand a bishop should use to carry his staff or the ceremonials and furnishings of the Church and you will fill the columns and engage the energies of Christian people for months on end. Meanwhile Christian comment on what we are doing to one another in an industry, or actually meeting our neighbours on common ground where we start to talk about Christ's claims or a project to discover and help those in special need in our own community — these go by default because there isn't enough time for them. We 'strain off a midge, and gulp down a camel'.[20]

Disastrous consequences inevitably follow in all directions. The reaction which followed the age when Christian put Christian to death for not affirming the right doctrine was to say, 'All doctrine is unimportant.' It bred a tolerance which was part good, but part bad too when it said, 'It doesn't matter what you believe.' That was not what Jesus was saying. The task of theology is not to make sure that every last hair is split on every subject as though all subjects were equally important. A major part of its task is to show which subjects are important. We must then be ruthless about limiting the number of man hours we give to the trivial in the city with all its great needs.

Otherwise disastrous consequences follow in matters of right and wrong. If it is really right to be as indignant about whether there are candles or no candles or more candles as about people being homeless, then God is like some erratic sultan, and morality simply follows His unpredictable whims. Any community which makes its own internal arrangements equally important with the 'weighty demands of God's law, like justice, mercy and good faith' is helping to destroy the basis of true morality.

A small congregation often feels powerless to take on the great issues which surround us in urban life. Often its members do not even open their minds to the groups which need understanding and the projects which could help bring them love, because they haven't got time. They might escape from the 'backs to the wall' attitude if they were more ready to acknowledge that the local congregation is not by itself the body of Christ. It is only a part of it. They should learn to ask for help from other Christians, whether in other denominations or in other parts of the city or of the world. And they may often need to go right outside the Church and find resources and allies in secular life.

The Elderly

For example, we became very aware of the needs of elderly people in Canning Town. A series of discussions and sermons about what value we placed on the elderly was followed by a congregational meeting. Twenty-three people between twenty and fifty years of age put their names down as wanting to do something about it. They used the skill of one staff member who asked the advice of an expert in secular community development about how best to discover the real needs. An enquiry showed that there was no evening club for elderly people in the district. Fifteen of the twenty-three agreed to launch initially a small club and to transport the elderly to it. The result was a club in which the elderly did not find themselves organised apart from other age groups but part of a club in which half the membership was under fifty. The fifteen came from several close-knit small groups, some of which had been accused of being cliques, and they discovered one another in serving elderly people. Others consulted a member of the welfare department of the borough. He agreed to run a course for members of several local churches who would be willing to visit on a regular basis elderly people referred by the welfare department. Four of the twenty-three signed up for this. This project fell down, partly because the right sort of continuing support was not maintained.

The Christian fellowship is for mission, and must never forget it. But it needs to strengthen its own common life. There would never have been the twenty-three potential helpers, unless attention had been given to building up the local congregation.

Small groups will be the setting in which people are most likely to discover one another. The Church has been redis- covering this all over the world and in a variety of different patterns. In the parish of St. Barnabas Cray, a large housing estate with clear boundaries (18,000 people, a mile and a quarter across in each direction) the parish was divided into nine sub-parishes in each of which there was a house Church. The whole teaching programme of the Church was geared to the subjects which the house Churches tackled.[21] Something so tidy and organised as this never seemed quite appropriate in Canning Town. Groupings which spring out of friendship, interests or work in the jumble of the inner city which has no very clear boundaries are much more hap- hazard. Moreover, there is a real danger that a small close-knit house group becomes a clique. I am prepared to take that risk, so that strong friendships may be formed and a sense of belonging established. But I have come to believe also in a changing pattern of groups which is much more kaleidoscopic. They come together for a limited period of time. They move around from one house to another. Perhaps they come together for a particular project or to dig deep into a particular subject for six evenings. Sometimes a group will rightly feel its life should continue indefinitely. It must then at regular intervals face the question itself whether its continued existence is furthering the task of mission or not. And it must not make such demands (as a weekly meeting would) on its members that they cannot belong for a while to some other group. To belong only to a group of a dozen or so is bound to mean after a while that it becomes a very like-minded group. It is good to realise that you belong also to a larger Church body which has a common life in which you can share.

Youth Work

The small group is often also the key to Christian youth work. A Church may decide to run its own youth organ-isations or open youth club, or it may choose to join in partnership with a secular youth club. Whichever is the case, young people of fifteen to twenty years of age need some sort of bridge where for them meeting, friendship and dis-covery can take place. It will need to be a mixed group. Often young people will prefer to sit on the floor of some-one's home, listen to records and talk about life than go to the best-equipped club which may be provided.

The open club has its point, but deep Christian dis-coveries are much more likely to be made in a small group which has something of a common life of its own. This can run parallel with a club or organisation or within it, without taking members away from it. Going away for weekends or holidays or for a Sunday ride in a van may all strengthen the common life.

The pattern of Sunday observance is an issue which points out sharply the difference between suburban, town, rural life on the one hand and urban life on the other. When I started work in Canning Town, it seemed to me important as a Christian to say something which was realistic about how a Christian should keep Sunday. As a cricketer it had been important for me to keep one day in seven as a different day and as a day especially for sharing in Christian fellowship and worship. Christians who valued Sunday in this way were happy to go for a walk in the country, to potter in the garden, to read a good book, to write letters, or to listen to classical music. I wondered what pattern would be right to suggest for children, young people and families in Canning Town. They couldn't go for a walk in the country except by going in a motor car; most had no garden; reading good books, writing letters and listening to classical music were not usual activities in most homes. It seemed to me important that the Church should itself offer some opportunity of expressing its fellowship on a Sunday, in a way which was not a long series of religious activities. It would include worship, it might include pop music, outings and a variety of activities which were different from week-night club activities, but which were within the normal patterns which were enjoyed.

Small Nucleus

The policy on which much Church youth work is based is first to build up a small Christian nucleus so that its members influence the others. This is fine, provided it is the right kind of nucleus. What often happens is that tidy programmed organisations by natural selection develop a nucleus of the 'nicer' type. They represent the minority in urban and industrial areas, and already have the firm intention of leaving the district when they marry. Such a nucleus will have little in common with the majority of young people in most open youth clubs, and will be unlikely to influence them. The better way may be for leaders to pray to be sensitive to some real sense of the Holy Spirit's leading to two or three natural groups of friends among the majority group of young people and to work for a nucleus from among them. There will be no more short cuts in this than in the bridge-building described earlier with adults.

If it is agreed that at the heart of the Christian learning process for older teenagers should be informal groups of the kind suggested, there are clear indications about the kind of children's work which should precede them. At one stage at the Mayflower, we found that the hardest group to integrate into our older teenage groups were those who had come up through the children's Church and the Bible class. By processes of natural selection in classes which emphasised reading, writing and good behaviour it was again only the 'nicer type' of youngster who stayed. Then we realised that we had allowed each section of our young people's work to develop on its own, without serious reference to what went before or what followed. We now brought the leaders together to talk about a total policy.

Christian discipleship seemed hardest among the older teenagers. We therefore felt the starting point for a policy must be with the framework which had developed for them and which we felt was appropriate. It meant a very informal common life and Christian discussion generally emerging from shared experiences within it. We agreed that we needed to change the policy of some of the younger groups in order to prepare their members better for the time when they would move into the older groups. It meant that Sunday morning for the children saw carefully laid out play activities, deliberately different from mid-week club life. In the middle of their time together there was half an hour of lesson, story, question time, singing. The helpers found that instead of sitting at the end of the row and trying to keep children quiet, they could make friends with them through the activities. Meeting, friendship and discovery became possible here. And the children were more likely to give full attention for the shorter, set teaching period. Those who were not good at books could find other ways of excelling and were noticed.

Teenage Vows

I should like to see the welcome into the worshipping community separated from Confirmation.[22] Without starting from any dogmatic view, we gradually found ourselves not presenting anyone for Confirmation under eighteen years of age. We knew that we would never allow children from a Moslem background to stand up publicly to make such vows. For that matter we would never have asked children from a lapsed Roman Catholic home to do so. It seemed almost as unreasonable to expect children from a totally unchurched home to make these great vows in public. Eleven year olds or fourteen year olds are likely to bring each other in as a group. This is fine if they are not asked to make any earth-shaking vows (which so often produce an earth-shaking reaction later). I would be very happy for eleven year olds to be welcomed to communion after due preparation, without being confirmed. In a country where fewer babies are being baptised, the question arises whether someone may be admitted to communion without having been baptised. The orthodox liturgical answer must be no. But the logic of the argument against encouraging youngsters to make such great vows without the support of their home is likely to be even stronger. I believe we should

welcome them unbaptised. 'It is better to be disorderly
saved than orderly damned.'

There is a special value in projects which need manual or
technical skills, because men who feel unable to bring any
worthwhile contribution to services or discussions can then
know that they are valued and significant members of the
community. Pastor Boiten and his wife went to live in a 'red
light' street in the old quarter of Amsterdam. Though there
were many churches in the quarter, there was no vicarage.
They bought a ruined house for £1,000. Local people helped
to repair it. The workers were mainly artists or students or
labourers. There were not many middle class people. Later
when they had completed the rebuilding and decoration,
more middle class people came, and the number of labourers
dropped off sharply. So they tried regularly to create new
projects which required manual labour.[23]

Everybody wants a faith in which he can express himself
according to his possibilities. The project does not have to
be on a vicarage or a church or a Church youth club. It can
be in some sort of service for the community. Many Church
members have become involved in play groups or in the
summer holiday projects for children which perhaps
demand two or three weeks of their time. They could
equally join, for example, in working groups which did up
rooms for elderly people in the borough.

Social Occasions

It fits the life of working class communities to make the
most of occasional social occasions. Parties in people's
homes or at weddings are events to support. We tried to
make sure that, at the Mayflower, there was some sort of
party at the centre to which all ages could come together
about every six weeks. This was run by different small
groups of local members. Three or four times during the

summer we raised all the transport we could and went out for a family day on a Sunday after the Communion Service in the morning. Holiday parties and weekends played an important part in strengthening the common life. This was true with youth groups, but also with families for whom we tried to run a holiday every other year. This has more recently been run by local people and is not a 'Church members only' party.

The common life of a Church ideally holds a balance between the atmosphere which is unjudging and accepting and the sense of challenge which provokes thought. Len said he used to think to himself about Church people 'if they were just a little more relaxing, how I'd love to go and listen'. The Christian fellowship which is learning to worship, is wrestling honestly with issues of life and trying to serve the community, has, by its very nature, a powerful challenge about it. It is not always necessary to create a deliberate head-on challenge to newcomers. In the accepting community, the Holy Spirit will issue His own challenges. They may not always be about the sins we should have picked out.

One girl at a Liverpool youth club used to get drunk on cheap wine most Saturday nights, and was often sick all over the club floor. She became a convinced Christian. Later the leader asked her what sin she was particularly aware of before becoming a Christian. 'Talking behind other people's backs', she replied.[24]

The talking group in which no one is made to feel silly is a powerful weapon in establishing the right sort of self-confidence. No one can seriously start feeling responsible about any matter until he has sufficient confidence in himself to believe that he could carry it through. It is as important that a group should have a Christian *structure* as that it should have a Christian *content*. For instance a Bible study group might have plenty of Christian content; but if it always deferred to one person's opinion, or if it discouraged its members from telling the truth to each other, because it assumes that Christians never disagree, its structure would be anti-Christian.

I have often doubted if I did the right thing at one meeting of the monthly discussion group which was called 'the Men of the Mayflower'. We used to talk about many issues at work. That month a rather bitter dock strike was dragging on. I knew that there were dockers present who held very strong and opposite views. I didn't raise the subject, because I feared that the division might break the group. I rather think I should have been willing to raise it with all the implications for following the matter through. Having to attempt to 'speak the truth in love' might have made the group a far more real body.

Disagreement

An unjudging fellowship ought to be able to take disagreement. Indeed it is a vital part of loosening up people's thinking processes to belong to a group where Christians disagree, yet stay together. The ideas of the group to which they belong have always been a major influence in the lives of many working class people. As new ideas are presented to them, they will naturally want to have a group which they can use as a sounding-board. For those who have grown up with little 'moral ballast', there is a special need for a 'communal conscience'. Yet immediately there are great dangers. What is acceptable behaviour to the group can quickly turn into as rigid a set of rules as any written code might do. Those who have not yet learned to think on their feet can too quickly snatch at clear rules. An unjudging yet challenging group will help individuals to 'stand back' and sift the true from the false in their conscience. It should help them to question the presuppositions which they bring about what is 'spiritual' or 'right' behaviour.

The content of a group is important as well as its structure. We are not to have fellowship simply for fellowship's sake, though enjoyment of one another's company will properly be one of a group's priorities. The agenda should come from the life of the group's members. Perhaps it needs two or three sessions of talking on subjects which everyone has some knowledge about. Then a 'brain-storming' session may throw up a series of subjects which matter to the group. When a subject has been opened up, the group's leader must hold it to asking what the Christian faith has to say about the matter and often to open the Bible to see how it relates. Many Christians feel that they are very ignorant of the Bible, but often, when they are pressed about what it has to say about a matter, they are excited to find that they know more than they expected.

In Silence

A group which knows each other well may dare to pray together or to share in silence together. The one part of our evening service at the Mayflower which was valued most of all was a minute of silence. It is in an intimate group which trusts each other that we are most likely to prove that spirituality is not confined to communities where 'everybody knows what it is like to move slowly, to walk solitary behind a plough'.[25]

In a house Church in East Germany, a moral question arose about a new conscription law. After two hours they were unable to see any right answer, either from their Bible study or their discussion. They broke off in order to share the Holy Communion, calling on one of their number, an engineer, to read the words of institution and to break the bread. Then they turned to the ordained men in their company with a list of questions of Biblical interpretation and Church history which they needed answering before taking up the discussion again at their next meeting.[26] They saw clearly the role of the professional.

The story raises the question of local leadership and local ministry.

LOCAL LEADERSHIP

ROLAND ALLEN'S book *Missionary Methods — St. Paul's or Ours?*, written in 1912, has rightly received much recent attention. His main thesis was that the modern missionary Church brings all the leadership, all the answers and all the money from outside, making the local Church dependent, and wasting its distinct and God-given gifts. By contrast, St. Paul founded a self-reliant Church in four provinces of the Roman Empire between A.D. 47 and A.D. 57. He appointed local leaders after what we would regard as a minimum of training.

It is a proper deduction from the New Testament to expect that, in any community in the world, Christ can build His Church, and that appropriate local leadership will emerge. Roland Allen needs to be taken seriously, but he misleads us when he argues from the speed of St. Paul's work, as though we too could see Churches firmly established after a missionary visit of at most eighteen months. Perhaps the clue to the difference in our situation is discovered at this point: 'St. Paul . . . so taught that no Church of his foundation was without a strong centre of respectable religious-minded people. These naturally took the lead, and preserved the Church from rapid decay.'[27] (Presumably he meant the Jews and the 'God fearers'.)

It is precisely the problem of the big city that there is district after district where the 'respectable, religious-minded people' have moved away every generation. We have to press Roland Allen's thesis further than he did himself, and believe that, in these districts, too, strong indigenous leadership can develop. But the time scale must be altered. It needed to be so in the mass movements in India among those with less educational and religious background. Bishop Azariah guided a mass movement with great skill for thirty years, aided by a number of 'exceptionally able and self-effacing European missionaries,'[28] in order to bring to birth an indigenous Church with its own leadership.

In the inner city there is a need for able and self-effacing staffs to come and stay for longer rather than shorter ministries. If they really believe that God can develop local leadership and want Him to do so, they will see it emerge — slowly.

A neighbouring minister asked if the local leadership which was emerging at the Mayflower was all dependent on the fact that we had a large staff. I answered by telling him about a row which had taken place the night before. A man who had been a Christian some three years and had begun to run a youth group himself had become very angry because his brother had been choked off by the senior youth leader. Two whole families said they were 'never coming round to the Mayflower again'. The senior youth leader was fairly new to Canning Town; the strongest support he received was from one local man who had been carrying responsibility in one group or another for eight years. Then another young man came in; 'When you've been here as long as I have,' he said, 'you'll realise that that sort of explosion happens every few months. They'll be back.' In due course his prophecy was proved right. He had been bearing responsibility in different groups for five years. The authority problems which had led to the row do not give way to a mature acceptance of responsibility in a year or two.

Taking Responsibility

One of the greatest lessons I learned from George Burton was about introducing those who had never previously taken a lead to accept responsibility. He never initially asked anyone to take charge as an individual. It was always two or three, perhaps even seven or eight. The group of friends gave confidence to one another, made it enjoyable and kept the momentum going when someone had a 'down' patch. Then sometimes individual acceptance of responsibility emerged. Particular tasks were often given in the first instance before someone had time to think and worry about it; 'Take charge for me in the swimming pool John', he said and left him to it. He was back twenty minutes later. Then he made a point of telling me more than once in front of John how he had accepted responsibility; or 'Take charge of the club for me tonight, Jim. I've got to go and visit someone.' Jim had been prepared for this moment by a series of tasks over quite a time.

The 'method' was to drop people in at the deep end, and then to stay very close in support. Many were introduced to accepting responsibility who would never have signed up for a course. The first huge hump of self-confidence had to be overcome before people could see themselves as those who could accept responsibility. Once the confidence is established, courses can begin to offer invaluable insights.

The emphasis on the word *leader* itself often draws us away to look in the wrong direction. The immediately reliable man, or the fluent speaker isolated from a group of friends, may be the least able to offer the kind of leadership which will be respected. We came to realise that we used the word 'leadership' very differently at the Mayflower. Everyone was expected to be a leader in our sense of the word. Leadership became a synonym for accepting responsibility. A research worker in a political organisation said, 'I'm suspicious about the way you Christians talk about leadership. To me leadership is found through a group of informed individuals arguing round a table.' In a community association or a trade union or a Church, working class leadership emerges in a strongly corporate way, when there is a task or project the group wants to achieve. Individuals within the group will then accept particular responsibilities towards that task.

Instrumental and Expressive Leadership

There will be 'instrumental' leadership and 'expressive' leadership. The secretary who makes sure that people know what is expected of them is an example of instrumental leadership. The man who can put into words the strong feelings of the group is an example of expressive leadership. We should not expect that both will always be found in the same individual. A more corporate view sets free varied gifts of leadership. Often the expressive leader is not interested in maintaining organisations. But he can be the one who foresees, dreams, discovers the vision which shapes the destiny of the group.

One of the problems of the wish for tidy democracy in the Church or anywhere else is that the committee system loads the dice so heavily in favour of those who live by diaries and are used to committee meetings at work. Again the majority group in working class areas is squeezed out. If leadership is the corporate and varied attribute I have been describing, it should not rest in one or two pairs of hands indefinitely. It should move round. Churchwardens, deacons, or Parochial Church Council members should not always be the same few. Simple patterns can ensure changes; for example many

Church Councils agree to the rule that one third should retire every year and not seek re-election for at least a year. Often Church affairs can be better conducted by having fairly frequent meetings of the whole congregation, especially where that is small — perhaps over the cup of tea after a service.

Part of the difficulties of trade unions could be ascribed to their dependence overmuch on communicating ideas from the centre through the institution with its central and branch committees. Often the strength of an unofficial liaison committee will be that it rests its life on frequent factory gate or shop floor meetings to which everyone can come. To be fair, part of its appeal is also that it doesn't have to act as responsibly as a union. Institutions in union life and in Church life are valuable. Their problem is to work out how continuity can marry spontaneity. They need to keep on learning the art of encouraging all their members to participate, and they must take every step which will help that to happen.

This means *ad hoc* working groups wherever possible rather than regular committees. It means drawing into the decision-making process those who would never endure a regular committee life — or changing drastically what a committee's life is like.

Steady Men

In many churches, as they are, it may be said that only one or two people answer to what I have described as the majority group in such areas. The Church majority is content with arrangements as they are. Thank God for the steady men and women who are regularly there at all the meetings! Many churches would collapse without them. But they must ask themselves if their ambition is to maintain Church life as it has been or to plan for how it might be. A committee made up largely of those who travel back from a suburb to which they have moved, and of those who do not 'feel' about life as the majority of the district feels, will be unlikely to plan the right kind of programme for a Church of and for the area. It would often be better for the 'Church that might be' — and for themselves and their new neighbours — if those who move out of a district to a quite different neighbourhood cut their links with their old Church. Our fear would be that it would then collapse; perhaps some organisations might have to close. But it would be a step in the faith that there can be a locally based Church.

If those who are not used to committee procedures and polite discussion begin to join in the decision-making process, we are in for some storms. This is as true in Church life as in secular community development. We must learn to welcome it, and to budget for the additional time that it will take and stress that it will cause.

Dave found it very difficult to discuss matters coolly. He was very antagonistic to the whole idea of committees. He could be pressed into joining a working group; if he felt strongly about a matter he would often make a sharp personal attack on those who held the contrary opinion. They would often answer him calmly. He would then want to crawl away, saying to himself, 'I'm too bad. I'm not like you Christians.' My task was to try to keep David and others like him in the ring. He had insights which the Church badly needed.

In many ways the best feature of British democracy is to pay the Leader of the Opposition a handsome salary with the duty of opposing the Government. If issues are to be debated fairly and fully, there needs to be coherent opposition. This is no less true in Church life. We need to believe that the Holy Spirit inspires the opposition. Nothing so inhibits honest discussion as the kind of Church council which says that it never takes a vote and expects all decisions to be unanimous. Such an attitude often causes those who don't agree with what they think is the vicar's line to keep silent or to withdraw. Part of the route to Christian maturity is to learn to hold strong convictions, to face others who hold different convictions, and to find the way through to genuine respect and partnership.

Changing Situation

The Church in the modern world is facing a constantly changing situation. How to organise ourselves to respond to change is a problem in all districts. Everywhere there will be strong motives for wanting to hang on to the institution as we have known and valued it in the past. The problem is in some ways greater for the church in working class districts. People are 'relatively less mobile'; they are more likely to know only one local Church; their experience of a variety of Christian ideas is likely to be limited. Clergy and ministers are partly responsible for this. We have been willing to open ourselves to different Christian viewpoints, yet have felt a need to shield 'our' people until they are 'more mature'.

Talking groups which follow the issues which matter most to their members are one great way of loosening up rigid attitudes. If anything can be on the agenda, even 'the way we've always done things here' can find a place. Most groups need someone from outside to help them hold up the mirror to see what are their own objectives and whether their Church life and organisations are serving those objectives effectively. 'If you clergy and ministers want lay people to get out and meet their neighbours, you must set us free from all these organisations', a woman told a commission on evangelism.

The right sort of 'consultant' who can help a Church set some objectives for the next year, and return to help them review their objectives each year, could do more for the mission of the Church than many visits by a bishop on great formal occasions. The problem for an Anglican bishop in an English diocese is that his span of care is so wide that he cannot offer that kind of time to each parish.

In Southwark Diocese in London a full-time borough dean has been appointed in each of the five inner boroughs in south London. His span of care takes in about thirty parishes, serving between 230,000 and 300,000 people. He is committed to the mission of the Church in that borough. If a parish comes to know and trust him, it might dare to ask him help them in a joint consultation about the mission they are called to and the way in which they are attempting it.

It is good to argue for strong local roots and responsibility. That should not lead to rejecting the professional skills a minister or priest may bring who has been trained in theological colleges, as the insights which someone like a borough dean may bring from outside his parish.

Small Steps

Much of this section has been dreaming of the Church as it might be. If we have faith and hope, we must take some practical if small-scale steps towards that Church. To take steps towards a Christian working class movement would both sound too grand, and might seem a sinful concept. To set out to produce a predominantly working class Church — or a black Church — is in isolation a sinful concept. But to enable some consciously working class groups to come together is, I believe, a proper response to the segregation which the development of big cities has brought about. The sin is not the consciousness of class or race. The sin is the segregation plus the assumption that one group is superior to the other. Groups who have received the wrong end of the stick in jobs, housing, schools and Church life need first to take confidence in one another.

We must always assert that this is not the last word. When

they have the strength and confidence a like-minded group gives them, they must then come to meet other groups on level terms. They must acknowledge that there is one Church and one human race. Paul needed to strengthen and fight for a Gentile Church, if it was ever to be able to meet the longer established Jewish Christian Church on level terms. Then he asserted firmly the truth that there is one Church and that each is poorer without the full contribution which the others can bring to the whole. The Church cannot identify wholly with any one race, nation or social group.

I invited some ten clergy and ministers from districts near my home in Peckham to discuss the possible value of bringing into being a pilot scheme of an 'inner city group' of lay men and women. The group would be made up of those who affirm rather than leave behind the working class culture of their district. It would be a talking group in which those who joined would take confidence from meeting one another. It might become a group which took on certain projects. It would decide its own agenda. Nine out of the ten agreed that this could be valuable. I then asked how many such laymen they might be able to name from each parish. The senior man present said, 'I could name one only. That says something by itself. He was confirmed a year or two ago. And perhaps that says something too about what Church life does to people.' Most of those present were able to suggest one or two, perhaps four or five. If our understanding was correct, and the numbers of mainstream working class people is so small in some of our best inner city congregations, it highlights our problem. These ones and twos have never belonged to a Christian group with others who feel the same way about life in their neighbourhood and at work. Within such a group a great deal of insight and ability might emerge which remains hidden while a man feels that he is alone in his views in the Church circle.

A Learned Ministry

The Churches in England have put much emphasis since the Reformation on the need for a learned ministry. We have wanted an objective yardstick by which to measure whether men have the right ability to be ordained or to be admitted as readers or as lay preachers. That yardstick has generally in recent years been men's achievement in written exams or in written essays. It loads the scales heavily against the local leaders who may emerge from churches in the inner city and from large council estates. It means that the Church accepts the judgment of the world that leadership belongs to certain groups who achieve well in school. If it is accepted that achievement in school is closely linked to social class we are denying that in Christ 'There is no such thing as Jew and Greek, slave and freeman, male and female'.[29]

That famous text doesn't simply mean that all those groups can equally be accepted by Christ, while each keeps his or her station in the ranking order. It meant in New Testament days a breaking of deeply held convictions among the predominantly Jewish church. Gentiles could be leaders in the Church as much as Jews. In Africa the Church dared to make an ex-slave a bishop. In Britain today the text challenges us to show that in Christ those with the appropriate ability should be given leadership whatever their social class or academic achievement — or sex — may be. I do not want to ordain dull men or women. They must be able to trade in ideas, to think on their feet.

The Church should dare to give a lead to society in recognising that there are other yardsticks and other ways of training than at present exist. The youth service has unwisely shut the door on those who have learned in the school of experience rather than in colleges of education. After the Albemarle Report in 1958 the door was left open to those who had served for five years in a grant-aided post. The minister could then decide what mixture of experience and training he would accept for a qualified youth leader. That door has been shut, though training courses now exist on which acceptance is measured by continuous assessment rather than by written exams.

Elizabeth Pepperell was a member of the Newsom Committee which in 1963 published its report on *Half our Future* in secondary schools. She told me that she began that enquiry holding the view that many of the ablest teachers in urban areas were those who, as older men and women, were given the short emergency course of training after the war. The view was very unpopular with the majority of the teaching profession. However, she finished the enquiry holding the view more strongly than ever. More than any other body, the Christian Church ought to take a lead in showing that we believe God can produce appropriate leadership in every community.

The Southwark Ordination Course has established that a non-residential training can be appropriate for many men. It has been under pressure to prove that its academic standards are the same as those of residential theological colleges. Exams and essays figure largely in its life. It has not therefore helped significantly more men from the groups I have written of into the ordained ministry.

Natural Leaders

When the Bishop of Stepney, Trevor Huddleston, ordained four local men from the parish of St. James the Less, Bethnal Green and St. Mark's, Victoria Park, it was spoken of as though it was something utterly new in the history of the Church. It would only be new if history were confined to the last four hundred years and to Europeans. In the New Testament Church, and widely in the world Church today, as well as in history, men have been ordained who are the natural local leaders.

In the New Testament there was an itinerant ministry (Paul, Barnabas, Timothy) — and an emergent, local ministry (elders in each congregation).[30] Roland Allen pointed out how, in China, concentrating all the functions of ministry in one man's hands limited the exercise of God-given abilities in a local Church. It silenced the natural local leaders or by sending them away to college cut them off from their own people, 'from whose intellectual and spiritual life they have been so long absent'.[31] The sometimes naïve judgments about industrial political issues of French worker priests coming 'from outside' might not have been made by worker priests who had never been withdrawn from working in that kind of job.

The rigid distinction that either a man is 'ordained' or 'not ordained' only arises in a Church which has lost the New Testament conception of 'varieties of ministry'.[32] Various distinctions must be drawn, not just the one between clergyman and layman. There is a distinction between the concept of a priest and of a clergyman. We have identified ministry with being a clergyman, a learned clerk in Holy Orders, belonging to a profession like other professions. The ordained presbyter or team of presbyters should be the focus of the Christian body in a neighbourhood or in a work situation or community situation in which people share. A man does not have to be paid and to live in a parsonage house to be an appropriate person to share in such a ministry.

What would they do? is the question which has regularly been pressed about every experiment of this kind. It is first a question about what the Church should be doing in any given situation. The question is not, How can some working class men be ordained? Rather it is, Given the company of Christians in any situation, how do we train them all, then select some and authorise some for particular ministries?

We need 'situational ministries'. Here is a modern university. What kind of ministers does it need? Here is a large urban parish with, for example, a considerable immigrant housing area, several factories, a settlement and a community development project. What kind of ministers are needed? The answer to each question must be different.

In Every Grouping

To ordain working class men without withdrawing them from their jobs, would be a sign that the Church takes seriously that leadership can develop in this section of the community. The truth about the Church is that it should be rooted in every nation and every social grouping. It is a right expression of this truth that some working class men should be ordained to what is seen to be an equal ministry with those who have been trained in colleges.

The most serious criticism is that this would damage a proper sense of responsibility among laymen — that they may say 'If he's a minister, I'll leave him to get on with it'. (This problem is not avoided when there are only traditionally selected clergy.) I believe it is more likely that laymen will say, 'If *he* can be ordained, perhaps I could lead a lay project, or join the neighbourhood council or lead a discussion group in my home.' The ordination of such men could help to close the gaps between local people on the one hand and professional clergy, social workers and teachers on the other. Christians are rightly concerned about the 'clergy line' which sets clergy apart from laymen. But the divisions in urban and industrial areas are less clergy/laity than professionals/working class people.[33]

A working party appointed by the Advisory Council for the Church's Ministry criticised proposals for local ministries, such as those in Bethnal Green and Bow. The value of speaking of an indigenous Church was sharply questioned. 'There is no Biblical or theological reason why the local manifestation of the Church has to be born in or native to a particular place, class or culture ... In post-colonialist countries it may be expedient to proclaim the doctrine of the indigenous Church, but it by no means follows that, except in the short run, it is healthy.' They also questioned whether the working class forms a separate cultural entity at the present time.[34]

Ultimate Goal

The whole of this book shows that I believe that there are, in fact, sharp and continuing divisions in our present society. I have acknowledged that the ultimate goal must be both universal rather than class solidarity and one Church rather than black Churches or predominantly working class — or middle class — Churches. But when there is as massive a gap as I know in working class London, 'the short run' of working for a proper indigenous expression of the Church may have to be not less than forty or fifty years. I do not argue that an 'indigenous' Church must be 'born in' or 'native to a particular place, class or culture'. After the Church has been at work in urban and industrial areas for a hundred years or more, the fact is that it still relies on an ordained ministry selected from every section of the population except the one made up by the majority in those areas. It has largely failed to root responsible, self-reliant congregations there. It is against that background that I am determined to work for indigenous Churches. By that phrase I mean that the Church's membership and leadership should properly reflect a cross section of the population. At present it does not. The Biblical doctrine of the Church has both a local, a congregational and a catholic principle to it.

The A.C.C.M. working party, having acknowledged that

ability and intelligence may not be properly assessed by academic yardsticks, returns to fears about 'lower standards', 'suitability of occupations' and 'the principle of congruity'. These phrases sound to me like the expressions of a Church which reflects the hierarchies of society rather than one which challenges them. It is determined that clergy should be professional men among other professional men.

The social significance of the priesthood was seen as one of the major factors in strengthening hostility to the French worker priests. People expected priests to be a professional class like other professional classes. Many laymen in Britain want to keep the clergy special, dignified and different. The first generation of local and factory floor ministers will have some particular difficulties to surmount. They will not be a class apart, except in the sense that all Christians should challenge the values of any social group, but some will expect them to behave as though they were.

If God-given and appropriate gifts of leadership are emerging in the local Church or among Christians in their work situation, we may ask who we are to withhold ordination? Peter asked, 'Is anyone prepared to withhold the water for baptism for these persons who have received the Holy Spirit?'[35] Central to Paul's idea of the Body of Christ is God-given charisma. The Church has narrowed down the kind of gifts that it recognises by ordination. If another style of leadership and another set of gifts is appropriate in working class areas, a widened selection should be held to be appropriate too.

The A.C.C.M. working party thinks of clergy as individuals apart, each holding the whole range of responsibilities in their hands. So long as we think in this way, we are right to be very cautious in selection, looking for safe, all-round men. Once it is accepted that a team of ministers is the norm, we may dare to widen the range of those whom we select.

Styles of Life

What would be the effect on a working class Christian of being designated as a leader in the Church, even if he were not withdrawn to a residential college for his training? When men are designated as trade union leaders, they sometimes change their style of life, and no longer see issues in the same way as their members. A man's frame of reference will be changed, if he spends a lot of time at party and international conferences, or alternatively at Church synods. When he is a designated leader, he takes on a new role. He is not simply reacting to decisions; he is making them.

Some of the French worker priests have argued against working class men being ordained for these reasons. It is a measure of their disenchantment with the Church that they assume that to hold any designated office in the Church and to receive any form of training for the ministry would drive a wedge between that man and his class. It is a serious objection. If his main 'reference groups' are embedded in working class life, a working class minister need not reject his class of origin, any more than many trade union leaders do. Further education of any kind will give him greater social mobility, greater degree of choice and wider terms of reference. To some extent he must face that these influences will set him apart from his fellows. If he then accepts promotion at work and spends most of his spare time with clergy chapters, social workers and Church members of a largely middle class group, he will gradually lose any sense of belonging to his neighbourhood, even if he still physically lives there. Suppose on the other hand, he belongs to a Christian group mainly comprised of working class laymen, is involved in local tenants' association life, is committed to trade union life at factory floor level, and suppose his social life includes a genuine meeting with his neighbours; then he is likely to

maintain a relationship with his fellows in which two-way
learning can take place.

'Ordination on the Cheap'

One of the fears is about lowering standards, about 'ordination on the cheap'. The four men from Bethnal Green and
Bow committed themselves to five years of training in the
evenings after work and at a number of weekends. They
were made deacon after three years and will be ordained
priest after five. Their training has focused mainly round
their vicar, but he has increasingly used other resources;
there has been a weekend with the Southwark Ordination
Course; there have been six evenings of small group experience with an experienced trainer from Chelmsford Diocese;
a variety of different men and women have come to their
training sessions. The strain of such a course on a man and
on his family is often much greater than the college years
which English clergy more normally experience.

These men knew when they began training that they
would be licensed to officiate for seven years. After that time
the bishop would consult with them, the vicar and the Parochial Church Council before renewing their licence. If they
move, they will not necessarily be given a licence to officiate
in another parish.[36] Some criticisms have made much of the
need for any ordained men to be comparable and inter-
changeable with any others. This bluff ought to be called.
More than half the present clergy in the Church of England
are quite incapable of ministering in urban and industrial
areas, and readily acknowledge it. No one believes that we
should refuse them ordination. Few, if any clergy are actually capable of a ministry in any and every kind of district.
No more should we refuse it to those we believe to have
appropriate gifts for these areas — or rural areas.

We can have no over-confidence that we know how to

provide appropriate training. Its objective should be to stretch a man to learn from his experiences, and to dig deep into the Bible, Christian history and contemporary Christian thought in order to be able to reflect theologically on those experiences. He must have sufficient confidence in his grasp of the Christian gospel and the Biblical material to be flexible enough to apply this to life. And he will need to develop personal maturity. He will share in providing a local ministry in partnership with the mobile professional ministry trained in theological colleges. Together they will have the task of enabling, teaching, supporting the Christian community.

THE FIVE CALLINGS

BELIEF in local leadership challenges the view of the ordained ministry which sees the minister or the priest doing all the work of the Church and perhaps asking laymen to help him. This has left some clergy confused about their role. Others have wondered if there is a man-sized job to be done. *All my experience leads me to believe that there is a vital and demanding task of lifelong ordained ministry to which men are rightly called.*

The five callings which Paul listed[37] are all highly relevant to ministry in urban and industrial areas:

1. *Apostles* — men sent on a mission, often to an area or to a group within an area where there is little Christian presence. We are called to live, to be.
2. *Prophets* — men with a word or an action for the

community, demonstrating along with local Christians
God's concern for all people there.

3. *Evangelists* — men who really believe in the living
   Christ, who along with local Christians will name the
   name of Christ to those who do not know Him.

4. *Pastors* — helping to be the anchor man, the elder, enabling Christians to develop their gifts, and offering
   pastoral care to individuals.

5. *Teachers* — injecting fresh ideas, stretching people to
   think about their experience, helping them towards
   deeply rooted Christian understanding.

These five callings are all 'to equip God's people for work
in His service, to the building up of the body of Christ'.
Clergy and ministers are not to try to do all the work themselves. They are essentially to be enablers to God's
people.

There are no short term answers and in these areas we
generally need ten year rather than three year ministries.
Father John Groser told me that, when he had been in Stepney for three years, a docker said to him, 'I suppose you'll
be off soon, like the rest of them.' This poses problems of
how a man and his family can be given the right sort of
support and stimulus to enjoy their ministry and to keep
professional standards and thought sharpened. Attitudes
have much to do with a man's ability to serve his area well.
He is not likely to be taken seriously by the people he wants
to serve, unless he respects them, expects to receive enrichment from them as much as he expects to give, and
comes to enjoy life there. We have overdone the sense of its
being some heroic sacrifice to go and make our home where
millions of our fellow countrymen have to live out their
lives.

A bishop said to a new vicar he was instituting to an inner
city parish, 'Don't bury yourself. Keep in touch, and we'll

find you something in about five years' time.' There has been an unspoken career structure for the ordained ministry; it is fine to go to the inner city or housing estates when you're young, strong and free, but, if you're any good, you should then move on to minister to a 'more thoughtful' congregation. Then when you are old, you go to a rural parish.

Urban and rural areas both suffer from this. The strong Churches receive much more than their share of what are judged as the most able and mature ministries. It is healthy to have some 'all-rounders'. It is healthy, too, to have some who specialise in understanding and serving urban or rural areas for most or all of their ministry.

Practical Steps

There are practical steps which the Church can take to support its full time staff.

Sensitive Episcopal Support

This can be given whether by an episcopal Church or not, and whether by a bishop himself or not. A Church can benefit from a consultant who understands and shares its task; so a priest or minister can benefit from setting some objectives and reviewing them at intervals with a bishop, a borough dean, a superintendent minister or a friend. Some see this as 'breathing down the neck' of the man, destroying his independence. That depends on whether any lessons about 'enabling leadership' have been learned. This requires the right touch to win other men's trust. It cannot be compelled. Such a joint work consultation often has the effect of 'loosing' rather than 'binding' burdens on a minister's back. Most ministers are inclined to be perfectionists and whip themselves for failures, which may not be seen as failures when looked at with a more objective eye. Many others don't dare look at their work, because they fear it may reveal failures they can't bear to face.

What is needed is not simply a shoulder to cry on and friendship to a man and his family. It is someone who understands the organisation well enough to be able to ask questions about a man's work, and to work towards removing some of the frustrations. Pastoral care and good administration are both parts of the support a minister needs.

In-service Training and Sabbaticals

The bishop who told the new vicar not to bury himself had no doubt seen many busy clergy who had stopped thinking long ago. One of the lessons I deduce from history is that we don't simply need great pastoral hearts in such areas. We need help to reflect on our work. We need to accept that education is a continuing process for ourselves. No less than those in other callings we need to go on being faced with new ideas.

In-service training courses are available on a great variety of subjects. Generally these are for 'the professionals', even though they may sometimes bring together ministers with teachers, youth leaders, community workers, doctors and social workers. In-service training may quite properly be for the purpose of stimulating and deepening the individual's own knowledge and thought. If its objective is to enlarge ideas of ministry to a particular neighbourhood, it must take each man's neighbourhood very seriously. One training project requires a written analysis of a man's situation before he comes on a course. Part of the course is to encourage him to produce a plan for ministry. One of the staff members of the course visits him later to help him assess how this is working out. And there are two two-day periods some months later when the course is re-assembled to review progress. Ministers are encouraged to bring some laymen with them on at least one of these.[38]

Another project plans to run its courses with equal numbers of those who have academic training and those who don't but are the people of the area. The objective of this is that local people and professionals should meet on equal terms and that urban training courses should not simply be comprised of professionals talking about what 'they' need.[39]

Practical problems of money can be overcome if in-service training is regarded as a priority. The bigger barrier lies in the attitudes of congregations and of ministers themselves. Often congregations judge their minister's performance by how busy he is seen to be. He returns from the stretching experience of a course, and they ask him if he has had a nice holiday. The minister himself will only believe that such courses should have high priority if he takes seriously the reality that he faces a rapidly changing world, that a major part of his calling is to trade in ideas, and that he is to remain a disciple all his life.

However great the practical difficulties, the Church must find ways of providing lengthy sabbaticals for clergy and their families. Few other professions demand that their members live on the spot where they work, bringing additional opportunities but also additional pressures. Many clergy and ministers move from a post because they feel played out. A sabbatical would often help them to come back with fresh insight to an area they have come to love and understand. It also enables a man to pull out of some commitments he's involved in, and to have some field of choice again when he comes back. At the Mayflower (where most of us lived on the premises) each member of staff was expected to have a long leave of three or four months every three or four years. One result was that during its first fifteen years it has had eleven staff members who have stayed seven years or more.

Team Ministry

The need is posed wrongly when people speak about the loneliness of the clergy. This provokes the retort, 'How can a Christian minister be lonely in a parish of 10,000 people?' Rather it is the lack of the sharpening effect of professional colleagues which can lead to loss of fresh thought and hope. I believe that the best team is found by local Christians bringing their insights and gifts into partnership with the particular skills the 'professionals' can bring. Sometimes large clergy teams have meant that local Christians have felt there was nothing left for them to do. We must not make that mistake over again. There is added strength to a team when it contains several different disciplines rather than being only a team of clergy — a parish worker, a youth leader, a secretary, a social worker, a community worker, a doctor . . . I shall discuss the question of formal team ministries under the heading of reorganisation. But, if we believe in working in teams, we need not wait for pastoral schemes.

If it is important enough, we shall find the time to meet. Sometimes a weekly meeting for prayer, discussion of issues and planning may be possible. 'Full-time' staff can meet in the day time. Otherwise it may have to be before and over breakfast or on a Sunday. Sometimes this will not be possible. Then an evening every six weeks together with an occasional Saturday or whole weekend together may make the team a reality.

If the money is not available for paid staff, a team of Christians, ordained or not, can form their own team. A solicitor and his wife lived in a terraced house in east London for thirty years. They didn't cost the Church a penny. But their commitment to the area, their vision and support meant that the minister of their Baptist church found 'exceptionally able and self-effacing' colleagues in them. They formed a housing association, as we did at the Mayflower. These associations mean that at least a few young couples from the district, who couldn't find housing elsewhere, but wanted to live in the district, were able to do so. So were teachers and social workers who wanted to live near their work and became part of the family centre or Church team.

Clergy Wives

We neglect many of the partners in ministry we already have. A vicar's wife is often expected to act as an unpaid parish worker. Whether she fits this pattern or refuses to do so, she lives on the spot. She probably has to answer telephone and door at all hours. Even if, like many clergy wives, she goes out to work, this is still her home. Often the nearest she comes to being consulted about anything is when she brings the coffee in to a staff meeting.

We are afraid of interfering Mrs. Proudies. But perhaps some women interfere just because they feel shut out. They frequently have to sit and hear their husband being criticised, have to carry the can for the policies the staff has made, and wait for him to come home late at night. Whether they come to all the staff meetings, as happened at the Mayflower, or not, I believe there should be some wider staff meetings arranged when they can come — as there should be for local ministers, readers, local preachers, churchwardens, and church deacons who may be employed elsewhere on week days, when staff meeting is most convenient for 'full-time' clergy.

A minister's wife and children are likely to feel both the enrichment and the pressures of a different social environment more keenly than the minister himself is. The family can play a very important part in 'earthing' him. It will make a great difference if the minister acknowledges to himself how valuable this can be to all that he is. For his ministry is to *be*, not just to *do*. Listening to local news and chatter, which his wife may hear much more freely than he does, will then not be a matter of listening because he thinks his wife needs it. Nor will it be wasting his time. It will help him to stand back from his work, to be able to be carefree as well as caring, to bring some humour and sense of proportion to his work. This will only happen if he makes time to communicate with his wife and children.

If his wife goes out to work, both must make determined efforts to find time for each other. High priority needs to be given to good holidays (he works a six day week and sometimes very long hours), a weekly day off which should be regarded as sacrosanct, and a family hour when he reckons to be with his family each day — perhaps from 5.0 p.m. to 7.0 p.m., or 6.0 p.m. to 8.0 p.m. Working from home has its advantages, but nothing is quite so tantalising for wife or child as to know that he is at home but never available.

Bridge People

The issue of 'identifying' with a district appears at several moments in this book. Nowhere is it more difficult to draw a clear line than in the life of a clergy family. What sort of house should the Church provide for them? How should they furnish it? In what style should they entertain? Where should the children go to school?

Providing a large detached house standing in its own garden in a parish of terraced houses, flats and maisonettes doesn't help. As far as the other questions are concerned, clergy families are 'bridge people' who have other relations and friends too. We shall feel the strains at both ends as bridge people are bound to do. By the same token we have the opportunity of the marvellously creative experience of being open to different cultures. We should acknowledge that because of educational and social background we have differences from our neighbours in a working class community. It would be phoney to pretend that this is not so. We must be ourselves. We must respect our neighbours and expect to learn much about life from them, as well as giving what we have to give. We can each be enriched, and so can our children, by the stretching experience of being bridge people. There is no most excellent way for families in such a situation to follow. We must each make our decisions about styles of life and schools to go to. We should certainly not judge one another.

RADICAL REAPPRAISAL

ATTITUDES are more important than structures. But structures have more influence on the kind of churches which develop than we like to admit. Take the case of a church which sees itself as the one representative of its denomination or distinctive tradition for a population of 100,000 people. It will find it very difficult to escape from developing an eclectic congregation, which will probably be like-minded culturally and socially, as well as in its Christian convictions. It will be very hard for such a church to be local in its mission.

Or take the case of a small congregation maintaining large buildings and all the organisations which go with 'lively church life'. It will be very difficult for its members to find time for mission and evangelism among those outside the institutions the Church runs. Loyalty to the Church seems to demand that their priorities are to maintain its organisations.

The painful and often bitterly contested process of pastoral reorganisation is only worth attempting if we agree that the way churches are organised affects the kind of Christians we are. I believe we could serve urban and industrial areas better with fewer large buildings and working more as teams than as separate parishes or churches with one priest or minister serving each.

Working in Teams

The Pastoral Measure (1968) has made it possible for the Church of England to form team or group ministries. The words have technical meanings; a group ministry brings a group of parishes to commit themselves to co-operate with each other. They form a group council. But each parish keeps its own vicar, its own boundaries, its own parochial church council. New appointments would not be made without consultation with the other clergy in the group.

A team ministry brings about a much more radical change. One parish is formed out of two or more. There are no formal boundaries within the new parish. There is a team rector and, according to size and needs, one or more team vicars. Rector and vicars are appointed for a number of years. The appointments can be renewed after consultation. There can be one or more parish churches and/or places of worship together with church or community halls.

There are few examples of team ministries as yet. The Pastoral Measure only came into existence in 1968. However in Southwark Diocese, for example, it is possible to consider the advantages and disadvantages of some of the large parishes established in the 1920s and 1930s on big housing estates; for example, St. John's, Southend, on the Downham Estate in Catford, St. Peter, St. Helier and St.

Lawrence, Morden. Each has a parish of about 30,000. Each has two or more places of worship. Each might be described as having team ministries before their time. They have done rather better than most churches in such areas in building up a Christian community of local families.

I asked one of these vicars to what he attributed his comparatively good number of local families in the church fellowship. He thought it was not so much any outstanding vicars as the consistent and generous provision by the diocese of good curates and priests in charge of 'daughter churches'. The official team ministry can do rather better; instead of priests in charge who are paid and housed as curates, and who have generally been expected to move on after three years, there can be team vicars, paid and housed as incumbents and expected to stay for a longer period of years.

Area of Experiment

It is possible to designate an area of ecumenical experiment. In such an area denominational disciplines are relaxed. It is also possible to enter into a legal sharing of churches agreement between denominations, in which either has its services at different times or they share in one service. When we talk of formal or informal teams, we ought to think as much about different denominations joining hands as neighbouring parishes. It is the dilemma of some Free Churches that they long to be a church of and for the area, yet are the only church of their denomination in an area far too vast to serve. Many Free Churchmen believe they would do best to plan along with other denominations, and determine to serve a limited locality.

Reorganisers who want tidy plans for each neighbourhood should recognise the distinctive convictions of Christians whether in their own denomination or in another.

Team ministry ought not to be an instrument of theological engineering. On the contrary it should provide a way of offering alternative styles of Church life and ministry in one area, which yet recognise and help one another. There is a danger which should be recognised by Church authorities; it is to regard the man who is 'co-operative' as being the 'good' priest or minister, and the individualist or the 'abrasive' character as being 'difficult'. What is more important is who cuts ice with the people of the district.

This is an argument for setting men free to make their distinctive contribution. It should not be regarded as a reason for opposing working in teams. My colleague George Burton was an abrasive individualist if ever there was one. When the pressures of having to work with other people became oppressive, he would indulge in his pipe dream of 'running my own mission hall'. He knew well enough that this was escapism. He would have been a disaster working on his own and, in any case, his influence would have been far more restricted. The team — at the price of facing up to some painful personal relationships — gave him the support he needed. He couldn't have done his work without us, and we couldn't have achieved nearly so much, or learned many important lessons, without him.

Different Corners

A team ministry need not mean that everything is concentrated in one big centre, with all the staff living there. It should more often have its staff living in different corners of the parish; it can have several centres of worship or of community life. Not all of these would attempt to offer the same provision. They would take each other's contribution into account. Rather than all run uniformed youth organisations or all run open youth clubs, as can happen when each works separately, they can make sure that a variety of provision is offered. Some areas can be better served by a small 'back street church' or by a coffee shop with a room for worship at the back and accommodation for a minister literally over the shop. It would not surprise me if such a centre develops a stronger Church life than that of the larger church or churches in a major parish.

Pastoral reorganisation is generally thought to be forced upon us by threat of shortage of money or manpower. I wrote a paper in 1964 on the need to look seriously at team ministeries in West Ham, because I believed they might serve parts of that borough better, not because I was thinking of any shortages. When some say that there is no evidence that team ministries will 'work', they choose not to look at the evidence of many years of the good men who have been broken or who have lost any vision by being put to work alone in an unworkable parish.

There is no one blueprint for urban areas. Team ministries will not be right in many districts. In each case the best form of ministry needs to be considered on its merits and in careful consideration with those who understand the area best. Formal schemes are not likely to mean much, unless the different congregations have worked together on different projects and worshipped together on occasions over some period. There are many very natural fears about 'take over bids' and loss of a particular parish's identity. These can only be allayed if the partnership is between groups who know each other to some degree.

It is often unreasonable to ask an older man whose whole training and ministry have equipped him to work alone to learn an entirely new pattern of ministry. Team ministry brings a bigger change to a man's way of working than is presumed. To have a colleague, or to be a colleague, is different from having or being a curate in the Anglican structure. Many have been quick to say of first tentative steps in team or group ministry, 'It doesn't work'. They cite examples where there was no careful attempt to look at the vastly different working relationship, and where it has all broken down.

One of the forms of in-service training greatly needed for our own sake is that which helps us understand the pressures and interworking of different groups. A new team ministry should very probably call in someone who has experience of small group work to help them face their new working relationships. And they might find that they actually like their colleagues.

Difficult Balance

A team which talks honestly to one another helps a Church to keep the difficult balance between maintaining continuity and organising for change. A Church ought to be able to enter on a new phase with some new objectives, without doing a right about face on its main goals. A gentle turnover of full-time staff, each bringing their different gifts, is one of the ways of maintaining this balance.

There are times when a minister working on his own ought to stand up to the congregation of the faithful. It can be very difficult when they press him that he should in effect act as their private chaplain, constantly visiting Church members and spending all his time preparing for and speaking to, or celebrating at, Church services and meetings. He may believe that he is called to minister to the whole parish. But he has to be a strong man to insist on the priorities he believes in, if his congregation put such pressures on him. It takes strong conviction to limit determinedly the time which should be given to the congregation; but it must be done if a minister, together with those Church members who will help, is to give proper priority to mission. He is not to give only half his attention to the faithful; he must give them the whole of his attention when he is with them, but it must be for a limited part of his time.

Working in a team helps a man to stand by his convictions without becoming a crank. He may need that support to stand up to the faithful; sometimes it may be to stand up to the community, if, for instance, his convictions are that certain pieces of work must have leaders who share deeply thought-out Christian convictions; sometimes he may need to stand up to the pressures which Church conferences — or bishops — put on him about patterns of Church life which may be quite inappropriate in his area.

Manpower, Money and Buildings

Reduced resources present some important questions to the Church of England and to other denominations. The Archbishop's Advisers' Report on Needs and Resources in 1972 predicted, from a careful study of the age of clergy and the numbers that the 13,000 clergy currently employed full-time in parishes would be reduced to 10,000 in 1980. If there were no joining together of parishes that would mean that in 1980 there would be no assistant staff in the whole of the Church of England. When a man was first ordained we should have to institute him to be vicar of a parish (which is what some Free Churches do now).

The discipline of money and manpower often compels us to answer questions we should have answered long ago. Many Church members have believed for years that we are running too many separate parishes, and maintaining too many buildings in Inner London. We could serve people much better if we had fewer units.

Church buildings should serve Christ's mission. Sometimes they dominate it. Time and money are eaten up by maintaining old buildings. It is always hurtful for a congregation to agree to see a building made redundant or demolished when it contains deep memories. Those who want to conserve beautiful and interesting buildings in a modern city naturally fight to keep strong legal safeguards against the demolition contractor. Memories and conservation are genuine values; but they must be measured against other values: the need to use land fully for housing and community use as well as for Church use; the burden of upkeep on the backs of a small congregation and the depressing experience for a small congregation of worshipping in a very large and cold building.

Laws should protect real architectural and historical treasures. But when it comes to measuring the value of conserving a fine example of a Victorian architect's work against the help redevelopment could bring to the living Church and the living community, the law seems to me to have weighted the case too much in favour of conservation.

Scarcity of Land

The scarcity of land in big cities has made us conscious in a quite new way that ownership of scarce land brings an obligation to see that it is as fully and well used as possible. A study of the use of Church property in multiracial areas of Bradford, Derby and Lambeth showed that Church halls are greatly under used. Sixty-six out of 115 Churches of all denominations did not have any outside group activities in their halls.

There is an extremely limited number of requests from community groups. This may be partly that such groups do not expect to be allowed to use them, and partly that the rooms may not be very suitable. Yet there is a great dearth of meeting places in these areas. From the Church side there are practical problems as well as the ideological ones of allowing groups to use Church premises, whose aims might not be approved of. The practical problems are that the minister and core of active members may already be overstretched in running activities in the buildings. Organising lettings might be the last straw. 'The key question seems to be "What is its role as a local Church?" After that comes the question "What buildings (if any) do we need for the fulfilment of that role?" '[40] If there is not a need for the buildings which exist, scarce land should be developed in whatever way might best serve the community and the Church. Not only the Church but local planners and preservationist societies need to examine more carefully 'the true cost of preserving old buildings in terms of opportunities lost of providing essential community services'.[41]

One church site was redeveloped. It had a nineteenth century church but no hall. Now there is a new church, a community and some forty flats on the same site.[42] Reorganisation is about what one generation hands on to the next. From what we know at present of the next generation of Christians and their attitude to institutions, it seems unlikely that they are going to thank us for leaving them the maintenance of the buildings we have today.

Beautiful Worship

We should give money and time to make worship beautiful. Like the woman who brought the very costly perfume to anoint Jesus's feet, we are then open to criticism for not giving the money to the poor. But we must not avoid the questions about where the proportions of our money go, and about whether we are indeed spending it on the worship of God or on ourselves and the Church life we have grown used to. It is hard to refute the charge that running the kind of Church we do, compels us to spend a disproportionate amount of time and money on ourselves.

We have very great resources, even if the predicted fall in

manpower comes. Suppose that in a large London borough of 250,000 people a new organisation was told it could have forty full-time workers living at strategic points all over the borough, it would seem like riches beyond their wildest dreams. But we have been spoiled. We see it only as a reduction perhaps from sixty to forty paid staff.

Perhaps it is God who is forcing such questions upon us. If so, our response should be to use the changes we shall have to make to give greater pastoral effectiveness. Rather than maintain the thin red line of isolated clergy stretched as far as possible we would do better to have fewer full-time clergy, better paid, better supported and better trained. It is no luxury to find money for in-service training and effective support. Nor should it be seen as opposed to the parochial dream. It actually makes the parochial dream possible.

THE ROLE OF THE WIDER CHURCH

MANY well-wishing members of strong congregations in suburbs, towns and country also feel powerless in the face of the big city. It doesn't help anyone to feel vaguely guilty about living in a pleasant house with a garden and space. There needs to be study, a change of attitudes and action. *The wider Church can acknowledge that it is part of urban society.* Economically, a whole nation is bound together. Those who take their money out of a city like London live as far away as Cambridge and Brighton. I visited a parish on the edge of the Greater London area. I said my subject would be 'Christian responsibility in the great city'. Someone said, 'We don't live in the great city.' I took a map with me of the Greater London Council area, and persuaded the hundred people who were there to call out the London borough in which they worked, or alternatively, to say Surrey or whatever other place they worked in. I marked them up on the map. The great majority worked in London. In their working life such a group already carry some very great responsibilities in the big city. Often the Church fails to help them to see how to work out those responsibilities.

One deanery synod in Surrey invited the senior chaplain of the South London Industrial Mission to come to them. They had often thought of S.L.I.M. as being something which happened in factories over by the river. Now they realised that its chaplains and lay members had been wrestling for years with trying to relate Christian understanding to some of the most traumatic questions which they faced in management. The follow-up was that a group from that outer suburban area asked to meet for some weeks with an Industrial Mission chaplain in the business centre of London. They understood the interdependent nature of a big city.

The wider Church can inform itself about urban and industrial areas. Alec Paterson, when he was in charge of the Oxford and Bermondsey mission took a young man from Bermondsey with him to speak to the annual meeting for supporters at Oxford. The young man was very nervous and tongue-tied. Eventually he scratched his head, looked round on the gathering of Fellows of All Souls and their like and said, 'Of course, you lot are all so ignorant.'

What the inner city has become owes as much to those who have left it and those who've taken their wealth from it as to those who live there now. We ought to take trouble to understand its pressures because we are all part of it and its problems. Interest in urban and industrial areas is often regarded as the curious concern of a few. It should be no more and no less so than interest in the Third World.

The wider Church can commit itself to the cause of

justice. Issues like housing, education and jobs cannot be adequately met by individual or voluntary action. Many changes can only be made through the ballot box, and through seeing that the right issues are raised at election time. Political decisions need to be worked for, which will, in the short term, be to the disadvantage of Church members, their children and their neighbours in many outer areas. Christians will be seen to care about equality of opportunity only if it is among their priorities to work for it. The Christian Church, its gospel and its Lord will not receive any credibility that it believes in the reign of God unless its members stand for justice, 'though it were to their own hindrance'.[43]

The wider Church can attend to comparable needs in its own area. Relative poverty, unequal opportunities and denial of a share in decision-making are not confined to urban and industrial areas. There are needy and deprived people in every community. Often causes will be more obvious in the inner city. 'Quick eyed love' will discover local needs which many in areas of comparative affluence do not want to notice.

The wider Church can establish relations of mutual help with churches or projects in urban and industrial areas. This is something which has to be approached delicately. The experience of too much condescension and 'slumming' has warned us of many pitfalls. But meeting on level terms can be established. Church members can share their experience of life and of Christ. Students can offer useful help in projects and at the same time learn a great deal.

The wider Church can encourage service in urban and industrial areas. The challenge to be teachers, community workers, social workers, planners, local government officers, nurses and clergy in these areas is none the less because of all that has been said about local responsibility. It calls for a more sensitive kind of service and leadership, and for a deeper understanding of the community in which professionals serve.

The wider Church can give money to Christian and other voluntary projects. There is a particular problem for some charities. It is not too difficult to raise money for those which help handicapped or poor people who are not very likely to challenge the present order of society. It is much more difficult to raise money for projects which set out to stop poor and powerless people being poor and powerless. If they are encouraged to change their life style, they may appear to threaten our life style and that of our children.

The wider Church can accept that there should be Priority Areas in Church life too. That means being unselfish about where the resources of money and manpower go. All the missions and Churches established in Inner London were over and above the settled ministry to the rest of England, not at their expense. The moment of truth about priority areas is coming soon, for a strong ministry will only be maintained in the largely unchurched areas of urban and industrial areas, if less clergy and ministers are allocated to the stronger Churches. Priority areas for somebody else means that you don't receive priority.

Many Church people in the church-going belt say, 'But we're weak and powerless too. We need a curate.' This is both true *and* untrue. Churches there need staff. But the weakness or strength of Church life is not comparable.

It is true that the population of the inner city has been gradually dropping. This has been matched by the need of new towns and new estates. Principles for deployment of clergy should include population figures. There will be other factors like chaplaincies to hospitals, or the number of churches in a parish. When comparisons about manpower are made they should include the total resources of all Christian denominations. Comparisons should also include the retired clergy and ministers who can play a large part but rarely do in the inner city or on housing estates. A large congregation may be said to need a large paid staff. This argument should perhaps be balanced by saying that a large congregation ought to develop its own local ministry, ordained or not, to minister to itself and its community.

Redemption

One Church leader used to say that we should put our resources where there was response. That meant Woodford and Buckhurst Hill and not West Ham. He would not have acknowledged that the blame for the different responses of different social groupings might lie at the Church's door. The parochial dream means that we believe we are called to serve a district whether there is response in church going terms or not. The Christian Church would have to have spent years of much more sacrificial commitment both to working class London in general and to the areas of greatest deprivation, before we could properly talk about shaking off the dust from our feet. Most people who live there have not yet seen the Church acting in terms which make Christianity a serious adult proposition.

One Christian said about work with youngsters in a deprived area, 'You're wasting your time with those kids.' Well, you either believe in redemption or you don't. I do.

Nine

THE GOSPEL FOR THE CITY

GOD'S PRESENCE IN THE CITY

WHAT is the Gospel for City Dwellers? believing in redemption in that which is built as a city, as anywhere else, we
can look in this last section at the nature of the Gospel for
city dwellers. This takes us into the realm of theology, but it
must be a theology that relates relevantly to all we have said
so far.

I believe that God is present in the city and ask just what
that means. I must try to understand what He is doing.
There are questions to be asked about the Incarnation of
our Lord and about personal and corporate salvation.

I walked slowly down London's famous Oxford Street
one day some years ago. I was trying out a slogan in my
mind 'We must go into the world to catch up with what God
is doing'. I noticed the great variety of fabrics, designs and
colours in the windows of all the stores and in the crowds
jostling each other along the pavement.

The great city need no longer be grey and dull. That is
good. From all around came snatches of conversation.
Every subject under the sun was being discussed. Many
languages were being spoken. Asian and African modes of
dress mingled with European. In a shrinking world, we can
rub shoulders with everyman and so learn from one another.
Colour, openness to other cultures, a cosmopolitan
city — all these result from natural processes at work in the
world. I believe that God smiles on these results of human
development, and that they are good.

I thought then about what was going on in many of the offices which look down on Oxford Street. There the rat race is in full swing. This also results from the processes at work in the world. It is not good. How do I decide which of the processes are good, and what God is doing, so that I may catch up with Him?

Marx would have said that I must give up my illusions about God before I could understand what was going on along Oxford Street. Religion was the heart of a heartless world. God was no more than a stand-by whom men had invented to come in from outside. Religion would offer answers about the suffering of the world without abolishing the suffering. Marx believed that 'matter' was all there was. In 'matter' he included animal and human life. It was in flux, in tension, in motion. Out of its torment 'life engendering life' was developing. Progress came only through the painful working out of the tensions in matter.

It is true that Christians have sometimes believed only in a God 'over against' the material universe, coming to the rescue from outside at moments of crisis. Along with this has gone an assumption that matter was evil so that machines and human 'progress' have been cursed as though they were to blame for exploitation and greed.

The Gospel must begin for all men with some understanding that there is a purposeful Creator and that He rewards those who search for Him.[1]

When the Apostles preached to Jews, they could assume that they had such an understanding of God from the Old Testament. So they could speak straight away about what God had done in Christ. But when they preached to Gentiles, who did not know about this purposeful, living God, their Gospel began by trying to lead them to belief in a good and loving Creator.

Two Speeches

The Acts of the Apostles includes two speeches to Gentile audiences. One audience consists of the dialect-speaking inhabitants of a backward agricultural area in Lystra. The other includes the philosophers of the cultural centre of the world, Athens. In both speeches the Gospel begins by correcting false ideas and establishing a true picture of the Creator. He is not like the idols they know. He shows kindness, sends rain for the crops. gives food and good cheer. Country people have experienced that. God is the universal giver of life and breath and all else. He made mankind of one stock — an ungratifying thought for the Athenians who liked to think of themselves as original inhabitants and thus superior to other Greeks who had migrated and to barbarians.[2] Men were to 'seek God, and it might be, touch and find Him; though indeed He is not far from each one of us, for in Him we live and move. In Him we exist.'[3] Paul met the Athenians on their own ground finding points of agreement with Epicurean and Stoic insights. He consistently searched for 'as much common ground as possible with his audience'.[4] He began where they were.

The majority of city dwellers that I know believe in God, but this believing should not be taken for more than it really means. The God who is generally believed in is often a welfare officer sort of God who comes in from outside at certain crisis moments of life. But He has nothing to do with bringing purpose and change for the good into work situations, housing and community life. The welfare officer God is not to be found there.

As in the days of the Acts the Gospel must begin by establishing a true picture of the Creator. This has often been left out, because those who preach and teach assume from their different experience that everyone in Britain believes in the living God. Christians have often made too sharp a division between the Proclamation (*Kerugma*) of the Gospel and the Teaching (*Didache*). The proclamation of the death and resurrection of Christ was made in the context of a continuing worshipping life of the Church, in which the teaching both of Jesus and of the Old Testament was regularly read.

Both proclamation and teaching begin with a purposeful Creator, who also continues to be the Sustainer of the Universe. The statement that 'all things are held together in Him'[5] (in His Son), suggests that if He ceased from His energising work, the Universe, as though it were a television picture deprived of its transmission, would cease. The material universe 'groans in all its parts in its birthpangs waiting with eager expectation for God's sons to be revealed'.[6]

God did not make matter as some backdrop to the human drama and then forget about it. He creates, renews, sustains, energises it. He gives to man not only the commission to go to work on matter but the brain and the muscle to do it. Man puts his life into matter and matter reacts on man. God is not a spectator or a neutral in all this. He has set Himself to 'reconcile the whole universe to Himself'.[7]

A Parable

Matter, the material universe, is The Thing which swoops down on two travellers in the desert in a parable of Teilhard de Chardin.[8] The travellers are mystics who wish to remain unspoiled by the world. From a distance it had seemed quite small, like a cloud of gnats dancing in the sun at evening; then at incredible speed it approached filling the whole world of space. First an irresistible rapture took possession of them, as if their tired bodies were being mightily refashioned. At the same time they felt an oppressive sense of peril that the thing was ambiguous, unquiet, the combined essence of all evil and all good.

The two temptations of the mystic are worked out in the parable. The first is to avoid the disturbing demands of the material world by keeping well away from it. The second is the temptation of the Pantheist; one man in the parable was almost seduced to lose himself in the breath that enfolded him. This would have been to deny self-consciousness and his responsibility as a man, and to drift along with all living things in the flux and flow of matter.

This is the temptation to those who insist that the way to personal maturity is above all through *experience*; they insist that they must be free to open themselves to every drive, to penetrate every height and depth. The Pantheist mistakes this god who is experience, for the living God who chooses one thing and not another, who sometimes commands and forbids. He is at work in men and in matter. He is also *other than* the flux and flow of matter, and *over against* the processes of human development.

Teilhard's traveller shakes himself from uncritical warmth to a harsh determination towards 'increased being'. Continuing evolution is at the centre of Teilhard's scheme; chaos — cosmos — life — simple consciousness — self-consciousness — cosmic consciousness. At the heart of the cosmos is Jesus. Cosmic consciousness is when men follow the way of Jesus and cease to be closed individuals whose souls are isolated from the Soul of the World.

I disagree with Teilhard when he seems to make the cosmic Christ emerge out of the evolution of man, as though there is a constant progress towards the good and the higher. Christ is present in the whole development of man; so are great forces of evil to which Teilhard does not give sufficient weight. Christ is not the topmost part of a pyramid of human goodness. He is present at the heart of all that is best and creative in the world. He is also over against the world as its Judge.

Disturbing Demands

Orthodox Christians have sometimes tried to avoid all the disturbing demands of the material world, by keeping away from 'worldly' activities. The New Testament writers sound serious warnings against love of the world. But it is important to understand what the word 'world' means.

St. John uses it in two senses. On the one hand he writes 'Do not set your hearts on the world or anything in it'.[9] This means the values and standards of the world as it is organised apart from God. The translators of the New English Bible have 'the godless world'; 'godless' does not appear in the text, but it is a fair commentary on what 'the world' means here. Its basis is greed or covetousness; its values are short term. Christians will be hated in the world as Christ was.[10]

In the second sense of 'world' Christ was no stranger to it; 'All that came to be was alive with His life ... the world, though it owed its being to Him, did not recognise Him.'[11] Here the word means all the life of the world, people, animals, matter. Evil is present in it too, and it has become a disordered world. The 'whole godless world lies in the power of the evil one'.[12] But God hasn't deserted it; He 'loved the world so much that He gave His only Son, that everyone who has faith in Him may not die but have eternal life'.[13]

This famous text is sometimes quoted to prove that the world is thoroughly good after all. This is to miss the point about God's love. It is the undeserved nature of His action which is the meaning of the grace of our Lord Jesus Christ. God's own proof of His love for us is that Christ died while we were still sinners.[14] He loves people, not because we are good, but in spite of the fact that we are sinful.

The big city appears to present all the opportunities the

world affords for man to develop. There is freedom to choose. But is there true freedom? High pressure advertising presses on him his need for commodities which will help him enjoy higher status, open the door to more escapism, offer him greater freedom to choose. In fact he is confused about whether this makes him more or less free. Christ calls him to be salt to the earth and life for all the world.[15] Yet evil threatens to engulf him when he goes into the thick of the life of the big city. So the temptation to try to get back to some state of innocence increases.

George Kelly suggests that man spends a good deal of his time trying to get back to innocence. Man had to choose between loneliness and companionship, and chose companionship. He had to choose between innocence and knowledge, and chose knowledge. He had to choose between good and evil and 'is still hung up on that issue'. Because man finds the responsibility for distinguishing good from evil in shifting circumstances unbearable, he tries to go back on his former decisions. Many psychiatric patients are trying to get back to choose loneliness instead of companionship and innocence instead of knowledge.[16]

Corporate Decision

Take, for example, the process of trying to develop corporate decision making in a big firm. Joint consultation is good. To get things done is also good. Endless consultation is bad. Unions are fearful of leaving their bargaining position. Time goes by. There is often then a return to autocratic decisions, which destroy the participation which was hoped for. Impatience, lack of trust, deceitfulness, build up a circle in which the Christian man feels, 'I only am left', and cannot bear facing the difficult task of being God's partner in changing things for good in the secular world. So he tries to turn back to innocence, keeping out of controversial matters at work and putting his energies into church life. Or he turns back to loneliness and goes to work in a small business by himself.

Christ a stranger — not a stranger; 'don't love the world' — 'God loved the world'. That tension must be maintained. If we let go the tension and think of the world and the flesh simply as the enemies of God, we shall expect Christians to be gathered out of the world into a Church which organises the whole of its activity and its learning apart from the world. Then we shall believe that God's truth has no connection with any other truth and perhaps say things like: 'The Church must guard the faith and teach it to the world; we have nothing to learn from the world.' 'If he's not born again, he won't know nothing.' 'Industry is rotten from top to bottom; our function is simply to preach the gospel to it.'

Costly involvement in the world is the Christian calling; 'Withdrawal to whatever degree is Pharisaic,' writes John Stott. 'As our Lord took on our flesh, so He calls His Church to take on the secular world. Otherwise we do not take the Incarnation seriously.'[17]

The God of the Bible is a living God. He doesn't simply smile or frown from afar at the processes of life. He is involved. He shapes events. He is the God of History. That is always easier to believe after the event (like Israel's deliverance from exile in Babylon or the Abolition of Slavery) than at the moment when history is being made. In our day it is being made through changes like the bringing of several cultures together to live cheek by jowl, or through something apparently as trivial as the extension of fashionable clothes to all classes in the population.

I asked some teenage Londoners if they thought God was interested in fashion. They thought not. We were away for a weekend in a beautiful country setting (part of sensible urban living). Soon we found ourselves discussing why He hadn't made the world in black and white if He wasn't interested in fashion.

Secular Men

If God is involved in the processes which I noticed in Oxford Street, He is not causing them to happen through Church activity. Rather it is through the intelligent, responsible activity of men in secular life, whether they acknowledge Him or not. The source of their intelligence is God. 'All that came to be was alive with His life.' So far as they work in harmony with God's natural law (for example by reverence for truth, whether it is scientific or moral truth) they will be adding to the works of the hands of God. The present day history they are making may be good planning and building of a new estate or making and working out a just law for industrial relations. God is at work in the world through them. He gives His common grace to all men. He 'makes His sun rise on good and bad alike, and sends the rain on the honest and the dishonest'.[18]

When we say that the Bible contains all things necessary for our salvation, we do not mean that God has done nothing and said nothing significant since Bible days. The revelation given in the Bible provides the yardstick, the criteria by which we may recognise the work of the hands of God in the world. And it shows the way to enter into conscious relationship with the living God.

Translators and theologians have frequently tried to get to the root of the meaning of the name of God given to Moses — the name Yahweh. Clearly there is something of a riddle about it. It contains within it the refusal of God to liken Himself to anything within His creation. He is not like a bull on a mountain, or the sun. 'I am: that is who I am.' It contains the claim that He will be the contemporary of every generation, 'The Eternal', 'I will be what I will be.' It includes the hint that He is the source of life and strength for men. He is not just the God who is there, to be admired and to smile on our work. 'I will be to you what I will be to you'. It suggests that God will act in history and that we shall not always be able to predict what He will do; 'Something important's going to happen. Look out! Don't miss it.'[19]

The Rat Race

So we go into the world to catch up with what God is doing. How do we know what He is doing? We must beware of becoming Pantheists here, and coming to believe that it is God who is causing every human process. The rat race proceeds just as much from the historical process as does willingness to learn from other cultures. If we say that love can be proved to be the best motive, Engels, among many, would contradict us. His contempt for love as a motivating force was total. But hate — ah, there he saw a motive to help get things done in the class war.[20]

It is, in a sense, a brave attempt to live by faith when a man says, 'I'm called to serve people on this new estate. I identify myself with them and their good. I can only find God and learn His will within this situation. Since ninety-nine per cent of those who live here have no Church background, sympathy or understanding, I will not find anything to help me in traditional Christianity. I will cut my links, however painful that may be, and learn from the living God who is here.' But there is a great danger that he will think that 'God is on our side', and that the word of the Lord will happen to be the same as the policy of the politically active members of the neighbourhood. To worship a God who is only to be found within the life of the housing estate, or the factory, or the big city is the modern equivalent of Pantheism. God is not the enemy of nature, nor of the developments of urban and industrial life. Nor is He their soul. He is their dynamo, their enabler, their rescuer and their judge.[21]

The Old Testament prophets dared to interpret what God was doing in their history — which was for them the present. The basis for their concern about society was their understanding of the character of God. For them He wasn't an unknown riddle, 'I will be what I will be.' He was the God of all the earth, wanting the good of all men and not only of the Jews. They appealed to natural law. If other nations didn't acknowledge the God of Israel, the prophets began where they were. For example, Amos did not condemn the war crimes of the Moabites, on the ground that they had fought against God's people. It was because they burnt the bones of the king of Edom for ash.[22] Even by the bloodthirsty standards of those nations, this was a barbaric and impious crime.

The prophets appealed also to God's character as it had been revealed in His dealings with His people. He loved mercy and justice and hated oppression and greed — and would always do so. Because there was something given, something revealed, about the character of God, they dared to be specific about God's attitude to particular situations.

The Christian has greater knowledge than the prophets. God has revealed His character supremely in His Son.[23] This does not mean that revealed truth should be seen as something altogether apart from understanding of the natural law. Jesus in Galilee began where people were, then tried to bring the fresh insights the Kingdom of God gave. He assumed that they could discuss serious issues before He attempted to say 'Repent and believe'. He discussed marriage and divorce, paying taxes to the Romans and the status-seeking of those who wanted the best seats at a party — all with those who were not within the Christian fold. We shall begin where they are, believing that the living God is there too, trying to discover His glory there. But the givenness of

God's revelation of Himself provides the yardstick which will help us to test how God is at work in a particular situation. We shall certainly affirm with confidence, against Engels, that it is always better to love than to hate, because we are aware of the Cross and the Resurrection. The man who wants to know what God's word in a situation is, should open his mind to three influences. As they interact on one another, they provide the yardstick against which we may test whether something is the work of God or not.

Three Influences

The first influence is the *Bible*. To live in its company means that a man holds the mirror up to see himself as he is, and that he soaks himself in God's dealings with men. This can be just a matter of curiosity, a glance at himself and off he goes, forgetting what he looks like.[24] He learns from the Bible if he really wants to know what it says to him. Sometimes it is treated as a lamp post is treated by a drunkard — for support, not for illumination — simply looking for some text to support our latest theory. Far different was Luther; 'my conscience is wrapped in the Word of God. I can do no other. God help me.' This means saying, 'If I am persuaded that the weight of scripture, properly read in its context, leads me to believe that a particular course is right, I will act upon it.' As we not only learn His truth but work it out in action in harmony with Him, our understanding of God's character will steadily increase.

The second influence is the *company of other Christians*. The Holy Spirit teaches us His mind through every member of Christ's body. The French worker priests found themselves torn in two by the tension between the way of life of most church members and that of a working class community. This tension tears others as well. But we are not to release ourselves from the tension. Disagreement between two Christians can be a way which forces both to think again what Christ's mind is, as each takes seriously the different insights the other has to offer.

The third influence is to be *open to the world*. Where the other two influences are present we can declare loudly, 'Let the world set the agenda.'

Placed in this context, responding to the world's agenda is far different from saying that the Church must follow the lead of the contemporary world. It is the living God who should set our agenda, and this He often does through the world. The trouble with slogans is that, by encouraging us to say whether we are for or against them, they pose us with a false choice of opposites. In the French worker priest debate, the foolish question has been asked, 'Should a priest be holy or up to date?' Another use of a slogan is to say that we mustn't expect the movement of God's activity always to be God — Church — World. If we reject that order of activity, we are in danger immediately of replacing it by saying that the movement is always God — World — Church. The living God will not be tied down to either formula. He may inject new ideas or action first through the existential situation which the world's agenda brings to us; or through the corporate learning experience within the Church fellowship; or through new understanding brought through exposition of the Bible.

An art the Christian needs to cultivate, as he lives with the world's agenda, is to spot Biblical insights in what people are saying or doing and to test his presuppositions against the values revealed in Christ.

The Present Christ

Christ is present and active everywhere. 'My Father has never yet ceased His work, and I am working too.' If we have eyes to see, we shall be filled with wonder at what He is doing.[25] Sometimes our testing against the Biblical revelation will show us that though He is present, men do not recognise Him. Often they reject Him, and His presence is then in judgment rather than in support of the process which is going on.

Christian attitudes to *progress* are divided. Sometimes we divide according to temperament. Our staff at the Mayflower Family Centre once considered the question: 'Are you more likely to be dazzled or depressed by progress?' We found that we were divided almost equally. Temperamental differences seemed the most likely explanation on that occasion rather than any sharply different theological insights. Sometimes, different theological insights do lead to different attitudes towards progress. Charles Kingsley blurred all the lines between the Kingdom of God and social utopianism. In his novel *Alton Locke*, Lady Ellerton says 'Call it the Church, the Gospel, civilisation, freedom, democracy, association, what you will — I shall call it the Kingdom of God.' F. D. Maurice did not share Kingsley's optimism about social progress. He said that God inspires in the whole of society — and that Satan corrupts, and that judgment falls.[26]

THE INCARNATION

THERE has been a long debate about how much should be built on the idea of *Christus Consummator*, Christ the consummation of human reason.[27] If the Son, the Logos of the prologue to John's Gospel, was 'the true light which enlightens every man',[28] then He has always been inspiring all truth, all good human reason, all honest endeavour. The Logos was active in the process of natural and of human development. Then He came into the world to show God's truth and love in terms all could understand. 'The Word became flesh: He came to dwell among us, and we saw His glory.'[29] His Incarnation, life, death and resurrection, was the truth which made sense of all the universe.

Jesus told Pilate, who didn't have the religious background of the Jews, 'I came to bear witness to the truth.'[30] This truth 'rings bells' for those who have already recognised natural law. But it is not just common sense. Peter wrote that a man was born anew by *obedience* to the truth. That truth was 'the word of the Gospel preached to you'.[31] Proclaiming the Kingdom of God means that God must be sovereign.

The Incarnation was the centre of faith to the young William Temple, because he saw it as making sense of a divinely ordered universe. As he grew older, he gave a much bigger place to the mystery of evil in the world than he had done earlier. He lived long enough to see the slump and the millions of unemployed in Britain and the Western world in the 1930s, and, before he died in 1944, a second and terrible World War. In his later years he said that the world must be changed by Christ to something very unlike itself, before a Christian map of it could be drawn. 'We used to believe in the sovereignty of the God of love a great deal too light-heartedly.'[32]

In a New Dimension

The Incarnation showed us goodness in a new dimension. A rich young man came to have a debate with Jesus on the basis that he had kept all the commandments from boyhood. 'Good Master', he began. 'Why do you call Me good?' came the reply. 'No one is good except God

alone.'[33] The moral-living young man was not meeting
someone who was one place ahead of him in the league table
of goodness. He was confronted by a whole new order of
goodness. It meant enlisting with Jesus in His kingdom, in
which the poor had a special place, and a special claim on
his money. It cut right across the static view of religion as
something you learn as a boy and then 'keep' in your own
private religious section of life. Instead Christ's kingdom
would make global claims on every part of his life. It meant
the personal relationship and obedience of, 'Follow me'. In
the face of this new order of goodness Simon Peter said,
'Go, Lord, leave me, sinner that I am.'[34]

The Incarnation spelled out not how close to God man
had made himself, but how far away he had gone. In the Old
Testament some men had learned this difference between
God and man (which we feel after when we talk about God's
transcendence) by a sense of distance, which made them talk
about a God 'up there' or 'out there': 'Come no nearer; take
off your sandals; the place where you are standing is holy
ground.' 'I saw the Lord seated on a throne, high and
exalted . . .' 'As the heavens are higher than the earth, so are
My ways higher than your ways and My thoughts than your
thoughts.'[35]

In Jesus, men saw God who is always present and at work
everywhere in the world (which we try to describe when we
talk about God's immanence) and also the transcendent
God. This is no contradiction, for transcendence stands for
difference, not distance from us. It is the opposite of Pantheism, not of intimacy.[36] The disciples learned an increased sense of a transcendent and holy God by knowing
Jesus as their intimate friend.

Talk about the Church as the 'extension of the Incarnation' has truth in it. In the company of Christians, Christ
is named. There should be conscious, intelligent response to
His revealed truth, which should lead to 'doing the truth'.

Nevertheless, the phrase can be misleading. It can make us
feel that the Church 'knows it all', goes on to teach without
learning from the world, expects 'outsiders' to fit into
Church ways, assuming that they are Christ's way. It can
make us forget that the Church too is under Christ's judgment. We are called to guard the treasure[37] of the eternal
gospel. We are also called to be disciples all our lives, continuing to learn from the living God through every agenda
He brings to us.

New Route to Freedom

In Jesus we see a new route to maturity and freedom. It is
through deliberately setting Himself to obey His Father's
will. So God's Peace, *Shalom*, is first restored, because Jesus
lives in perfect harmony with His Father. It extends, like
ripples on a lake, as more men respond to His Peace and are
brought into right relationship with God and with their
fellow men.

Christ's freedom is responsible and mature. It is not the
maturity of an individual found through selfish experience,
but through having His Father at the centre of His life and
wanting no progress for Himself without the good of His
human brothers being furthered. So He says, 'Abba Father,
Not my will, but Yours',[38] in mature dependence and in
free obedience. It has delivered Him from worshipping any
tradition, any good cause, any power — even if that would
bring Him all the kingdoms of the world.

God calls us to grow up. Christians have sometimes emphasised the child/father relationship to such a degree that
they remain immature children. To look always for complete guidance 'from outside' a man's own thinking, or to
say 'working class people like things simple; they like to be
told with authority where they stand', these make people
dependent, like children under a strict governess. That was

only meant to be until Christ came. Now we are to grow up, to make moral choices and stand by our own responsibilities. But God does not say, 'You're on your own now.' The authentic mark of having ceased to be a child under the governess of the Old Testament Law, and of having become an adult son of God is that 'God has sent into our hearts the Spirit of His Son, crying, Abba! Father!'[39] Our maturity, too, should have the Father at the centre of our life. We, too, should want no progress without the good of our human brothers being furthered. Our freedom, too, will come by setting ourselves to do the Father's will.

As we grow, we shall understand that the Father's part is different from what in human relationships we have scathingly called 'paternalist'. God the Father is the great enabler, stimulating us to develop our gifts to the full. We may learn something about God's Fatherhood if we try out some of our best thoughts about enabling leadership in community work. It is to stimulate and help sustain responsible action by others.

An enabling leader may sometimes need to challenge views strongly, at the same time leaving people free to accept or reject his challenge. His task is to be at different times: sustainer, enabler, resource man, and at certain moments, rescue man and hate bearer. All these roles are played by God as He calls us to grow up to be mature sons, working in partnership with Him.

The Call to Discipleship

Jesus's call to discipleship always treated people as responsible beings. All people have a contribution to make; all can and should have eyes to see the significance of His love. His healing miracles were without strings attached. They were an expression of His uncalculating love. But they were also signs of the coming of His Kingdom which demands a response from men. He healed ten lepers. He was disappointed that only one came back and gave praise to God.[40] He showed no condescension in His dealings with 'the common people'. His sharpest words about commitment being costly in terms of 'goods, fame, child and wife' were said to the crowd as well as to the disciples.[41] After the feeding of the five thousand the crowd wanted to make Him a king, crowding round the shore to follow Him. Jesus said they only came looking for Him because their bellies were filled. They came for what they could get out of Him. His response was not to attach strings, and say, 'only those who've paid Judas the Treasurer can come to the next miraculous feeding.' But there was a sharp edge to His love, which wouldn't let poor and needy people think that they must always be the objects of a charitable hand out. He said they should have had eyes to see that the miracle was a sign.[42] It signified that God was at work in their world. It meant His Kingdom was at hand. The Kingdom demanded intelligent response from all men.

Stories of 'how good God's been to me' are often used as a buffer to keep the searching demands which the living God might make at arm's length. They belong to the circle of ideas which goes like this: we know God doesn't hear sinners — He's answered my prayers (to get me out of trouble or sickness) — I've lived a respectable life — I've been a hard working man, not a drinker — I've done the right thing by my family — what more do you want?

The Church is responsible for much of this reaction, specially among working class people. It has expected so little of people, when Jesus expected so much. God's kindness is meant to lead to a change of heart. This change of heart calls all of us to become responsible partners with Christ in working for His Kingdom in the whole of life. Our preaching too often confines both righteousness and sin to our private lives and to the small circles where we have obligations. The Church's gospel generally teaches that Christian morals have to do with the family, colleagues at work and those who come to the local church where we belong. Frequently it stops there.

SALVATION — PERSONAL
AND CORPORATE

IN the big city, many people feel helpless and vaguely resentful because they feel unable to change things for good. A Gospel which is only a personal and family Gospel ignores the fact that God has deliberately made the world corporate. Only corporate action can bring about many of the changes which are needed.

The word 'salvation' in the Bible has a corporate sense as well as a personal sense. It is concerned with removing everything which spoils what J. V. Taylor calls 'God's Kingdom of right relationships'.

The most important Old Testament word for salvation is *yash'a*. It provides Jesus's own name: 'You shall give Him the name Jesus (Saviour), for He will save His people from their sins.'[43] The root meaning of *yash'a* is 'bringing into a spacious environment', 'being at one's ease, free to develop'. It is the opposite of the verb *tsarar*, 'to be in discomfort, in cramped or distressing circumstances'.[44] We need a lot of salvation in the big city in every sense of the word, if people are to be made whole. Jesus said that faith would move mountains. God wants to move mountains of many different kinds.

I have grouped some examples of the kinds of mountain I believe He wants to move under four main headings. These four mountain ranges keep many city dwellers in cramped or distressing circumstances.

Personal and Inter-personal Problems

    Writing off people who hurt you.
    Personal authority problems.
    Selfishness in sexual relationships.
    Family rows.
    Despair at frequent failures.

Problems of Community Structures and Institutions

    Bad relations at work between management and labour.
    Poor schooling available in the district.
    Lack of good hospital treatment.
    Overcrowded housing.
    Old people feeling undervalued by the community.
    Unemployment of black school leavers.

Global Problems

    Inequalities of opportunity between rich and poor nations.
    Population explosion.
    Racialism.
    War.

Problems of Eternal Destiny

    Fear of death.
    The groaning of the whole created universe.

Relationship with God

In the Gospels the same word is used to describe both *spiritual salvation* and *physical healing*. Through faith in Jesus, men are brought into right relationship with God. They are made whole.[45] God is concerned to move all these mountains, and, as His fellow workers, we should be concerned about them too. Some Christians say we must tackle personal and inter-personal problems *first*. Others exactly reverse this, and say that it is a waste of time 'tinkering' with personal problems unless we *first* change the structures of society.

God's salvation is concerned with all four mountain ranges. The right reaction is not for each individual to try to balance his priorities and time exactly between the four. But he ought to be worried, if he sees that the Church corporately is ignoring one or other group of mountains. The salvation he believes in and preaches must be concerned with all four because they interact on one another. Lack of humility in personal relationships, for example, is likely to affect the way the council official or a factory manager operates the structures of his institution. And inequality of opportunity between rich and poor nations reacts on the attitudes unemployed black youths learn. They in turn affect their personal authority problems.

Christian people are often troubled and resentful at the complexity of modern urban life. They cling fiercely to the hope that all life is simply a series of relationships between individuals. They will generally believe that it is important for the Church and its members to fight battles to defend family life. There is deep concern for this, because the family is the basis of society in the Bible. You don't find an army of social workers paid out of heavy taxes there. It is worth asking why not. What you find in the Bible is the 'extended family', something very different from what we

generally think of when the word family is used. It would
have been difficult, for example, to house Abraham's family
in a flat on the twentieth floor of a modern point block.
There might have been a hundred of them or more. Families
in Britain, we are told, have 2·4 children each. This 'nuclear
family' is very different in kind when it is cut off from the
extended family. When someone dies, or is unable to cope
with life, who comes to the rescue?

The Extended Family

In the Bible the duty of coming to the rescue is laid on the
family — the extended family. Take the case of Ruth. The
'redeemer kinsman' was obliged to buy the land, and also to
marry the dead man's wife. This was presumably to guard
the widow, and to perpetuate the name of the dead man by
the birth of a child. Here the extended family is guarding its
future and its weak member. So he redeems her. Or, suppose
your brother becomes poor and sells himself as a slave; 'the
brother, uncle, cousin, or any blood relation of his family
may redeem him, or if he can afford it, he can redeem himself.'[46] In much of our society, with its emphasis on individuals standing on their own feet, the man would have been
expected to sort out his own problems. In the Bible, as in
rural countries today, orphans and old people would not be
a charge on the community at large, because the extended
family came to the rescue.

The first fact of life in the big city is that the links of the
extended family break down. Sometimes they survived in
old streets. They are often seen in the first generation of city
dwellers, as for example with West Indians who live in a
house, because their cousin came to London first and has
found rooms for different members of the family. But it
does not survive long. Separate households, rebuilding, mobility of one kind or another break up the organism which

was once a family. If we take seriously the importance the Bible gives to the extended family, we must ask seriously what takes its place in modern urban life?

Clearly what is needed is *a caring community*. With the terms of reference of the Kingdom of God, the Church should have special concern to strengthen such a sense of community. What God requires of us is to loose the fetters of injustice, to set free those who have been crushed, to share your food with the hungry, to take the homeless poor into your house ...[47] In the areas of Britain where the greatest concentrations of homeless poor live, the churches are generally very weak in numbers. Much of their members' leisure-time energies are taken up in keeping church organisations going, because there's no one else to do it. So they dare not get involved in anything more. 'One thing leads to another. You don't know how to say No.' And if you live in a council flat or house, you're not allowed to take homeless poor, or any other lodger, into your house. Nevertheless, some Christians welcome individuals in need into their homes. Many more perform kindly acts. Others again are working as professional social workers.

Picking Up Casualties

All this is picking up casualties on the road. It is not necessarily doing anything about producing the kind of caring community which will prevent so many people from becoming casualties. Some Christians who see the need to be involved in the local community ask despairingly if there is any community to relate to. Often in a great city, and especially on estates in the first ten years of their life, the answer will be no. The priorities of God's Kingdom of right relationships suggest that many Christians are likely to be called by God to be enablers, helping secular communities to come into being.

It is of the nature of a city, and of life, that we are all involved together in the bundle of life. If we tolerate lack of community spirit we shall all pay the price; literally in taxes, and also in lonely old age, in fatalism which refuses to get involved in anything new, in vandalism and crime. 'It's the home and the family influence', we say. It might be more Biblical to say, 'It's the community and our failure to play any part in giving it life.' Judgment— or blessing — falls on us together; it happened in Jerusalem:

'Then it will be the same for priest and people
 the same for master and slave, mistress and slave girl,
 seller and buyer,
 borrower and lender, debtor and creditor.'[48]

If we want to get things changed, we have to acknowledge the corporate nature of urban life, and go in for corporate action. If I want to love my neighbour, and I discover that his needs are to do with housing, it is very unlikely that I can do anything for him as an individual. I can only help if I am prepared to join with others already involved, or perhaps bring some group together to take a fresh initiative.

Politics

This will probably mean politics at a local or wider level. It does not necessarily mean party politics, but it may mean the politics of pressure groups concerning themselves with particular issues. Many Christians say that they are apolitical. This probably means that they think politics is a dirty game in which their hands would be found to get dirty. It is questionable if on that ground it is a Christian attitude to leave it to others to risk their immortal souls, rather than risk your own.

Any involvement in the real world risks being caught up by evil motives and movements. Niebuhr said that politics is the place where conscience and power meet.[49] We naturally shrink from the corrupting influence of power. But we can't have it both ways. If we stay out of the affairs of men, we cannot go on complaining that we feel so impotent to 'do anything about it'. When Christians criticise others for taking part in politics, and claim that they themselves are apolitical, they probably mean that they are broadly content with things as they are. If they don't feel passionately that things are wrong, they will leave well alone. But that is not an apolitical attitude. It is as classic and decisive a political position as socialism. Historically laissez faire was a specific policy on which governments were frequently elected.

As far as getting your hands dirty is concerned, another uncomfortable truth about modern urban life has to be faced. It is that we live in a pluralist society. That is to say, there is not one code of principles and interests but many. Therefore if coherent political action (local or national) needs two or three party groupings rather than forty, we shall find ourselves having to join hands with men who have different approaches to many issues from us. If you belonged, for example, to a parliamentary political party, you would be lucky if you agreed with 75% of its programme. The problem of integrity in what you do about the remaining 25% is one which every man involved in responsible corporate action (in State or Church) knows. The ability needed is a cool enough head to distinguish between the issues we can go along with because we feel only sixty to forty against them, the kind of issues we would fight against in private and keep quiet about in public, and the issues over which we would resign. Corporate action means listening to other points of view, and often coming to compromises which are not weak but honourable, namely the programme which as a mixed group you feel able to accept.

The Biblical question about involvement in politics that is hardest to answer is Paul's failure to condemn slavery. He seems to have accepted it as part of the scenery, calling individual masters and slaves to make the best relationships they could within the given framework of society.

Bonhoeffer said that the Church finds itself at different times in its history in different relationships to the state.[50] At times — and the New Testament era was one of these — the Church is what he called a 'congregation in the catacombs'. This is its present situation in Russia, for example. Anything the Church says is unlikely to have any impact upon an avowedly anti-Christian government. By contrast, in local and national issues in Britain the Church is in a position to make its voice heard when it argues for justice.

This was the situation in the Old Testament. The prophets had a chance of being heard, and they spoke to their rulers and to the rulers of surrounding nations about changing the given framework of society, when they believed it was unjust. When the Church has this opportunity, it has a responsibility to speak out about matters which dehumanise or oppress people.

Where are the Prophets?

Who are the sons of the prophets today? Few if any are likely to claim, as the Old Testament prophet did, 'Thus says the Lord.' A rough and ready comparison of the New Testament experience of the Holy Spirit with that of the Old Testament may be instructive. Broadly it can be said that, in the Old Testament, the Holy Spirit came upon some men (like the prophets) some of the time. In the New Testament, the Holy Spirit is poured out on all Christians for all of the time. If the Church takes the prophets seriously, it means that all Christians should be concerned with the kind of issues about which the prophets spoke — issues which are very much within the terms of reference of God's Kingdom of right relationships.

In many shop stewards' meetings or board rooms or town hall committee rooms, it will be the layman who speaks the prophetic word — or keeps silent. Often he doesn't speak up because he feels so alone, or because he has never been given the opportunity to thrash the issues out with other Christians. If he has thought out a clear doctrine of the Creator, he will expect to find allies among those who are not Christians but think responsibly about life. But the fact remains that the Church betrays many of its laymen who could speak the prophetic word because we allow them to feel ill-equipped and unsupported. They need to belong to a group of fellow Christians where political, neighbourhood and work issues are seriously grappled with, in the context of a brotherhood which is strong enough to cope with disagreements. The love of the brotherhood is a springboard from which Christians can take off to obey the still more taxing command to love neighbours who may be on the other side of the table in any industrial or political dispute.[51]

Some feel that it is never the function of the ordained minister, or of the congregation as a whole, to speak or act in a political context. This is a dangerous view of a minister, for so to speak, it 'unmans' him. He is still a citizen. He may be the best informed and best equipped person to act in a particular situation, whether it is in private discussion or in public utterance. The Church will be operating out of balance if he alone exercises a 'prophetic ministry'. Similarly, it will be off balance if he never has anything to say about the hard issues of community life. There is a parallel in the way the evangelistic ministry should be carried out. It is the task of the whole *laos*, the whole people of God. If the minister thinks it his task alone, the body will not be functioning properly. On the other hand if he never attempts to evangelise or speaks about evangelism, he must not be surprised if the laity are not enthusiastic about it either. If there is a clear issue, it may well be appropriate for Christians corporately to show their views, especially if it is standing up for someone else's rights. But there is no one clear Christian viewpoint on thorny public issues.

Two Alternatives

This leaves two alternatives. One is that Christians enter the public arena locally and nationally and sometimes disagree with each other with the pain which that brings. The other is that we keep silent. The voice of Christian prophecy is then silenced. We must not stay silent. We must enter the ring, not in a triumphalist way which will tell the world what to believe, but with fear and trembling, standing up to be counted on issues of justice.

The preaching of the Gospel of the Kingdom calls men into personal relationship with Christ. Its challenge does not stop there. It is to lift up our horizons to what God wants this world to be like, and what He wants us to be like as His responsible partners. If a man dares to join Him in His work of overcoming and casting out whatever hinders God's purpose for the world, 'Then he will discover how much there is in himself from which he needs to be cleansed and set free.'[52] Man only realises that he has a great need to be forgiven, when it dawns on him that God is truly good and calls him to use to the full the gifts he has in responsible service. Then he understands what it is to come short of the glory of God.[53]

We often fail to see our need of Christ's redemption because we have set such low objectives for ourselves. We withdraw from involvement in meeting the needs of people at work or in the community, because we say we wouldn't be able to cope. God's purpose for us is greater; 'He has made us little lower than gods, while our highest ambition is to be a little above the Joneses. We are looking for a sensible, family-size God.'[54]

THE SINS OF THE CITY

GOD's love is greater than that. Therefore He has greater purposes for us and for the city we live in. And therefore His love expresses itself in judgment against much of what He sees in it and in us. Judgment and wrath, sin and guilt are words which many thoughtful Christians shrink from using. Such words seem to them to misrepresent the God of love.

To take first the concepts of God's judgment and wrath. Part of the problem is that we confuse any idea of wrath with what so often happens within ourselves when we are angry. Yet we have learned from behavioural studies to look carefully even at the anger in ourselves and not necessarily to suppress it. Parts of our anger, far from being evil, are expressions of love.

If we see eight year olds left outside to play by the lifts at eleven o'clock at night, silent tolerance is not likely to be the highest expression of our love towards their parents. If we see members of an affluent society holding firmly on to their advantages and indifferent to others' disadvantages in housing, jobs and education, it is not loving to accept things as they are. Indignation, perhaps being very angry until something is done about it, may be much more Christ-like. And if men understand what needs to be done and persistently refuse to do it, love must be implacably opposed to them.

The burning, holy love of God will not come to terms with ruthless greed and indifference to others' needs. Though they offer countless prayers, He will not listen, as long as they refuse to pursue justice, to champion the oppressed, to give the orphan his rights, to plead the widow's cause.[55]

In the Gospels Jesus shows anger and indignation, which is far removed from petulance. This appeared, for example, when He was confronted by the hardness of heart which put the letter of religious law before the need of a man in trouble, or at those who turned the small children away from Him, or at people grabbing the best seats at a party. In His parables the master is rightly angry at his servant's refusal to forgive his fellow servant. In another parable, the master is angry with the lazy servant who would not use the talent which he had been given.

The more people knew of God's purposes, the sharper Jesus' words were when He saw them failing to live up to their knowledge. Those who knew less often found, to their great surprise, that His attitude was one of acceptance, when they had expected judgment. Anger is an appropriate reaction to seeing eight year olds playing outside a block at eleven o'clock at night. But before we assume that God's holy love is as angry with the parents as we are, perhaps we need to know the parents as well as God does. One clergyman found himself feeling very angry with the parents of some of his youth club members, because he realised that they were being given no sort of experience of firm love at home. When he came to know the parents, he started to like them and to make allowances for them.

Savagely Scarred

My colleague George Burton's personality had been savagely scarred as a boy in the Glasgow of the Depression. It remained scarred till his death, though there was a great measure of healing in him. It was not possible to tell him to forgive and forget in the way that someone with a secure upbringing could do. His jealousy of anyone he conceived to be a rival was a kind of lashing out because an open wound of insecurity had been touched. It would be true that some of the scars in his personality were the result of self inflicted wounds. In his case it wouldn't have explained much to say 'I blame the parents'. His mother worked heroically to provide love in his home. It is a much more complex question to ask who was to blame for the lack of education which blocked a brilliant child, and gave him chips on his shoulder against 'You educated people' for more than half his lifetime.[56] Or to ask who built the slums of Glasgow's Townhead, and who tolerated their continued existence. Industrialists, shareholders, governments, voters, teachers, Church people, both by greed and by doing nothing created Glasgow of the 1920s. Similar scars are being caused in children's personalities today, particularly in priority areas of big cities.

God's love knows about people's opportunities for understanding and for doing. I believe that He 'makes allowances'. That is not the same thing as believing that He expects nothing of those who are disadvantaged and regards them as cases for treatment. His respect for men means that He treats all of us as responsible beings. We experience His judgment when we consciously and deliberately turn our backs on what we know to be good, true, loving and human; when we know at the same time that God bore the experience of the Cross, because He so much wanted us back as His partners, we begin to realise how much sin matters.

There is a tangled jungle to clear away, before we can see clearly what really matters to God and what doesn't. A false conscience has often been stimulated which makes people feel guilty about trivial matters. A seventeen year old in east London said that she had been made to feel terrible when she was at school for sliding down a corridor, forgetting her books and having an untidy desk. The whole majesty of authority's disapproval was exerted to make her feel guilty about matters like these. She could see clearly the danger that when she saw that that sort of crime didn't matter very much, she might in the same breath say, 'So nothing matters.'

False conscience can paralyse people with guilt. A woman's husband has not been in long from work. He comments that the meal is a little late. She promptly bursts into tears. She feels terrible about the chaos the kitchen is in — the breakfast hasn't been washed up — the beds haven't been made — there's still a pile of ironing — she only has one child and her friend has four, and still keeps her flat spotless, as well as helping with the play group. She feels guilty about everything, and in the end responsible about nothing.

All That Wrecks and All That Falls Short

At the risk of producing a great catalogue, I am going to set out some of the forms of sin which seems to me to do the most damage in the big city. They come under these two headings.

All That Wrecks

Ruthless greed,

especially when it exploits others for its gain. It is blatant when lorry drivers bring teenage girls from Liverpool to London, and when a procurer pays the driver his price; when big business exploits a woman's body for pornography — or for advertising.

The lines are not so obviously drawn when advertising creates consumer demand for something valueless.

Or when a developer holds on to land and then sells to the highest bidder, when he knows the housing needs of a district.

Or when a father encourages his son to believe that he must keep up in the rat race, instead of asking, 'Who wants to be rats anyway?'

Contempt for others

This is obvious when it is backbiting at a neighbour who isn't there to speak up for himself, and when mindless violence attacks a tramp or an old lady as though they are fair sport.

It is not so obvious when people talk about yobbos, or scroungers, without bothering to try to understand what has made them what they are.

Prejudice against other groups

The segregated city leaves some groups ignorant of others. That's when prejudice flourishes. It is prejudice when people write off 'these dockers, always striking for more', quoting unverified figures, without acknowledging the fact that they themselves earn as much as the dockers, and have vastly greater security and real wealth.

It is prejudice when militant leaders repeat old stories about bosses and question their motives in order deliberately to keep old distrust strong, and to keep their own position of personal power.

It is less obviously prejudice when employers refuse a job to black people or youths with long hair because, they say, other workmen wouldn't like them

What the ancient Greeks called hubris — overweaning pride

Hubris leads planners to assume that they know what is best for a district and that it would only waste their time to ask local people to join in the planning process.

Hubris is when teachers do not believe that parents could help them understand how best to educate their children, if they gave them time.

It is a less obvious form of *hubris* when a parent encourages his son to believe that he and his kind are the leaders of society, and should not expect to learn from the less academically able.

All That Falls Short

Withdrawal

People fall short of living up to their God-given gifts when they say, 'I wouldn't be any use', when they haven't even tried to see what they could offer to a community group that needs help.

It falls short of a man's capabilities when he withdraws from a group he helped to start, because it isn't going well, or because he is insulted or not praised.

Withdrawal falls short of what human beings can achieve when they say of the estate/the factory/the city, 'It's too big and complicated. My job is to work as much overtime as I can for my family's sake.'

It is withdrawal which blames 'them' for bad policies, but refuses to participate in making decisions when the opportunity is offered.

Indifference

It is falling short of simple humanity to take no notice of colleagues or neighbours who obviously need a friend to talk to.

Refusal to take seriously the cause of a less powerful community group or union, when it needs help, is a falling short of human solidarity.

Indifference to the disadvantages some people face in the same city is falling short of being members one of another.

Asserting that anyone who deserves it can enjoy the same affluence as we do is frequently falling short of love.

Wilful Ignorance

The city is difficult to understand, but some ignorance is wilful, when human beings are being deprived of the opportunity to develop God-given potential.

It is wilful ignorance to say that because powerlessness comes from complex forces, we cannot understand or do something about any of them.

It can become wilful ignorance to assert, in the face of much evidence, that all children in our country who work hard have equal opportunities to achieve well.

Reality Of Evil

Perhaps we can dismiss some sins as trivial. If so, we cannot include sins like these among them. They wreck the city which could be a place of partnership and human warmth. By withdrawal, indifference and wilful ignorance, the relatively powerful leave the powerless to fend for themselves.

Whatever the origin of evil, its reality confronts us. The mystery is deeper than the sum of individual acts of selfishness, and indeed of corporate guilt from a long past. I believe that behind flesh and blood are principalities and powers, superhuman forces of evil.[57]

Helmut Thielicke preached a series of sermons in Stuttgart during the weeks of fierce American and British bombing. He said they had in their time had far too much contact with demonic powers to laugh the 'evil one' out of court. They had observed how an alien spirit could ride those who had been quite decent and reasonable persons, driving them to brutalities, delusions of power and fits of madness.[58]

I have not discovered a better way of describing the power of evil after eighteen years ministry in London than the Bible's name of *Satan*. Hard work at planning for a neighbourhood, a model factory, extra resources for youth work have in turn seemed to make little headway against the forces which divide and dehumanise. The dark power in the New Testament seems far more uncanny than, for instance, in the Book of Job.[59] It is not helpful to see a personal devil lurking round every corner at all times. Yet demonic intelligence seems to lie behind so much evil which confronts us.

REDEMPTION

WE understand the Incarnation best when we see that Christ came to undo the devil's work. It exposed evil for what it is, and was the first costly step on the road to the Cross. Christ's coming was not first and foremost to explain things more clearly, but to make things right which had gone terribly wrong. God's First Plan was that the world should be a place of partnership and harmony. The great variety of gifts He had given to human beings were all to be used to the utmost for the common good. Truth, beauty and justice were to reign.

Redemption is not, so to speak, some Second Plan of His. It is God's determination to the death that His First Plan has not been abandoned. Evil remains a mystery. In the

Cross God takes it with deadly seriousness. And God's love wins. The mystery of evil is still there, but in the Cross and Resurrection there is the clue to a victory to which faith can hold on. When Christians have looked at the Cross, they have been aware of judgment, of acceptance and of victory. No theory, no illustration is adequate to explain what God was doing on Good Friday. They can only point us in some directions which may help.

We are aware of judgment. 'Christ died for our sins once and for all. He, the just, suffered for the unjust, that He might bring us to God.'[60] The once and for all claim makes us ask how this one death could be so special. The answer depends upon what you believe about Jesus Christ. If He is in a special and unique sense God's only Son, we have started to talk about the dealings of a personal God with His children.

Christ is truly man, facing all our tests, yet coming through with perfect obedience to God. He is Himself God's First Plan restored. He is also God working in man for reconciliation. The holy God Himself met the sin, entered into its costliness, suffered redemptively in His own Son. Here was no overlooking of guilt or trifling with forgiveness; no external treatment of sin, 'but a radical, a drastic, a passionate and absolutely final acceptance of the terrible situation, and an absorption by the very God Himself of the fatal disease so as to neutralise it effectively'.[61]

Jesus was no outwardly triumphant martyr, smiling to His death. 'Now is My soul in turmoil . . . take away this cup from Me . . . My God, My God, why have You forsaken Me?'[62] Sin is judged. We know sin hurts innocent people. Now we see in the Cross what our personal sin, and the corporate sin in which we share, did to the only perfectly innocent One. Because of the way we have lived, *that* had to happen to the One who was altogether good.

A Nightmare

Kafka's man on trial cannot get at authority. He doesn't
know what he is being tried for. The law is rigid, impersonal,
totally external to his life. 'I don't know this law', he says.
Yet he is caught up in its authority and its judgment. *The
Trial* is a nightmare. Yet it has too much in common with
the experience of many in the big city who feel that they are
powerless and do not know the procedure or the right
people. They feel that authority is remote, emerging with its
rigid set of rules from the world of 'them'. Sadly, God and
the Church are often connected mentally with such authority.

A prison chaplain meets the man on trial, Joseph K., in
the cathedral. He goes into the pulpit in order to talk to him.
'Won't you come down here?' said K, after the chaplain had
told him more about authority's view of his case, 'You
haven't got to preach a sermon. Come down beside me.' 'I
can come down now,' said the chaplain. 'I had to speak to
you first from a distance. Otherwise I am too easily
influenced and tend to forget my duty.'[63]

I sat in a juvenile court while Tony aged sixteen stood in
front of the magistrates. The way the clerk asked him if he
pleaded guilty or not guilty left him confused. 'Yes', he said.
Eventually it was agreed that he was guilty of taking and
driving away a scooter, and that the scooter had not been
taxed. They dealt with him in a kindly fashion, and lectured
him about the seriousness of the offence in a language he
clearly did not understand. But how could they know that
his mother who sat there helplessly was ill, and would be
dead within a year; that his father had already given up, and
would soon be £150 in arrears with the rent, that nobody
bothered to get Tony and his brother up in order to go to
work? They knew a bit on paper, as I knew it, but could

they, or I, *feel* what new actions were really possible for a boy like that? The feel and reality of our worlds were poles apart.

We see a new kind of authority on the Cross. It is no longer distant, bound by a set of rigid rules, emerging from the world of the powerful. It has become personal in Jesus. He experienced what it meant to be the victim of what was expedient policy to the government in distant, impersonal Rome and to those who wanted to keep their balance of power in Jerusalem. He did not know any of the right people with access to power. He knew what it was to have authority against Him. He experienced the personal hurts of betrayal and desertion by all His friends.

The one who hung on the Cross is the only Person who can understand what is possible and what is not possible for someone like Tony. He alone can justly judge — and can therefore justly forgive. Like anyone who has been wronged and seeks a personal reconciliation, he bears the pain and loss Himself.[64]

Acceptance

In the Cross we are aware of God's *acceptance*. The robber dying beside Jesus mocks, when he sees the words above Jesus's head — 'This is the king of the Jews'. Then he begins to wonder. He had never seen anyone carry himself more like a king should. And He doesn't continue the vicious circle of hate and revenge. He actually prays for His enemies. His love is undeserved, uncalculating. So an instinct draws the robber, as it has drawn many others who have understood little of Christian theology, and he says, 'Jesus, remember me when you come to your throne.' There is no rebuff. There are no conditions. 'Today you shall be with Me in Paradise.'[65]

The robber experienced the same surprise which many

who condemned themselves felt when they met Jesus. There is no pretence that he is really a good man deep down, who has been damaged by his environment. All that may be true, but he is a responsible person facing real goodness and real justice for the first time. As best he can, he faces Christ, and says, 'Here I am, Jesus. I'm sorry.' The genuine wish for reconciliation was enough. Repentance, a change of heart, settles all accounts. Jesus will not keep him waiting, nor put him on probation, nor will He spoil His gift by bringing up old sores from the past.[66]

A question has haunted us all along as we have seen the pressures which the big city at its worst puts upon people. Does a right environment have to be established before they can become Christians? Is Christianity only for those who've already been through some primary school of culture?

Justification by faith says no. A group in our flat at the Mayflower was discussing over a period of six weeks some of the pressures which make us behave as we do. Dave said, 'Well I believe that Christ accepts me just as I am. And if that's not true, I've got no chance.' A neighbouring vicar who was leading the discussions said, 'Yes, I believe that. But I also believe that Christ meets me in judgment. He wants me not to stay just as I am, but to come on a bit further with Him.'

When I have thought about George Burton, who was such a study in contradictions, I have often remembered the part in Paul about God's treasure being put in earthenware pots.[67] George was very earthy. The bursts of temper, the brash boasting, the personal fears, remained part of his make up until his death, though many of these were partially healed. But George knew what it was to be a man accepted in Christ, and he was confident that that undeserved love would never be withdrawn. He knew he was not on probation. The pot was earthy, but the treasure was in it. There was an astonishing tenderness, a jump ahead in knowing what others feared, a powerful faith in Christ, when at ease an ability which was quite out of the ordinary to handle the roughest youngsters, taking their hates and bringing about riotous fun, lifting their horizons of what life could be in east London.

Misunderstood

The belief that Christ accepts us by an uncalculating love has often been misunderstood. It has been suggested that all it asks of a man is that he correctly believes the proposition that he is justified by faith, or that he keeps taking the medicine called grace. 'It's an easy religion, yours,' a friend said to me. 'You get in the lift. You push the button and up you go. You sin and then you apologise. You sin again and you apologise again. And so it goes on.' He didn't understand that we are speaking not of a contract, but of a personal relationship, a love relationship.

The nearest human experience is in marriage. A man may say something, or do something which hurts his wife. She forgives him, though he doesn't deserve it. Her love is such that he believes that, if he were to do it again, she would forgive him again. The logic to that would be to go on doing it, because he could expect to 'get away with it'.

Uncalculating love always takes the risk that people may take liberties, because it does not put them on probation. Because these are personal relationships, a love relationship, changes of attitudes begin to happen. Nothing makes you feel so small, and nothing so much makes you want to be different, as to be forgiven when you don't deserve it by someone whose love you have hurt.

Perhaps for most Christians it is true that they are only conscious of sin being something truly hurtful and destructive, when they have experienced for some time what it

is to receive love that is not deserved. Karl Barth said, 'Sin
scorches us when it comes under the light of forgiveness,
not before. Sin scorches us then.'[68] Grace is not a medicine
you take. It always means undeserved love, and should never
be thought of apart from the grace of God and of our Lord
Jesus Christ.

In the Cross we see too God's *victory*. The way of love
wouldn't be any good, we say, unless everyone agreed to
start living by it at once. 'It's all very well for you. You don't
know what people are like round here', 'It just isn't possible
to live that way — not where I work'; 'What good can I do,
all by myself, if I try to take on the system.' Jesus chooses to
be stripped of all the trappings of power. He no longer
knows the top people; remote Rome and its political needs
influence Pilate, when he nearly does the right thing; He is
exposed to the whole snarling pack. He makes Himself
nothing; He is a man, a slave, accepts even death — death on
a cross.[69] The principalities and powers of the world are
against Him. They are exposed for what they are. Naked evil
wants to tear good to pieces. He doesn't retaliate by smash-
ing their teeth in. He goes on living by the love which we say
is impossible in our situation. It proves to be the toughest
commodity in the world. Perfect obedience to His Father's
will is worked out until He can say, 'It is accomplished.'[70]
He faces all the impersonal and personal pressures we have
to face. From within the alienated human situation He wins
through.

Paul used a vivid picture, suggesting that He disarmed His
executioners and judges, and marched them off in His
triumphal procession leaving the judgment against human
sin nailed to an empty Cross.[71] John saw the Cross as the
moment of glory to which the whole of Christ's life moved.
This was 'the hour' for which He came. He was 'lifted up',
so that the gallows became a throne.[72]

Living Lord

For John and the other New Testament writers, the Cross and the Resurrection were seen as one. Indeed, we could not talk about *Good* Friday if there was no Easter Day and Pentecost to follow. Reconciliation and peace flow from the Cross, but they would not be personal, love relationships, if Christ were not a living Lord. We should still be on our own with the pressures of a disordered world. But He is alive and with us by His Holy Spirit. He calls us to be responsible partners, no longer slaves receiving orders from afar, but friends sharing His confidences. We can experience both the power of His Resurrection, and share His sufferings in the situation where He has placed us.

THE CHANGES WE NEED

CHRIST'S victory on the Cross has implications for the whole of creation. 'God chose to reconcile the whole universe to Himself, making peace (*Shalom*) through the shedding of His blood upon the Cross.'[78] Because of texts like this, it has been claimed that the victory of Christ has *already* brought the whole world out of bondage.

It is sometimes said, using F. D. Maurice's phrase, that 'the whole world is in Christ'. Maurice went on to say that men could shut themselves out by conscious rejection of God and His values. Yet the phrase 'The whole world is in Christ' remains misleading. It leads to such statements as, 'Every man has been made a member of the new mankind,

because of Christ's resurrection.'[74] It is as though humanity
is a group of loving, caring people, taken without being consulted, to the top of a hill. All we have to do is to remind
them to be what they are, take the brake off, and point out
those causes which need their care most, as they free-wheel
eagerly down the hill. The mystery of evil and the twists in
human nature are forgotten. The reality of the world is that
frequently the car is at the bottom of the hill, and that the
engine won't go, which would carry them to this caring activity.

The death and resurrection of Christ are for the whole
world. But man's personality remains unviolated. His co-
operation in the Kingdom of God has to be willing. Like
Nicodemus, he must be born over again, if he is to enter the
Kingdom of God.[75] However much people may be victims
of the worst of urban life, and however much they feel solidarity with a group, God treats them as responsible human
beings, not as helpless 'cases'. Each individual stands before
God; each individual is summoned by God to decision according to the understanding he has.[76]

Christians are tragically wrong to manipulate people to
obtain a 'decision'. They are equally wrong if they do not
make them aware that a conscious response is needed. 'It is
as if God were appealing to you through us: in Christ's
name we implore you, be reconciled to God . . . we urge this
appeal upon you.'[77] God's infinite respect for men made in
His image allows the possibility that some, who steadily turn
their backs on what they know to be true and good, will
eventually, as Herod did, find Him silent, with His back
turned on them. That is indeed the defeat of the Almighty,
the defeat of love. But it is because He is the *Father* Almighty, and His love does not impose its will by force. So He
weeps over the city: 'How often have I longed to gather your
children, as a hen gathers her brood under her wings; but
you would not let Me.'[78]

Man's response needs to be repentance, that is a complete change of heart. It may or may not happen first at one decisive moment in time. It does not mean floods of tears, 'I've sinned, I've sinned. I'll make up for it. I'll never do it again.' Rather, Christ suggests that I stop, turn round and look at myself and what I've done. Then I must sift away the parts for which I am not properly to blame, and acknowledge those parts for which *I* rather than the devil, society or ulcers am to blame. It means looking realistically at what I am going to do when I face similar situations again.

But repentance is more than determining to stay out of trouble. It involves the will to 'go straight', as an ex-prisoner might put it. So our response also includes the positive determination to serve in His Kingdom.

More Honest

Christians have sometimes spoken too glibly about continuous 'victory' in their lives. This claim has sometimes been made possible only by avoiding all the most threatening parts of living in the thick of the world. Our generation is more ready to be involved, and to be more honest about our failures. That is healthy. But we are too afraid of believing that we can experience Christ's power. So we say to ourselves, 'Yes, I believe God defeated all the principalities and powers of the Universe, and raised Jesus from the dead. But I don't believe He can alter anything in my situation this week. That's too hard for Him.'

Our unbelief often springs from our misunderstanding of what kind of Kingdom God's is. Its triumphs are not generally written in the history books, cannot usually be measured in terms of profits or national growth rates or in personal recognition. But when the Kingdom of God begins to come in a particular situation, subtle and pervasive changes come about. We must train ourselves to have eyes to see the right kind of differences and to work for them.

John the Baptist, lying in prison, no longer the big figure, desperately trying not to lose his faith, sent a message to Jesus, 'Are you the one who is to come, or are we to expect some other?' There was no great victory, no mass movement, no protection against Herod, and death loomed up in front of him. 'Go and tell John what you have seen and heard,' Jesus told the messengers, 'How the blind recover their sight, the lame walk, the lepers are made clean, the deaf hear, the dead are raised to life, the poor are hearing the good news.' It was a restatement of the terms of reference He had set out in His first sermon at Nazareth. There was a 'not yet' about the coming of the Kingdom when all wrongs would be righted. John the Baptist would not yet be rescued, and would not yet be raised from the dead. No total victory yet swept all before it. But Christ was beginning to undo the devil's work. Broken lives were being mended; those who had never counted before were hearing the good news.

The Church, like Christ, has a dual role in its ministry to a disordered world. We have to work to remove sufferings and injustice since they are hateful to God. It is also our ministry, 'when they are overwhelming and there is no escape from them, to transfigure them and use them as the raw material of love'.[79] Often our position has to be somewhere in between these two roles. We have to set short term and medium term objectives, taking realistic account of what the raw material is.

A planner has to be conscious of the constraints which his raw materials of limited land and cash place upon him. Yet he must not forget the dream of the city that might be. The parent or the teacher has to remember what the realities of life are going to be at work. But he must not forget the dream of how God really wants the child's potential to be used.

A young man who worked in the docks saw vividly, in a

conversation, the implications of belief in a God who was extremely interested in the whole quality of life in the docks. Immediately he said, 'But what could I possibly do in the docks?' At that moment I felt for the first time that I understood the parable of the mustard seed. The smallest of seeds grows to a tree, big enough for the birds to come and roost among its branches.[80] The mustard seed is every act of obedience to God, however small. No one knows what influence it may have. If he really was to begin to be what he believed God wanted him to be in the docks, there would be few obvious results. But response to the Kingdom has to begin somewhere; it is impossible to calculate what effect on the network of relationships which make up an industry each person can have who rejects withdrawal and tries to work out Christ's dreams in his situation.

Life Through Death

Christ's way is of death and resurrection, life through death. His attitude facing the city may be contrasted with that of a Psalmist. The Psalmist faced violence and strife in the city. It was alive with rumour and scandal. Its public square was never free from violence and spite. His response was withdrawal; 'Oh that I had the wings of a dove to fly away and be at rest! I should escape far away and find a refuge in the wilderness.'[81] Jesus faced a very similar city. 'Now my soul is in turmoil, and what am I to say? Father, save me from this hour? No, it was for this that I came to this hour . . . A grain of wheat remains a solitary grain unless it falls into the ground and dies; but if it dies, it bears a rich harvest.'[82] His way in which He asks us to share, is not withdrawal but life through death.

In the Gospels, the Kingdom of God is central to understanding the mission of Jesus. Wherever He is, the Kingdom has drawn near. He drives out demons 'by the finger of

God', and therefore the Kingdom of God 'has already come upon you'.[83] If what they see is the finger of God at work, there may also be the implication that His strong right hand is just round the corner. There is both the sense that the Kingdom has come, and that it is not yet.

The Kingdom of God is not the same as the Church. This has already come into being with the choosing of the twelve and the seventy and Peter's recognition of Jesus as the Christ. The 'little flock' is in being; the Father has chosen to give them the Kingdom.[84] Therefore, they are to start to live according to the values which are important in the Kingdom of God. The ethics Jesus teaches are in response to the coming of the Kingdom — if God's Kingdom is here, what kind of lives ought we to be living in the whole community? The Kingdom of God is not the same as the Church. But it is not unrelated. We 'enter the Kingdom of God by being born anew from water and spirit'.[85] Personal faith in Christ needs the stimulus and encouragement of this Christian fellowship. That fellowship is called to serve the needs of the Kingdom.

The coming of the Kingdom in power is the event towards which the first three gospels move, like the 'hour' in John. It is coming in 'this generation'. The gospels will not allow us to banish all the teaching about the Kingdom come in power to a second coming at the end of history.

One of the most remarkable features of the New Testament is that the phrase 'the Kingdom of God', which is so central to everything in the first three Gospels, scarcely receives a mention in the Acts of the Apostles or in their Letters. It is as though the Kingdom has already come and they are looking at it from the other side. Central to everything in the first preaching of the apostles were 'the mighty acts' of God — the death, resurrection and exaltation of Jesus and the pouring out of the Holy Spirit.

From Now On

In John the hour towards which everything moves is the death and resurrection of Jesus. There are strong clues which suggest that these mighty acts are regarded as the coming of the Kingdom in the first three Gospels too. There is a strong sense of 'From now on'. For example, when the High Priest, the supreme authority in the earthly court, put Jesus on oath, 'Are you the Messiah, the Son of God?', Jesus's answer, if we dare to put Mark and Matthew together, was 'I am. But I tell you this: from now on, you will see the Son of Man seated at the right hand of God and coming on the clouds of heaven.'[86]

We have grown so used in religious imagery to connecting the clouds of heaven with Christ returning *from* heaven that we have forgotten that the Son of Man in the Book of Daniel came *to* the Ancient of Years to the higher court where he was vindicated. This is surely the movement. Jesus suffers and is vindicated. Sovereignty, glory and kingly power is given to Him. He pours out His Spirit upon His people.

The Gospels and the Acts have a further dimension to the coming of the Kingdom. 'This Jesus will come in the same way as you have seen Him go.'[87] John's Gospel, which sees the mighty acts of God fulfilled in the death and resurrection of Jesus ('realised eschatology'), still speaks of a last day, 'when all who are in the grave will hear His voice and come out: those who have done right will rise to life; those who have done wrong will rise to hear their doom.'[88]

The first three Gospels have a doctrine of the last things too, which is not yet fulfilled. For example, the wheat and the tares are to grow together *until harvest*. The Church of apostolic days believed that all the dreams of the Kingdom would one day be fulfilled. There would be new heavens and a new earth, the home of justice;[89] there would be the holy city, new Jerusalem.[90] When it seemed to a suffering Church that only disorder and gloom lay ahead, 'Paul's answer was clear and definite. The world is not moving on to chaos: it is moving on to Christ.'[91]

Part of the promise has bothered modern man — the resurrection of the body. But to leave this out would be to contradict all that we have said about the material world being God's creation, and that it too is to be redeemed along with men. We have no gospel of wholeness for a man with a twisted body or half a mind, unless it includes the resurrection of the body. We do not know precisely how this resurrection will shape us. This much can be said — faith, hope and love are three things which last for ever. Together with them, all that is good and true will be caught up, and somehow made greater in the Resurrection. Personality will be real, not absorbed into the ocean of matter. Paul suggests that all we know now may be compared with a world of seeds.[92] If we only knew shelves of seeds in their packets, we should never have seen the bloom of a rose or a full-grown tree. The new world will be that much greater than this one; it will apply to all our knowledge and experience. 'Now we see only puzzling reflections in a mirror, but then we shall see face to face.'[93]

A World to Come

Christians who insist that the whole answer must be in this world are frequently reacting against a false use of belief in a world to come. A friend told me she didn't believe in any resurrection, because she had so often heard belief in a life to come used wrongly. It had been used to justify doing nothing in this life about the terrible injustices she knew in her country. In fact the logic should argue the other way. If we believe that God's future kingdom will have justice and peace as features of its life, it is a powerful argument to work with all our strength to bring those features into action now. An example of this appeal to eschatology as a basis for dockyard ethics comes from Georges Velten.[94]

There was a strike in St. Nazaire and the Mission provided an old hall for meals for strikers and their families. 'To hell with this filthy kitchen,' shouted La Chope, one of the dockyard workers, 'a friend of mine will pinch half a dozen steel brushes for us in the shipyards. We'll have a beautifully clean kitchen and no one will be in danger of breaking his neck.' 'I don't hold with pinching', said Georges Velten. 'But everybody does it from the ship's boy to the captain.' Velten persisted, 'Do you think we're always going to have a world like this, one with sometimes the need to go on strike for weeks to get management to negotiate?' 'We won't. Society has to change and will.' 'I, too, think it will. Should pinching be going on then?' 'I hope not. It has more disadvantages than usefulness.' 'I hold the belief,' said Velten, 'that the world will change radically through Christ, and Christ tells us that if we really want a new world, we had better behave today as citizens of the world we would like. That is why I think we should not pinch those steel brushes we so definitely need.'

Belief in the City of God which will be made perfect one day, leads me to say that God has a purpose for the big city now. Our programme must learn something from the terms of reference of Jesus's mission. Its marks are the mending of broken lives and the proclaiming of good news to the poor. He set Himself alongside those who didn't have influence with the authorities, with the victims of principalities and powers. He was a realist about the evil influences in the world, as we have to be if we are serious about winning some battles in the city. He expected no cheap victories. His way was through suffering and death to a Resurrection which was only known to a minority. He promises that His Resurrection is only the first fruits of a harvest to come.

EPILOGUE

We are meanwhile to set ourselves limited aims in the city where we live. We are to encourage Christian expectations in the city; love really is the toughest commodity in the world; life comes through our smaller 'deaths', as it does through His Cross; people can be enabled to achievements far beyond what they expect, and we can be set free from some of our present day enslavements.

We shall find, as Jesus found, that we should not try simply to come to terms with some patterns of urban community. because when we look at them carefully we shall see that they are expressing non-community and non-life.[95] For example, we are not simply to teach people how to fit in to some huge new housing development or to the jobs which industry offers. The Kingdom of right relationships challenges people to believe that they can bring about changes in community and in industry. Then people can be people, families can be families, neighbours can be neighbours and workers can be workers.

We must hold on to the dream that it is possible for a place to be built as a city, and to know in the thick of its life right relationship beween men and with God.

NOTES

NOTES

PART ONE

1. *The Lambeth Conference* (S.P.C.K. and Seabury Press, 1958), p. 267.
2. Zechariah 3:10. New English Bible. All Bible quotations are from this translation unless otherwise stated.
3. Proverbs 8:3 Revised Standard Version. Psalm 8:6. Genesis 1:28.
4. Harvey Cox, *The Secular City* (S.C.M., 1965), p. 73ff.
5. Jacques Ellul, *The Meaning of the City* (William B. Eerdmans, 1970), p. 151.
6. Psalm 8.
7. Gavin Reid, *The Gagging of God* (Hodder and Stoughton, 1959), p. 35.
8. Richard Hoggart, *The Uses of Literacy* (Chatto and Windus, 1957), cf. pp. 141–202.
9. Edited W. R. Niblett, *Higher Education: Demand and Response* (Tavistock Publications, 1972), p. 222. Quoted in John Poulton, *A Today Sort of Evangelism* (Lutterworth, 1972), p. 30.
10. Lederer and Burdick, *The Ugly American* (Corgi, 1959).
11. Charles Reich, *The Greening of America*, 1970 (Penguin Books, 1971) describes Consciousness III which many young people in particular have embraced in reaction against Consciousness I and II. It rings many bells for me. But it is significant that the core group is always white, well educated and middle class. They seem to have no answer to industrialised work except to reject it (p. 204). The trouncing of Senator McGovern in the 1972 Presidential election could be read as the alliance of white collar and blue collar workers against what they saw as Utopian idealists. The criticisms of Consciousness I and II are shrewd and right. The idealist must not relapse into disillusion, but go to work to see how the ideals can effectively transform life in an urban and industrial society.
12. Jurgen Moltmann, *Theology of Hope* (S.C.M., 1967), p. 180. Quoted in J. V. Taylor, *The Go-Between God* (S.C.M., 1972), cf. p. 76ff.

13. Jacques Ellul, *The Meaning of the City*, op. cit., see pp. 158–63, 170, 181.

14. Richard Hare, 'Community and Communication' in *People and Cities* edited by Stephen Verney (Fontana, 1969), p. 160.

15. Alan Bullock, *The Life and Times of Ernest Bevin* (Heinemann, 1960), vol. 1, p. 551.

16. Peter Willmott and Michael Young, *Family and Class in a London Suburb* (Routledge and Kegan Paul, 1960).

17. D. Lockwood, 'Sources of Variation in working class images of society', *Sociological Review*, 14, 1966, pp. 249–68. See also Gordon Rose, *The Working Class* (Longmans, 1968).

18. Professor Colin Buchanan, 'Living in Cities' in *People and Cities*, op. cit., p. 150.

19. R. Dahrendorf, *Class and Class Conflicts in Industrial Society* (Routledge and Kegan Paul, 1963), p. 112f. 'Social mobility has become one of the crucial elements of the structure of industrial societies, and one would be tempted to predict its "breakdown" if the process of mobility were ever seriously impeded.'

20. John H. Goldthorpe, David Lockwood, Frank Bechhofer, Jennifer Platt, *The Affluent Worker in the Class Structure* (Cambridge University Press, 1969), pp. 26–8 and 163f. I find their history of the debate on the working class (pp. 1–30) the clearest brief description I know.

21. R. Dahrendorf, op. cit., p. 117.

22. F. Engels, 'The English Elections' 1874 and 'Trade Unions' 1881 referred to in Goldthorpe, Lockwood, Bechhofer, Platt, op. cit. p. 3.

PART TWO

1. I Corinthians 9:19, and see Romans 1:14 where Paul says that he is under obligation to Greek and non-Greek, to learned and simple.

2. Romans 12:5 (Authorised Version).

3. Ibid.

4. Alan Dawson, *A Sociological Study of Attitudes to the Church in Urban Areas*, unpublished M.A. Thesis, Liverpool University, 1967.

5. F. Boulard, *An Introduction to Religious Sociology*, translated M. J. Jackson (Darton, Longman and Todd, 1960), p. 60f.

6. Owen Chadwick, *The Victorian Church* (A. and C. Black, 1966), pt. I, pp. 271–5.

7. Owen Chadwick, *The Victorian Church*, op. cit., pt. I, p. 273f.

8. Quoted in The Religious Life of London (Hodder and Stoughton, 1904), edited R. Mudie Smith, p. 401f.

9. W. W. Daniel, *Whatever happened to the Workers in Woolwich?* (P.E.P., 1972), A survey of redundancy in South East London, p. 114f.

10. Gibson Winter, *The Suburban Captivity of the Churches* (Doubleday and Company Inc., Garden City, New York, 1961), p. 72f.

11. David and Jean Hewitt, *George Burton: A Study in Contradictions* (Hodder and Stoughton, 1969).

12. Isaiah 1:18 and see verse 17.

13. I Corinthians 10:32f.

14. *The Youth Service in England and Wales* (H.M.S.O., 1958), p. 37.

15. John Benington, *Culture, Class and Christian Beliefs* (Scripture Union, 1973), p. 24. This is a sensitive and important attempt to try to probe into the way things *feel* to those who have grown up altogether outside church culture and life.

16. John Pollock, *Billy Graham* (Hodder and Stoughton, 1966), p. 269f.

17. And see *On the Other side* (Scripture Union, 1968), p. 183. A report of the Evangelical Alliance Commission on Evangelism. This shows the results of a 1967 questionnaire put to 5,000 members of Evangelical Churches of different denominations. The proportion in the 'higher' social classes was more than double the national figure. The proportion among skilled, semi-skilled and unskilled manual workers was about one third of the national figure.

18. Mark Hodson, Bishop of Hereford in *Cosmos*, the journal of the Royal Foundation of St. Katharine, Spring 1966.

19. Nicholas Stacey, *Who Cares?* (Anthony Blond, 1971) gives an honest and perceptive account of his years as Rector of Woolwich.

20. Christian Lalive D'Epinay, *Haven of the Masses* (Lutterworth, 1969), cf. pp. 38, 47, 134f.

21. D'Epinay, op. cit., p. 136.

22. Walter Hollenweger, *The Pentecostals* (S.C.M. Press, 1972), p. 78f.

23. Bryan Wilson, *Sects and Society* (Heinemann, 1961), p. 106f.

24. Clifford Hill, *Black Churches* (Community and Race Relations Unit of the British Council of Churches, 1971), p. 13.

25. *Clifford Hill*, op. cit., p. 9.

PART THREE

1. Colin Marchant's major sources are: Copies of the *Stratford Express*; Frank Sainsbury, *West Ham — 800 years*; Donald

McDougal, *Fifty years a Borough 1886–1936*; E. G. Howarth and M. Wilson, *West Ham*, a study in social and industrial problems; Handbook of the Churches, *London over the Border*.

2. C. F. G. Masterman, in *The Religious Life of London*, edited R. Mudie Smith (Hodder and Stoughton, 1904), pp. 192, 199, 209.

3. Edited A. Amos and W. W. Hough, *The Cambridge Mission to South London* (Macmillan and Bowes, 1904), p. 88. W. W. Hough was Missioner of the Corpus Mission near the Old Kent Road. He was later Bishop of Woolwich.

4. *The Cambridge Mission to South London*, op. cit., p. 63. A sermon preached in Trinity College Chapel, Cambridge in 1885.

5. G. Kitson Clark, *The Making of Victorian England* (Methuen, 1962), p. 192.

6. George Potter, *Father Potter of Peckham* (Hodder and Stoughton, 1955).

7. Kathleen Heasman, *Evangelicals in Action* (Bles, 1962), p. 58.

8. See *The Problem of East London*, op. cit., Percy Alder's contribution to *The Religious Life of London*.

9. The dangers of accidents and disease caused by industry before the Factory Acts had their effect is reflected in the fact that a man's expectation of life was much higher if he was a pauper than if he was a worker. R. F. Wearmouth, *Methodism and the Working class Movements of England 1800–1850* (Epworth, 1937), p. 248.

The figures he quotes for the average life of a labourer in 1843 are:

in Liverpool	15 years
in Manchester	17 years
in Leeds	19 years
in London	22 years.

If you survived to be twenty-one, you were likely to live for rather more than double those figures. In London the average life of labourers was forty-nine and of paupers sixty.

Christians were closely involved in demanding better conditions for factory workers. Parson Bull of Bradford became known as the Ten Hour Parson because of his campaign to limit the hours of work for women and children in textile factories. This Act was passed in 1847 after fierce controversy. Factory legislation began in 1833. Factory Acts were often ignored and Lord Shaftesbury was still campaigning to stop the use of little boys as chimney sweeps in 1875.

10. cf. K. S. Inglis, *Churches and the Working Classes in Victorian England* (Routledge and Kegan Paul, 1963), pp. 194–214.

Richard Collier, *The General Next to God* (Collins, 1965), pp. 191–5.

11. I owe this description to a note from Dr. Maldwyn Edwards.
    Lord Donald Soper has commented, 'The founders of the Central Halls designed them to be as unlike churches as possible — and they certainly succeeded.'

12. Owen Chadwick, *The Victorian Church*, pt. I, op. cit., pp. 455–68.

13. *Second Report of the Royal Commission on Friendly and Benefit Societies*, 1872, vol. L 6. I owe this information to the Revd. Ronald Crewes.

14. This is a Londoner's comment and may not hold good for other cities. For instance, Kirby New Town would seem to represent a 'decanting' much more comparable with Dagenham than Harlow, as far as the population who moved there is concerned. Kirby could be described as a large slice of Inner Liverpool transferred to a New Town. In its church-going habits it far more nearly resembles inner Liverpool (or Dagenham) than, say, Wigan or St. Helen's. These smaller industrial towns have a more comprehensive cross section of social classes and have an identity which in any case takes many years for a new town to develop.

15. Owen Chadwick, *The Victorian Church*, pt. II (A. and C. Black, 1970), p. 279.

16. Quoted in Stephen Mayor, *The Churches and the Labour Movement*, p. 323. George Lansbury, who was unusual among Labour leaders in being a practising Anglican, also said once that the Settlement Movement never substantially affected the cause of working class advancement.

17. I owe this to Dr. Kitson Clark. See *Melvin Richter, The Politics of Conscience. T. H. Green and his Age*, p. 322.

18. For the setting of this debate in France see, Alec Vidler, *A Century of Social Catholicism* (S.P.C.K., 1964), pp. 112–40.

19. R. Mudie Smith, *The Religious Life of London*, op. cit., p. 207.

20. Romans 13:1–6.

21. Norman Cohn, *The Pursuit of the Millennium* (Paladin, 1970).

22. Gordon Rupp, *A Small Birth of Freedom*. Firth Memorial Lectures no. 4. Christian History and Western Civilisation.

23. *The Victorian Church*, pt. I, op. cit., p. 373f.

24. R. F. Wearmouth, *Methodism and the Common People of the Eighteenth Century* (Epworth, 1945), pp. 217–38.

25. R. F. Wearmouth, *Methodism 1800–1850*, op. cit., p. 15f. and p. 211f.

26. *Methodism 1800–1850*, op. cit., p. 158.

27. *Methodism 1800–1850*, op. cit., p. 185.
28. Quoted, op. cit., p. 227.
29. op. cit., pp. 221–35.
30. op. cit., p. 194.
31. Owen Chadwick, *The Victorian Church*, pt. I, op. cit., pp. 370–91.
32. Owen Chadwick, *The Victorian Church*, pt. I, op. cit., p. 352f and p. 350.
33. Edited Frederick Maurice, *Life of Frederick Denison Maurice* (Macmillan, 1884), vol. II, 365. Quoted in A. M. Ramsey, *The Gospel and the Catholic Church* (Longman's Green and Co., 1936), p. 211.
34. cf. Colossians 1:20.
35. Owen Chadwick, *The Victorian Church*, pt. II, op. cit., pp. 277–83.
36. Edmund Arbuthnott, *Joseph Cardijn, Priest and Founder of the Y.C.W.* (Darton, Longman and Todd, 1966), p. 11.
37. Scott Lidgett, *My Guided Life*, p. 170.
38. Aileen Nash, *Living in Lambeth 1806–1914* (Lambeth Borough Council). I owe this information to the Revd. Ronald Crewes.
39. Owen Chadwick, *The Victorian Church*, pt. II, op. cit., pp. 155–7.
40. K. S. Inglis, op. cit., p. 27. Committees of the Canterbury and York Convocations, reporting in 1889 and 1892, found that most of the clergy were opposed to dividing parishes. They believed it was better to have resident curates in various parts of a large parish.
41. 1972 mid-year estimates of the Registrar General based on the 1971 Census:

Southwark	253,260
Lewisham	262,920
Greenwich	216,180

42. Charles Booth, *Life and Labour of the People of London* (Macmillan, 1902), Third Series: Religious Influence, vol. 7, chapter 10, paragraph 1.
43. C. F. G. Masterman in *The Religious Life of London*, op. cit., pp. 196–9.

	Population	Church attendance	Percentage of population
Walworth	99,261	6,644	6·5
Dulwich/Sydenham	32,096	9,833	30·6

Masterman noted that a number of church-goers travelled then as now from the suburbs to churches in the inner area; also that tradesmen and middle class people who lived in the bigger houses, for example, along the Walworth Road were the most enthusiastic supporters of many churches. On this basis he said that adult church attendance by the working class and the poor was 2%.

44. R. A. Soloway, *Prelates and People: Ecclesiastical Social Thought in England 1783–1852* (Routledge and Kegan Paul, 1969), p. 5.
45. Charles Smyth, *Cyril Forster Garbett* (Hodder and Stoughton, 1959), p. 180.
46. *Stratford Express*, November 8th, 1919.

	Population	Communicants	Percentage
Essex	1,350,000	68,903	5
West Ham	296,000	6,814	2·3

PART FOUR

1. See Plato, *The Republican* (Penguin Classics Edition), p. 160 and pp. 109–12.
2. J. W. B. Douglas, J. M. Ross, H. R. Simpson, Peter Davies, *All Our Future*, 1968.

   Marcus Worsley, M.P. for Chelsea asked in a parliamentary question in 1973 how many children leave secondary schools without taking either the General Certificate of Education 'O' level exams or the Certificate of Secondary Education exams. The answer was that of the 613,000 pupils who left schools in England and Wales in 1970/71 269,000, or 44% had attempted neither the G.C.E. nor C.S.E. examinations.
3. Edited A. H. Halsey, *Educational Priority. E.P.A. Problems and Policies* (H.M.S.O., 1972), vol. 1, p. 11.
4. Luke 10:26, 10:36, 12:14, 12:57.
5. John 1:42.
6. Luke 5:8.
7. A phrase used in a talk by Michel Quoist.
8. Paulo Freire, *Pedagogy of the Oppressed* (Penguin Edition, 1972), p. 92. This book has an intriguing description of dispelling the low self-picture of many peasants in Brazil and of problem-posing methods of education.
9. Edited A. H. Halsey, *Educational Priority*, op. cit., p. 117f, and

see Youth Service Development Council, *Youth and Community Work in the 70s* (H.M.S.O., 1969), pp. 75–77.

10. Denis Lawton, *Social Class, Language and Education* (Routledge and Kegan Paul, 1968), pp. 77–103.

11. A. T. Ravenette, *Intelligence, Personality and Social Class*, an unpublished thesis in 1963 describes some research done by Bernstein in West Ham.

Over 600 children were involved, some 9% of the total school population within their age group (12½, 13½ and 14½). Intelligence tests were used to produce a score for verbal (spoken language) ability and non-verbal or perceptual ability.

Only at the lowest level of intelligence were the verbal intelligence scores higher than the perceptual. The higher the intelligence the larger grew the gap between the perceptual and the verbal scores. For example:

> Perceptual score: mean IQ 98
> Verbal score: mean IQ 91
> Perceptual score: mean IQ 130
> Verbal score: mean IQ 108

12. Wyn Williams, 'The Proper Concerns of Education' in *Education for Democracy* (Penguin Books, 1970), edited by David Rubinstein and Colin Stoneman, p. 161.

13. *Half Our Future*, The Newsom Report (H.M.S.O., 1963).

14. Evidence from London Comprehensive schools of 1966 leavers includes:

Nine boys who left Peckham Manor School and gained university places had all been given IQs below that usually required for entry to Grammar Schools.

John whose IQ was 91 gained five G.C.E. 'O' levels.

Jack whose IQ was 103 gained six G.C.E. 'O' levels.

Jean failed eleven-plus. Gained eight 'O' level passes, then three 'A' level passes.

David failed eleven-plus. Won a Trevelyan scholarship at Christ Church, Oxford.

Andrew came from the bottom stream of a central school, passed three 'A' levels, went to university.

See *London Comprehensive Schools*, 1966, pp. 97–101. Quoted in *The Comprehensive School*, Robin Pedley (Pelican Revised Edition, 1969).

15. Basil Bernstein, 'Compensatory Education' in *Education for Democracy*, op. cit., pp. 110–21.

16. *Educational Priority*, op. cit., p. 117.

17. Leila Berg, *Risinghill: Death of a Comprehensive School* (Pelican, 1968), p. 270.

18. Michael Young and Patrick McGeeney, *Learning begins at home* (Routledge and Kegan Paul, 1968), p. 42f.

19. *Educational Priority*, op. cit., pp. 125–7.

20. *Half our Future*, op. cit., p. 23.

In areas which the Newsom Report described as 'slums' only thirty-three out of one hundred of the women and fifty-two out of one hundred men stayed more than three years. In all schools the figures were fifty out of one hundred women and sixty-four out of one hundred men. In addition there was only an even chance that a woman who joined the staff later than the beginning of the Christmas term in 1958 would still be there three years later; for men the odds were two to one against.

PART FIVE

1. Luke 4:18.

2. Circular 11/67, August 1967. Quoted in *Educational Priority*, edited A. H. Halsey, op. cit., p. 48f.

3. *Educational Priority*, edited A. H. Halsey, op. cit., p. 29f.

4. John 12:24.

5. The story was told by Bob Lambourne and quoted in the *C.M.S. Newsletter* by J. V. Taylor, October 1972.

6. R. H. Tawney, *Equality* (George Allen and Unwin, 1964), Fifth edition, for a classic discussion of equality especially pp. 48–56, 120f, 173, 227f.

7. Philip Mason, *Patterns of Dominance* (Oxford University Press, 1970), p. 321.

8. David Newsome, *Godliness and Good Learning* (John Murray, 1961), p. 220f.

9. cf. Brian Jackson and Denis Marsden, *Education and the Working Class* (Routledge and Kegan Paul, 1962).

10. Robin Pedley, *The Comprehensive School*, op. cit., p. 101.

11. Sir William Alexander, *The Sixth Form College in Practice* (Councils and Education Press, 1972).

12. See Michael Young and Harringay Parents' Group, *Why Our Susan?*, 1969, for a discussion of these conflicting principles, which arrives at the opposite conclusion from mine.

13. John Greve, Dilys Page, Stella Greve, *Homelessness in London* (Scottish Academic Press, 1971), p. 247.

   Inner London contains about 6% of the population of England and Wales. It has 37·5% of the registered homeless. In its forward look the Greater London Council hoped that the 1972 figure of some 550,000 'unsatisfactory dwellings' might be reduced to 300,000 by 1974. Of this, the crude shortage between housing stock and the number of households will still be 100,000. A further 200,000 will be regarded as 'unsatisfactory'. The greater part of these are in the Inner London areas.

14. Anthony Crosland, *Towards a Labour Housing Policy* (Fabian Society, 1971).

15. Leviticus 25.

16. Isaiah 5:8.

17. Leviticus 25:29f.

18. Leviticus 25:23.

19. John O'Grady at a seminar, The Future of Employment in Southwark, 1972, p. 32.

20. Dr. David Eversley at the same seminar, p. 11.

21. Octavia Hill, *Letters on Housing*, p. 60.

22. Peter Wilmot and Michael Young, *Family and Kinship in East London* (1957 Penguin Edition, 1962), p. 93.

23. W. G. Runciman, *Sociology in its place* (Cambridge University Press, 1970), p. 134.

24. R. E. Pahl, 'Poverty and the Urban System' in *Spatial Problems of the British Economy* (Cambridge University Press, 1971), edited Chisholm and Manners.

25. Dr. David Eversley in *The Future of Employment in Southwark*, p. 7. Between 1966 and 1970 employment in London declined from 4·6 million jobs to 4.2 million. London's population was also dropping but, in order to keep a balance between population and employment, the reduction of jobs should have been 35,000 a year. In fact, nearly three times as many were being lost.

26. W. W. Daniel, *Whatever happened to the Workers in Woolwich?* (P.E.P., 1972).

PART SIX

1. David Donnison, *Micro Politics of the City in London: Urban*

patterns, problems and policies: eds. David Donnison and David Eversley (Heinemann, 1973), p. 398.

2. *Training for the Future*, Department of Employment, 1972.

3. Alexander Paterson, *Across the Bridges* (Edward Arnold, 1913), Second Edition, p. 46.

4. Edited Victor H. Vroom and Edward L. Deci, *Management and Motivation* (Penguin Modern Management Readings, 1970), p. 17.

5. 'We are becoming quite certain that, under proper conditions, unimagined resources of creative human energy could become available within the organisational setting.' Douglas M. McGregor, *The human side of enterprise*. Quoted in *Management and Motivation*, op. cit., p. 307.

6. Mary Morse, *The Unattached* (Pelican, 1965), p. 225f.

7. John Macquarrie, *Principles of Christian Theology* (S.C.M. Press, 1966), e.g. p. 103, 110.

8. Mary Morse, op. cit., p. 127.

9. Rodger Charles, *Man, Industry and Society* (Stag Books, Sheed and Ward, 1964), p. 441.

10. I Corinthians 12:25f.

11. See Richard Hare, *Community and Communication: What are cities and what are they for?* in *People and Cities*, ed. Stephen Verney (Fontana, 1969), pp. 155–63.

12. An article by Lloyd E. Ohlin and Martin Rein, *Social Planning for Institutional Change*.

13. Edited by Tom Burns, *Industrial Man* (Penguin Modern Sociology Readings, 1969), p. 263.

14. Luke 4:18.

15. Colossians 3:5.

16. Luke 6:20.

17. Matthew 6:24.

18. See Herbert J. Gans, *Poverty and Culture* in *The Concept of Poverty*, edited Peter Townsend (Heinemann, 1970), pp. 146–64.

19. See S. M. Miller and Pamela Roby, 'Poverty: Changing Social Stratification' in *The Concept of Poverty*, op. cit., p. 139f.

20. *Homeless Single Persons in Southwark*. Report of a working party of the Camberwell Council on Alcoholism, 1972, p. 10. The Report compares the number of registered Common Lodging house beds in 1960 and 1972.

	1960	1972
London	6,405	4,708
Manchester	1,535	1,325
Birmingham	807	485

21. John Benington, Director of the Home Office Community Development Project, Coventry. Articles in *Municipal Journal*, 22nd and 29th January, 1971.

22. See T. R. Batten, *The Non Directive Approach in Group and Community Work* (Oxford University Press, 1967), p. 47.

23. See W. G. Runciman, op. cit., pp. 157–75. He took a thesis of Max Weber about 'charisma' and its 'routinisation', and studied how it might be applied to Nkrumah's Ghana in 1949–62.

24. R. E. Pahl, *Poverty and the Urban System*, op. cit.

25. Clowland and Piven quoted in *The Cross Roads for Social Work*, Martin Rein, p. 24.

26. David Donnison, *Micro Politics of the City*, op. cit., p. 384

27. David Donnison, op. cit., p. 394.

28. Gerry Williams in *Cambridge House Report* (Camberwell, 1971).

29. Quoted in Rodger Charles, *Man, Industry and Society*, op. cit., p. 129.

30. *Man, Industry and Society*, op. cit., pp. 55–7.

31. A Ministry of Labour enquiry reported that at the end of 1954 there were 297 undertakings operating schemes of profit sharing on a pre-arranged basis (excluding co-operatives). These 297 firms employed over 500,000 persons of whom 344,792 were taking part in the profit sharing schemes.

32. Fred H. Blum, *Work and Community. The Scott Bader Commonwealth* (Routledge and Kegan Paul, 1968).

33. George Goyder, *The Responsible Company* (Blackwell, 1961), p. 89. He suggested that a general Purposes Clause should be required in the Memorandum of Association of the bigger public companies.

34. Dr. A. W. Pearce, *Involvement or Negotiation in Industrial Participation*, Autumn 1972, pp. 7–13.

35. Violence in Southern African (S.C.M., 1970), p. 68.

36. William Blake said 'He who would do good to another must do it in minute particulars'.

PART SEVEN

1. Max Weber, *The Protestant Spirit and the Spirit of Capitalism*, 1904.

2. Quoted in R. H. Tawney, *Religion and the Rise of Capitalism*, 1922 (Pelican, 1961), p. 244.

3. Owen Chadwick, *The Reformation* (Pelican, 1964), p. 184.

4. H. F. R. Catherwood, *The Christians in Industrial Society* (Tyndale Press, 1964), p. 2, p. 13.
5. Mark 8:35.
6. Alan Bullock, vol. I, op. cit., p. 253.
7. Ferdynand Zweig, *The Worker in an Affluent Society* (Heinemann, 1961), p. 79f, 210–12
8. John H. Goldthorpe, David Lockwood, Frank Bechhofer and Jennifer Platt, *The Affluent Workers in the Class Structure* (Cambridge University Press, 1969), cf. p. 164f.
9. Mark 12:24, 27
10. Frank Deeks, *Shop Floor Christianity* (Inter Varsity Press, 1972), p. 78.
11. Georges Velten, *Mission in Industrial France* (S.C.M., 1968), p. 8.
12. Richard Taylor, *Christians in Industrial Society* (S.C.M., 1961), p. 69f.
13. I Corinthians 15:45.
14. John 8:39.
15. John V. Taylor, *The Primal Vision* (S.C.M., 1963), p. 115.
16. See for instance Hugh Montefiore, *Doom or Deliverance* (Manchester University Press, 1972).
17. Victor Obenhaus, *Ethics for an Industrial Age* (Harper and Row, 1965), p. 217.
18. See Professor Galbraith Interview in *Observer Review*, November 22nd, 1970.
19. John V. Taylor, 'Enough is Enough', *C.M.S. Newsletter*, September 1972. cf. Leviticus 19:9f.; Deuteronomy 24:19–22; Deuteronomy 22:9; Exodus 23:10f.; Leviticus 25:1–7; Exodus 22:29, 23:16; Deuteronomy 26:1–11.
20. Luke 12:15.
21. Dr. E. F. Schumacher, *Crucible* (May, 1969).
22. *Intermediate Technology*, the bulletin of the Intermediate Technology Development Group.
23. Dr. E. F. Schumacher, op. cit.
24. Dr. A. W. Pearce in *Industrial Participation*, Autumn 1972.
25. Cf. Alan Richardson, *The Biblical Doctrine of Works* (S.C.M. 1963 edition), pp. 11–30.
26. Psalm 104.
27. Zechariah 8:3–19.
28. Genesis 3:19.
29. Romans 8:18–25.
30. Edited David Edwards, *Priests and Workers* (S.C.M., 1961), p. 37f.
31. Luke 10:7.

32. Matthew 25:21; Luke 19:12–28; Luke 12:15, 21.
33. Karl Marx, 'Alienated Labour' in *Economic and Philosophical Manuscripts of 1844.* Quoted in Goldthorpe, Lockwood, Bechhofer, Platt, op. cit., p. 180, and see p. 54.
34. Quoted in a sermon by Leopoldo J. Niilus, 1969.
35. Victor Obenhaus, *Ethics for an Industrial Age*, op. cit., pp. 189–206.
36. Luke 12:13, 57.
37. James 5:1–6.
38. Alexander Solzhenitsyn, *Cancer Ward* (First published The Bodley Head, 1968; Penguin, 1971), p. 225.
39. Colossians 2:15.
40. Matthew 24:14–30.
41. Leviticus 25:8–34.
42. Neil Wates, 'Business and the Salvation of the World', Article in *Frontier*, November 1970.
43. Ezekiel 34:3–6.
44. E. R. Wickham, *Church and People in an Industrial City* (Lutterworth, 1957), pp. 238–61.
45. E. R. Wickham in *Priests and Workers*, op. cit., p. 135.
46. H. L. Ellison, *From Tragedy to Triumph. Studies in the Book of Job* (Paternoster Press, 1958), p. 83f.
47. Mark 10:31, 44.
48. Luke 1:52f.
49. *Christians in an Industrial Society*, op. cit., p. 67f.
50. Gregor Siefer, *The Church and Industrial Society* (Darton, Longman and Todd, 1964), p. 171f.
51. op. cit., p. 52.
52. op. cit., pp. 65, 67.
53. André Collonge in *Christians in an Industrial Society*, op. cit., p. 62.
54. Gregor Siefer, op. cit., p. 59 and note p. 120.
55. op. cit., p. 54.
56. Emile Poulat, 'Reflections' in *Priests and Workers*, op. cit., p. 95.
57. André Collonge, 'The Partners' in *Priests and Workers*, op. cit., p. 40.
58. E. R. Wickham, 'Appraisal' in *Priests and Workers*, op. cit., pp. 124–52.
59. Kenneth Mason, *The Priesthood of Priest workers: Comments after Conversations*, an unpublished article 1972.
60. *Report of the Belgium Worker Priests to their Bishops and Superiors*, December 1970.

PART EIGHT

1. Roundshaw Ecumenical Experiment. Working Paper no. 3.
2. A paper by Cecilia Goodenough.
3. Horst Symonowski, *The Christian Witness in an Industrial City* (Collins, 1966), p. 37f.
4. 1 Peter 2:9.
5. Isaiah 44:28, 45:1, 4.
6. Roger Sainsbury, *From a Mersey Wall* (Scripture Union, 1970), p. 93f.
7. Romans 1:25.
8. Donald Reeves, *The Church and Community Development or The Next Bandwaggon.* An article 1973.
9. Jacques Ellul, *Violence* (S.C.M., 1970), p. 67.
10. Isaiah 42:1f.; John 13; Isaiah 49:2; Isaiah 50:4.
11. See John Poulton, *A Today Sort of Evangelism*, op. cit., pp. 61, 91.
12. Acts 22:1-22; Acts 24:24f.
13. Luke 14:1-24.
14. Harvey Cox, *The Feast of Fools* (Harvard University Press, 1969), pp. 59-62, 111.
15. I Samuel 3:9.
16. John Skinner, *Prophecy and Religion* (Cambridge University Press, 1955), pp. 2f., 138f., 185f.
17. Jeremiah 5:1, 7:17.
18. Leslie Davison, *Pathway to Power*, p. 41.
19. Gordon Rupp, *Patterns of Reformation* (Epworth, 1969), pp. 276-9.
20. Matthew 23:24.
21. This is described in John Tanburn, *Open House* (Falcon, 1970).
22. I agree largely with the arguments set out in *Christian Initiation, the Report of the Commission on Christian Initiation* (Church Information Office, 1971).
23. *Frontier* Magazine, Summer 1967.
24. Roger Sainsbury, *From a Mersey Wall*, op. cit., p. 62f.
25. Michael Hare-Duke, 'Getting into Groups', *New Christian*, August 10th, 1967.
26. Horst Symonowski, *The Christian Witness in an Industrial Society*, op. cit., pp. 84-86.

27. Roland Allen, *Missionary Methods — St. Paul's or Ours* (1912, World Dominion Press, 1960), p. 24.

28. Stephen Neill, *A History of Christian Missions* (Pelican, 1946), p. 479f.

29. Galatians 3:28.

30. Acts 14:23.

31. Roland Allen, op. cit., pp. 99–107.

32. I Corinthians 12:6.

33. *See Local Ministry in Urban and Industrial Areas.* The Report of a Working party under the joint chairmanship of the Bishop of Stepney and the Bishop of Woolwich (Mowbrays, 1972), p. 13.

34. *The Place of Auxiliary Ministry, Ordained and Lay* (Church Information Office, 1973), pp. 13–17.

35. Acts 10:47.

36. See Ted Roberts, *Partners and Ministers* (Falcon, 1972), for a description of the supplementary ministry in Bethnal Green and Bow.

37. Ephesians 4:11.

38. *Urban Ministry Project.* Details from St. Peter's Vicarage, Bishopsford Road, Morden, Surrey.

39. *Evangelical Urban Training Project.* Details from 96 Burleigh Road South, Liverpool L5 1TW.

40. Ann Holmes, *Area Surveys — Final Report.* 1973 British Council of Churches Working Party on the use of Church properties for community activities in multi-racial areas, p. 57.

41. *The Use of Church Properties.* Interim Report of the British Council of Churches Working Party, 1972, p. 22.

42. *There Comes a Time.* British Council of Churches Housing Trust, 1971.

43. Psalm 15:4. Prayer Book Version.

PART NINE

1. Hebrews 11:6.

2. Michael Green, *Evangelism in the Early Church* (Hodder and Stoughton, 1970), pp. 125–9 and see note 125 on p. 311.

3. Acts 17:27.

4. F. F. Bruce, *The Book of the Acts* (Marshall, Morgan and Scott, 1954), p. 336.

5. Colossians 1:17.
6. Romans 8:19, 22.
7. Colossians 1:20.
8. Teilhard de Chardin, *Hymn of the Universe*, quoted in R. C. Zaehner, *Dialectical Christianity and Christian Materialism* (Oxford University Press, 1971).
9. I John 2:15f.
10. John 17:14, 17.
11. John 1:3, 10.
12. I John 5:19.
13. John 3:16.
14. Romans 5:8.
15. Matthew 5:13, 14.
16. Brendan Maher, *Clinical Psychology and Personality. The selected papers of George Kelly* (John Wiley and Sons, 1969), p. 169.
17. J. R. W. Stott, *Christ the Controversialist* (Tyndale Press, 1970), p. 191.
18. Matthew 5:45.
19. Exodus 3:14. This is E. R. Wickham's suggestion of its meaning.
20. See F. Engels, *Ludwig Feuerbach*, pp. 38, 47, quoted in R. C. Zaehner, op. cit., p. 654.
21. See C. S. Lewis, *Miracles* (Geoffrey Bles, 1947), pp. 131–58.
22. Amos 2:1.
23. Hebrews 1:1.
24. James 1:23–5.
25. John 5:17, 20.
26. A. M. Ramsey, *F. D. Maurice and the Conflicts of Modern Theology* (Cambridge University Press, 1951), p. 102.
27. The history of this debate in England is worked out in A. M. Ramsey, *From Gore to Temple* (Longman's, 1960).
28. John 1:9.
29. John 1:14.
30. John 18:37.
31. I Peter 2:22–5.
32. A. M. Ramsey, *From Gore to Temple*, op. cit., p. 160.
33. Luke 18:18–27.
34. Luke 5:8.
35. Exodus 3:5; Isaiah 6:1; Isaiah 55:9.
36. A. A. Vogel, *The Next Christian Epoch* (New York, Harper and Row, 1966), p. 78. Quoted in A. M. Ramsey, *God, Christ and the World* (S.C.M., 1969), p. 29.
37. II Timothy 1:14.

38. Mark 14:36.
39. Galatians 3:23–4:7.
40. Luke 17:11–19.
41. Mark 8:34f.; Luke 14:25f.
42. John 6:26.
43. Matthew 1:21.
44. Michael Green, *The Meaning of Salvation* (Hodder and Stoughton, 1965), p. 15f. and see pp. 96–118.
45. Michael Green, *The Meaning of Salvation*, op. cit., pp. 119–35.
46. Leviticus 25:48.
47. Isaiah 58:6.
48. Isaiah 24:2.
49. Reinhold Niebuhr, *Moral Man and Immoral Society* (Charles Scribner's Sons, 1936), p. 4.
50. Dietrich Bonhoeffer, *Ethics*, edited Eberhard Bethge (S.C.M., 1955), p. 290.
51. See Stephen Neill, *The Christian Society* (Nisbet, 1952), p. 13f.
52. Leonard Hodgson, *Sex and Christian Freedom* (S.C.M., 1967), p. 29. Quoted in J. V. Taylor, *The Go Between God* (S.C.M., 1972), p. 36f.
53. Romans 3:23.
54. J. V. Taylor, *The Go Between God*, op. cit., p. 48.
55. Isaiah 1:15–17.
56. David and Jean Hewitt, *George Burton — A Study in Contradictions*, op. cit., is a sensitive study, warts and all, of the differences salvation made and had not yet made in the life of a brilliant and disturbing man.
57. Ephesians 6:12.
58. Helmut Thielicke, *The Prayer that spans the World* (James Clarke), p. 133.
59. Emil Brunner, *The Christian Doctrine of Creation and Redemption: Dogmatics* (1949, Lutterworth, 1952), vol. II, p. 136.
60. I Peter 3:18.
61. C. F. D. Moule, *The Sacrifice of Christ* (Hodder and Stoughton, 1956), p. 28.
62. John 12:27; Mark 14:36; Matthew 27:46.
63. Franz Kafka, *The Trial* (1925, Penguin Modern Classics), p. 234.
64. T. M. Kitwood, *What is Human?* (Inter Varsity Press, 1970), p. 110f.
65. Mark 15:32; Luke 23:39–43.
66. H. R. Mackintosh, *The Christian Experience of Forgiveness* (first published 1927, Fontana Books, 1961), p. 86.

67. II Corinthians 4:7.
68. Quoted in James Stewart, *A Faith to Proclaim* (Hodder and Stoughton, 1953), 1962 Edition, p. 58.
69. Philippians 2:6–8.
70. John 19:30.
71. Colossians 2:15. See James Stewart, *A Faith to Proclaim*, op. cit., p. 95.
72. cf. John 12:32.
73. Colossians 1:20.
74. Thomas Wieser, *Planning for Mission* (Epworth, 1966), p. 54.
75. John 3:3.
76. See Emil Brunner, *The Christian Doctrine of Creation and Redemption*, op. cit., vol. 11 p. 96.
77. II Corinthians 5:20f.
78. Matthew 23:37.
79. A. M. Ramsey, *The Gospel and the Catholic Church* (Longmans, Green, 1936), p. 41.
80. Matthew 13:31f.
81. Psalm 55:10f., 6.
82. John 12:27, 24.
83. Luke 11:20.
84. Luke 12:32.
85. John 3:5.
86. Mark 14:61f.; Matthew 26:63f. I owe this suggestion to Bishop J. A. T. Robinson in his Cambridge lectures on the Gospels in 1954. cf. Daniel 7:13.
87. Acts 1:11.
88. John 5:28f.
89. II Peter 3:13.
90. Revelation 21:2.
91. James Stewart, *A Man in Christ* (Hodder and Stoughton), 1935, p. 318.
92. I Corinthians 15:35–40.
93. I Corinthians 13:12.
94. Georges Velten, *Mission in Industrial France*, op. cit., p. 51.
95. A paper by Cecilia Goodenough.

INDEX

INDEX